A Guide to Florida's Historic Architecture

LIBRARY PRESS@UF

AN IMPRINT OF UF PRESS AND
GEORGE A. SMATHERS LIBRARIES

A Guide to
Florida's Historic Architecture

EDITED BY THE FLORIDA ASSOCIATION OF
THE AMERICAN INSTITUTE OF ARCHITECTS

LibraryPress@UF
GAINESVILLE, FLORIDA

ISBN 978-1-947372-19-1 (pbk.)
ISBN 978-1-947372-22-1 (ePub)

LibraryPress@UF is an imprint of the University of Florida Press.

LIBRARY PRESS@UF

AN IMPRINT OF UF PRESS AND
GEORGE A. SMATHERS LIBRARIES

University of Florida Press
15 Northwest 15th Street
Gainesville, FL 32611-2079
http://upress.ufl.edu

The Florida and the Caribbean
Open Books Series

In 2016, the University Press of Florida, in collaboration with the George A. Smathers Libraries of the University of Florida, received a grant from the National Endowment for the Humanities and the Andrew W. Mellon Foundation, under the Humanities Open Books program, to republish books related to Florida and the Caribbean and to make them freely available through an open access platform. The resulting list of books is the Florida and the Caribbean Open Books Series published by the LibraryPress@UF in collaboration with the University of Florida Press, an imprint of the University Press of Florida. A panel of distinguished scholars has selected the series titles from the UPF list, identified as essential reading for scholars and students.

The series is composed of titles that showcase a long, distinguished history of publishing works of Latin American and Caribbean scholarship that connect through generations and places. The breadth and depth of the list demonstrates Florida's commitment to transnational history and regional studies. Selected reprints include Daniel Brinton's *A Guide-Book of Florida and the South* (1869), Cornelis Goslinga's *The Dutch in the Caribbean and on the Wild Coast, 1580–1680* (1972), and Nelson Blake's *Land into Water—Water into Land* (1980). Also of note are titles from the Bicentennial Floridiana Facsimile Series. The series, published in 1976 in commemoration of America's bicentenary, comprises twenty-five books regarded as "classics," out-of-print works that needed to be in more libraries and readers' bookcases, including Sidney Lanier's *Florida: Its Scenery, Climate, and History* (1875) and Silvia Sunshine's *Petals Plucked from Sunny Climes* (1880).

Today's readers will benefit from having free and open access to these works, as they provide unique perspectives on the historical scholarship on Florida and the Caribbean and serve as a foundation upon which today's researchers can build.

Visit LibraryPress@UF and the Florida and the Caribbean Open Books Series at http://ufdc.ufl.edu/librarypress.

Florida and the Caribbean Open Books Series Project Members

This book is reissued as part of the Humanities Open Books program, funded by a grant from the National Endowment for the Humanities and the Andrew W. Mellon Foundation.

A Guide to Florida's Historic Architecture

Florida Association of the American Institute of Architects
104 East Jefferson Street
Post Office Box 10388
Tallahassee, Florida 32302

Compiled by:
F. Blair Reeves, FAIA

Editors
Mary Nell Reeves
Diane D. Greer

Art Direction
Peter Mitchell Associates

Printing
Boyd Brothers

Contributing Authors
Richard Garfinkel, AIA
Mike Kelly
Tom Van Cleave
Matthew Ploucha, AIA
Linda Stevenson, AIA
Susan Turner, AIA
Reed Black
Keith Silas
Robert Ray, AIA
Vincent Nicotra, AIA
Robert E. Forsythe, AIA
Frederick Cale
Frank Comarati
Ivan A. Rodriguez, AIA
Michael Maxwell, AIA
Russell Hope, AIA
Michael Gordon, AIA
Michael Clary, AIA
Jerry Mills
Sandy Johnson
Bill Bauer
Peter Jefferson, FAIA

Eugene Pandula, AIA
Sidney D. Corhern
Gar Barkman, AIA
Robert C. Broward, AIA
E. Wendell Hall, AIA
F. Blair Reeves, FAIA
Diane D. Greer
Les May, AIA
Al Dompe, AIA
Edward E. Crain, AIA
Peter E. Prugh, AIA
Ronald Haase, AIA
William Hunter, AIA
Richard H. Morse, AIA
Bertram Y. Kinzey, AIA
Anthony J. Dasta, Architect
Rocke Hill, Architect
David E. Ferro, Architect
Walt Marder
Tim White, AIA
Charles F. Morgan
Edward D'Avi, AIA
Eric Wiedegreen, AIA

George Scheffer, AIA
Robert Heffernan, AIA
William Bean, AIA
Steve Jernigan, AIA
Rick Barnett, AIA
Jeff Fuller
J.P. McNeill
George L. Chapel
Patrick Hartlaub, AIA Asso.
Elizabeth H. Sims
Ed Butler
Evonne V. Cline
Cauley Copeland
Julian Cranberry
Jo Allie Downing
Junius Downing
George Griffin
Perry Hill
James Hurst
Sharon McCall
Kathryn McInnis
Leon Ward

FA/AIA Executive Committee

President
John Ehrig, AIA
4625 East Bay Drive
Clearwater, Florida 34624

Vice President/President-elect
H. Dean Rowe, FAIA
100 Madison Street
Tampa, Florida 33602

Secretary/Treasurer
Larry Schneider, AIA
25 Seabreeze
Delray Beach, Florida 33483

Past President
John Barley, AIA
5345 Ortega Boulevard, Suite 9
Jacksonville, Florida 32210

Regional Directors
Mark Jaroszewicz, FAIA
331 Architecture Building
University of Florida
Gainesville, Florida 32611

James Greene, FAIA
254 Plaza Drive
P.O. Box 1147
Oviedo, Florida 32765

Vice President for Professional Society
R. Jerome Filer, AIA
250 Catalonia Avenue, Suite 805
Coral Gables, Florida 33134

Vice President for Governmental Relations
Bruce Balk, AIA
290 Coconut Avenue
Sarasota, Florida 33577

Vice President for Professional Development
Rudolph Arsenicos, AIA
2560 RCA Boulevard, Suite 106
Palm Beach Gardens, Florida 33410

Vice President for Public Relations/Communications
Raymond Scott, AIA
601 S. Lake Destiny Road, Suite 400
Maitland, Florida 32571

FA/AIA Board Of Directors

Henry C. Alexander, AIA
James H. Anstis, FAIA
Rudolph M. Arsenicos, AIA
William L. Awodey, AIA
Bruce Balk, AIA
John M. Barley, AIA
Richard R. Barnett, AIA
Michael A. Byrd, AIA
Charles E. Block, AIA
John R. Cochran, AIA
Charles Cole, AIA
Javier F. Cruz, AIA
Thomas C. Culler, AIA
Don W. David, AIA

John P. Ehrig, AIA
R. Jerome Filer, AIA
Alfred W. French, AIA
Joseph A. Garcia, AIA
Richard M. Garfinkel, AIA
Robert B. Greenbaum, AIA
James A. Greene, AIA
William P. Greening, AIA
Jeffrey Gross, AIA
Thomas H. Gyllstrom, AIA
Randolph C. Hansen, AIA
Troy Hawkins, AIA
Charles D. Heller, AIA
Jerry L. Hicks, AIA
Samuel C. Holladay, AIA

Mark T. Jaroszewicz, FAIA
Robert Koger, AIA
H. Samuel Kruse, FAIA
Mary Marsh Lasseter, AIA
David C. Leete, Jr., AIA
Richard W. Morris, AIA
John W. Page, AIA
Harry Parkhurst, Asso.
David Perez, AIA
Richard D. Pritts, AIA
Norman N. Robson, AIA
H. Dean Rowe, FAIA
Angel Saqui, AIA
John J. Schlitt, AIA
Larry M. Schneider, AIA

Raymond L. Scott, AIA
Frank Sheehy, AIA
Roy D. Smith, AIA
Ross Spiegel, AIA
Ludwig Spiessl, AIA
Linda D. Stevenson, AIA
John W. Szerdi, AIA
John L. Tennison, AIA
John Tice, AIA
Terry L. Tougaw, AIA
Daniel M. Urbanus, AIA
Calvin T. Weese, AIA
Kenneth H. Woolf, AIA
Mitchi Yamaguchi, AIA
Emilio Zeller, AIA

Financial support for this project was obtained from the Florida Association of the American Institute of Architects, the Research and Education Center for Architectural Preservation at the University of Florida and two matching grants from the Florida Department of State, Division of Historical Research. In addition, the following architectural firms and individuals made generous contributions to support the project.

George Bail, AIA
Charles F. Harrington, AIA
Leslie Divoll, AIA
William Faust, Architect, PA
Homer F. Daniel, AIA
KSD Architectural Associates
Marion, Paluga & Associates
Fleischman Garcia Architects
Dorothy A. McKenna, AIA
Jerome A. Goebel, AIA
John H. and Sue Lind
William Morgan Architects
Bullock Tice Associates Architects
Fullerton and Associates Architects
Urban Design Center Inc.
Mark Ramaeker Architects, Inc.
Gottfried & Garcia Architects

Theodore R. Majdiak & Asso..
Hoon & White Architects
McCormick Construction Co.
Richard M. Garfinkel, AIA, Architect
ODELL Associates Inc.
James J. and Joan Jennewein
Vickrey/Oversat/Awsumb Associates
Schwab & Twitty Architects
Nichols Carter Grant Architects
Collins and Associates
H. Maxwell Parish, Architect
Kenneth Hirsch Associates
C. Trent Manausa Architect
Shepard Associates
Flad & Associates
Digby Bridges, Marsh & Asso.
Robert A. Harris, Architect

Alfred French & Asso.
Spillis Candela & Partners
Rowe Holmes Hammer Russell Architects
Frasuer Knight Asso.
Frederick Lee Vyverberg, Architect
E. L. Hunt
LaVerne E. Hoon
Edward D. Stone and Asso.
Daniel Perez-Zarraga, AIA
Cuhaci & Peterson Architects
Russell C. Chase, Architect
Charles Sharrod Partin Architect
Emilio Zeller III, Architect
The Evans Group ADP Associates
Edge Group, PA
Historic Ocala Preservation Society
Mark V. and Mary B. Barrow

FOREWORD

This *Guide to Florida's Historic Architecture* was prepared by the Florida Association of the American Institute of Architects and is dedicated to all people who find pleasure and satisfaction in learning more about Florida's architecture and historical heritage.

Each county is represented with an architectural history, examples chosen for their historic and architectural significance, and a location map. Each example is identified by a photograph, name, address, and brief description. Only major and easily identifiable features are mentioned. Style nomenclature, for instance, is used only as a means for recognition.

Because much of Florida's historic architecture incorporates innovational interpretations of academic styles and often combines one stylistic feature with another, identifying buildings by style alone can be confusing. In this guide, to help the reader quickly identify each entry, academic architectural styles are often combined into major categories. For instance: Victorian Revival style implies architecture inspired by building forms popular during the nineteenth century reign of Queen Victoria. In Florida vernacular, this style often includes Gothic Revival, Italian Villa, Romanesque, Italianate, Stick Style, Eastlake, Shingle Style, English Tudor, or Queen Anne elements. Buildings in clearly identifiable academic styles are noted with appropriate descriptions.

GUIDELINES

This guide to the historical architecture of Florida, a diverse assembly of buildings reflecting the rich heritage of the state, is divided into zones and each zone into counties since the geographic geometry of the state is sometimes a problem for the uninitiated.

Each county is represented with an architectural history, a list of historic sites, and a map locating the sites. The structures were chosen for historic and architectural significance to the area. Each guide entry is identified by a photograph, name, address, and brief description. Only major and easily identifiable features are mentioned.

ACKNOWLEDGMENTS

The Herculean task of researching, writing, photographing, and assembling this guide was accomplished by members of the Florida Association of the American Institute of Architects. Chapter preservation officers appointed architects to study each county within their chapters' areas. This appointment required a very generous donation of time and effort. Using data prepared by graduate students in the Department of Architecture, University of Florida, architects criss-crossed Florida's counties and met with local authorities to identify, locate, and photograph examples and then prepare an archi-

Ringling House — Sarasota

tectural history of each county. In several cases, where architects were unavailable or otherwise occupied, other authorities gathered data and prepared guides. Personnel from the Division of Historical Resources of the Florida Department of State checked the histories and examples for accuracy. The guide was coordinated and edited by F. Blair Reeves, FAIA, and Mary Nell Gibson Reeves. Diane Greer, editor of *The Florida Architect,* was responsible for its final design and overall production.

GOOD TOURING MANNERS AND LIABILITIES

The privacy of people occupying the buildings listed in this guide should be respected at all times. Since many of these buildings are in rural areas, poison ivy, snakes, and watchdogs should be avoided. Occupants and owners who enjoy their privacy may become irritated by inconsiderate tourists. (There is nothing quite like the feeling of being ordered off a property by someone making his point with a double-barrel shotgun!) With this in mind, no one connected with this project will assume liability for any sort of damage or inconvenience caused by this guide. Nor will anyone be held responsible for inaccurate information which may have inadvertently been included in the text. It is our sole intention to provide a workable guide to Florida's historic architecture.

F. Blair Reeves, FAIA

CONTENTS

FOREWORD
    Guidelines
    Acknowledgments
    Good Touring Manners and Liabilities

FLORIDA: ARCHITECTURAL HISTORY AND PRESERVATION

FLORIDA NORTHWEST CHAPTER

FLORIDA NORTH CENTRAL CHAPTER

FLORIDA NORTH CHAPTER

JACKSONVILLE CHAPTER

DAYTONA BEACH CHAPTER

MID-FLORIDA CHAPTER

FLORIDA CENTRAL CHAPTER

FLORIDA GULF COAST CHAPTER

FLORIDA SOUTHWEST CHAPTER

PALM BEACH CHAPTER

INDIAN RIVER CHAPTER

BROWARD CHAPTER

MIAMI CHAPTER

FLORIDA: ARCHITECTURAL HISTORY & PRESERVATION

Florida's architecture for over three centuries has responded to the physical and social evolution of the state. Houses, churches, forts, schools, railroad stations, courthouses, stores, hotels, spas — the diversity of buildings speak from the past in a language which can be understood by all. The more they become known, the more they tell about the history of this state.

While knowledge of prehistoric architecture is limited to mystical remains of ceremonial mounds and archeological interpretations of early sites, examples of Spanish colonial architecture are found in the substantial construction of Castillo de San Marcos, Fort Matanzas, and Fort San Carlos and in the town plans of St. Augustine and Pensacola. Domestic architecture remaining from the second period of Spanish occupancy is heavily influenced by British and American building traditions. Preservation efforts, especially those using restored and reconstructed buildings within the Historic District in St. Augustine, present a thorough interpretation of Spanish and British colonial life when coquina, tabby, and small amounts of lumber were the basic material of the colonials.

Settlers moving into north Florida from Georgia and the Carolinas brought their traditions of log houses with porches on two sides and a wide hall at the center. Built of heart pine shaped with broad axes and foot adzes, raised off grade, and protected by wide roof overhangs, these expedient structures were threatened only by fire. Kitchens were soon housed in separate structures to limit potential danger, but most houses had to have one or two mud and stick fireplaces and chimneys for heating.

Along the coast, builders had access to milled lumber, bricks, and hardware processed elsewhere. However, traditional braced frame construction continued in use until the mid-nineteenth-century advent of balloon framing and wire nails. Building styles in these coastal communities reflected the influences of New England, the Carolinas, and the Caribbean. As railroads crossed the state from Fernandina to Cedar Key and later from Jacksonville to Pensacola and Tampa, the indigenous architecture of pioneers was replaced with designs reflecting the latest styles and technological advantages. Even so, building styles continued to be influenced by local lifestyle and climate and a sense of rigid individualism.

From the 1870s to the 1900s Floridians benefited from inexpensive housing and growing home ownership stimulated by popular and technical journals, pattern books such as *The American Builder, The Cottage Builder's Manual,* and the catalogues of prefabrication mills. During early building booms, Sears, Roebuck, and Company expanded its mercantile business to include house components. Other firms developed prefabricated dwellings and institutional buildings. Almost overnight housewrights and carpenters became general contractors and speculative builders causing great changes throughout all building trades. House plans also changed with spaces set aside for new functions. Parlors, pantries, and porte-cocheres became normal elements of turn-of-the-century Florida houses.

Architects of commercial and institutional buildings were quick to utilize the newly available materials, elements, and techniques of building. Brick, stone, cast iron, sheet metal, and concrete came into common use. Carrere and Hastings, architects for Henry M. Flagler's Ponce de Leon Hotel in St. Augustine, used cement from Belgium, terra cotta from New Jersey, and tile setters from Italy. Henry Plant's Tampa Bay Hotel was built of brick in a Moorish style using horseshoe windows, domes, and minarets. Collegiate Gothic was the style selected for Florida's universities built of brick, tile roofs, and terra cotta and cast stone trim.

The Biltmore — Coral Gables

Florida's architecture in the first part of the twentieth century was stimulated by both disasters and development. The 1901 fire in Jacksonville, while a catastrophe, caused a new city core to be built of Neo-Classical and Prairie School architecture. Flagler extended his railroad and hotel chain to Palm Beach and finally to Key West. In Palm Beach earlier wood frame cottages and large Victorian Revival style hotels were replaced by magnificent concrete structures when Addison Mizner introduced his version of Spanish Revival style. His use of roof tiles from Cuba, interiors salvaged from European palaces, and antique tile, hardware, and furniture from Spain caused a transformation of architecture of Florida's lower east coast. Viscaya, designed by Hoffman and Chalfin for James Deering, is Italian Baroque in style. In George Merrick's Coral Gables, Fink and Paist designed their version of Norman and Chinese villages, African colonial dwellings, and Venetian pools. In Sarasota, the Ringling museum and residence were built in an Italian Renaissance Revival style; and, in Opalaka, a city hall was built in a decorative manner inspired by *The Arabian Nights.* This was an era of new life patterns, optimistic development, and flamboyant interpretation of architectural styles.

Florida architecture, especially in boom towns stimulated by land speculation and tourism, presented interesting and innovative adaptations of academic styles. Elsewhere in the state, when growth was less spectacular, the bungalow slowly replaced Victorian Revival cottages and then evolved into other styles utilizing features inspired by Classic Revivals, Art Deco, Art Moderne, Prairie School, and finally modern. Commercial and institutional work continued to be in conservative academic styles until after World War II when population growth, new lifestyles, technological advancements, and changing values demanded a new architecture.

Frank Lloyd Wright's designs for Florida Southern College provided a new environment for educational processes in a mid-Florida locale, and Paul Rudolph and Ralph Twitchell designed Sarasota residences using new materials and systems to work within a tropical environment. While other competent Florida architects provided thoughtful designs to solve local building problems, the simultaneous availability of air-conditioning and standard building components often led to expedient solutions which misunderstood or ignored climate and location. As interstate highway systems penetrated the state and changed traditional travel patterns, some communities were isolated or divided. Commercial centers moved from downtown to a new cluster of congestion near interchanges which were dominated by regional shopping centers or ubiquitous eateries and motels. Large corporations, with heads and hearts elsewhere, called for an architecture of national appeal with little Florida accent, perhaps to make newcomers or two-week vacationers feel they never left home.

Cuban Club — Ybor City

St. George Street — St. Augustine

Marjorie Kinnan Rawlings House — Cross Creek

In the last two decades rapid changes in the built environment, especially the thoughtless demolition of buildings and neighborhoods once considered to be of lasting value, stimulated the growth of public and private preservation efforts throughout Florida. The state legislature established advisory boards and guidelines to protect historic districts in St. Augustine, Pensacola, Key West, and other locales. Stimulated by federal preservation legislation and programs, the Florida Division of Archives, History, and Records Management was created to conduct state-wide inventories, to direct nominations to the National Register of Historic Places, and to assist local preservation programs. The Historic American Building survey returned to Florida with field offices to record buildings from Fernandina to Key West to Pensacola. Architectural students and faculty at the University of Florida and University of Miami prepared inventories and documented buildings in their locales. In 1972 the University of Florida established the Research and Education Center for Architectural Preservation (RECAP) to offer multi-disciplinary programs to professionals wishing to specialize in preservation. The Florida Trust for Historic Preservation, created in 1977, provided a focus for preservation efforts in the private sector. The Florida Association of the American Institute of Architects reestablished its system of preservation officers who, in their latest project in cooperation with the Research and Education Center for Architectural Preservation and the Division of Archives, History, and Record Management, prepared this guide to Florida's Historic Architecture. Diverse influences such as Florida's celebration of the Bicentennial with its emphasis on the state's heritage, the nostalgic pleasures of the streetscapes of Disney World, and the diminution of natural resources have caused reappraisals of architectural motives and solutions. The latter part of the 20th century may be remembered as a period of return to a Florida vernacular architecture involving both tradition and innovation.

ESCAMBIA

ROBERT HEFFERNAN, AIA, FLORIDA NORTHWEST

Escambia County, located in the extreme north-western part of Florida, is bordered on the north and west by Alabama, on the east by Santa Rosa County, and on the south by the Gulf of Mexico. When Florida became part of the United States in 1821, the county extended east from the Perdido River to the Suwanee River. Because of its strategic location, this area was also considered a valuable acquisition by Spain, France, England and the Confederacy.

After Tristan De Luna's unsuccessful attempt to settle the Escambia area in 1559, the land changed hands thirteen times under the dominion of five flags. Each era of occupation left its mark. Spain left a rich heritage of names, customs, and traditions as well as modest houses reflecting Caribbean building traditions. The British imposed a town plan, replaced swamps with planted gardens, and erected additional fortifications which included Fort George and Gage's Hill.

The United States began its occupancy by establishing a Naval Yard in 1925, building coastal fortifications and a lighthouse, and proposing a railroad from Pensacola to Columbus, Georgia. Following the Civil War and Reconstruction, railroads were completed to serve the north part of the county and to bring lumber and naval stores to Pensacola's busy waterfront of piers, warehouses, and terminals. Despite an 1880 fire which destroyed more than a hundred buildings in the business district, Pensacola was Florida's third largest city by the turn of the century. Although the Navy Yard was closed in 1911, the facilities reopened in 1914 as the first naval aviation training station in the nation. This important installation continues to influence the growth and movement of Escambia's population. During the Florida boom of the 1920's, Pensacola experienced prosperity and municpal expansion but not at the escalating scale of South Florida.

After World War II, commercial, institutional, and residential architecture moved from the waterfront towards the Naval Air Station and northeast along Pensacola Bay following US 90 and later Interstate 10. Access by US 98 across Pensacola Bay and population increase stimulated rapid development of the beach-front communities of Gulf Beach and Pensacola Beach, and Gulf Breeze in neighboring Santa Rosa County. Since most of Escambia County is composed of forest uplands, agricultural wetlands, and water, Pensacola and Century are the only incorporated municipalities.

Pensacola's concentration of significant historic architecture has attracted the attention of local and state preservationists. Small preservation groups were consolidated when the state established the Historic Pensacola Preservation Board in 1967.

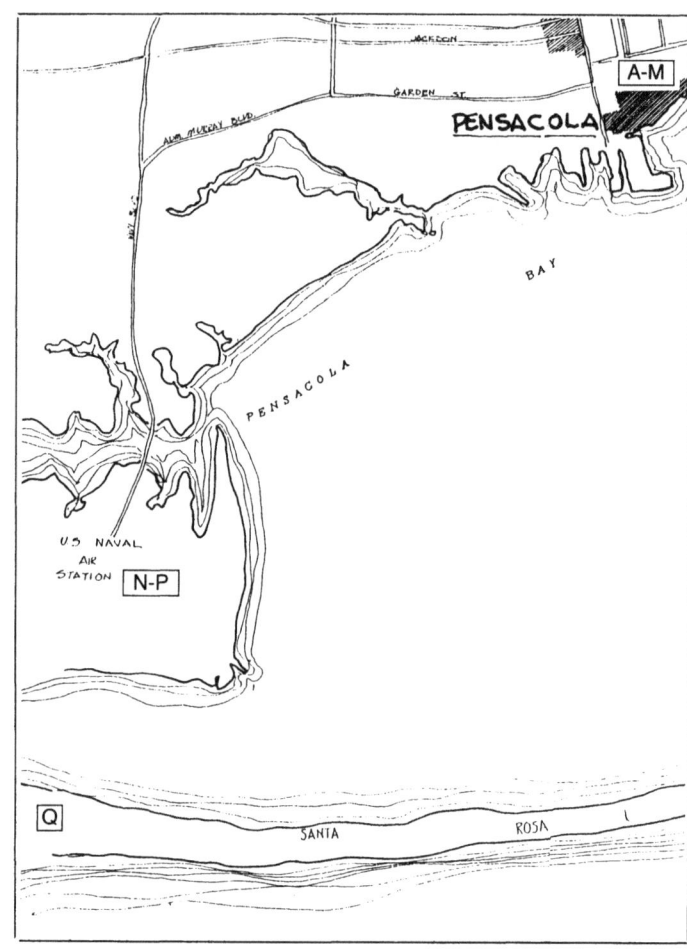

The City of Pensacola was authorized by state legislation in 1968 to establish the Pensacola Historic District, an area of 36 blocks stretching from Plaza Ferdinand past Seville Square to Ninth Avenue on the east and from the waterfront to St. Michael's Cemetery on the north. Summer field offices of the Historic American Buildings Survey documented buildings in this Historic District and on the Naval Air Station. In 1972, a new historic district was created in the North Hill District and was listed on the National Register of Historic Places in 1981.

The Palafox Historic Business District, established in 1977 by a city ordinance, placed this commercial area under an architectural review board. Stimulated by governmental action, the business committee responded by initiating preservation projects involving salvage, rehabilitation, and adaptive use. In this partnership between the public and private sectors, Escambia County has provided inspiration for the rest of Florida.

A
NW corner Garden St. and Palafox St.
Pensacola

San Carlos Hotel, built from 1909 to 1910 by C.H. Turner Construction Company. Good example of Mediterranean Revival style with pebble dash exterior wall surfaces and cast stone building detailing over a primary masonry building. Interior two-story central lobby with art glass dome and marble walls. Significant for preeminent role in cultural, social, and economic life of Northwest Florida in early 1900's.

B
SW corner Garden St. and Palafox St.
Pensacola

Blount Building, completed in 1907. Fine example of turn-of-the-century commercial architecture in Pensacola. Exterior differing significantly from artist's rendering of 1906 but upper six floors not modified in past 75 years.

C
S. Palafox St.
Pensacola

Saenger Theater, built by C. H. Turner Company in 1925. Spanish Baroque Revival style reflecting impression of mid-20's "Grand Experience of the Theater." Interior lobby, main auditorium, balcony, and offices, modified and restored in 1979 to accommodate live theater.

D
S. Palafox St.
Pensacola

Citizens and Peoples National Bank. Classical Revival style structure built in 1906 as new home of Pensacola's First National Bank.

E
Plaza Ferdinand VII
Pensacola

Pensacola City Hall, built in 1907. Earliest example of Spanish Colonial Revival style in Escambia County. Unique architectural character, designed by Frederick Ausfeld and built by C.H. Turner Construction Company.

F
Downtown
Pensacola

Plaza Ferdinand VII and Seville Square, tangible remnants of Spanish Florida. Plaza Ferdinand VII, site of 1821 transfer of Florida to the United States. Seville Square, focus of historic district encompassing 30 blocks of buildings in old city area.

G
SE corner Zarragossa St. & Barracks St.
Pensacola

Tivoli High House, built in 1805 by John Baptiste Cazenane, Pedro Bardinave, and Rene Chandiveneau. Originally High House, a small kitchen, and Tivoli ballroom. Prominent in early social life of Pensacola. Used as a dwelling, then barracks for Union soldiers during Civil War, and finally a boarding house. Demolished in 1930's, but documented by photographs, sketches, and archeology. Reconstructed as a Bicentennial project. Now housing Historic Pensacola Preservation Board.

H
221 E. Zarragossa St.
Pensacola

Dorothy Walton House, originally built at 137 W. Romana St. by Gabriel Hernandez or original grantee Madame Del Junco, wife of Governor Folch, who sold the house in 1812. Used by Dorothy Walton, wife of the signer of the Declaration of Independence and mother of Col. George Walton, after Florida became a U.S. territory in 1821. Moved to present site in 1966.

I
Seville Square
Pensacola

Old Christ Church, built in 1832, oldest Protestant church building in Florida. Constructed of local brick believed to be made at Bright Brick Plant, with ceiling beams of heart pine. Building used as Union barracks, hospital, and stable during Civil War and as public library from 1936 to 1960. Now Pensacola Historical Museum directed by Pensacola Historical Society.

J
Seville Square
Pensacola

Clara Barkley Dorr House, built in early 1870's by Mrs. Clara G. Dorr, daughter of George W. and Clara Louise Garnier Barkley, for her five children. House located in Pensacola's most prestigious residential neighborhood of the 1870's and 1880's.

K
Tarragona St.
Pensacola

L&N Marine Terminal Building, built in 1902-1903, designed by railroad engineers and constructed by Alexander V. Clubbs. Originally located near port, moved to present location in 1969 by Pensacola Preservation Board.

L
E. of Seville Square on Pensacola Bay
Pensacola

The Barkley House, east of Seville Square, built about 1835 by George Barkley, a prosperous merchant, for his wife, the former Clara Ganier. Symmetrical building with brick masonry walls sixteen inches thick at the base tapering to twelve inches at the gable and curved plastered chimney pieces serving four fireplaces downstairs and two upstairs.

M
Alcaniz St.
Pensacola

The Desiderio Quina House, one of Pensacola's early apothecaries run by Quina, a native of Genoa, Italy, who came to North America as a Spanish soldier. House typical of raised cottages with apron porch, gable roof, double fire chimney, and ample doorways and windows to provide cross ventilation.

N
Naval Air Station
Pensacola

Fort San Carlos y Barrancas, located on waterfront in Naval Air Station, composed of semicircular water battery built by Spain during its second period of control (1783-1821) and Fort Barrancas built by the United States (1839-1844). Of special interest, groins of brick vaults caused by irregular polygonal plan of fort.

O
Near Ft. San Carlos
Pensacola

Pensacola Lighthouse and Keeper's Quarters, constructed in the 1820s to mark entrance to Pensacola Bay. During Civil War light apparatus removed by retreating Confederates and recovered only after war. Now automatic light, administered by United States Navy, limited access.

SANTA ROSA

WILLIAM BEAN, AIA, FLORIDA NORTHWEST CHAPTER

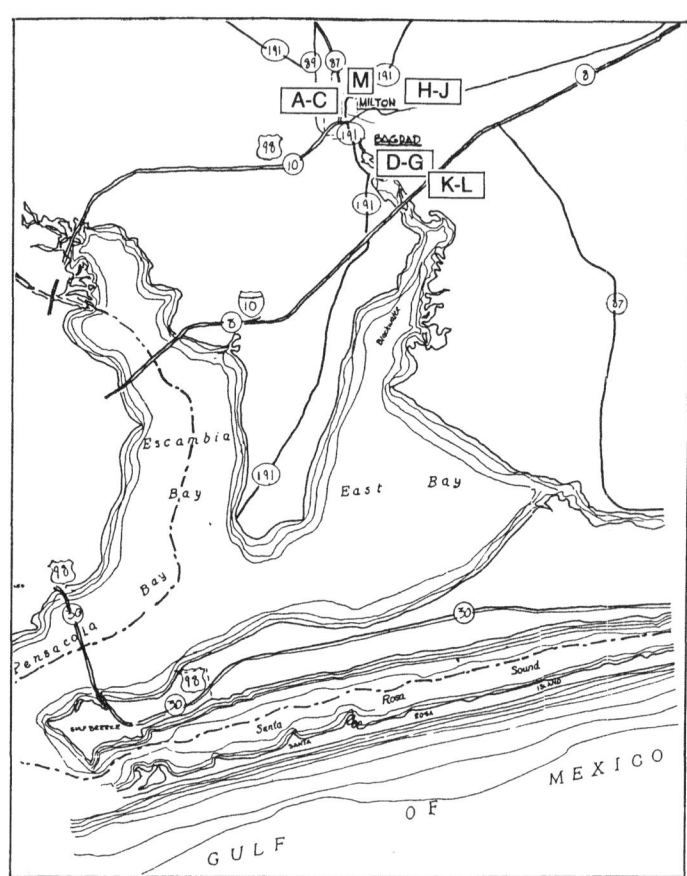

Santa Rosa, established in 1842, was Florida's twenty-first county. The name was derived from Santa Rosa Viterbo, a saint of the Roman Catholic Church and patron saint of a chapel at Viterbo, a small city near Rome. Located in the extreme northwest section of Florida, the county is bordered by the Gulf of Mexico, Alabama, and Escambia and Okaloosa counties. The county seat, Milton, was founded on Blackwater River in 1825 as a trading post. For many years this locale was accessible only by riverboat or by stagecoach along the Geneva-Pensacola road. Before the Civil War, Milton was a collecting point for cotton and wool to be shipped down river to Pensacola and across the Gulf to northern points.

The area's primary resource until the 1930's was timber, enormous stands of cypress and yellow pine. In the early nineteenth century a scout for General Andrew Jackson erected a sawmill and brickyard on the north side of the mouth of the Blackwater River and the area's prosperous industry began. Ships from all over the world sailed into Gulf Coast waters for this region's lumber. Early settlers included John Hunt, who built kilns for a brickyard on the Blackwater River in the 1820's and planted lotus, cedar, and pecan trees on his plantation; Joseph Forsyth, who came from New Orleans to the Hunt brickyard and then purchased land from a Spaniard in 1827 to establish a sawmill north of Pond Creek at Arcadia; and the Simpson brothers from North Carolina, who joined Forsyth to create the lumber firm of Forsyth and Simpson. Because of transportation problems, these pioneer lumbermen constructed a new mill at the mouth of Pond Creek on the northwestern tip of Blackwater Bay. This location was the site of mill operation until 1939 and also the site of a growing community, Bagdad, which claimed Forsyth as founder.

By the 1840's Blackwater Bay shipbuilding firms and other lumber mills lined the shores of the river and bay from Milton to Robinson Point. During the Civil War Union forces in Pensacola made an expedition in October of 1864 to the Blackwater Bay and River to capture the valuable lumberyards in that area. Confederate forces burned the yards and fled. After the war, the Bagdad mill was reconstructed. Name and ownership of the mill changed several times over the years. From 1912 to 1939 when it finally closed, the business was known as the Bagdad Land and Lumber Company. Depletion of timber resources caused the early 20th century decline of the area's lumber industry. Reforestation has been practiced since that time.

Badgad (the ancient Mesopotamian city's name was given the lumber company and the town because of the location between the two area rivers, the Escambia and the Blackwater) played an instrumental role in shaping the history of this northwest Florida region. While the mills prospered, so did the town. The commissary catered to mill employees. Mill superintendents built their houses on Forsyth Street. On Church Street, the next street over, mill foremen had their homes. Laborers lived on School Street. Limit Street, the farthest street out of town, was reserved for slaves. Many of the old houses, and even some of the old families, still remain. Milton and Bagdad are served by US 90 and a railroad, but Interstate 10 passes through the county to the south to leave this area in relatively quiet isolation.

The southern portion of Santa Rosa County, lying between East Bay and the Gulf, is an active area which includes the thriving beach resort settlements of Gulf Breeze and Oriole Beach. Santa Rosa Island, while sharing the county's name, is not part of the county area.

Architectural preservation in Santa Rosa County has been mostly confined to the private sector with individuals and organizations such as the Santa Rosa Historical Society taking initiative. The condition of remaining structures indicates that the architectural heritage of this locale could be in jeopardy. Buildings could be lost because of vacancy, poor maintenance, and careless development.

A
Milton

Saint Mary's Episcopal Church, built in 1867. The first Episcopal Church in northwest Florida. Mentioned by Frank Lloyd Wright in his book, *The Aesthetics of American Architecture,* when he wrote: "Saint Mary's is a jewel created in the purest tradition of the Gothic revival. It survives today with its pure lines intact, its muted colors untouched. Purity, it is without a blemish."

B
302 Elmira St.
Milton

Exchange Hotel, constructed in 1914 by S.F. Fulghum and Company of Pensacola to house a telephone system, office rooms, and bachelor apartments. After building's completion, telephone exchange moved to new wood frame building next door. Building converted for use as hotel. Rectangular in plan, building constructed of red brick with four chimneys on north wall and four on south, high parapet arched over entranceway, and windows with white concrete lintels. Renovated in 1983 and operated as bed and breakfast inn in mid 1980's.

C
Milton

L & N Railroad Depot, built in 1907 to replace 1880's depot building which burned. William Jennings Bryan and President Woodrow Wilson among speech-makers at depot which served railroad and community until Milton agency closed in 1973. Building has exposed supporting beams, intersecting hip roofs, and oak floors.

D
Bagdad

Bagdad Methodist Church, established in 1832, originally met in a "bush arbor" or temporary building. Existing building of ship-lapped method of construction with underpinning wedged with wooden pegs, a technique used by shipbuilders. Altar rail originally at center of building separating men and women. Recent construction restoring cedar-shake roof and natural wood interior and addition of replica of porch to enclose the communion table behind altar.

E
Thompson Street
Bagdad

Bagdad Post Office, built in 1894 nearer water but moved to present location when lumber mill expanded operations. Front portion original with additions in rear. Postmaster General James A. Farley visitor in 1930's to present Emma Joyner, retiring postmistress, an award. Still in active use in mid 1980's.

F
Church & Allen
Streets
Bagdad

Emma Fournier Forcade-Donald Youngblood House, built in 1919 by Exie Fournier for his sister and her husband. Curved shingled wall receding into the gable on either side of balcony above front porch. Continuation of shingle band below the soffit down either side of house. Dormer on the north end encasing chimney. Heart pine from Bagdad mill used throughout house. Sold to present owner in 1952.

G
Forsyth Street
Bagdad

Benjamin W. Thompson House, believed to have been built by Thompson sometime between 1840 and 1850 (county records destroyed by 1869 fire), one of oldest houses in Bagdad. Originally overlooked Pond Creek, moved two blocks to present location in 1912. Constructed of heart pine; windows original rolled glass; notable nineteenth century door and window trim. Bathrooms and kitchen additions. During restoration Union Civil War graffiti discovered on parlor walls. Horseshoe prints imbedded on stairs.

H
302 Pine St.
Milton

Ollinger-Cobbs House, built 1870. Unique in area because of tower room overlooking Pine Street which gives house imposing facade. Broom-handle picket fence.

I
Canal at Pike Street
Milton

Masonic Hall, Santa Rosa 16 F.A.M. Lodge, built in 1855 on the site of Canal Street School which is now site of Pensacola Junior College Milton Campus. Moved to present location in 1915. Lodge used continuously since 1855 except for the years of 1863 and 1864 when presence of Union troops inhibited public gatherings.

J
Oak Street
Milton

St. Mary's Rectory, built in 1860's by Rev. Charles E. McCougall, M.D., who served St. Mary's in Milton from 1876 until his death in 1916. Story-and-a-half house constructed of native pine, oak, and cypress, a legacy to the Episcopal Church. Basically unchanged except original kitchen and dining room separated from main house by open porch renovated at turn of the century.

K
Limit Street
Bagdad

Slave House, originally constructed as slave quarters before Civil War. Board and batten construction. One of several slave houses in area. Some still inhabited.

L
Allen Street
Bagdad

McNair House, built in 1900 by McNair family who had a welding and machine shop in Milton. House well-maintained by owners since its construction.

M
Clara St. at Alice St.
Milton

Mount Pilgrim Baptist Church, built in 1916. Church established in 1866 with original building located on Canal Street. The 1916 building was the only brick church structure in Santa Rosa County at the time of its construction. Bell and tower added in 1920's and stained glass windows in 1970's.

WALTON

STEVE JERNIGAN, AIA, FLORIDA NORTHWEST

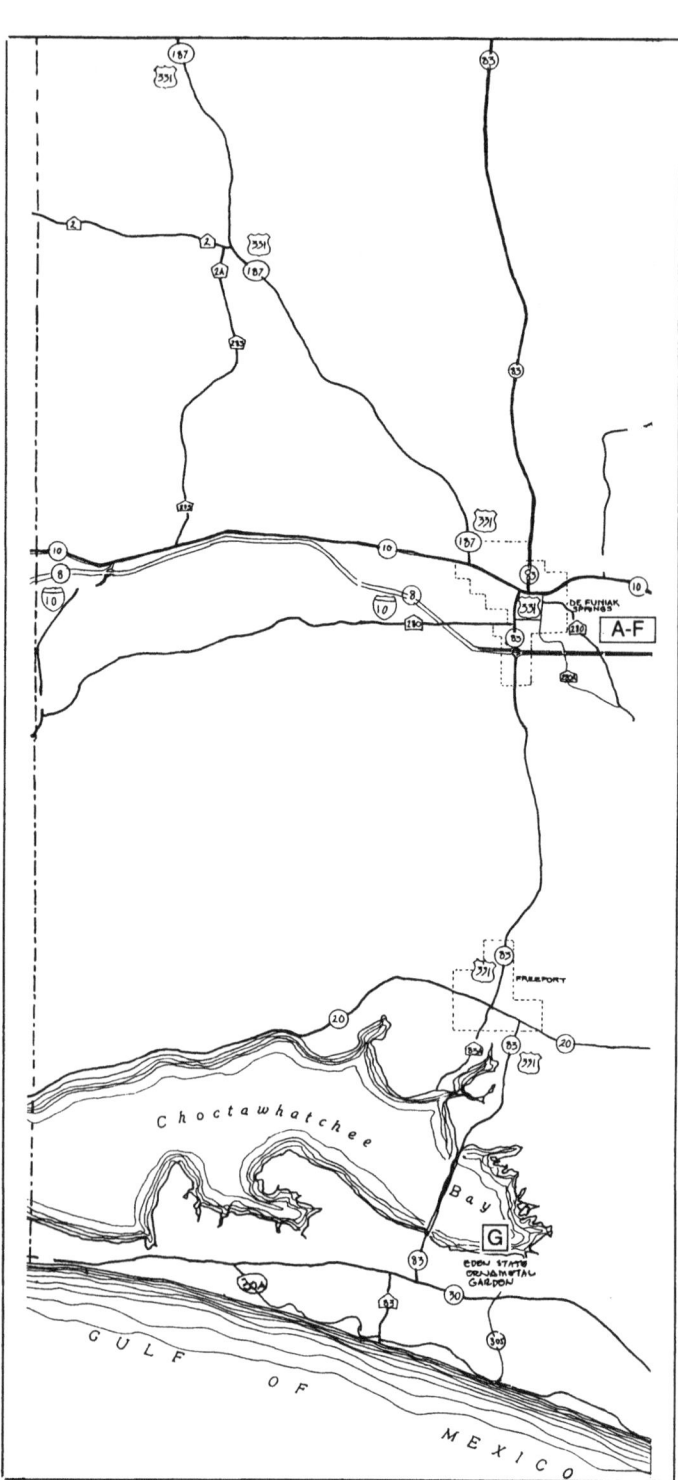

Walton County, established on December 29, 1824, as Florida's eighth oldest county, was named for Colonel George Walton who was Secretary of the Territory of West Florida during Andrew Jackson's term as governor and the son of George Walton, a signer of the Declaration of Independence and governor of Georgia.

The county is bordered by the Gulf of Mexico, Alabama, and the counties of Holmes, Okaloosa, Washington, and Bay. The Choctawhatchee River and Bay and the Gulf of Mexico are the significant natural boundaries. Much of the west portion of the county is included in Eglin Air Force Base. (Jimmy Doolittle's Raiders received special training at this base for their Tokyo mission during World War II.) The county is served by US highways 90, 98, 301 and Interstate 10.

Both Indians and whites settled in this area because of the abundance of fish and shellfish and because of the transportation potentials due to ample waterways. Wild life continues to be abundant, especially in management areas throughout the county. DeFuniak Springs is the county seat named for Colonel Fred DeFuniak who was an official of the Louisville and Nashville Railroad. The spring, known in earlier days as Open Pond, is bordered by the business district, residential areas, and recreational facilities.

The economy of Walton County has been based on lumber and wood products and truck crops throughout most of its history. Regional architecture reflects this with the most impressive buildings located in DeFuniak Springs. Recent population increases are occurring in the southern part of the county, due to the recreational facilities being developed on the bay and the Gulf.

Preservation efforts are especially noticeable in DeFuniak Springs where individuals and institutions are caring for their properties. The Chatauqua Building was restored as a project sponsored by the American Revolution Bicentennial Commission. Residential properties are being preserved through careful maintenance.

10

A
Live Oak Ave at
US 331
DeFuniak Springs

Sidney J. Catts Residence, built between 1886 and 1890. Home of Florida Governor Sidney J. Catts. Two-story wood frame building with an octagonal tower on one corner and porches at both floors.

B
Circle Drive
DeFuniak Springs

Chautauqua Building, built in 1890 for Chautauqua, an organization developed in New York for adult education. Classic Revival style meeting hall with wood frame construction, three classical porticos on the front facade, and each pediment supported by four Doric columns. Central rotunda cupola with dome roof and lantern. Auditorium removed following damage by 1975 hurricane.

C
Circle Drive
DeFuniak Springs

Walton-DeFuniak Springs Library, built in 1886. Small one-story wood frame building constructed as a library. Said to be the oldest original library building remaining in the state. Clipped gable roofs and portico at entrance.

D
DeFuniak Springs

Van Kirk-Henry House, built in 1900. Unusual square tower set at a forty-five degree angle to the rest of the house. Two-story wood frame, hip roof with dormers, porch at first and second floor with shed roof and square columns.

E
Circle Drive
DeFuniak Springs

Thorpe Residence, built by D. W. Burke for the Thorpe family around 1900 as DeFuniak Springs was being developed by the Lake DeFuniak Land Company. Queen Anne style structure with delicate porch balustrades.

F
Circle Drive
DeFuniak Springs

A. F. Bullard House, built around 1905 by a builder named Graves for the Bullard family. Greek Revival style home with massive porticos and simple detailing and an unusual red clay roof. Balconies at second floor under porticos.

G
Point Washington

"Eden," William Wesley Residence, Eden State Ornamental Gardens, on Choctawhatchee Bay. Built in 1895 by Wesley as the hub of a large complex which included a lumber mill with docks. Exact copy of "Dunleith" in Natchez, Miss. Lumber cut and seasoned on site. Originally two identical homes built by the Wesley family. The surviving "Eden" restored by Lois Maxon from New York and later donated to state as park.

NOTES

11

BAY

JEFF FULLER, FLORIDA NORTHEAST CHAPTER

B Bay County derives its name from St. Andrews Bay. Originally occupied by several Indian tribes, this area around a natural harbor was inhabited at different times by settlers from France, Spain, England, and the American colonies. Easily accessible to the Gulf of Mexico, St. Andrews Bay provided the potential for shipping, trade, and industry.

The first settlement in the county after the United States acquired Florida from Spain in 1819 was LaFayetteville, a log cabin town. The area developed slowly because of continuous skirmishes between the Indians and the white settlers. In 1835 the town of Austerlitz was established on 80 acres (now the town of Parker) by William Loftin, a surveyor from North Carolina who also platted the town of St. Andrew (now Panama City, the county seat).

In 1836 James Watson built one of the area's first sawmills in the town then known as Millville. Several other sawmills were constructed, and timber milling became a major industry in Bay County. During the Civil War, the Confederacy engaged in running a Union blockade and utilized the bay as an export center for cotton. In the town of St. Andrew, on the east side of the bay, saltworks to supply the Confederates were constructed. This development drew workers to the area, especially since employees at the works were exempt from combat duty. When Union forces blockaded the bay in 1861, the saltworks and the town of St. Andrew were destroyed.

With the end of the Civil War and Reconstruction, Bay County began to grow with many new inhabitants coming from the north. The pleasant climate and availability of inexpensive land attracted Union veterans. Much of the land in the St. Andrews area was platted in 1887. Many of the lots were less than thirty feet wide and sold for $2 each. W. H. Lynn, a magazine publisher from Washington, D.C., became a land promoter and developed the town of Lynn Haven on the east shore of North Bay as a settlement for Union veterans. The town was officially platted in 1911, a bank was established, and later a branch railroad constructed.

In 1905, a town site near St. Andrews was platted by George Mortimer West, a land promoter from Chicago, and named Panama City in honor of the construction of the Panama Canal. This town and adjoining communities, St. Andrews and Millville, were merged and incorporated as Panama City in 1909. In 1908 the railroad was linked with Panama City and the fishing industry revolutionized by the introduction of ice manufacturing plants. Between 1906 and 1909, more than five hotels were constructed in Panama City. The Atlanta and St. Andrews Bay Line Railroad reached Panama City in 1908. Expansion of the railroad and state highway systems brought new growth to Panama City. By the late 1920's, the town had developed into a sprawling, decentralized community.

The economic pressures of development have taken their toll on early structures in Bay County. In Panama City many surviving buildings are either not used efficiently or modified without consideration of the original design. However, the downtown area still maintains a good stock of early structures and a cohesive streetscape which offers the potential for impressive revitalization programs. There is a growing awareness of the need for organized preservation activities in Bay County, particularly in Panama City. The Bay County Historical Society has initiated a listing of area historic structures and sites and published booklets on important aspects of county history.

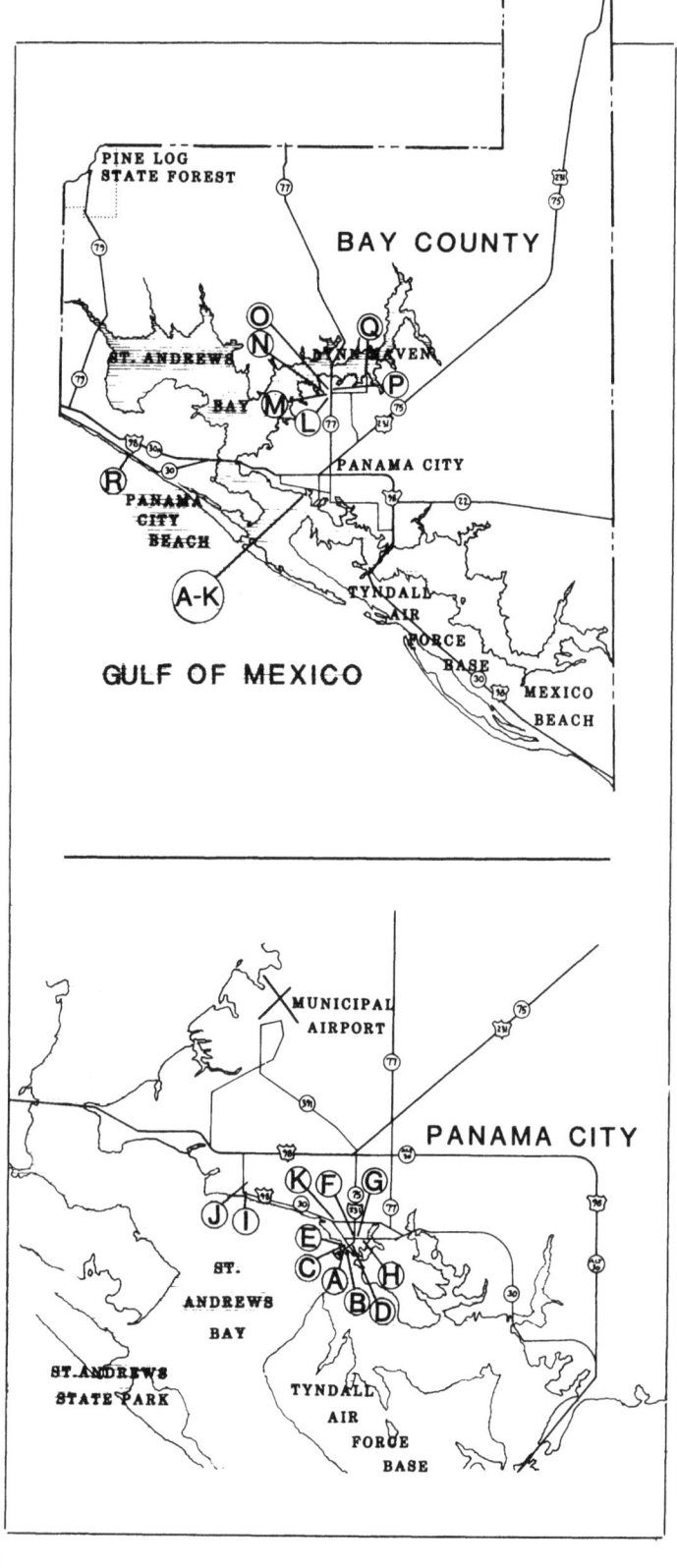

A
13 Harrison Avenue
Panama City
Dyer building, built in 1910 on Sandy Creek and floated to Panama City by Joseph Dyer. First building constructed of brick in Panama City.

B
100 Harrison
Panama City
Bank of Panama City, built of brick from Joseph Dyer's Brickyard in 1911. Housed the first bank in Panama City, later offices of the Gulf Coast Development Company.

C
101 Harrison
Panama City
First National Bank. Painted terra cotta commercial building of Neo-Classical style. Used for F. A. Black Insurance office in mid 1980's.

D
200 Harrison
Panama City
Wilkerson Building, built in 1915. Housed Post Office, Panama Jewelry Co., and the telephone company. Large pine poles used as corner posts to support weight of second-floor telephone equipment.

E
227 Harrison
Panama City
Commercial Bank, built in 1926. Constructed of buff-colored brick, an adaptation of Sullivanesque architectural style.

F
409 Harrison
Panama City
Ritz (Martin) Theatre, built in 1940. Art Moderne style with glass veneered facade still intact. Vacant in mid 1980's.

G
19 E. 4th Street
Panama City
Bay Humanities building, built as city hall in 1926. Exterior finish of mixed ground glass and stucco.

H
4th and McKenzie
Panama City
Courthouse, built in 1915 to serve as Bay County Courthouse, burned in 1920. Renovated without original domed clock cupola.

I
1000 Beck Avenue
Panama City
Bank of St. Andrew, built in 1908 as first bank in Bay County. Only bank of original three to survive until the 1940's. Used as St. Andrew Bakery. Vacant in mid 1980's.

J
1134 Beck Avenue
Panama City
Panama City Publishing Co., built in 1930 as the St. Andrews Publishing Co. Later the home of the St. Andrews Bay News.

K
Beach Drive and 6th
Panama City
Bayline Depot, built in 1911. Originally serving as depot for Atlanta and St. Andrews Bayline Railroad. Important in early industrial growth of Panama City.

L
Georgia and 9th NW
Lynn Haven
Presbyterian Church, built in 1911. Interesting architectural study in scale and massing.

M
8th and Georgia SE
Lynn Haven
Yankee Monument, built in 1920. One of few monuments to Union soldiers south of the Mason-Dixon Line.

N
Florida and 10th SW
Lynn Haven
Lynn Haven Bank, built in 1911. Bank first established by W. H. Lynn when he founded the town for northern Civil War veterans.

O
Florida and 10th SE
Lynn Haven
Lloyd's Country Store, built in 1911 as Robert's Hall to serve as site of civic meetings and entertainment center.

P
Ohio Ave. and 10th
Lynn Haven
City Hall. Mediterranean Revival style building serving as city hall and housing police and fire departments.

Q
NW Harvard and 12th
Panama City
Bob Jones College Ruin. Interdenominational liberal arts junior college founded by Bob Jones, evangelist, in 1926. College moved to Tennessee in 1931. Ruins of one building remaining.

R
Alt. Rt. 98
Panama City Beach
Palmetto Motel, built in 1921. First motel built on Panama City Beach. Served as catalyst for growth in recreational development of the beach area.

13

WASHINGTON

J. P. McNEILL

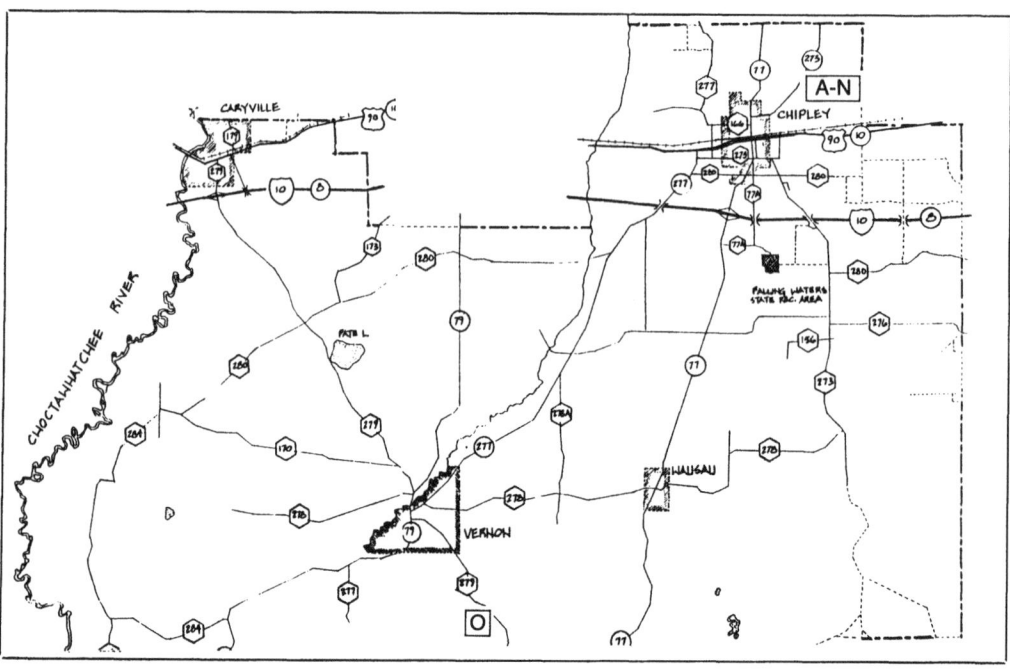

Formed in 1825 as the state's 12th county, Washington County stretched from Alabama to the Gulf Coast, comprising much of the Panhandle, until legislative acts reduced the area to its present 585 square miles. Chipley, the county seat, lies in the center of the Panhandle.

Early in the 19th century, the United States was involved in a two-part war against the British and the Indians. General Andrew Jackson was in the Gulf Region defending against the British and preparing for the battle at New Orleans. Groups of Indians fled Alabama and Georgia to seek refuge in the dense forest and swamps of West Florida. The increased activity in the Panhandle caused Jackson great concern. Hearing of Indian activity in the Choctawhatchee Basin and Holmes Valley, Jackson ordered a group under Maj. Uriah Blue to dislodge the Indians.

Following his defeat of the British at New Orleans, Jackson returned home believing that the trouble in Florida was caused by the British. Holding to the belief by many Americans that the U.S. would never be safe without controlling Florida, he armed a force to invade the state and marched his men for eight days, crossing Holmes Creek near the Reddick Mill. Jackson continued across Washington County and the state, killing Indians, burning villages, and raising havoc with British subjects. On May 28, he captured Pensacola and two days later returned to Tennessee a controversial American hero.

Two forts were built by the U.S. army as protection against the Seminoles. One on the site of the present day Moss Hill Church served as a school, courthouse and church. In 1825 the Holmes Valley Methodist Church was established and was named the head church for West Florida and most of the surrounding areas. Soon after the formation of the Holmes Valley Church, the Moss Hill Church was built. Founded by some of the first settlers in the area, the church was on a hill under moss-covered oaks. The first county seat of Washington County was named after the church. The plentiful moss of the area afforded the Indians and white settlers a versatile form of clothing, padding for beds, and, eventually, the county's first industry. Although the moss industry thrived for some years in West Florida, it was shortlived in Washington County.

Today Washington County residents are still turning to the forests for a living. Approximately 83 percent of the county consists of woodlands containing abundant stands of longleaf pine, live oak, cypress, poplar, magnolia, and sweet gum. Another major industry is farming. Crops include corn, cotton, and watermelons.

Washington County is realizing the historic importance of its buildings. Though the restoration of structures is minimal, citizens are becoming aware of their presence. National trends to recapture the richness of the past and tours of homes organized by local community groups have helped this architectural awareness.

(Condensed from *The Bicentennial Guide to Florida*, 1976, "Washington, 'Cradle of Christianity,'" by F. D. Hessey; published by the *Florida Times-Union*, Jacksonville, Florida, pp. 115 and 135.)

A
West Jackson Ave.
Chipley
Washington County Courthouse, built in 1932. Classical Revival style, red brick masonry structure with white trim. Flat roof with parapet and dentil cornice. Two-story portico of six columns. Entry doorway with broken pediment.

B
West Fifth St.
Chipley
Chipley Presbyterian Church, built 1902. Simplified Victorian Revival style with brick masonry, gable roof, tower entry, and pointed arch windows. Buttressed walls and original stained glass.

C
Chipley
Old City Hall-Library-Chamber of Commerce, built in 1924. Mediterranean Revival style, two-story brick masonry structure with curvilinear parapet wall at round-arched entry doorway, round-arched windows, hip roof, with tower with hip roof.

D
West Jackson Ave.
Chipley
Chipley Methodist Church, built in 1906. Unusual interpretation of Romanesque Revival style with unequal towers, gable roofs intersecting at crossing, and onion-shaped finials on vertical elements at gable ends of transept.

E
Railroad Ave.
Chipley
Porter Building, built in 1920's. Victorian Revival style building with elaborate corbeling patterned in street facade wall. Stepped parapet with pyramid finials on projecting elements marking bays. Segmental arched windows. Modern first floor facade detracts from original design.

F
105 S. Fifth St.
Chipley
Old Florida Bank Building. Three-story brick masonry commercial building. Mansard roof with dormer windows and decorative trim. Masonic Hall originally upstairs. Once housed headquarter offices of Birmingham, Columbus, and St. Andrews Bay Railroad.

G
West Jackson Ave.
Chipley
First Baptist Church of Chipley, built in 1898. Oldest brick masonry church in county. Severe Victorian Revival style with intersecting clipped gable roofs, short square tower, pointed windows, and decorative buttresses.

H
530 S. Third St.
Chipley
Dekle Residence. Victorian Revival style, wood frame construction with shingle and horizontal wood siding finishes. Intersecting gables roof, octagonal tower set into roof, and shed porches.

I
Corner S. Sixth St.
and S. Railroad Ave.
Chipley
Farrior Drug Store, built in 1900 for Dr. J. R. Farrior. Served as Farrior Drug Store until 1936. Asymmetrical facade with corner entrance, corbeled brick cornice. Segmental arched windows.

J
S. Fifth St. and
Railroad Ave.
Chipley
Calleway Building. Plain rectangular two-story brick commercial building. Facade extensively reworked. Previously housed third oldest Ford dealer in the state.

K
100 Church Ave.
Chipley
J. R. McAferty House, built in early 1900's. Hip roof with protruding dormer. Strict symmetry in plan and decorations. Delicate porch ornament including scroll-sawed brackets on turned and tapered columns, scroll-sawed cornice, and turned balusters.

L
West Jackson Ave.
Chipley
Watts Residence. Originally housed telephone service but then made residence of the first mayor of Chipley, Watts, who also was responsible for bringing telephone service to the area. (His house next door burned and the telephone service had been sold and moved). Simple L-shaped, gable roof structure. In disrepair in mid 1980's.

M
N. Fifth St.
Chipley
Judge J. J. Jones Residence. Classical Revival style. Two-story wood frame building. Horizontal wood siding, gable roofs, two-story porches at front and side. Frontispiece with central door and transom and sidelights of beveled glass.

N
307 S. Sixth St.
Chipley
Lloyd Haycox House, built in 1902. Two-story wood frame house with a porch off the first and second floors. Lap siding and metal roof. Decorative verge boards, porch cornices, and balustrade.

O
CR 279
Vernon
Moss Hill Methodist Church, south of Vernon, built about 1857. Reputed to be the oldest remaining building in Washington County and the second to have glazed windows. Constructed with hewn timber, braced frame, horizontal siding, stepped brick pier foundation, and gable roof. Two entries at gable end with chancel opposite end. No electricity or plumbing.

HOLMES

J. P. McNEILL

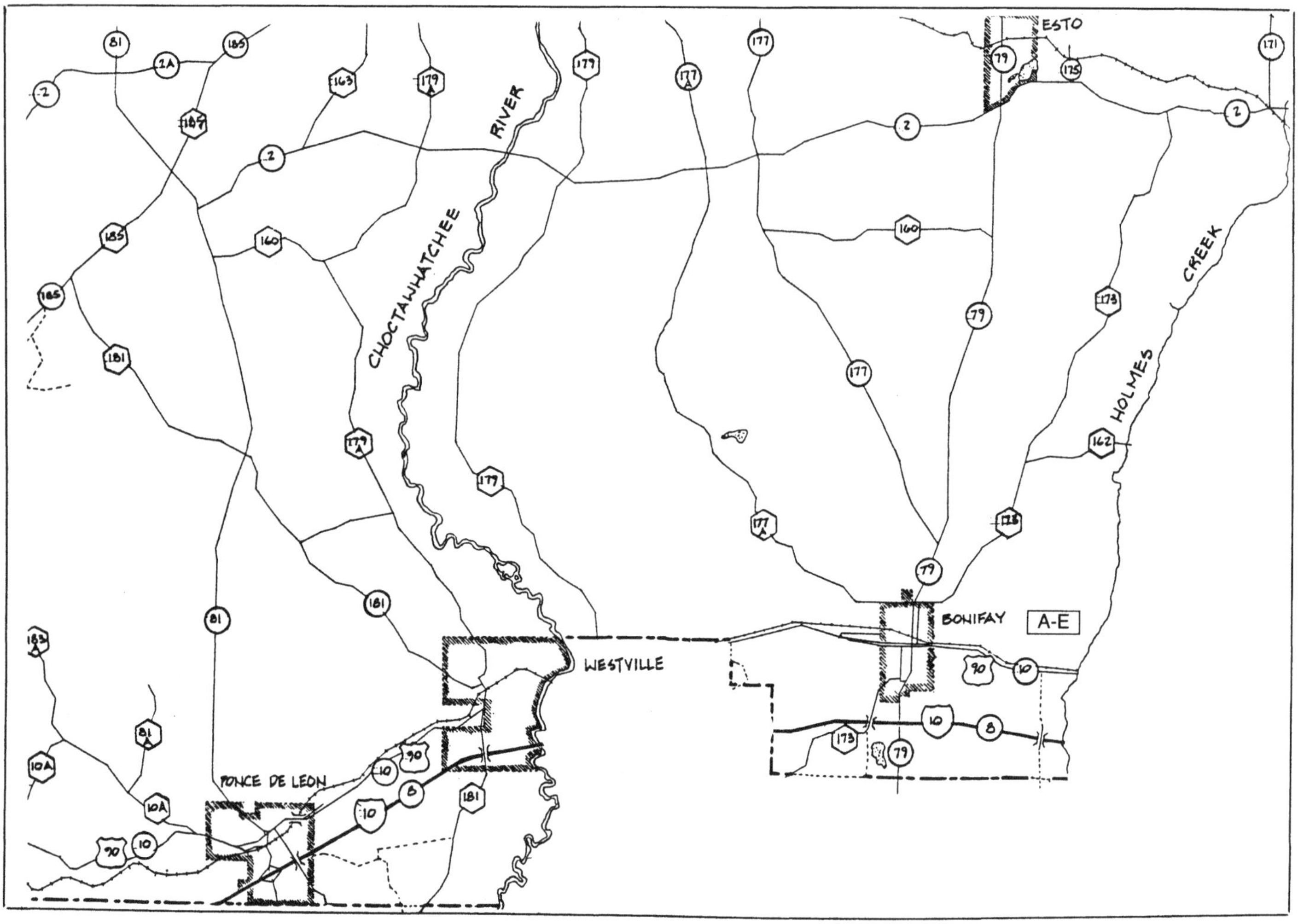

Holmes County was established in 1848 with Alabama to the north, Jackson and Washington counties to the south and east, and Walton County to the west. Choctawhatchee River and Holmes Creek are the major waterways. Hewetts Bluff or Bear Pen, Cerro Gordo, and Westville were county seats until Bonifay was selected in 1905.

When the Spanish first came to Florida in the sixteenth century, the area between the Choctawhatchee and the Chattahoochee-Apalachicola rivers was the home of the Chatot Indians. In 1639, the Spanish governor, Damian de la Pardo, arranged peace between Chatot and their neighbors, the Apalachicola Yamassee and Apalachee Indians.

During the Revolutionary War (when Florida was under the control of the British), David Holmes of Pensacola was sent by Colonel John Stuart to help defend St. Augustine. He started his journey at the upper end of Escambia Bay and traveled across West Florida, making friends with Indians

and securing them as reinforcements. There is speculation that Holmes County was named in honor of him. Others believe the county was named for an Indian chief who had been given the English name or for Thomas J. Holmes from North Carolina who settled in the area in 1830.

Holmes County economy has depended primarily on agricultural pursuits involving lumber and wood products, truck crops, cotton, peanuts, and livestock. The architecture of this locale is modest, built at an intimate scale, in the few small communities which exist in this county. The two major communities, Bonifay (once known as the "Crossroad of Gospel Singing") and Ponce de Leon, provide services required by adjacent rural areas. The Louisville and Nashville Railroad, US Highway 90, and Interstate 10 have been major transportation arteries during the county's history.

Preservation of historic structures in Holmes County has occurred where profitable economic conditions have allowed continued use. The history and landmarks of the area are recorded in the words of the citizens themselves. As in most small rural communities, the people are well versed in the events and who's who of the area. The individual pride of the owners themselves has preserved the important structures of the county.

16

A
411 Tracey St. North
Bonifay

Residence built in early 1900's. Wood frame structure, blue with white trim, novelty siding, and gable roof. Said to be oldest residence in Bonifay. Recently renovated.

B
209 Kansas St. East
Bonifay

Residence built in 1920's is local interpretation of Mediterranean Revival style. Wood frame structure with wood siding and ceramic tile roof. Recessed porches at first and second floors. Porch at first floor with fluted Doric columns. Porch at second floor with round arched openings.

C
803 Waukasha Ave.
Bonifay

Residence built in early 1900's. Bungalow style building with hip roof, clipped gable roofs on dormers, shed roof at porch, and paired wood columns on brick piers.

D
105 Waukasha Ave.
Bonifay

Residence built in the 1920's. Simplified Bungalow style, one-story wood frame with hip roof and hip roof dormer. Paired porch columns on brick piers.

E
Pennsylvania Ave.
and S. Waukasha St.
Bonifay

Commercial Buildings. Block typical of late nineteenth and early twentieth century small-town commercial buildings. One-and-two-story brick buildings modified to meet stylistic and merchandising changes. Many offer facade restoration potential.

OKALOOSA

STEVE JERNIGAN, AIA, FLORIDA NORTHWEST

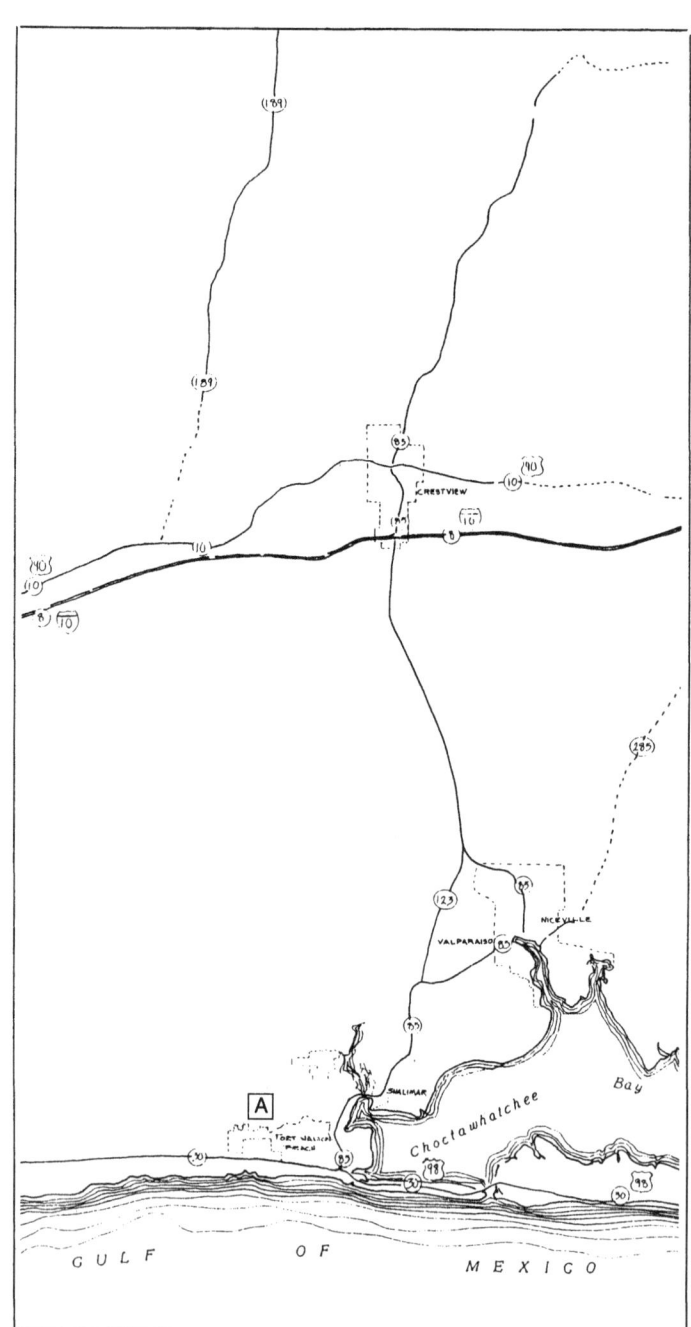

Established on June 13, 1915, Okaloosa is Florida's fifty-second county, extending from Alabama to the Gulf and lying between Walton and Santa Rosa counties. The word "Okaloosa" comes from the Choctaw Indian words of "Oka," meaning water, and "lusa," meaning black. The name probably referred to the Blackwater River which runs through part of the county.

Although Crestview is the county seat and a commercial center, most of the county's population is in the communities of Valparaiso, Niceville, Shalimar, Fort Walton Beach, Destin, and other coastal sections. Eglin Air Force Base, a major employer, occupies almost half of the county's area; Blackwater State Forest protects natural resources in the northwestern section.

Downtown Fort Walton Beach is located around burial and ceremonial sites of the Choctaw tribes that inhabited the region. John L. McKinnon, in his *History of Walton County*, describes an 1861 excavation of a large mound in which skeletons of men were found. Many of these were removed by Confederate soldiers and displayed in one of the buildings of the fort. Federal gunboats shelled the building, caused fires, and destroyed the collection. Artifacts discovered in other excavations are on display in a museum on the site (illustrated).

Preservation activities in Okaloosa County are limited to sites threatened by development, sites not included in public lands. Concentrated efforts by both the public and private sectors are necessary if these efforts are to be successful.

A
Ceremonial mound

The Fort Walton Temple Mound, built by Indians occupying area until c. 1700 A.D.; designated as National Historic Landmark; interpretive museum adjacent.

TAYLOR

ELIZABETH HAMBY

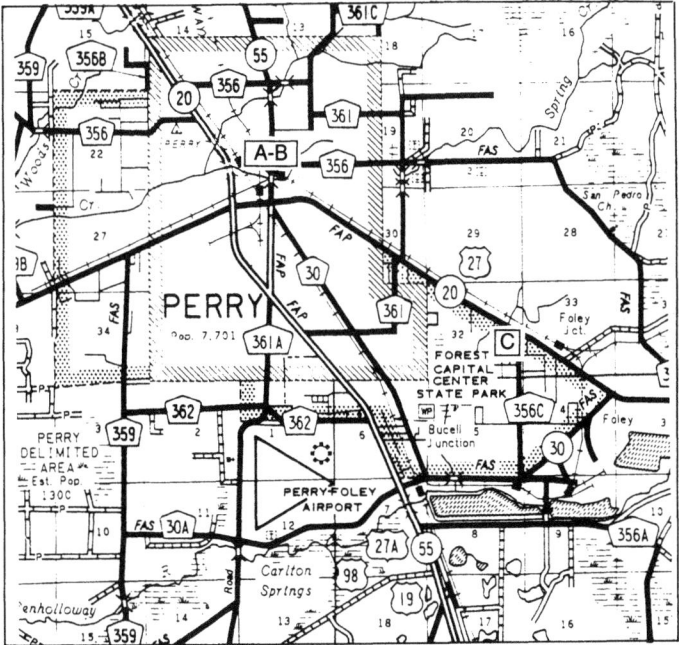

It wasn't until the Spanish American War period at the turn of the century that the grand stands of virgin timber were noticed by the rapidly expanding industrialists of America. From that time to the present, trees have been the basis for the county's economy. Nature's way of producing rosin and turpentine was improved upon with planned slashing and Taylor County became the home of the largest single naval stores industry in the world.

With the advent of railroads, there came sawmills into the area. In 1914, Burton and Schwartz Cypress Company erected a mill in Perry. In time this mill was developed into the largest cypress mill in the world. Logging camps began to spring up throughout the county to supply these mills. As was the custom of the day, a company town included all the necessities of life including homes, stores, schools and entertainment.

In 1951, Buckeye Cellulose Corp. moved into the county and established a pulp mill which was to grow to become one of the most modern industrial plants in the state. It produces over 400,000 metric tons of pulp each year.

For many years, Taylor County has been the focal point of the travelling public in North Florida. Four federal highways and five state roads converge at the county seat of Perry. During the post World War II years, Perry became a favorite stopover for north-south travelers and many motels were built to handle the tourists. Although the construction of the interstate highway system has siphoned off some of the traffic, Perry still enjoys the reputation as the motel center of north Florida.

The history of Taylor County has been colorful, to say the least. Located in the deepest indention in the Gulf of Mexico coastline in North Florida's Big Bend, its 673,000 acres have been identified with forests and forestry from its earliest known days.

The Spanish explorer de Narvaez passed through its tall timberland in 1528 in search of gold. Historians believe that deSoto passed through the northern part of the county in 1539. There were several primitive forts built during the Seminole Indians Wars including Fort Brooke near the mouth of the Steinhatchee River.

Throughout the 17th and 18th centuries, pirates and freebooters of all nationalities frequented Deadman's Bay off the mouth of the Steinhatchee River. In 1816, the forces of General Andrew Jackson fought the Seminoles at the Natural Bridge on the Econfina River, but it wasn't until General Zachary Taylor, commander of all U.S. forces in northwest Florida, instituted a campaign that lasted from 1835 to 1842, that the land was made safe for settlers.

Taylor County was formed from part of Madison County on December 23, 1856 and it was named for General Zachary Taylor who had cleared out the hostile Indians a decade earlier. On October 2, 1857, the County Commissioners of Taylor County purchased for $75 forty acres from the State of Florida on which to build a town. A courthouse of rough logs was erected and they named the town Rose Head. Common dwelling of the era were one-room log cabins or hipped-roof log homes with a kitchen built away from the house. In 1860, there was only one frame house in the community and it was located on Rocky Creek.

By 1870 the population of Taylor County had risen to 1,453. It jumped to 2,279 by 1880 when there were two post offices in the county, one in Fenholloway and one at Rose Head. In 1879, Rose Head was changed to Perrytown in honor of Florida Governor Starke Perry.

A
201 E. Green St.
Perry
Taylor County Post Office. Completed in 1935, this Mediterranean-style building serves an historic landmark in the area.

B
Corner Main and Washington Streets
Perry
Taylor County Historical Society Headquarters. Built in 1903 as the Bank of Perry, this Classic Revival building has housed the historical society since 1967.

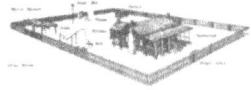

C
204 Forest Park Drive
Perry
Forest Capital State Museum. This museum interprets the history of Florida's forest industry. Hours are 9 to 5 except major holidays. Most interesting is the Cracker Homestead Interpretive site which includes the house and outbuildings of a typical Florida cracker farm.

JACKSON

DIANE D. GREER

E Established on August 12, 1822, Jackson County Florida observed its sesquicentennial in 1972. It is Florida's third oldest county and it was created by an act of the Territorial Legislature while meeting near Pensacola. The county originally stretched from the Choctawatchee River to the Suwannee River and from Alabama and Georgia to the Gulf of Mexico.

After a bitter and extended controversy, Marianna became the permanent county seat of government in 1829. Marianna was founded in 1827 by Robert and Anna Maria Beveridge, who purchased three eighty-acre tracts of land on a bluff along the Chipola River. They, together with associates, donated land and built the first of four courthouses which were to eventually stand on the same square.

In the late nineteenth century pioneers poured into the rich, fertile Chipola River area to establish homesites. Typical of the deep South, cotton eventually became "King" and numerous large plantations thrived on this economy. Though the cotton kingdom was to be crushed during the Civil War and the changes that it brought, wealthy families and a rich heritage remained.

After statehood in 1845, there came secession and the War Between the States. Jackson County's John Milton served as governor of Confederate Florida. One of the most tragic events in the county's history occurred on September 27, 1864, when Marianna was raided by a band of Federals from Union Headquarters in Pensacola. A battle ensued, primarily in the environs of St. Luke's Episcopal Church. The church was burned and the community plundered.

After a bitter Reconstruction ordeal, Jackson County began its return to normalcy. Recovery ushered the people into the twentieth century and a return to prosperity. Though growth has never been spectacular, Jackson County's communities have been stable, the economy largely based on agriculture.

Some of the finest Greek Revival architecture to be found in Florida is located in Jackson County along with an interesting collection of very elaborate Victorian residences.

20

A
Lafayette St.
Marianna

St. Luke's Episcopal Church and Cemetery. The present church, built in 1947, is the fourth to stand on this site. The names of many distinguished Marianna families can be found on tombstones in the cemetery.

B
217 E. Lafayette St.
Marianna

Holden House. This house was probably built between 1849 and 1851 and it has never gone out of the Holden family. The house is vernacular in style and well suited to the Florida climate.

C
10 W. Lafayette St.
Marianna

Joseph W. Russ House. Constructed in 1892-96, much of the original fabric of this Stick Style house remains intact despite alterations that were made around the turn-of-the-century.

D
403 Putnam Street
Marianna

Slade West House. This 1840 house, which bears characteristics of both the Classic Revival and Victorian periods, is associated with the life of its builder, prominent physician Theophilus West.

E
State Rd. 71, at the main intersection
Greenwood

Pender's Store. This typical rural commercial structure was built in the late 1800's and has served as a general store ever since.

F
State Rd. 71
Greenwood

Great Oaks Plantation, just south of junction with State Rd. 69. Built in 1857, and fully restored to its original appearance, this house is one of the finest antebellum structures in Jackson County.

G
Fort Road immed. east of intersection
Greenwood

Erwin House. This rural residence built in the early 1900's, is a transition colonial house with a central hall plan. The family cemetery is immediately to the north of the house.

H
242 W. Lafayette St.
Marianna

Ely-Crigler House. This National Register property was built around 1840 as a Greek Revival house. Later, Victorian railings and trim were added, as were the wings. Francis Ely, who built the house, was one of Jackson County's earliest settlers.

NOTES

CALHOUN

WALT MARDER

On January 26, 1838, Calhoun County came into existence. Occupying an area that began as Escambia County and then became part of Fayette County (the only Florida county to have completely disappeared), Calhoun was named in honor of John C. Calhoun, the senator from South Carolina. Fourteen years earlier, on January 2, 1824, the Blount Reservation had been established here. John Blount, a Seminole chief, was a signer of the treaty establishing the reservation and it was for him that Blountstown, the county seat, is named.

Calhoun County figured prominently in the early history of Florida. Before the Civil War, the Apalachicola River was a major shipping route. Thousands of tons of cotton were sent from Alabama and Georgia to the port of Apalachicola. On route, Blountstown was an important stopover for ship's crews on their long journey. The pilings from long forgotten wharves still dot the river bed.

The major growth in Calhoun County has been agricultural and crops such as tobacco and vegetables, along with cattle and lumber, have helped the economy flourish. Its favorable climate, coupled with its rich soil, give it some of the finest farmland in Florida.

At Torreya State Park, one of the most impressive antebellum homes in Florida has been preserved and is open to the public. The Gregory Mansion, built in 1834, was brought across the Apalachicola River into Liberty County in the 1930's as a part of a part of a Civilian Conservation Corps project that helped establish the park.

The first train in Calhoun County began running between Marianna and Blountstown in 1909. The 29-mile route was the shortest in Florida. The railroad provided mail, freight and passenger service until 1929, connecting with the L & N in Marianna. During its heyday, the M & B ran special excursion trips to the West Florida Fair, charging fifty cents for a round trip ride.

Below Torreya, State Rd. 20 crosses the Apalachicola River outside Bristol and descends into the river valley as a beautiful truss bridge which was built in 1940. Continuing on, the road passes through the Blount Reservation and approaches Blountstown where the Calhoun County Courthouse, one of the finest Romanesque Revival buildings in Florida, comes into view. Built in 1904, the courthouse has recently been restored. Across the street, in the new courthouse, is a small museum devoted to the Indian settlements in the area and the early history of the county.

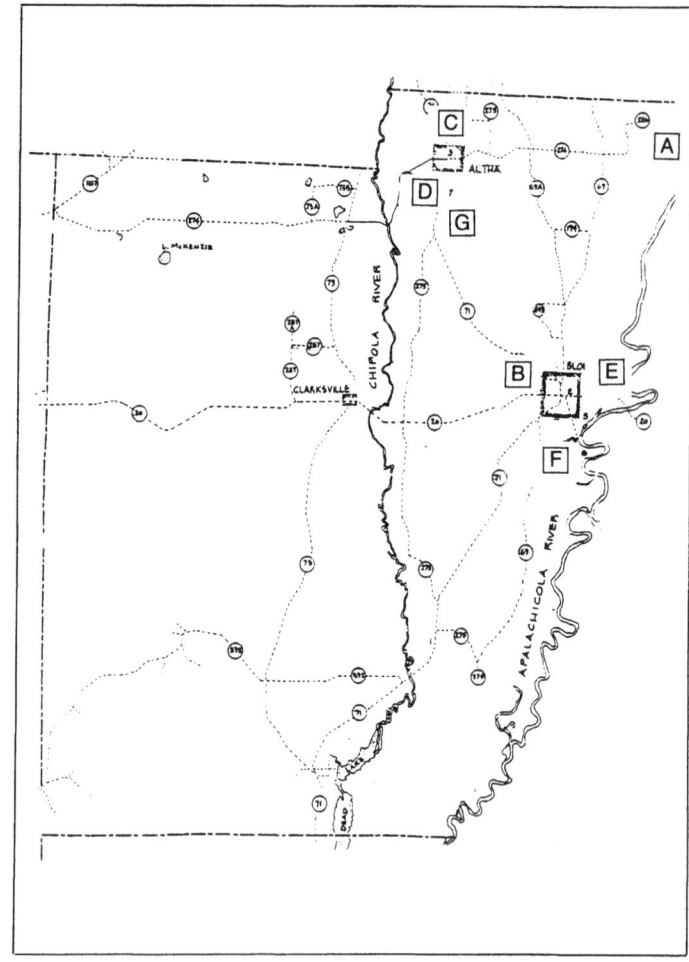

Leaving Blountstown, only the tiny village of Clarkstown to the west interrupts the miles of wilderness. To the north is Altha, another farming community and along the river, both north and south, are small towns which serve as reminders of the last century.

Calhoun County remains aloof from the fast pace of a growing state. In 1838, the first convention for the organization of state government took place in Blountstown and the town was even considered for state capital. Now, however, those politically important days are all but forgotten.

A
Torreya State Park
Calhoun County

Jason Gregory House. Built circa 1834, this mansion was removed from the eroding piece of land it was built on to its present site overlooking the Apalachicola River in Torreya State Park. The building is open to the public.

B
314 E. Central Ave.
Blountstown

Old Calhoun County Courthouse. Designed by architects Benjamin Smith and Frank Lockwood of Montgomery, Alabama, this 1904 building is one of two Romanesque Revival courthouses extant in Florida. The red brick building has recently been restored.

C
Route 71
Altha

Altha School. The Altha School has served this small rural community continuously since its construction in 1922 with only modest repairs.

D
Route 71, 1.5 miles
south of Altha

Log structure. This single pen log dwelling was constructed of pine logs with corners saddle notched. Built in 1880, the house was originally sited farther back from the road, which has since been moved several feet.

E
Along SR 20
S. of Blountstown

Cayson Mound and Village. Built A.D. 900-1500, this represents one of the best preserved temple mound-village complexes in Florida. The site appears to have served as the socio-political center for numerous farmsteads along the Apalachicola River. It contains the mound, a village site and the plaza.

NOTES

GULF

RICK BARNETT, AIA, FLORIDA NORTH CENTRAL

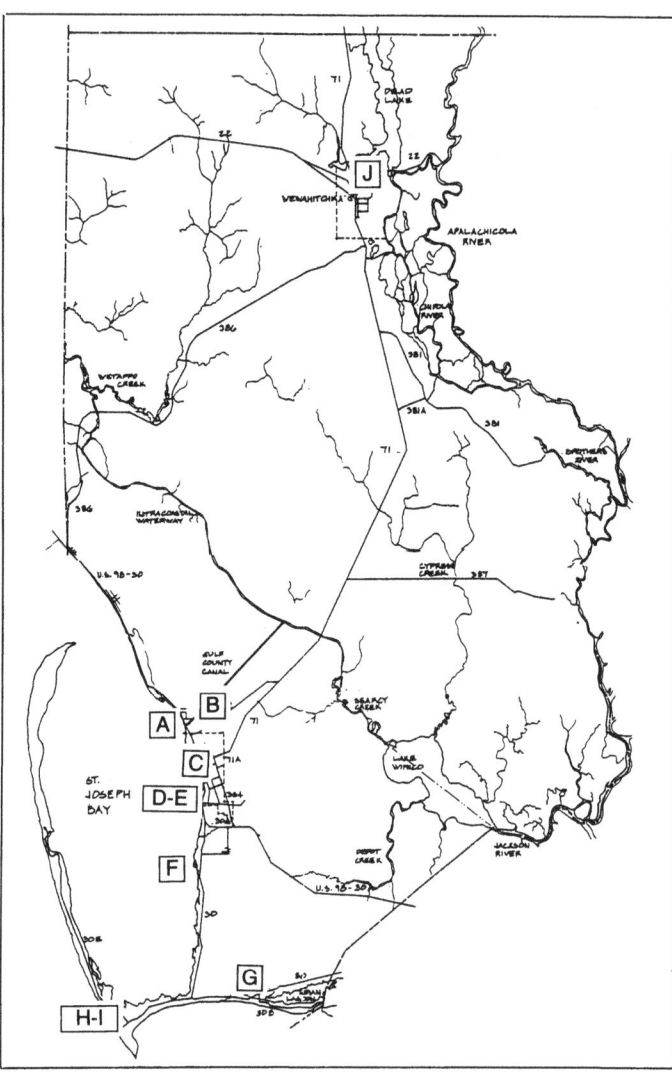

Several thousand years before Europeans planted their standards on the Gulf Stream of Florida and St. Joseph Bay, the area was inhabited by prehistoric Indians. Natural resources provided ample food supply for a small, but well distributed, population whose economy was based on hunting, fishing, and gathering of shellfish and wild fruits. Evidences of long habitation by these people can be found in the numerous Indian mounds in Gulf County.

Early French, Spanish, and English settlers were attracted by the land-locked waters of St. Joseph Bay where they built fortresses to secure territorial control of the Gulf of Mexico. In 1819, the United States purchased Florida from the Spanish who relinquished control of the territory in 1821. In 1835 the United States Supreme Court declared the Forbes Company legal owners of about 1,250,000 acres of land in the Apalachicola region, and many settlers were forced to give up their holdings in that area and move northwest. This was the beginning of the historic city of St. Joseph.

The settlement period became a boom era in St. Joseph as wealthy planters, merchants, and industrialists built cotton mills, ship and brick yards, luxurious hotels, wharves, and businesses. Due to efforts of Peter Gautier, a newspaperman, Florida's 1838 Constitutional Convention was held in St. Joseph. This important convention, which helped chart the future of Florida, created a place for St. Joseph in state records, but, the historical city was shortlived. Economic panic in the 1830's, epidemics of yellow fever brought from the West Indies, and a devestating hurricane in 1841 brought the development of St. Joseph to an end.

After the Civil War, steamboating became the major source of transportation, not only for economic markets, but also for passengers and livestock. During this riverboat era, many Confederate veterans migrated to the Wewahitchka region, the first permanent settlement in Gulf County. The hardy, industrious people cleared the land, planted citrus, and furnished timber for the sawmills.

With the advent of the railroads at the turn of the century, a greater influx of people moved into this Gulf Coast region. Soon there were churches, schools, stores, and, some of the early families, including those of T. H. Stone and A. M. Jones, built handsome dwellings. The Port Inn, a large wooden building which stood where Motel St. Joe is now, was the hub of social life. This building burned. The old Woman's Club, a spacious log building which served as a community center, was replaced by the Garden Club. With the completion of the railroads, increased development brought more docks, wharves, saw mills, sugar cane mills, ice plants, fisheries, oyster packeries, and tobacco growing.

The present industrial expansion began in 1938 when the St. Joe Paper Company completed a pulp and paper mill to utilize the abundant supply of pulpwood. As the company grew, so did the mill and the community. A box plant was added. Three chemical manufacturing companies moved to the county. In the 1980's, the region is gaining stature as an industrial area by supporting such enterprises as timber production, cattle raising and shipping and fishing. At the same time, the natural beauty of beaches, lakes, and forests continues to attract vacationers, tourists and new residents.

In 1955, the Florida Museum at Port St. Joe was founded to depict the brief history of Florida's constitutional city. Since 1960, St. Joe Historical Society has played a major role in preserving the region's past as members collect old maps, photos and papers to document this coastal community's heritage.

A
Hwy. 98
Port St. Joe

St. Joe Paper Mill, built in 1938. Industrial complex of raw materials yards, processing buildings, and stacks. Chief industry in Gulf County.

B
Hwy. 98
Port St. Joe

Executive Offices of St. Joe Paper Company and Apalachicola Northern Railroad. Three-story brick building with trim delineating bands of windows and stairwells.

C
304 Monument Ave.
Port St. Joe

Florida National Bank. Commercial building with decorative panels emphasizing street entry.

D
5th Street
Port St. Joe

A. M. Jones Home. One of the earliest homes in Port St. Joe. Typical wood-frame, single-story, late nineteenth century style house with front porch wrapping around part of side elevations and pyramid roof with dormer.

E
8th Street
Port St. Joe

St. Joseph Catholic Mission Church, built in 1925. Oldest church in city. Simple wood-frame, single-story building with gable roof, masonry piers, square tower with pyramid roof and louvered openings, and an entry porch with gable roof. Used by St. Joe Garden Club in late 1980's.

F
Port St. Joe

Old Beacon Hill Lighthouse, 2 miles off Hwy. 98 toward Indian Pass. One of area's oldest lighthouses. Two-story building with verandas on four sides at first and second floors. Double exterior stairways over first floor entrance, hip roof with cupola. Relocated and adapted as residence.

G
Port St. Joe

Indian Pass Trading Post and Post Office. Earliest post office and mercantile business. Wood frame, single-story building with gable roof. Front bay providing covered service area.

H
Cape San Blas

Cape San Blas Lighthouse, 14 miles east of Port St. Joe, built in 1847. Relocated. Space-frame construction supporting circulation cylinder from second floor level to deck and room with light housing above.

I
Cape San Blas

Cape San Blas Coast Guard Housing, Cape San Blas. Two-story, wood frame building with gable roof. Shed-roof porch on four sides of first floor.

J
Wewahitchka

Old Gulf County Courthouse, built in 1927 by H. H. Taylor. Neo-Classical Revival style, two-story building with attic and flat roof. Portico with four columns and gable roof.

FRANKLIN

GEORGE L. CHAPEL

Franklin County was established February 8, 1832. It was named after Benjamin Franklin. Its two principal communities are Apalachicola, which is the county seat, and Carrabelle.

The name Apalachicola come from a Hitichi Indian word "Apalachi," meaning roughly "land of the People Beyond." To the Creek Indian nation the Apalachicola River flowed into the "land Beyond," currently called Apalachicola Bay.

At one time the area supported Indians of various tribes. In 1527 Panfilo de Narvaez became the first European to view that part of Florida. In 1705 the French set up Fort Covocer on St. Joseph's Bay, but were ousted from there by the Spanish who established San Marcos de Apalache a year later. A trading post was built in 1790 and in 1803, John Forbes and Company received a 1,250,000 acre land grant from the Seminole Indian chief Hopoeithle Micco. The "Forbes Purchase" included the site of the present city of Apalachicola.

With Andrew Jackson's acceptance of the transfer of West Florida from the Spanish in 1821 came economic change. Shipment of cotton began on the Apalachicola River in 1828, and within a few years, steamers were cruising daily. In that period, Apalachicola became the second largest American port on the Gulf.

In 1832, Franklin County was inaugurated as the name of the territory. A post office was built and the first postmaster was William D. Price. Dr. John Gorrie followed as second postmaster in 1834, and George F. Baltzell became the third in 1837. In the 1840s, Dr. John Gorrie discovered an artificial method for freezing water and built the first ice machine. Dr. Gorrie's statue is one the two from the state of Florida in the Hall of Fame in Washington, D.C.

At the outbreak of the War Between the States, Franklin County supplied men for the Confederacy. Apalachicola was fortified in preparation for war, and was bombarded once by Federal gunboats.

Apalachicola, and, by implication, Franklin County, achieved its heyday in the days of King Cotton. During the 1860s, Apalachicola's importance as a port declined after railroads were built, but in the 1870s, it became a saw mill center for the Apalachicola River basin. After all the timber was logged (around the early 1930s) the seafood and oyster industry rose to its present importance.

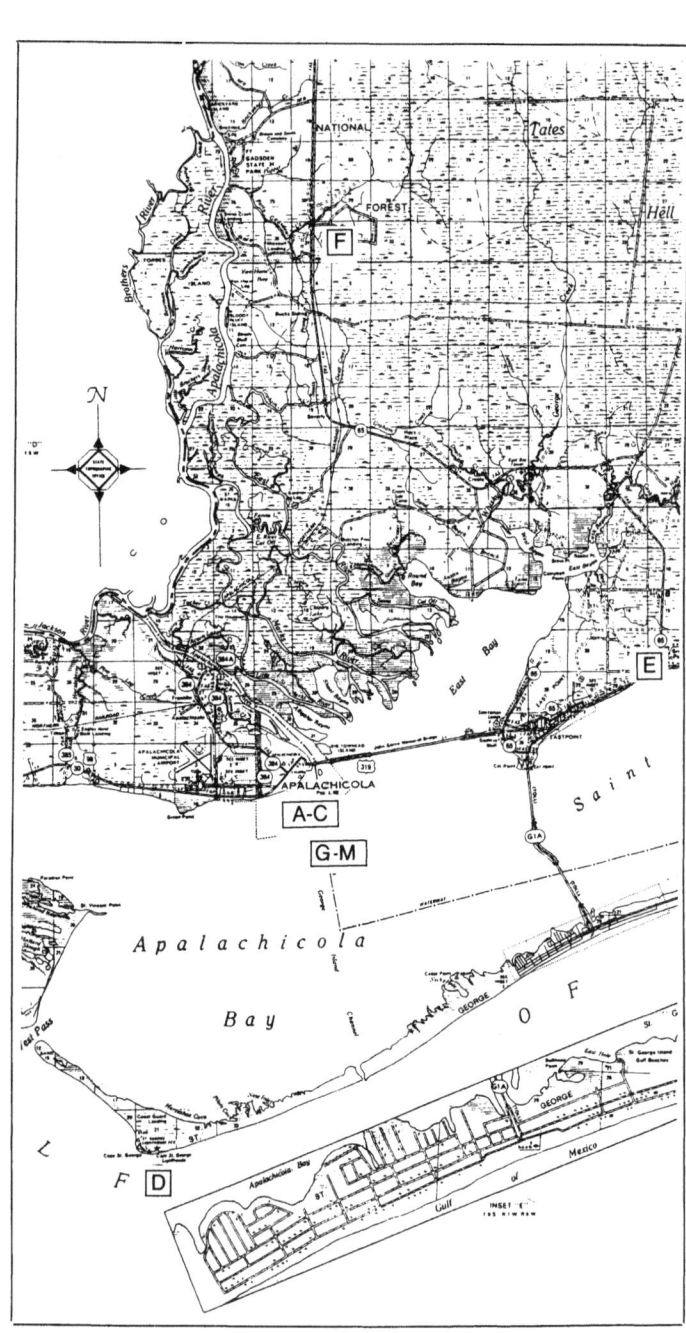

A
Historic District
Apalachicola

This district includes most of the 1836 town plan and a remarkable concentration of 19th and 20th century residential and commercial buildings. Most of the pre-1860 buildings are concentrated along 5th and 6th Streets. Most of the commercial area along Market and Commerce Streets dates from the early 20th century. The district is on the National Register of Historic Places.

B
SW corner Market &
Avenue F
Apalachicola

David G. Raney House. A Greek Revival, two-story, wood frame house built by a leading merchant at the height of Apalachicola's prosperity as a leading cotton port.

C
Avenue D & Sixth St.
Apalachicola

Trinity Episcopal Church. This structure was prefabricated in New York and shipped to Apalachicola by ship where it was assembled in 1841. It is Greek Revival style and one of the oldest Episcopal churches in Florida.

D
West end of
St. George Island

Cape St. George Light at southernmost point of Little St. George Island. The present tower, built in 1852, replaces two which preceded it and were destroyed by storms. Although damaged during the Civil War, the light was repaired and continues to serve today as an operative light.

E
City Park on Hwy 98
Carrabelle

Crooked River or Carrabelle Lighthouse. This wrought iron skeleton tower was built in 1895. The increase in the lumber trade necessitated the light. The light is still active today and visible from seventeen miles.

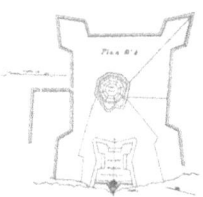

F
6 miles sw of Sumatra
Franklin County

The Negro Fort and Fort Gadsden were both situated on the east bank of the Apalachicola River where they could control water traffic. Fort Gadsden was decribed by an aide to Andrew Jackson as "a temporary work, hastily erected of perishable materials." Today the site of the forts is operated by the Florida Department of Recreation and Parks.

G
Avenue B
Apalachicola

Richard G. Porter House. Built in the early 1900's, this is a well-maintained example of local Victoriana, complete with rounded porch and turret.

H
Corner Broad St. &
Chestnut Avenue
Apalachicola

Chapman House. The home of Dr. Alvin W. Chapman, a botanist and author of international importance, the Greek Revival house was built c. 1840.

I
Chestnut Street
Apalachicola

Chestnut Street Cemetery. Dating from 1832, many local Confederate soldiers are buried here.

J
Water Street
Apalachicola

Cotton Warehouse. In 1838, the Apalachicola Land Company built 43 cotton warehouses, each 30 feet in width and three stories tall. Only two remain today.

K
Avenue B
Apalachicola

Hoffman House. This Gulf Coast Cottage was moved from St. Joseph by boat in the 1840's.

L
Locust Street
Apalachicola

Whiteside House. An 1878 example of Gothic Revival architecture.

M
Avenue B
Apalachicola

George Ruge House. An 1896 example of Queen Anne architecture.

N
Historic District
Apalachicola

Norvell Cottages. Built in 1886, these are rehabilitated Gulf Coast Millworker's cottages.

Other sites of significance in Apalachicola include the completely restored Gibson Hotel, the Gorrie Museum and grave on Gorrie Square, the Sponge Exchange and Chapman Elementary School, the only known example of Egyptian Revival architecture in Florida.

LIBERTY

TIM WHITE, AIA, FLORIDA NORTH CENTRAL

L Liberty County was chartered on Dec. 15, 1855, after a Gadsden County citizen, with the last name of Dismukes, proposed a bill for its creation. The county was formed from territory included in the Forbes Grant, a Spanish grant given in 1803 to an Englishman as compensation for destruction of his trading post by Indians under Spanish rule. This grant to Forbes included approximately all of what is now Liberty, Franklin and Wakulla counties. Early Indian inhabitation of the area remained evident in the many Indian names used and the number of Indian mounds found.

After the United States purchased Florida from Spain, pioneers bought homesteads from the government and settled in Liberty County. However, according to the purchase treaty, all Spanish grants before 1821 were to be honored. Heirs to the Forbes Grant, then living in Scotland, claimed the land. The settlers were forced to buy their land again or to leave. Among those making the claim were members of the Bruce family, descendents of a former king of Scotland. The old Bruce home, where three bachelor brothers lived, is on Road Number One outside the city limits of Quincy.

Rich soil, a fine range for stock, and wild animal game brought settlers to Liberty County from Georgia and South Carolina. First cultivated by the Indians, the farmland was some of the best in Florida. Crops included corn, cotton, beans, forage, peaches, figs, pecans, blueberries, peanuts, sugar cane, and sweet potatoes. Principal industries developed by those moving to the area were turpentine distilleries, naval store plants, sawmills, and shingle mills. The rich forest resource was reflected in the twentieth century when a large portion of the county was included in the Apalachicola National Forest.

The county seat is Bristol, originally called Riddeysville but renamed in 1858. The town had few of the services normally available at such a location, according to a 1914 speech made by Mrs. V. O. Carson when she was remembering Liberty County sixty years before that time. She recalled that the county seat had one hewed log dwelling, one store building, one courthouse, one church building that belonged to everybody but was not deeded to any particular denomination, no post office, no doctor, no jail, so little county business that county officers spent most of their time away from the courthouse, and no store with goods (the population traded in Quincy or ordered goods from Apalachicola and Columbus, Ga.). There were few frame buildings. Most dwellings were double-hewn log houses with stick and clay chimneys.

Liberty County's first post office, established in 1918, was located at Coe's Mill which was built by Emanuel Sikes to grind grits, clean rice, and saw lumber. Coe's Mill became a social center and eventually was renamed Hosford in 1907 to honor Senator R. F. Hosford who promoted the building of the county railroad. The Apalachicola Northern Railroad connected Liberty County with the rest of the southeastern states and encouraged the growth of population, towns, and industry.

The oldest city in the county was Rock Bluff where a relative of Andrew Jackson lived. (Unfortunately all that is left of Dr. Jackson's home is a chimney). One of the battles in county history involved the Indian massacre of a Scottish-immigrant family, the Laslies, on June 20, 1838. During the Civil

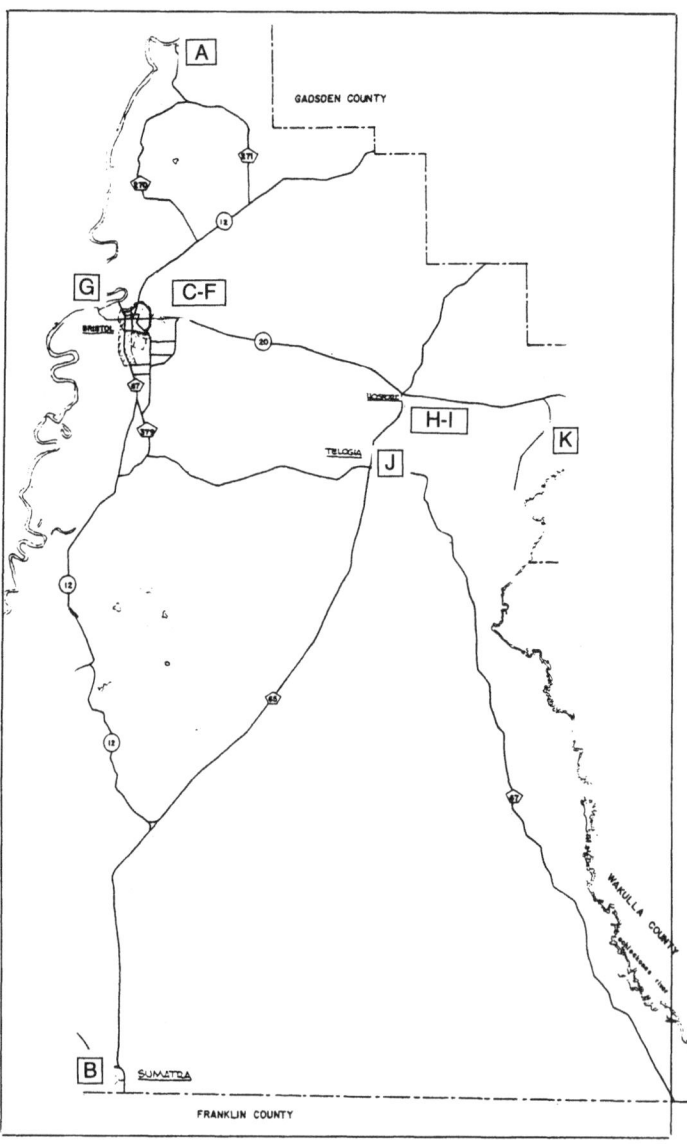

War, Confederates built two half-moon trenches with cannon emplacements north of Bristol on palisades along the Apalachicola River to halt the advance of the Union Army.

In the late 1930's, the building of the bridge across the Apalachicola River had a major effect on economic and social development in the county real estate sales and architectural growth increased dramatically. Development in Liberty County is guided by the Liberty County Planning Board and the Apalachicola Planning Council.

A
SR 271
Bristol

Jason Gregory House, 13 miles northeast of Bristol, built in 1849 at Ocheesee Landing on Apalachicola River. Pine and cypress house on five-foot brick piers, constructed by slave labor. Moved to Torreya State Park in 1930's and restored.

B
Hwy.65
Sumatra

Dr. Spence House, built in 1906. Two-story Neo-Classical style, house of cypress and pine with 5,000 sq. ft., sheet metal roof, and layer of sand between floor and ceiling as fire retardant.

C
Highway 20
Bristol

Liberty County Courthouse, built in 1940 with Jack Cullpepper as architect. Brick Neo-Classical style.

D
Central at Main
Bristol

Bristol State Bank, built in early 1900's. Survived 1930 fire which destroyed most of Bristol. Commercial use in 1980's.

E
Central Street
Bristol

Stockade, built in 1930's as stockade with iron bars within some walls. Adapted by Liberty County as office space.

F
Central Street
Bristol

Bristol Free Press, built in late 1800's. Wood-frame structure with sheet metal roof and unique light source in roof. First newspaper office in Bristol, original printing press.

G
Highway 20
Bristol/Blountstown

Apalachicola River Bridge, between Bristol and Blountstown. Constructed of steel and concrete piers in 1937-38 by Wisconsin Iron and Bridge Co.

H
Hosford

Westlian Church, built about 1900. Primitive Victorian Revival style building with wood frame. First meeting held in 1913.

I
Hosford

Graves Lumber Company, built in 1900's and closed in 1927. Known for constructing railroad to haul products. Brick vault remaining.

J
Telogia

Bass Store, intersection of Roads 65 and 67, built in 1927 as country store. Wood-frame structure with sheet metal roof.

K
Blue Creek Rd.
Liberty County

Blue Creek Church, off Hwy. 20, built in late nineteenth century by Daniel Stoutamire. Wood-frame building on cypress log posts. One of earliest churches in county.

NOTES

29

GADſDEN

DIANE D. GREER

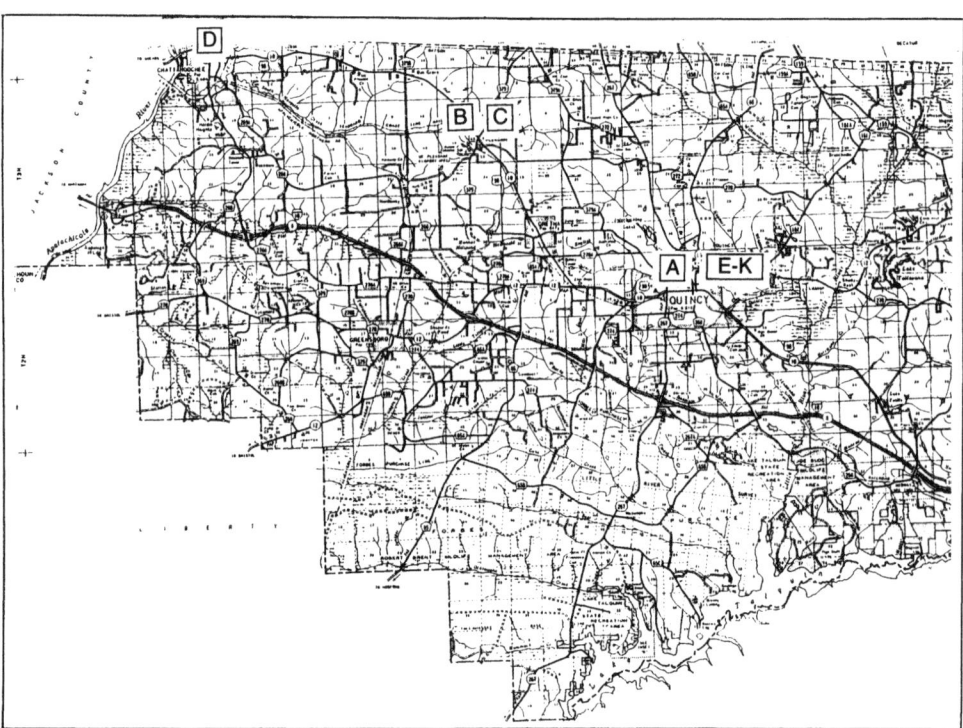

G Gadsden County was settled during Florida's territorial period by planters who migrated with their families and slaves from Virginia and the Carolinas. Lured by the possibility for successful cotton and tobacco cultivation, these early settlers established plantations throughout the region. Although most plantations in the county were small, there emerged an influential planter class that attempted to transplant the culture of their former tidewater region to Florida's frontier.

On June 24, 1823, just two years after Spain ceded Florida to the United States, the Legislative Council approved the creation of Gadsden County. In 1825, Quincy was established as the seat of county government and the first courthouse on the public square was erected in 1827. Since then at least two other courthouses have been built on the same site and have visually symbolized the continuity of public life in the county.

Quincy in 1830 was a small village inhabited by some merchants, doctors and a dozen or so citizens living in frame and log houses. But, the town soon became the site of the county's early social clubs, schools and churches.

Gadsden county's planters had concentrated on cotton production, but in the late 1820's some Virginia planters brought with them the knowledge and skill of tobacco culture. One settler, John "Virginia" Smith, who owned a plantation a few miles south of Quincy, brought with him some Virginia tobacco seeds. When the Virginia plant was cross-pollinated with a Cuban tobacco, which had previously been cultivated in the county, the resulting hybrid became known as "Florida wrapper leaf." The new tobacco plant was used in the manufacturing of cigars and produced a small local cigar industry in the area.

The town of Quincy flourished during the 1840's and many of the homes that had been built earlier received elegant Classic Revival additions which reflected the town's growing prosperity. By the 1850's, although still a small town, Quincy's future looked bright. The Civil War, however, abruptly ended the region's progress. The loss of slave labor and capital crippled the tobacco plantations and recovery did not take place until the mid-1880's. During the Civil War, Quincy served as the Confederate military headquarters for the Middle Florida District. The town also served as a commissary depot and hospital station with the Episcopal Church, Courthouse and Quincy Academy used as makeshift medical centers.

By the 1890's, however, Northern tobacco leaf dealers and cigar manufacturers had begun investing in tobacco plantations in the county. Overproduction and the nationwide panic in 1893 ended the short-lived economic boom. During the next few years experiments to find a more marketable tobacco leaf led to the development of a new artificial shade tobacco process. Shade tobacco brought great wealth to the region as speculation produced inflated land values and sensational wage increases. Two and three-story brick tobacco packing and storage warehouses were built in Quincy between the late 1890's and 1920.

By 1907, due to overproduction, the instability of tobacco cultivation temporarily caused major financial problems in the county. Left without working capital, both large and small tobacco companies were forced to merge into one corporation called the American Sumatra Tobacco Corporation. The period between the merger and 1920 were profitable years for the county and a new courthouse was built in 1913 on the public square in Quincy. This building, along with many others dating from as early as the 1840's, survive in the Quincy Historic District.

A
Historic District
Quincy

The Quincy Historic District, which lies within the bounds of the original township plat, is a 16-block area around the historic public square. It contains 145 structures which are visual links to Quincy's past.

B
Hwy 90, nw of
Mt. Pleasant

Joshua Davis House, northwest of Mt. Pleasant on Hwy 90 at a point 2¼ miles west of the junction of County Road 379. Built in 1827 by Thomas Dawsey, the property was later owned by Joshua Davis and used as a stagecoach station. The house gains its significance from the fact that the log portion of the building is the oldest documented structure in Gadsden County.

C
North of Hwy 90
Mt. Pleasant

Malachi Martin House, one mile northwest of the Mt. Pleasant Methodist Church, 1/4 mile north of U.S. Hwy 90. Built between 1870 and 1884, the Martin House is an unusual and unique example of a vernacular copy of the Octogon Mode which was popularized in the mid-19th century. This house is one of only two period octagons in Florida.

D
US Hwy. 90
Chattahoochee

United States Arsenal & Florida State Hospital. Completed in 1839, the arsenal was used for mustering the Confederate troops into service at the beginning of the Civil War. In the Spring of 1862, the Florida Infantry was organized here. In 1876, the buildings were taken over by the Florida State Hospital for the mentally ill.

E
205 N. Madison
Quincy

E.B. Shelfer House. This is a transitional building that retains Victorian articulation in combination with Neo-classical decoration. Built in 1903.

F
300 N. Calhoun
Quincy

Quincy Woman's Club, Old Washington Lodge No. 2. Built in 1852-53, this Classic Revival building is typical of the work of Charles Waller, a builder of local importance. Originally built as a Masonic hall, the building has been in continuous use since it was constructed.

G
219 N. Jackson
Quincy

E.C. Love House. Built c. 1850, the Love House is significant as the extant example of a type of house that was common in the Quincy vicinity prior to the Civil War. The house is Georgian in plan and decoration.

H
303 N. Adams St.
Quincy

Quincy Academy. Built in 1850, this building is basically utilitiarian and strongly influenced by the Georgian and Federal styles. The present structure retains most of the original architectural elements and the devices used to keep the sexes separate in school provide a glimpse into the attitudes of the period.

I
121 N. Duval St.
Quincy

Stockton-Curry House. This 1845 house is a surviving example of antebellum Classic Revival architecture.

J
212 N. Madison St.
Quincy

Methodist Parsonage/White House. Built in 1843, this building is an excellent example of Classic Revival architecture.

K
305 E. King St.
Quincy

John Lee McFarlin House. This 1895 house served as a residence to J.L. McFarlin, who was one of the largest independent tobacco producers in the Florida-Georgia shade district. The house is the most exuberant piece of Victoriana remaining in the county.

LEON

DAVID E. FERRO, ARCHITECT

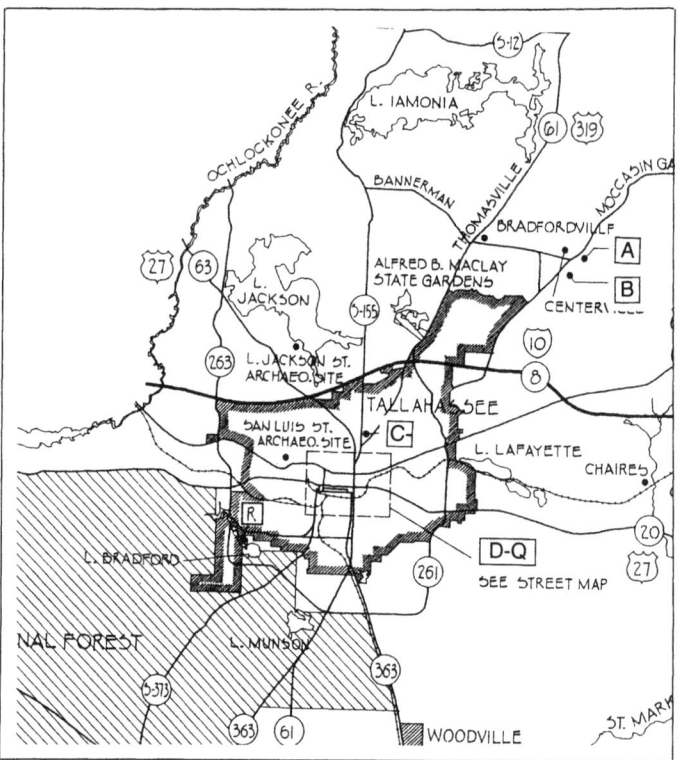

L ong before recorded history, Leon County was occupied by Indians, predecessors of the Chero-kee and Seminole. Fertile lands, numerous streams and lake and a temperate climate led the Apalachee to establish a village and, in time, cultivate a wide variety of crops. Initial Spanish contact occurred in 1528. Eleven years later, explorer Hernando de Soto wintered in the region on his way to discovery of the Mississippi. By the middle of the 17th century, the Spanish had established a string of missions and forts in the Apalachee country of northwest Florida. San Luis, founded in 1633, was the largest, with a population eventually reaching 1,400. British invaders eventually drove the Indians out of the area and with the burning of San Luis the Spanish era in Leon County ended. Soon the land was consumed by wilderness, a province of abandoned villages, the meaning of the word "Tallahassee" in the Apalachee language.

Soon after the American acquisition of Florida in 1821, a site near the old Indian village of Tallahassee was chosen as the new capital of the Territory. In the Spring of 1824, settlers began moving in and the town was laid out with Capitol Square at its center. Leon County was established in 1825. Named for Juan Ponce de Leon, it originally extended from the Gulf of Mexico to Georgia and from the Suwannee River to the Ocklocknee. By 1842, with the creation of Jefferson and Wakulla counties, it was reduced to its present 696 square mile area.

The area soon developed as an important addition to the Cotton South and the undisputed political and social center of Territorial Florida. A plantation economy developed and Tallahassee immediately became a center for trade in the region, with St. Marks as its port. In 1837, a railroad line was completed from Tallahassee to St. Marks. This was the state's first successful rail line, in continuous service until its abandonment in 1984.

Florida's first permanent Capitol building was begun in 1839, but not completed until 1845. This 3-story Greek Revival building forms the core of the recently restored Old Capitol. Several other territorial buildings survive in Tallahassee.

By the early 20th century, it was clear that the future prosperity of the area would not be built on agriculture. By mid-century, the state government and two institutions of higher learning, Florida State University and Florida Agricultural and Mechanical University, had become central to Tallahassee's economy and purpose. FSU, which has its roots in the West Florida Seminary, began as a college for women. It has a nucleus of fine Collegiate Gothic style buildings constructed between 1907 and 1950. The legislature established the Tallahassee State Normal School for Colored Students in 1887. This institution, now FAMU, occupies a commanding site south of the Capitol and continues to grow in size and prominence.

Tallahassee remained a small, agriculturally-oriented community until well into the 20th century. The Florida boom of the 1920's had little material effect on the character of Tallahassee and there are few of the Mediterranean Revival style buildings which are so dominant throughout the rest of the state.

As Florida has grown, so has state government. By the late 1890's, the state had outgrown its Capitol. In 1978, a 22-story tower designed by New York architect Edward Durrell Stone was built as Florida's new Capitol. The Old Capitol, restored to its 1902 form in 1982, provides an important architectural and historical complement to the new houses of state.

(The author gratefully acknowledges the assistance of Kevin McGorty and Larry Paarlberg of the Historic Tallahassee Preservation Board and Michael Zimny of the Bureau of Historic Preservation, Florida Department of State, in the preparation of this guide.)

A
State Road 151 and
Moccasin Gap Road
Tallahassee
Bradley Country Store Complex. The store and sixteen farm buildings built between 1893 and 1927 reflect the development of the small cottage industry in this area. Architecture is rural vernacular.

B
SR 151
Tallahassee
Pisgah United Methodist Church, 1.6 miles north of State Road 154. Built in 1859, this Classic Revival frame building has served as a social, cultural and religious center for the Centerville community for 150 years.

C
1513 Cristobal Drive
Tallahassee
Woman's Club of Tallahassee. Edward D. Fitchner was the architect on this 1927 building, one of only two Mediterranean Revival structures in the Los Robles subdivision built on 37 acres of the original Lafayette Grant.

D
Duval St at First Ave.
Tallahassee
The Grove. Florida Territorial Governor Richard Keith Call built this as his home in 1836. Adjacent to Florida's Governor's Mansion, the house is architecturally distinguished as a provincial adaptation of the Greek Revival style.

E
329 N. Meridian St.
Tallahassee
Brokaw-McDougall House. Built 1856-60 by a successful Tallahassee businessman, this well-crafted Classic Revival house has Italianate features. The property is now owned by the State of Florida and it serves as the headquarters for the Historic Tallahassee Preservation Board.

F
211 North Monroe St
Tallahassee
St. John's Episcopal Church. Built 1881-87, this church is one of few brick Gothic Revival style structures in Florida.

G
102 North Adams St.
Tallahassee
First Presbyterian Church. Built 1835-38, the original design influenced by classical architecture. An earlier steeple was replaced by the present 3-tiered tower and spire in 1932.

H
110 W. Park Ave.
Tallahassee
U.S. Post Office and Courthouse. Designed by architect Eric Kebbon and built in 1935, this was the most significant Works Progress Administration project in the Tallahassee area. Neoclassical Revival style structure.

I
301 East Park Ave.
Tallahassee
Knott House Museum .This two-story residence with classical details was built between 1843 and 1928, having been enlarged a number of times. Built by William V. Knott, State Treasurer and Comptroller of Florida, the house is now owned by the State and will soon operate as a museum.

J
201 South Monroe St.
Tallahassee
Exchange Bank Building. Designed by architects Edwards and Sayward of Atlanta and built in 1927, this six-story Commercial style building features ornament which includes Egyptian papyrus columns and Classical swags and eagles.

K
100-102 E. Jefferson
Tallahassee
Gallie's Hall/Munro Opera House. Part of a complex of three historic buildings constructed between 1873 and 1920 as Masonry Vernacular style commercial buildings. Completely restored in 1983. 104 E. Jefferson now houses the headquarters of the Florida Association of the American Institute of Architects.

L
College Ave. &
Copeland Street
Tallahassee
Westcott Building. Built 1910-11 with Edwards and Walter of Columbia, S.C. as architects, the Collegiate Gothic style building is the administration building for Florida State University.

M
Apalachee Parkway
and Monroe Street
Tallahassee
Old Capitol. Built 1839-45, design of the original 3-story building is assigned to Cary Butt of Mobile, Alabama. 1902 enlargement by South Carolina architect Frank Milburn. Building was vacated in 1978 and restored to its 1902 appearance by Florida architect Herschel Shepard, FAIA.

N
SE corner Apalachee
Pkwy and Monroe St.
Tallahassee
Union Bank. Constructed in 1841 at 106 S. Adams St., this antebellum building was moved to its present site in 1971 to save it from demolition.

O
E. Gaines Street &
South Gadsden St.
Tallahassee
Old City Waterworks. This utilitarian structure was built c. 1909 and is a designated civil engineering landmark by the American Society of Civil Engineers.

P
Near the intersection
Gamble & Boulevard
Tallahassee
Carnegie Library. This Classic Revival building was completed in 1907 with funds provided by Andrew Carnegie. It is on the campus of Florida A & M University

Q
3945 Museum Drive
Tallahassee
Bellevue, Tallahassee Junior Museum. Frame vernacular style plantation residence of Catherine Murat, widow of Prince Archille Murat, nephew of Napoleon Bonaparte. Built before 1847, it was moved in 1967 and restored in 1971.

WAKULLA

DAVID E. FERRO, ARCHITECT

A At the time of Spanish contact in Florida, Apalachee Indian villages and hamlets were well established in area now known as Wakulla County. As a chain of missions was developed in the region, Spanish authorities soon realized that a coastal port was needed to maintain communication with St. Augustine and handle waterborne commerce. To protect their interests, the Spanish first built a log fort at the confluence of the St. Marks and Wakulla Rivers in 1679. A stone fortress, San Marco de Apalache, begun by the Spanish in 1739, was only about half finished when Florida was transferred to the British in 1763. The British maintained a garrison at the Fort until Florida was ceded to Spain in 1783. In the same year, the first British trading post, Panton, Leslie and Company, was established above the fort on the Wakulla River.

By 1824, the Americans had abandoned the fort. Tradition has it that the nearby St. Marks Lighthouse (1829-31) was constructed of stone quarried from the abandoned fort. A federal marine hospital for yellow fever victims was constructed on the site from limestone salvaged from the fort. The hospital was completed in 1858, three years before Confederate forces occupied San Marco, renaming it Fort Ward. Today the earthworks thrown up during this occupation are clearly visible.

Shortly after American occupation, the Spanish seaport village of St. Marks was resurrected as the main shipping point for this vast agricultural area. During the early 1830's the merchants of St. Marks petitioned the Territorial legislature for a railroad charter as a means of capturing a larger share of the lucrative cotton trade. The rail line connecting Tallahassee and Port Leon, a community near St. Marks, was chartered in 1834 and not abandoned until 1984. Today, through the State of Florida's "Rails to Trails" program, its historic roadbed provides a recreational link between Tallahassee and St. Marks.

Various communities were established in Wakulla County for reasons of commerce, politics and eventually even tourism. The first of these was Magnolia in 1827. Port Leon and Newport followed and although each had a period of prosperity, little or nothing remains of the towns today. Crawfordville, named for John L. Crawford, a State Legislator and Secretary of State, did prosper and survive to become the county seat.

During the last years of the 19th century, communities along the Gulf coast became centers for commercial fishing and seafood production. Tourism also began to mature as an industry in the region. However, lumber and naval stores production ranked as the chief economic influence in Wakulla County in the post-Reconstruction years. Curtis Mills and Smith Creek on the Ocklockonee River were important mill towns. Sopchoppy housed several large turpentine operations, one alone employing over 100 workers. Panacea was known as Smith Springs until renamed by Northern investors who purchased the land surrounding the area's five springs in 1893. Their Panacea Hotel soon became a popular retreat for Tallahasseans.

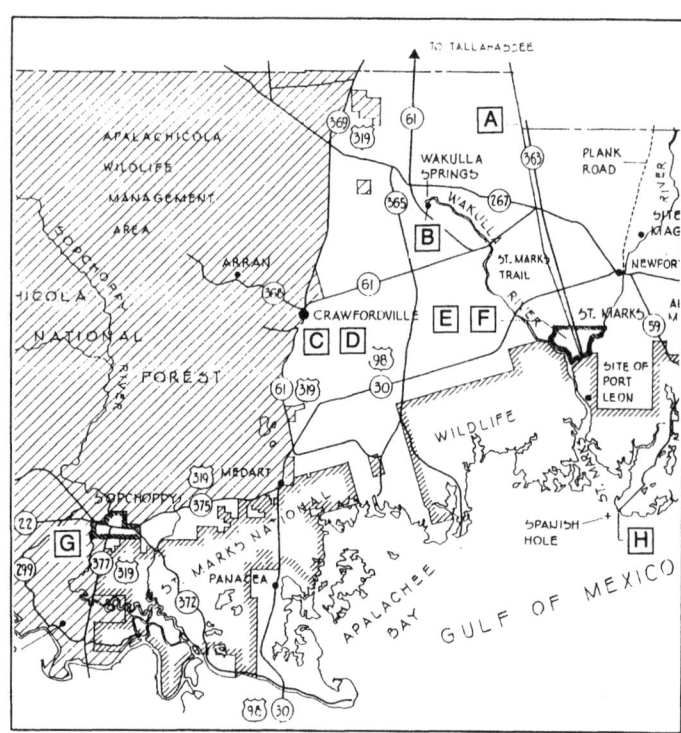

Today, approximately 65% of the county's 600 square acres is under Federal stewardship. St. Marks National Wildlife Refuge established in 1931, encompasses 65,000 acres of uplands and protects 32,000 acres of Apalachee Bay. In 1938, over half of Wakulla County's land area was added to the Apalachee National Forest. Wakulla Springs, a spectacular natural wonder with a depth of 250 feet and a rate of flow of over 600,000 gallons per minute, is said to be the deepest and largest spring in the world, and is designated a National Natural Landmark. In the mid-1930's Edward Ball, a financier conservationist, developed the Springs as a retreat. He built a clubhouse and hotel and established a 55-acre park within a 4,000 acre wildlife sanctuary. In 1986, the State purchased 2,900 acres of the sanctuary, including the Spring and hotel property, for development of the Edward Ball Wakulla Springs State Park.

The early history of Wakulla County is marked by conflict, prosperity, tragedy and depression. It is an area of great significance to the early development of the state, and is equally important today for the unsurpassed natural beauty of its savannas, salt marshes and hammocks, the outstanding recreational opportunities it provides and the vital industries it supports. The fact that few historic properties are included in the following guide is more a reflection of our limited knowledge of the cultural resources of the county than of its offerings. To date, there has been no systematic survey of the historic and archeological resources of the county. With the area's increasing growth, both as a bedroom community to Tallahassee, and as a tourist destination and recreation area, it is imperative that these resources be identified and evaluated to ensure their preservation for future use.

A
W. of SR 363
**Tallahassee
to St. Marks**

St. Marks Trail. Roadbed of the original 24-mile narrow gauge rail line constructed 1834-37 by the Tallahassee Railroad Company from Tallahassee to Port Leon over the drawbridge on the St. Marks River. Acquired by the State of Florida in 1986 and developed as 22-mile linear park through the "Rails to Trails" program.

B
SE of intersection of
SR 267 and SR 61
Wakulla Springs

Wakulla Springs Hotel. Two-story Mission Revival style retreat and resort hotel on the south bank of the Wakulla Spring. Designed by Jacksonville architects Marsh and Saxelbye and completed in 1937. Owned by State of Florida and operated as park and conference center.

C
1 blk. w. of Church St.
& U.S. Highway 319
Crawfordville

Old Wakulla County Courthouse. Designed by surveyor-builder G.W. Tully and constructed in 1893-94, the Wakulla County Library is housed in the first floor offices. Second floor courtroom remains intact. Moved approximately one block in 1948 to permit construction of a new courthouse and restored during the Bicentennial.

D
South of Arran Road
(SR 386) at Towles Rd.
Crawfordville

Crawfordville Elementary School. Constructed under WPA in 1933-34. Vernacular style classroom building. Still in use.

E
S. end of Canal St.
St. Marks

San Marcos de Apalache Archeological Site and Museum. Site of Spanish log fort built in 1679, stone fort built in 1739. Marine hospital built within ruins of the fort in 1857-58. Hospital abandoned after Civil War. Present Museum building constructed on foundations of marine hospital in 1966.

F
Intersection SR 363
and Old Fort Drive
St. Marks

Posey's Oyster Bar. Two-story frame vernacular building typical of 1920's-30's commercial development in the region.

G
One half blk. north of
Rose St. on First Ave.
Sopchoppy

Abandoned commercial buildings among many, mostly wood frame, reflecting town's prominence as a center for naval stores production in the early 20th century.

H
St. Marks

St. Marks Lighthouse, at termination of County Road 59, north side of Apalachee Bay. Constructed in 1829-31 by Winslow Lewis from brick and local limestone. Keeper's house constructed in 1853. Masonry vernacular style structure. Light automated in 1960.

(The author gratefully acknowledges the assistance of Mr. Larry S. Paarlberg of the Historic Tallahassee Preservation Board and Mr. Michael Zimny and Dr. William Thurston of the Bureau of Historic Preservation of the Florida Department of State, in the preparation of this guide.)

35

JEFFERSON

PATRICK HARTLAUB, ASSOCIATE AIA

During the early part of the 16th century, the famous Spanish explorers de Narvaez and DeSoto made their way through what is now Jefferson County. Here they found fierce resistance from the Apalachee Indians who inhabited the region. All attempts at establishing a mission ended in failure. Half-a-century later, the Spanish were back in Florida, at the request of the Indians, to prevent the French from expanding into the region and to establish a permanent colony for Spain. Throughout the 17th century, the Spanish maintained numerous missions in North Florida, several of which were in Jefferson County.

By the end of the 18th century, the relatively calm existence between the Spanish and the Indians began to break down. The War between Spain and England, and later the British possession of Florida in 1763, caused increased tension between the Indians and the white settlers. By the beginning of the Seminole War, a continuous border war was in effect.

Once Florida became a territory of the U.S. in 1821, a large influx of settlers arrived. In 1827, Jefferson County was established after having been situated through the years in both East and West Florida and in the counties of Escambia, Jackson, Gadsden and Leon. The county was named in honor of Thomas Jefferson and its county seat, Monticello, in honor of the former president's home in Virginia. In 1828, the town of Monticello was laid out with two main streets and a central courthouse square. While there were a few frontier homesteads around Waukeenah and Lloyd at this time, the majority of the people resided in Monticello. During the territorial and early period of Florida's statehood, Monticello gave political, economic and social leadership. Florida's first governor, William D. Mosely, was from Jefferson County.

The end of the Seminole Wars brought many more settlers into Florida and many of them took up residence in the northern counties where the cotton plantation system prospered during the years before the Civil War. There were a number of large plantations in Jefferson County at this time and the homes the planters built displayed high levels of architectural skill.

The years following the Civil War saw economic and social change in the county. Other agricultural products began to take the place of cotton as important cash crops. Among these were pecans, tobacco, citrus, watermelon, lumber and later, sawmills sprung up. New railroads were built, wooden stores were replaced with brick buildings and in 1890, an opera house was built making Monticello the social center of the county. The first telephone system was installed in 1901.

While many civic and commercial buildings were constructed during the late 19th century, this era also produced some of the best examples of domestic architecture to be found in Florida. With a diverse and flourishing economy, houses were built in Italianate, Queen Anne and Stick styles that were popular at the time.

The severe deflation of farm prices in 1920 coupled with the economic depression of the 1930's seriously damaged the county's economy. Even after World War II when Florida experienced explosive growth, Jefferson County's population decreased.

Jefferson County has an exceptional collection of architecture from the 19th and early 20th centuries. The Jefferson County Historical Society has played a role in preserving many of the significant buildings. At the core of the town is the Monticello Historic District which is listed on the National Register of Historic Places.

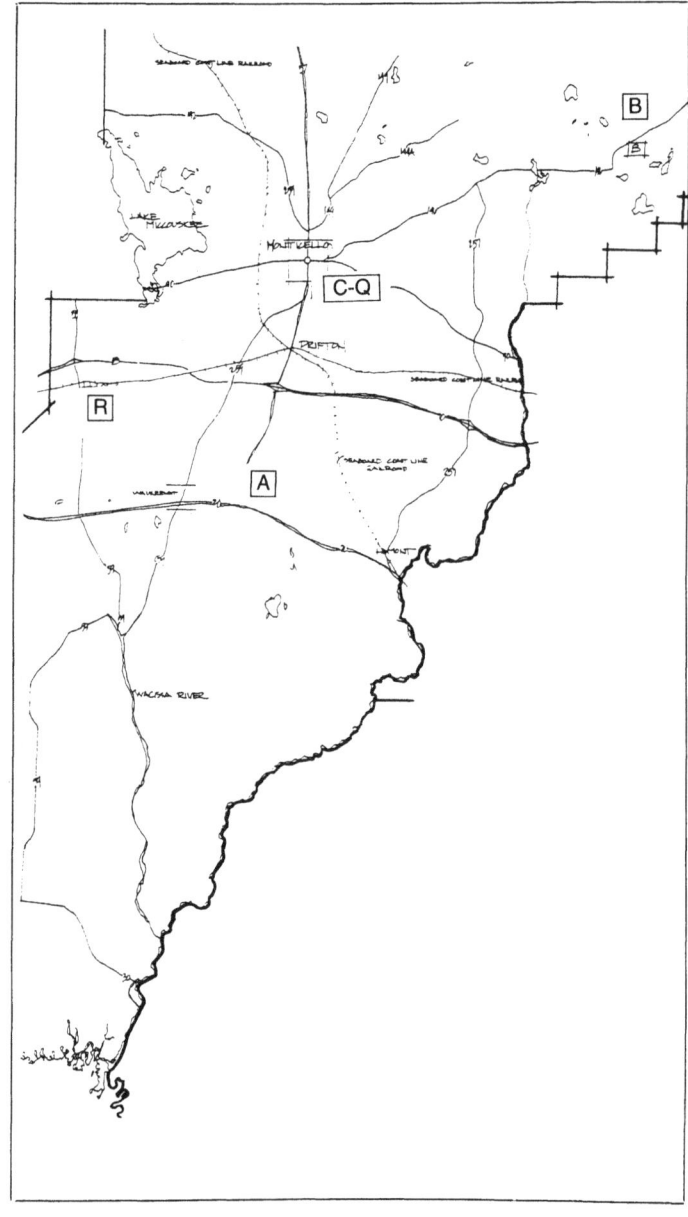

A
US Hwy. 19
Near Capps
Asa May Plantation, 9 miles south of Monticello. Built c. 1840, this simple Greek Revival farmhouse is in nearly original condition.

B
State Road 146
Near Ashville
Lyndhurst Plantation, 15 miles northeast of Monticello. This 1850 structure is one of only two remaining two-and-a- half story brick Classic Revival structures in the state.

C
North Jefferson and Pearl Streets
Monticello
Wirick-Simmons House. C. 1833, This Greek Revival house was built by Adam Wirick, one of the first Methodist circuit riders in Florida. Now serves as headquarters and museum for the Jefferson County Historical Society.

D
North Jefferson and High Streets
Monticello
Christ Episcopal Church. Architect J.W. Ferguson designed this Stick Style church in 1885. The corner tower rises one-and-a-half stories above the church proper and facade has quadrupled lancet windows filled with stained glass.

E
N. Jefferson and Madison Streets
Monticello
Bailey-Eppes House. This highly embellished Stick Style house was built in 1889.

F
Dogwood Street
Monticello
Jackson Drugs and Harris Grocery, between North Jefferson and Cherry Streets. This 1878 building is a good example of commercial Classic Revival architecture with 3-bay gable ends and pediments facing the street.

G
Washington Street at Courthouse Square
Monticello
Monticello Opera House (formerly the Perkins Opera House). This Romanesque Revival-style building was constructed in 1890 and has been completely restored for use as a 250- seat opera house and theatre.

H
Washington and Jefferson Streets
Monticello
Jefferson County Courthouse. Architect E.C. Hosford designed the courthouse in 1909. It is a Neo-Classical structure which still houses the main functions of county government today.

I
Dogwood and Waukeenah Streets
Monticello
First Presbyterian Church. Built in 1841, and rebuilt in 1867, this is one of the few surviving Greek Revival religious structures dating from the mid-nineteenth century in Florida.

J
Washington and Hickory Streets
Monticello
Finlayson-Kelly House. Though built fairly late in the Victorian period, 1909, this is a fine example of Queen Anne architecture.

K
East Dogwood and Rhodes Street
Monticello
Girardeau - Walker House. John H. Girardeau was Jefferson county's first game warden and he built this Queen Anne-style house in 1890.

L
885 S. Waukeenah St.
Monticello
Girardeau - Durst House. A two-story wood frame Italianate-style house built in 1882.

M
Washington and Waukeenah Streets
Monticello
Dilworth-Turnbull-Anderson House. This Classic Revival house is one of the earliest surviving residences in Monticello. It was built in 1853 for a prominent Monticello attorney.

N
555 Palmer Mill Road
Monticello
Denham-Lacy House. Built c. 1873, the house is a two-story wood frame Italianate style. It has bracketed eaves and an octagonal lantern atop the roof.

O
Madison and Mulberry Streets
Monticello
Turnbull-Evans House. 1880, Italianate style house.

P
Madison and Hickory Streets
Monticello
Bailey-Brinson House. Businessman and State Senator Edward Bailey built this Italianate-style house in 1885.

Q
Jefferson & York Sts.
Monticello
Budd-Braswell-Pafford House. This Classic Revival cottage-style clapboard house was built in 1833. Its style is sometimes called "Gulf Coast Vernacular."

R
Near junction SR 49 & 158
Lloyd
Lloyd Railroad Depot. Built in 1856, this one story brick building has a heavy timber gable roof and brick pilaster with segmented arches over windows and doors. Currently houses the local post office and volunteer fire department.

MADISON

BY ELIZABETH H. SIMS

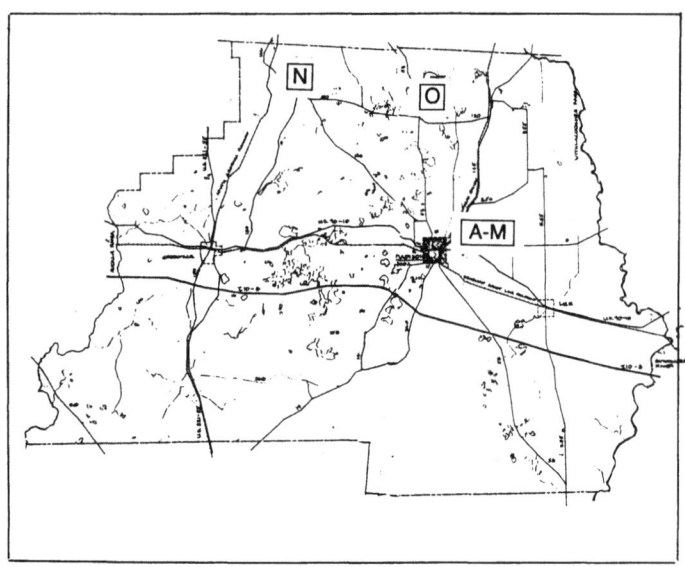

Madison County contains evidence of habitation dating back ten thousand years, as shown by artifacts recovered by the State Department of Archives and History from the Hutto Pond site. The Timucuan Indians inhabited the area at the time of early Spanish exploration. In the middle 1600's, three Spanish missions were established. One of these, San Pedro de Protohiriba, was excavated by the state in 1972; and, charred remains of three buildings were uncovered with evidence of the site being burned by the British in 1704.

With the establishment of the territory of Florida in 1821, settlers particularly from Georgia and South Carolina, began to migrate to the area. In December, 1827, Madison County was established with borders including the area between the Aucilla and Withlacoochee and Suwannee Rivers from the Georgia border to the Gulf of Mexico. The land was partitioned from Jefferson County which had in turn been divided from Leon County less than a year before. In 1856, when Taylor and Lafayette counties were created, Madison County was reduced to its present size.

The first county courthouse, built of logs with a huge end fireplace, was constructed in San Pedro on the Bellamy Road, the military route from St. Augustine to Pensacola. Only an historical marker, sponsored by the San Pedro Bay Sportsmen Club, marks that courthouse site. The town no longer exists. In 1838, the county seat was moved to what is now the city of Madison, and Adoniram Vann constructed a wooden courthouse in 1840 which burned in 1876. A new brick courthouse, built in 1880, burned in 1912. The present courthouse was constructed on the same site.

Madison County and its residents played an important part in Florida's early political history. The president of the Florida Secession Convention, John C. McGehee, built a mansion between San Pedro and Moseley Hall; but, as happened to many of the early rural residences, the building was destroyed. In 1860, area construction of the railroad marked a period of prosperity and growth for residents. During the War Between the States, Madison served as a refugee destination and a supply point with farms providing needed food and a shoe factory producing thousands of pairs of shoes. The first post-Reconstruction "home-rule" governor was George F. Drew of Ellaville whose sawmill at the junction of the Withlacoochee and Suwannee rivers shipped lumber all over the country. His mansion also was destroyed by neglect, vandalism, and finally fire.

Madison County has been noted for its educational institutions. The St. Johns Seminary of Learning, founded in 1850, evolved into the Madison High School. Established in 1907, the Florida Normal Institute became an outstanding teacher-training institution for a large region until its closing in 1927. North Florida Junior College, one of the six original state-sponsored junior colleges, was founded in 1958.

Religion has also played an important part in the life of the county with a Baptist Church being established in 1835, and other churches founded soon after. The Florida Baptist Convention was organized at Concord Baptist Church in 1854. When the town of Madison was plotted, lots on Meeting Street were designated for churches.

During the 1930's, the years of national economic depression, the county was the site of a federal rehabilitation project. Cherry Lake Rural Industrial Community was designed to involve up to 500 families in living and working on a community farm of 15,000 acres which was to include craft projects. Homes were built by participants' labor. Water and telephone systems, a sugar mill, and a community center were constructed. The social experiment did not succeed. Only the houses remained, and these were sold to whomever would buy them. Many were moved to other areas in the county.

At present there are three incorporated areas in the county — Lee, Greenville, and the county seat of Madison. County population has remained around 15,000 for a number of years. The Chamber of Commerce is working to attract new industries to the county. The City of Madison, through its revitalization committee, is making an effort to preserve the turn-of-the-century downtown heritage while encouraging business growth. The Madison County Historical Society has published a county history and is planning to establish a museum to preserve historical artifacts.

A
W. Base St. (US 90)
& N. Washington St.
Madison

Wardlaw-Smith House, built for Benjamin F. Wardlaw about 1860 with William Hammerly as architect. Greek Revival style house remodeled by C.H. Smith in 1902; restored by William Goza in 1978; owned by University of Florida in 1980's.

B
105 E. Marion St.
Madison

Dial-Goza House (Magnolia Hall), built about 1880 as town house of Major William M. Dial and restored in the 1970's by William Goza. Residence of Mr. and Mrs. Charles Bassett in 1980's.

C
Corner W. Pinckney &
S. Orange Streets
Madison

Old First Baptist Church, constructed in 1898 with Stephen Crockett as architect and W. T. Davis as builder. Queen Anne style building moved from original location on opposite side of block in 1956.

D
304 W. Marion St.
Madison

King Home, constructed in 1849 probably for Nathan P. Willard who established second cotton factory in Florida. Oldest house in city, restored by Mr. and Mrs. Maurice King.

E
302 N. Range St.
Madison

S. A. Smith Home, built in 1894 by W. T. Davis for Dr. and Mrs. Chandler H. Smith. Late Victorian style private residence which has remained in the same family.

F
405 W. Pinckney St.
Madison

Old Jail, built about 1900. In 1953 adapted for public library. In 1988 assigned to Madison County Historical Society for museum and meeting place.

G
501 W. Base St.
(U.S. 90)
Madison

G. Whitlock Home, built about 1990 for Mrs. Ida Whitlock. Bought in 1987 by Madison County Farm Bureau for adaptive use as offices.

H
202 N. Duval St.
Madison

Tri-County Building, constructed about 1910 by city as dormitory for Florida Normal Institute students and later used as school building. In 1950 purchased and adapted for office use by Tri-County Rural Electric Cooperative, Inc.

I
111 N. Range St.
Madison

Manor House, constructed about 1905 by W. T. Davis as Merchants Hotel. Served briefly as social center for North Florida Junior College. Converted into offices and apartments by new owner, Mrs. Virginia Rowell, in 1978.

J
E. Base St. (US 90)
Madison

Courthouse, built in 1913 to replace earlier building destroyed by fire. Standpipe in background erected in 1894 for city water system.

K
S. Range St. at
Railroad
Madison

Warehouse, Florida Manufacturing Co., built about 1890. Surviving structure of what was world's largest long-staple cotton processing plant acquired by J&P Coats in 1890's. Ceased operation in 1916. Used as feed store in 1980's.

L
Corner W. Base and
N. Harry Streets
Madison

Madison Guest House, constructed about 1900 and rebuilt in 1922 after fire. Building used as Dr. D. H. Yates' sanitarium which pioneered in use of electrical treatment. Used later as hotel, bus station, restaurant, and then retirement home in 1980's.

M
212-214 S. Range St.
Madison

W. T. Davis Building, built about 1890 by W. T. Davis with opera house on second floor. Converted to law offices.

N
off CR 150
Madison

Concord Baptist Church, about 14 miles northwest of Madison, constructed in 1887 to replace log building dating from church founding in 1841. Typical of rural church architecture in county.

O
Post Rd. off Hwy. 53
Madison

Cherry Lake Project House, 9 miles north of Madison, built in 1936. Typical board and batten house built by Cherry Lake Resettlement Project. Remodeled at one time but unoccupied in 1986.

DIXIE

ED BUTLER, EVONNE V. CLINE, CAULEY COPELAND, JULIAN CRANBERRY, JO ALLIE DOWNING, JUNIUS DOWNING, GEORGE GRIFFIN, PERRY HILL, JAMES HURST, SHARON McCALL, KATHRYN McINNIS, LEON WARD

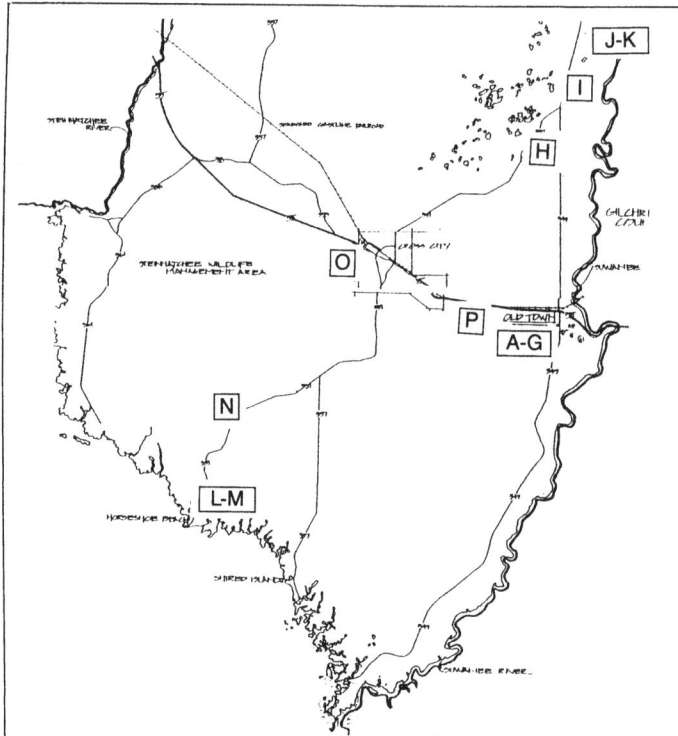

Dixie County's first known inhabitants were Indians who lived on Shired Island from about 1,000 B.C. until 500 A.D. After that time migratory Indians often visited the area. When European explorers arrived in the sixteenth century, Timucuan Indians were the region's inhabitants. Coastal Indian sites are marked by mounds of shells, especially oyster shells, left by these prehistoric Floridians.

General Andrew Jackson came through the area in 1819 while pursuing Chief Billy Bowlegs who had been attacking Georgia settlers. It is believed that Jackson and his troops crossed at Steinhatchee Falls and camped at the future site of Hitchcock. From there Jackson went to Old Town, the home of Bowlegs. No Indians were found, but a British trader was arrested and sentenced to death at St. Marks for aiding the Indians. Jackson's route became a main thoroughfare to the coast. In the 1820's George Miller, a settler from North Carolina, met the father of Suwannee and Bowlegs, Chief Tigertail, near present-day Tallahassee. The chief gave him a track of land around Old Town. Miller was buried in 1833 behind the Old Town Elementary School.

In 1828, the first post office in the area was built at Jena with Silas Overstreet as postmaster. In the early 1840's, Colonel J. L. F. Cottreal bought all the land in and around Old Town and built a large plantation. In 1854, James McQueen, brother of Mrs. Cottreal, moved to the area and also bought extensive acreage. By the late 1850's, Old Town Methodist Church was constructed under the leadership of Robert Barnett, a church circuit rider.

During the Civil War, salt furnaces were operated along the Gulf Coast. The product, sold to the Confederates, was considered so important that southern workers were exempt from military duty and Union soldiers attempted to destroy the salt works. (In 1947, an estimated 100 salt wells could still be found on the coast between the Suwannee and Steinhatchee Rivers.)

Following the war, Jim Johnson brought the first cattle from South Carolina to an area which began to attract settlers and was later called Hitchcock. The period 1865 to 1900 was a time of growth with many pioneer families moving to the county, including Tom Peter Chaires, who married McQueen's daughter and built on the McQueen estate, and the Chavous family. The first Masonic Lodge, located in Summerville near Old Town, surrendered its charter in 1880. The second, Joppa Lodge number 4 at Governor Hill chartered Jan. 19, 1882, is still in existence.

In 1900, lumber and naval-store industries began to boom with resin hauled to markets in Georgia and South Carolina. The Atlantic Coast Line Railroad line was constructed through Cross City from 1905 to 1907 (Cross City had been known as Cross Roads until this time since the town was at the intersection of two salt traffic roads during the Civil War.) The area led the southeast in production of lumber and naval stores from 1928 to 1938.

Dixie County had been created in 1921 from land that had been part of Lafayette County after a dispute over a bond issue for roads and the location of transportation facilities. There was also a bitter political battle over the location of the county seat which was first temporarily located in Cross City. Cross City, Eugene, Old Town and the Chavous homesite were on the first ballot. Cross City was the permanent designation in a run-off with Eugene. Other settled communities in the county, besides those competing for county seat, included Shamrock, Rocky Creek, and the fishing villages of Salt Creek, Jena, and Horseshoe.

Education has always been important to Dixie residents. Included in the many early schools were Pine Hill School, First District (still standing); Cross Road School (Fletcher School) near Adolphus Currie Home; and Summerville School (located at site of New Prospect Baptist Church where the lunchroom is still standing). Black students had their own schools at Hines, Shamrock, and Old Town.

In the 1920's Putnam Lumber Company moved to Shamrock and built what was said to be the world's largest sawmill with a full camp which had a hotel, homes, dairy, ice house, and commissary. Little conservation was practiced. Putnam Lumber left the county in the late 1940's when its holdings were sold at $14 an acre to Hudson Pulp and Paper Company. The late 1940's were economically difficult for county residents. Two-thousand people left the area during this period.

Since 1950, the county has been growing gradually. The 1980's population was 9,521. Principal regional products include pine and cypress lumber, mulch and pulpwood chips, seafood, farm crops, livestock, and Great Bear Clothing Factory merchandise. Employing many county residents are governmental institutions which include the Cross City Correctional Institute.

A
Old Town
Francis Cambridge Robinson House, Black Jack Community. Built of pine lumber.

B
Old Town
W. D. Finlayson House, half mile south of Old Town Elementary School. Pine Construction.

C
Old Town
Thomas Peter Chaires House, adjacent to Old Town Elementary School. Still occupied by a member of the Chaires family.

D
Old Town
McQueen Chaires Homestead, half mile south of Old Town Elementary School. Pine construction.

E
Old Town
George Miller Grave. Marble grave commemorating the son of Colonel Stephen and Winifred Miller who was born in 1801 in North Carolina and died in 1833 in Old Town.

F
SR 349
Old Town
Old Town Elementary School, one mile south of U.S. 19. Built in 1910 on land donated by McQueen and Ruby Chaires. Auditorium constructed by George Levingston. School still in operation with 381 students in late 1980's.

G
Old Town
Old Town Methodist Church. Built in 1890 by Ed and Charlie Hill. Church used as annex in late 1980's.

H
SR 349
Old Town
First District Community Building, 10 miles north of Old Town. Built in 1931-32 with WPA money. Used for political rallies, a voting precinct, 4-H meetings, and community social events.

I
Off SR 349
Old Town
Milas Bush Homestead, 12 miles north of Old Town. Built by Milas and Rosa Gornto Bush. Constructed of pine lumber without knots. Wooden shingle roof sealed inside with tongue and groove yellow pine siding.

J
CR 340
Old Town
Pine Hill School Lunchroom, one mile off SR 349. Built in early 1920's.

K
CR 340
Old Town
Pine Hill School, one mile off SR 349, built in early 1900's.

L
Horseshoe Beach
Jack Locklear Homestead. Built over a hundred years ago of cypress lumber. Wooden shutters with no screens.

M
Horseshoe Beach
Charlie Polk Home. Built in 1920's from lumber used in original hotel commissary.

N
Horseshoe Beach
James D. Butler Homestead, approximately six miles north of Horseshoe Beach. Built over 140 years ago of virgin pine. Shingle board roof. No nails used in building home. Blocks under house original. Chimney built of stone and lime mortar made by Butler from burning oyster shells to obtain lime.

O
Shamrock—
Putnam Lodge (part of Putnam Lumber Company mill camp). Complex once included homes, dairy, ice house and commissary.

P
Cross City
Original Eugene School Bell, marking site of old school, five miles south of Cross City. Bell turned upside down in cement. Site now occupied by New Prospect Baptist Church.

(Information for this history was gathered by Dixie County residents: Ed Butler, Evonne V. Cline, Cauley Copeland, Julian Cranberry, Cauley Copeland, Julian Cranberry, Jo Allie Downing, Junius Downing, George Griffin, Perry Hill, James Hurst, Sharon McCall, secretary and photographer, Kathyrn McInnis, chairman and photographer, and Leon Ward.)

HAMILTON

EDWARD E. CRAIN, AIA, FLORIDA NORTH CHAPTER

Hamilton County, named for Alexander Hamilton, was established as Florida's fifteenth county in 1827. The Alapaha River runs through the center of the county which has as its boundaries the Georgia state line on the north, the Suwannee River on the south and east, and the Withlacoochee River on the west.

In the early nineteenth century, missionaries visited the Indians in this area. Daniel Bell, the first settler, did not arrive until 1824 when he and his family were guided by Indians to land near Micco, an old Indian village on the Alapaha River.

Inexpensive land sales and governmental land grants increased the number of settlers. Transportation depended primarily on rivers and paths following Indian trails. Early records mention ferries crossing major rivers. In 1865 the Pensacola and Georgia Railroad (now the Seaboard Air Line) was extended from Live Oak, Florida, through Hamilton County to Dupont, Georgia. The Georgia, Southern and Florida Railroad was built in 1889-90. A paved road (now highway US 41), constructed in 1917, served as a main north-south traffic artery and stimulated commercial development until highway I-75 by-passed county towns in the 1970s.

Hamilton County's governmental center, Jasper, was incorporated in 1840 and named for Sgt. William Jasper, a Revolutionary War hero. In the late nineteenth century, Jasper was a thriving community. Today, only one cotton gin remains. However, many of the large homes built by merchants and politicians survive. In 1890 Hamilton County built a large brick courthouse and jail which are still standing.

Jennings, in the northern part of the county, was founded by George Jennings in the mid-nineteenth century and incorporated in 1900. The town's business district, constructed of wood and brick, was a center for shipping of turpentine, lumber and cotton.

White Springs developed as a resort town in the southern part of the county. The spring had been praised for its medicinal properties by Indians and early settlers. By the early twentieth century seven luxury hotels had been built to accommodate the tourists who came to enjoy the spring waters. In 1911 fire swept through White Springs destroying most of the buildings. This fire, coupled with the declining timber industry, caused many people to leave. Today one of the major attractions is the Stephen Foster Memorial which honors the composer of the state song and hosts folk arts and crafts festivals.

Sea Island cotton was raised by most of the settlers until the boll weevil destroyed the crop. Later, short grain cotton was introduced, revitalizing many farms. Sawmills and turpentine distilleries flourished until 1915 when the timber supply was depleted. Today Hamilton County's flue-cured tobacco crop is second to none in the region as are the cotton and tree farming industries. Even more important to the county are Occidental Chemical Company's phosphate mines and chemical plants near White Springs.

Hamilton County's history is depicted by many buildings of local architectural and historical significance which have not been demolished or severely altered, often because of few growth pressures. The Bath House at White Springs was documented in drawings and photographs for the Historic American Buildings Survey before it was razed. The United Methodist Church of Jasper is listed on the National Register of Historic Places.

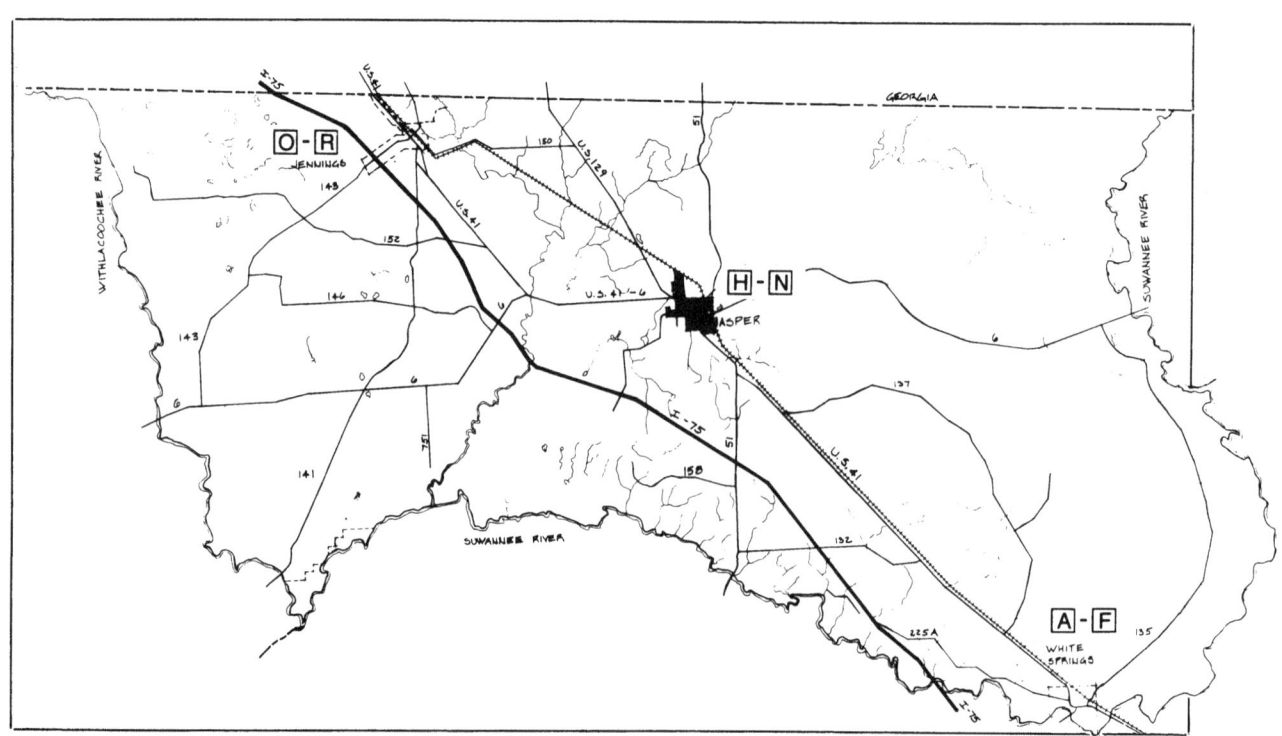

A
Corner of Bridge St. and River St.
White Springs

Adams-Saunders House, built in 1865 by R. W. Adams, Confederate captain who established mercantile store after war. Two-story Victorian home, closely massed "L" shape with two-story verandas and projecting bay window in front.

B
River Street
White Springs

Telford House (Jackson House), hotel built in 1902 of local limestone with brick trim, originally two-story verandas on all sides. Featuring acetylene-powered lighting, only hotel to survive fire of 1911.

C
Corner of Highway 41 and Bridge Street
White Springs

Adams Store, built in 1890. Typical example of rural commercial structure with false facade built before the turn of the century.

D
Highway 41
White Springs

Bath House Site, a poured concrete wall, the only remains of a three-level wood frame bath house which was designed in 1900 by McClure and Holmes, architects, to surround the spring. Wide walkways, dressing rooms, and medical examination and treatment rooms in original structure.

E
Corner Highway 41 and Camp Street
White Springs

Camp House, built in 1898 by B. F. Camp, owner of lumber company. Queen Anne derivative with wide porch, octagonal tower, and wrought iron fence surrounding yard. Still occupied by Camp descendants.

F
Highway 41
White Springs

Stephen Foster Memorial and Museum (on bank of Suwannee River), museum complex honoring Stephen Collins Foster. Building in Classical Revival style housing antique musical instruments and diaramas; 200 foot Carillon tower.

G
Throughout county

Tobacco Barns of Hamilton County, built throughout county with similar design to allow tobacco to dry by natural means or gas burners for acceleration of curing process.

H
501 NE First Ave.
Jasper

Hamilton County Jail, built in 1893 by Peter and John Pauly. Originally two-story "T" shaped building with one-story additions added later. Romanesque Revival features of massive brick walls, arched windows, corbelling along eaves, and three story hanging tower.

I
408 NE Central Ave.
Jasper

Jasper Ginning Co. Warehouse, built in 1906. Housed eight long and short staple cotton gins before boll weevil invasion destroyed cotton crops. Converted to grind meal and rice.

J
102 Hattey Street
Jasper

Commercial Bank, built in 1904, typical of brick commercial buildings in small southern towns. Characterized by plain brick walls with arched or pedimented windows placed symmetrically and corbelled brick cornice.

K
Corner of SE 1st St. and Central Ave.
Jasper

W. Y. Sandlin House, built in 1899 as designed by George A. Davis. Brick house with original veranda and balustrade details and etched glass, marble sills, and cherry woodwork.

L
306 Central Avenue
Jasper

W. R. Drury House, built in the mid-nineteenth century with frame construction on brick piers. Central hall with two rooms on both sides and regularly spaced windows. Front porch possible addition.

M
Corner of Central and SE Fifth St. Ave.
Jasper

United Methodist Church, built in 1878. Small rectangular church with bell tower centered on entrance facade. Later trancepts added to create Latin cross plan and in early 1930's a small country church moved and attached to northeast corner of church building.

N
208 First Avenue SW
Jasper

Kirby L. Sandlin House, built 1895, basically unaltered. Fine example of house with typical Victorian Revival ornamentation such as arched brackets and scroll sawed palings at second floor veranda.

O
Highway 141
Jennings

Jennings Post Office, built 1910 as bank. Beaux-Arts Classicism example with concrete Ionic columns supporting metal cornice and balustrade.

P
Highway 141
Jennings

Mercantile Stores, built at turn of century. Unique because of pressed metal facades which still bear name of manufacturer, G. L. Mesker and Company.

Q
S-150
Jennings

McCall Bates House, built in 1860, by Ben McCall. Ornamented two-story veranda, scroll-sawed brackets connecting column and cornice and turned balusters. Double door entry with sidelights. Two small gables at north gable roof. Wood frame with flush siding.

R
Dirt road off 141
Jennings

Apalahoochee Bridge, built in 1911 by Roanoke Bridge Company, second oldest steel truss bridge in Florida. Span of 75 feet. Channel bars braced with cap and stay plates, angle bars, and steel rods and supported by lally column piers.

SUWANNEE

PETER E. PRUGH, AIA, FLORIDA NORTH CHAPTER

In 1539, when Hernando DeSoto's party of Spanish adventurers came to the area now known as Suwannee County, the region was inhabited by the Timucuan Indians. The Spanish named the river bordering the north, west, and south of the county Rio San deGuacara, a name later corrupted to Suwannee and made famous by Stephen Foster's popular song, *Old Folks At Home.*

The Spanish established three missions in Suwannee County along the old Spanish trail connecting St. Augustine and Pensacola, but, by the beginning of the eighteenth century, attacks by the English had destroyed these. A hundred years later Georgia settlers followed the old salt road to the Gulf of Mexico where boiled sea water could provide a source for essential salt. After the War of 1812 and the acquisition of Florida by the United States from Spain in 1821, American settlers began to move into north Florida. Conflicts with the Seminole Indians led the U.S. Congress to construct a military road which followed the old Spanish trail across north Florida. In 1824, the first permanent settlers, the Ruben Charles family, came to Suwannee County and began the operation of a ferry and trading post at the junction of the new Bellamy Road and the Suwannee River about five miles south of today's Dowling Park.

To protect the new settlers from Indian raids, forts were built in the area. Steamboats opened the river to commerce in 1837. With the conclusion of the Second Seminole Indian War in 1842, settlers flooded into North Florida, and new counties were formed with Suwannee County established in 1858. The 1860 federal census listed the county population as 2,303. Frontier architecture, a response to a rigorous lifestyle, used indigenous materials and expedient building methods.

While Suwannee River steamboats brought commerce to the county by carrying cargo and passengers and operating as floating general stores, the building of railroads changed the area by moving development away from the river. In 1861, the Florida and Atlantic and Gulf Central Railroad linked Jacksonville and Pensacola. During the Civil War, the Confederacy constructed a north-south rail line through the county to DuPont, Georgia. The station at the intersection of these railroads became the site for the new community of Live Oak which was made the county seat in 1868. With railroad transportation available, sawmills, turpentine stills, cotton gins, and manufacturing brought booming commerce. Lumber and wood products were a major part of the county's growth, and cotton was the main agricultural product until the boll weevil disaster of 1915.

Regional architecture changed with the growth of the area. Wood frame buildings such as the 1866 Hull-Hawkins House (the hub of a 1,580-acre plantation ten miles south of Live Oak on Highway 49) were constructed. Reflecting the popularity of the Victorian Revival style of the late nineteenth century,

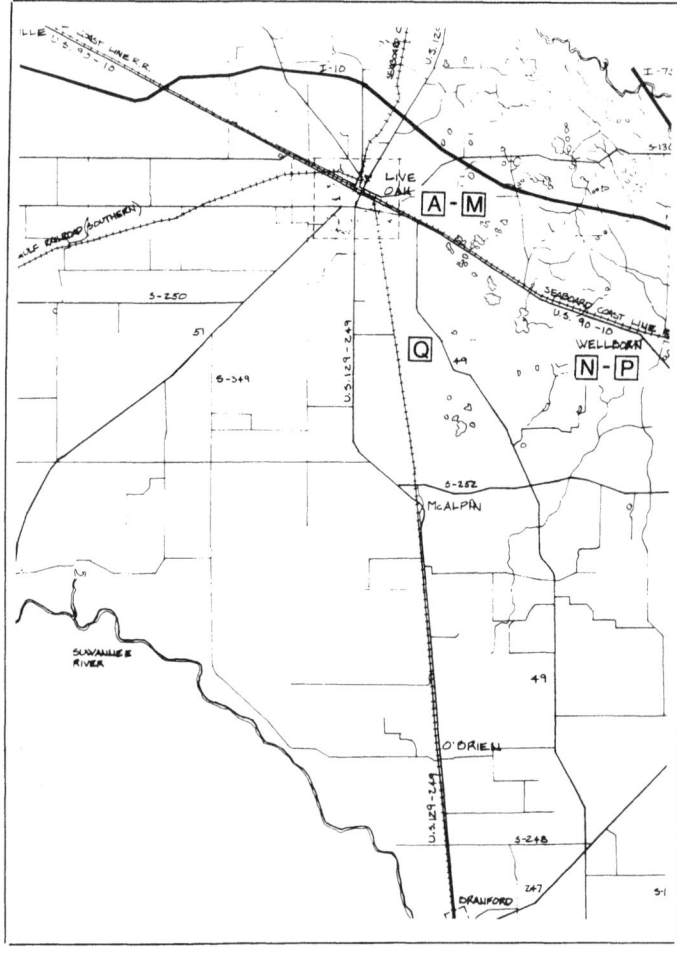

commercial structures were built in Luraville, Wellborn, and Live Oak. In 1897 a new water plant replaced mosquito-infested individual home cisterns in Live Oak, and streets were paved in 1906.

Highway construction after World War II, especially the completion of I-10 in the 1970's, changed social and economic structures that had shaped the county for a century. While still a major agricultural center, Suwannee County expanded and diversified the industrial sector as highway systems allowed construction of new plants throughout the county. The Suwannee River gained influence as a major recreation and tourist resource.

Renewed interest in preserving the architectural heritage of the county was evident in Live Oak as many of the homes with Victorian Revival features were saved. The turn-of-the-century courthouse was restored, many downtown commercial structures were renovated, and the old train station was moved in 1985 to save it from being demolished. However, valuable examples of early regional architecture in the rural areas deteriorated, and Wellborn had residences and commercial buildings in need of preservation. Collectively these structures offer an accurate record of late nineteenth and early twentieth century architecture in north Florida.

A
105 North Houston Avenue
Live Oak

Mayor Broome House, built at turn of century by former mayor. Featuring Victorian Revival decorative elements, one of few remaining houses in town area primarily inhabited by railroad workers.

B
Ohio Avenue
Live Oak

Old Live Oak City Hall-Police Department and Suwannee County Museum, built 1908 with square plan, tower, and central hall. Decorative elements in Italianate style.

C
202 East Duval Street
Live Oak

Dr. White House, constructed 1904 with Hildreath as architect and builder, a wedding gift from Judge White to son. Four square plan with porch on two sides, Queen Anne style, attic story bedrooms and back addition added in 1910.

D
406 East Duval Street
Live Oak

Dowling House-Senior Citizen's Home, built 1904 by Thomas Dowling, lumber and railroad entrepreneur. Wood frame building with double gables and Greek Revival characteristics of massive wood columns on three sides supporting prominent cornice.

E
Ohio Avenue and Haines Street
Live Oak

Live Oak Station, designed by the Office of the Chief Engineer of the Seaboard Airline Railroad and built for $13,129 in 1909. Relocated in 1985 to avoid demolition.

F
South Ohio Avenue
Live Oak

Suwannee County Courthouse, built about 1900 of yellow brick with stone quoins and detailing. Recently restored, Queen Anne style featuring elaborately detailed ornamentation, entrance ways, and fenestration and clock tower with metal dome.

G
South Ohio Avenue and Parshley Street
Live Oak

Live Oak Post Office, built 1915. Neo-Classic Revival features of low hip tile roof, elaborate brick details, and belt courses. Palladian-inspired windows on two sides arranged in formal facade with central entry.

H
110 Parshley Street
Live Oak

Blackwell-Airth House, built 1886-89 by B.B. Blackwell, banker and state legislator. Masonry structure with pronounced segmental drips over windows, moved to present site in 1910 to make way for new post office.

I
626 South Ohio Ave.
Live Oak

Williams House, built by Thomas Dowling for a daughter in 1900. Typical north Florida wood frame structure with brick piers, four square plan, central entry, and porch on two sides.

J
704 South Ohio Ave.
Live Oak

Kirby House, built by Thomas Dowling for a daughter, in 1900. Wood frame structure with projecting front bay, slender wood Corinthian porch columns, and turned balusters in connecting balustrade.

K
702 Pine Street
Live Oak

McDowell House, built before 1900. Constructed of masonry to base of gables with flush siding in pediment, colonets supporting porch roof, hexagonal turret at corner with bell cap roof with flaired eaves.

L
Corner of Suwannee Ave. and Highway 51
Live Oak

Rogers House, built 1900. Projecting bay windows, polygonal turret topped by flattened bell-shaped cupola, and porch surrounding two sides supported by square Doric columns in brick piers.

M
Corner of Ohio Ave. and Duval Street
Live Oak

Masonic Lodge #43, built 1922. Example of classical influence on institutional architecture of modest scale with elaborate brick pilasters, stone belt course, carved panels, and intricately detailed pedimented entry with flanking Corinthian pilasters.

N
North of railroad
Wellborn

McLeran Stores, financed by trading cotton for lumber 1897 by A. W. McLeran. Now vacant, one of few surviving wood frame nineteenth century commercial buildings. Pitched roof behind a parapet wall and two bay windows projecting into front porch.

O
County Road S-137
Wellborn

Brick Commercial Structure, south of railroad. Example of brick masonry commercial architecture with arched openings on side walls, iron frame with wooden infill on main facade, and center entry flanked by two iron columns.

P
South of railroad
Wellborn

Walters House, built in late nineteenth century, several additions. Originally four square plan with central entry, Victorian Revival ornamentation with modified Chinese chippendale balustrades on porches at both levels.

Q
Highway 49
Live Oak

Hull-Hawkins House (10 miles south of Live Oak on west side of Highway 49), built 1866 as hub of 1,580 acre plantation by Noble A. Hull, state legislator when Ordinance of Secession passed. Two story wood frame structure, porches recently enclosed.

R
Corner of Hwy. 51 and Luraville Road
Luraville

Dr. McIntosh House, built late nineteenth century by physician as home with office in one-story wing connected by porch. L-shaped frame two-story Neo-Classic structure with intricate scroll-sawn wood palings and brackets on porches.

LAFAYETTE

WILLIAM HUNTER, AIA, FLORIDA NORTH CHAPTER

One of Florida's smallest counties in size and population, Lafayette County was created by an act of the General Assembly of Florida on December 23, 1856, from an area which had been part of Madison County and was named in honor of the Marquis de Lafayette, an American Revolutionary War hero. Dixie County was created from the lower part of Lafayette in 1921. The county's inhabitable area is a narrow strip of land between the Suwannee River, which is the county's east-northeast border, and Mallory Swamp, which extends into neighboring Dixie and Taylor counties. The county seat was first located in McIntosh and then Troy and moved to Mayo in 1893.

The Spanish explorer Narvaez crossed the Suwannee River on May 17, 1528, near Oldtown. In 1539, Hernando DeSoto searched for gold in the region, and the Spanish established missions north of Lafayette in 1637 to make Christians of the area's inhabitants, the Timucuan Indians. Later British invasions destroyed many of the Spanish and Indian settlements.

During the early 1800's, settlers from Alabama, Georgia, and the Carolinas moved to northern Florida to become traders or plantation owners, many with slaves. In 1818, General Andrew Jackson led a military group of American regulars, Creek Indian allies, and Tennessee volunteers to drive out the Seminole Indians along the Spanish Florida border. In 1826, five years after Florida was ceded to the United States by Spain, land was surveyed and could be bought cheaply. However, by 1835 the Seminole Indians had moved back to Mallory Swamp, and palisade forts were built in the Lafayette County region to provide protection so that settlement of the area was not discouraged during the 1835-42 Seminole Wars. Before the Civil War, Suwannee River trade had provided opportunities for prosperous settlers to exchange livestock for tools and dry goods; but during the Civil War, many homesteads were destroyed by freed slaves and Confederate and Union soldiers.

After the Civil War, in 1885, a freeze influenced farmers to switch from citrus to other crops. The Suwannee River provided shipment of cotton and vegetables by steamboat. The lumber industry was spurred on by the building of a railroad from Live Oak to Luraville. By 1910, steel bridges spanned the Suwannee so the railroads could better serve the area.

More recently tobacco, livestock, dairy and poultry, pine timber, pulp and hardwood products have become vital to the county's economy. Outdoor recreational opportunities are provided by the river, lakes, and springs. The Steinhatchee Wildlife Management Area protects wildlife in 100,000 acres.

In the mid-1980's preservation in Mayo and Lafayette County was limited to efforts of individual property owners. The structures that remain in the county were saved more by minimum area growth than organized preservation activity. Many buildings suffered from lack of maintenance.

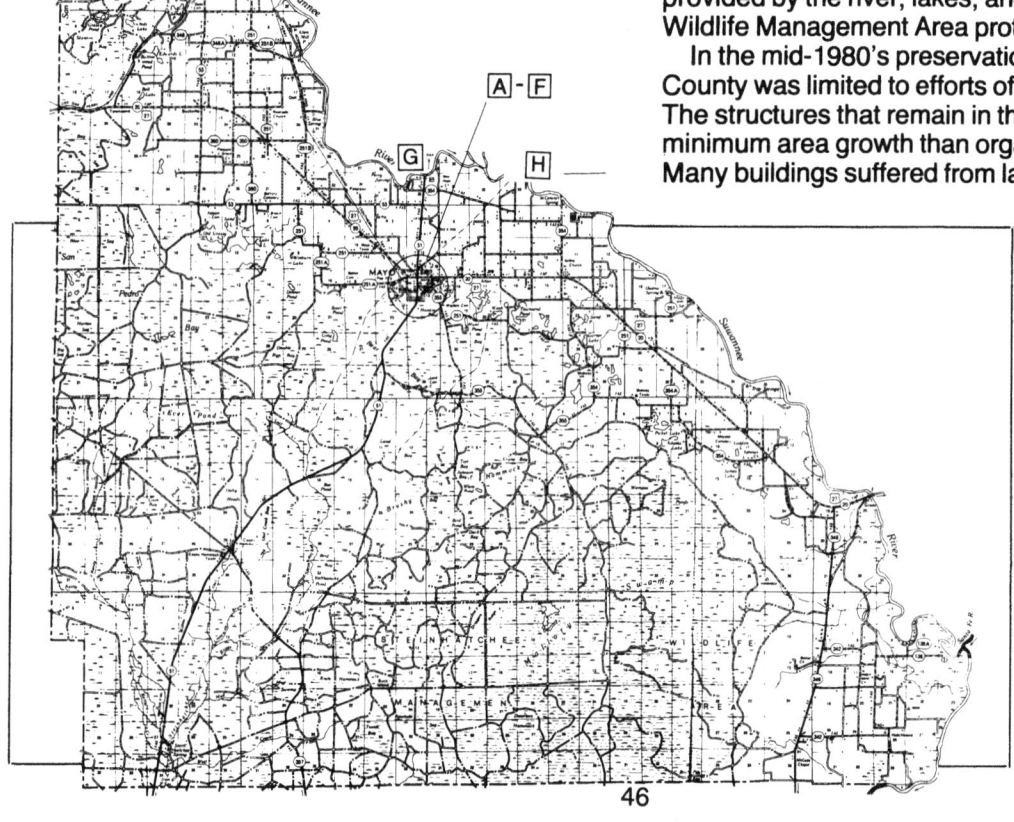

A
Corner of Fletcher &
Main Streets, N.W.
Mayo

New Lafayette County Courthouse was built in 1908 by
Mutual Construction Company of Louisville, Ky., with
E. C. Hasford Company of Atlanta, Ga., as architects.
Two-story structure of Neo-Classical style with intersecting central halls. Significant architectural features
of balustrades, porticos (two one-story porticos and one
two-story portico), and clock tower. Built of Indiana limestone for fire-proofing with cast-iron and wood interior.
Materials sent by rail to O'Brien, then by wagon to Mayo,
crossing at Grant Ferry North of Troy Springs.

B
Corner of Monroe and
Main Streets N.W.
Mayo

M. Pico Building was built in 1915 on site of lodge building destroyed by fire. Focal point for central business
district. Structure decorated with brickwork cornice,
three feet high, formed by vari-colored as well as protruding brickwork.

C
Fletcher Street
Mayo

Old Mayo Free Press Building, next to old courthouse,
built in 1888 to house Mayo Free Press (Lafayette
County's oldest continuous business, now a weekly
newspaper housed in brick building off Main Street).
Granny's Country Store, mid 1980's occupant of this
twenty-by-forty-feet, wood frame building.

D
Corner of Fletcher
and Bloxham Streets
Mayo

Old Lafayette County Courthouse, built in 1893-94 as
courthouse for Lafayette County, moved to present site
in 1909 when commissioners voted to build fire-proof
courthouse. One of most massive buildings in Mayo with
later addition of large two-story verandas extending
around three sides.

E
Corner of Clark and
Bloxham Streets NW
Mayo

House of the Seven Gables, designed by James
Mitchell after reading Nathanial Hawthorne's *House
of Seven Gables* and built in 1880's by Mack Koon,
builder. Octagonal-shaped main section with seven
free standing gables, eighth side extending into rear
wing which originally contained kitchen and dining
rooms. Rest of house divided into four pie-shaped
rooms, one living room and three bedrooms. Originally
porches surrounding seven of eight sides of house,
exterior decoration of diagonally cut wood shingles in
herringbone pattern, and eves of each of gables decorated with small sawn teeth placed along edges.

F
Corner San Padre
and Main Streets NW
Mayo

Brick Office Building, built in 1916 as drug store, later
housed Mayo Free Press, now unoccupied. Decorative
brick and arched windows.

G
State Road 51
North of Mayo

Hal W. Adams Bridge at the Suwannee River, built in
1947 to span the Suwannee River and to connect
Suwannee and Lafayette counties. A four-hundred and
twenty-three foot span, first suspension bridge in
Florida.

H
State Road 51
South of Mayo

Drew Bridge at Suwannee River (left at first paved road,
travel four to five miles, turn left at sharp curve onto dirt
road, left at "T, next right to river), built in 1907 as swing
bridge, first bridge to connect Lafayette and Suwannee
counties, not used in mid 1980's.

NOTES

47

COLUMBIA

RONALD W. HAASE, AIA, FLORIDA NORTH CHAPTER

Modern history of Columbia County dates back to the sixteenth century with evidence of an early Spanish mission located on the shores of Lake Alligator. Significant inland populations did not develop until the eighteenth century when the British made positive efforts to settle families in Florida. By the time of the American Revolution, several prosperous plantations were established in what is now Columbia County.

As late as 1817, the present site of Lake City was an Indian village named Alligator after a Seminole chief. By 1824, after Andrew Jackon's First Seminole War, several white families were known to live in the area. When Columbia County was officially established in 1832, the town of Alligator was designated as the county seat. Fresh water lakes, forests, and fertile land led to rapid growth and development during the county's early history. In 1859, residents became dissatisfied with the name Alligator and officially incorporated the town as Lake City.

About this same time the extension of the Florida, Atlantic, and Gulf Central Railroad to Lake City encouraged further economic growth in the area and allowed the use of mass-produced building materials and mill work. Cotton was the main attraction to permanent settlers in this part of Florida; but tobacco, lumber, naval stores, and citrus production (until the freeze of 1895) made Columbia County a growing and prosperous place at the turn of the century. Most of Columbia County's significant architecture dates from this era. The structures reflect the effect of mass production, standardization of building materials, and response to commercial and institutional development.

The State Agricultural and Mechanical College was established in Lake City in 1893. After the college was elevated to the status of the University of Florida in 1905, the location was moved to Gainesville. On the original Lake City college site, a Veterans Administration Hospital now functions and provides employment for many area residents.

Columbia County is bordered by the Suwannee River to the northwest and the Olustee and Santa Fe rivers to the south. A major portion of the county lies in Sandlin Bay Pinhook Swamp and Osceola National Forest. Farming and phosphate mining dominate the remaining open landscape. Only two metropolitan areas are incorporated: Lake City with a population over 12,000 and Fort White, a small community named after a Seminole War fort. The 1980 census listed Columbia County's population at 35,399. U.S. highways 90 and 41-441 provided major east-west and north-south traffic routes until interstate highways 10 and 75 were constructed north and west of Lake City. I-75 stimulated growth along U.S. 90 west of Lake City but removed highway traffic from downtown.

Both the Columbia County Historical Society and the Historic Preservation Board of Lake City and Columbia County take an active role in preserving the area's past. *The History of Columbia County* and *A Century in the Sun: Lake City 1859-1959* document the story of this county.

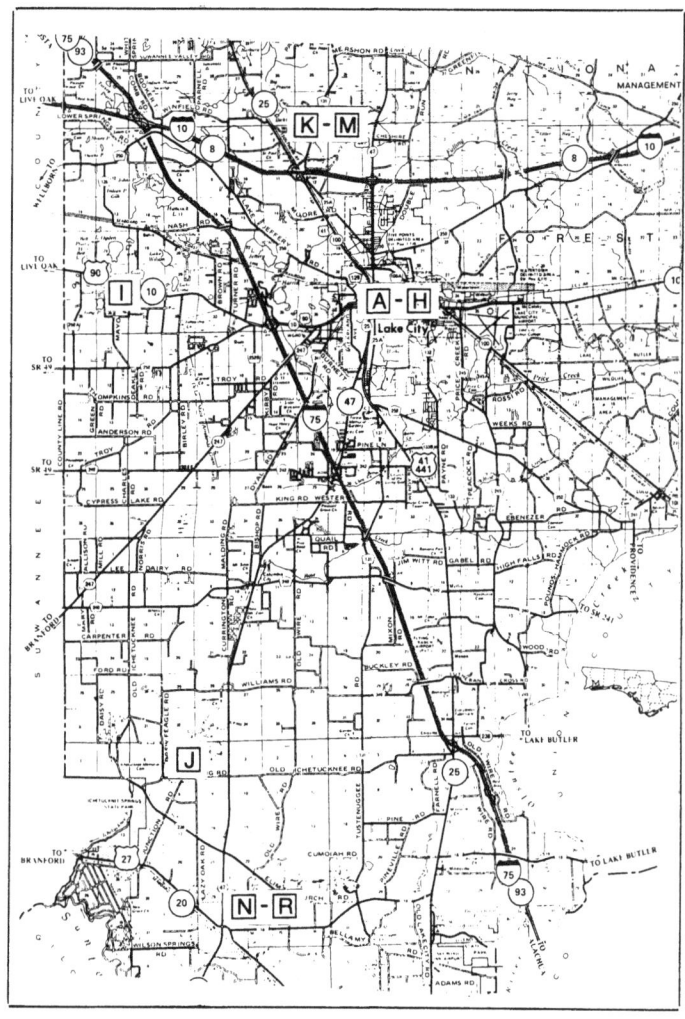

A
North Hernando St.
Lake City

Columbia County Courthouse, built in 1905 with Frank P. Milburn as architect. Classic Revival style with cupola and dome removed and parapet modified at later date.

B
North Hernando St.
Lake City

Old Post Office, built as 1932 Works Progress Administration project. Mediterranean Revival style civic building now used as courthouse annex. Architect: James A. Wetmore.

C
200 North Marion St.
Lake City

Hotel Blanche, built in 1902, named after owner's daughter. Social center for Lake City and popular tourist stopping place registering Governor Fred Cone as resident and, at one time, Al Capone as guest. Brick masonry building with three stories, three bays, quoins, and bracketed cornice. Now converted to business and office use.

D
502 North Marion St.
Lake City

Old Columbia County Bank, well-maintained Neo-Classic building. Governor Fred Cone, one of founders in 1912.

E
203 West Desoto
Lake City

Old Courthouse, built in 1874-75 and moved from its location on Olustee Square in 1902. Now a rooming house. Porch added later.

F
207 South Marion
Lake City

Marcello-Henderson House, built at turn of the century. Elaborate Victorian Revival style with a Moorish motif expressed in ornamentation, especially on second-floor porches.

G
105 South Hernando
Lake City

May Vinzant Perkins House, built in 1865, burned and rebuilt in 1890. Two-story wood frame house, four-square plan with verandas on three sides. Building being restored by Historic Preservation Board as Civil War museum.

H
202 West Duval
Lake City

Duncan-Herlog House, begun in 1907 for Horace A. Duncan. Queen Anne style residence of brick and stone masonry which initially also served as funeral parlor. Recently restored and converted to offices.

I
U.S. 90 (3 mi. west of I-75)
Lake City

Birley-Gray Plantation, built in 1898 by Henry R. Birley. Second floor added in 1917, several early out-buildings.

J
Herlong Road (west of US 47)
Lake City

Watkins Estate (Penwood), built before Civil War as plantation house, acquired by Watkins family in 1909. Classical Revival portico added by Isaac Watkins. Edgar Watkins said to have shot Belle Starr.

K
Corinth Road (north of US 47)
Lake City

Corinth Methodist Church, estimated construction, 1860, built on foundations of old house.

L
US 131 (12 miles north of I-10)
Lake City

Falling Creek Church and Cemetery, built in 1899, gable-ended wood clapboard church with metal roof. Interesting 1910 decorative wood fence surrounding grave in cemetery.

M
US 27 at US 47
Fort White

Fort White Bank, built in 1860's as primary bank in area but closed during 1930's depression. Currently real estate office.

N
US 27
Fort White

Old Post Office, one block east of US 47, built in 1850's and used as post office until 1964. Now a gift shop.

O
US 27
Fort White

J. R. Terry Grocery, one block west of US 47, built in 1890's by grandfather of Senator Lawton Chiles, original commercial buildings known as "The Chiles Store," one of three remaining.

P
North Byron Street
Fort White

Stevenson House, built in 1870's by McKinney, local designer-builder of other structures still standing in Fort White.

Q
Fort White

Fort White School, built in 1915 by A. J. Greene with W. J. Sneil as architect. Italianate style, closed in 1967 when consolidation led to centralized high school in Lake City.

UNION

RICHARD H. MORSE, AIA, FLORIDA NORTH CHAPTER

Union County, the smallest county in Florida, has an area of 248 square miles and a 1980 population of 10,532. Its natural boundaries are the Olustee, New and Santa Fe rivers. In the one hundred years before formal designation as a county, the area had been part of St. Johns, Duval, Alachua, New River, and Bradford counties. When this area was part of Bradford County, the county seat drifted back and forth between Lake Butler and Starke without resolution. To avoid the problem of county seat location, area leaders decided to divide Bradford County; and, in 1921, the state legislature established Union County with Lake Butler as the county seat.

Located in the crown section of north central Florida, Union County's flat terrain has an abundance of pine woodland which promoted turpentine and lumber as major industries in early area history. Even today the lumber industry is a major economic factor with the Owens-Illinois Corporation owning 74,707 acres of pine forest, almost half the area of the county.

The land was suitable for growing Sea Island cotton. At the turn of the century, cotton was a booming industry in the county with one cotton gin reporting a quarter of a million dollars in business in the Lake Butler area. When the boll weevil moved into the county in 1919, the cotton industry was halted. Growers turned to lumber, cattle, poultry, and food crops.

In the developing years of the region before the turn of the century, the railroad's passing through a town was a guarantee of growth and prosperity. In 1880, the Georgia Southern and Florida track was laid across Union County on its way west from Jacksonville and passed through Lake Butler. Some years later the Atlantic Coastline Railroad was also routed through Lake Butler. Passenger service declined after World War II, but railroad freight business still has an active role in the economy of the region. Important highway systems bypassed Lake Butler.

As the area developed in the latter half of the 19th century, the architecture changed from simple structures built of indigenous materials to compositions of spindel columns, brackets, and jigsaw traceries which were possible because of accessible sawmills, turning lathes, and mass-production of windows, doors, and decorative elements.

Today, major economic forces in Union County include the prison and correctional facilities near Raiford (Lake Butler Reception and Medical Center, Union Correctional Institution, and Florida State Prison) where many county residents work. Others commute to larger cities such as Jacksonville or Gainesville.

Lake Butler, the largest town in this small county, has the greatest number of historic buildings in the area.

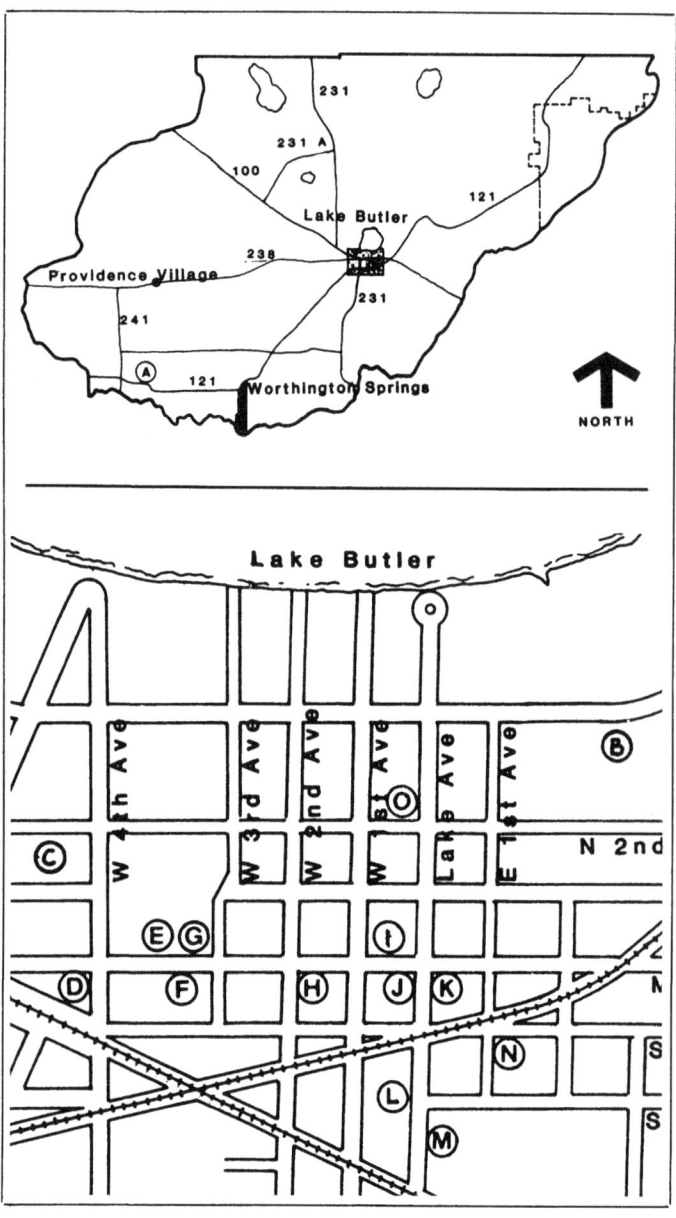

A

SR 121
Worthington Spring

First United Methodist Church, built in 1893. Vernacular Victorian Revival church architecture, single-hung sash replaced arched windows usually associated with this style.

B

283 Northeast
Third St.
Lake Butler

Lake Butler Women's Club, building constructed in 1923 as county's first courthouse on present courthouse site, moved to present location in 1936, and later given to club. Wood frame construction with porch addition, original embossed metal siding still in place on old building which has been renovated and remodeled.

C

Between West Fourth
& Fifth Avenues and
North First & Second
Streets
Lake Butler

1910 Jail on private property, two cells with iron grate doors and small barred windows on north, brick-vault roof with three iron tie rods at spring line and stucco finish inside and out.

D

410 West Main St.
Lake Butler

Commercial Building, built as drugstore in 1890's by J.W. Townsend, used as drugstore until 1950's then as restaurant, upper level burned in 1983, currently vacant. Brick arches over curvilinear wood sash windows on east facade, metal projecting cornice and metal vase-like ornaments on east side and north front, present canopy not original, cast iron details at entrance. Originally easternmost building in a block of two-story buildings with continuous sidewalk metal canopy for entire block, other buildings demolished.

E

345 East Main Street
Lake Butler

First United Methodist Church, built in 1920, oldest church building in town, Victorian Revival style with battlements on parapet of entrance tower, stucco on brick.

F

340 West Main Street
Lake Butler

Strickland House, built in 1912 by M. L. McKinney, ownership assumed by Strickland family in late 1920's. Two-story wood frame with gable roof and two projecting gables on front, porch roof supported by plain round columns on brick pedestals. Porch on three sides of house with projecting gazebo at north-east corner, steep sheet metal conical roof emphasizing gazebo, projecting gable defining entry. Renovated in late 1970's for day care center, now vacant.

G

324 West Main St.
Lake Butler

Old School House, built in early 1890's. First public building, used as school until 1908, now the Masonic Hall. Metal hipped roof, two double-hung windows at second level blocked up.

H

190 West Main St.
Lake Butler

Fowler Brothers Building, built in 1907. Typical turn-of-the-century commercial building, brick arched window openings with double-hung sash. Original cast-iron work at front entry replaced with aluminum store-front assembly.

I

55 West Main St.
Lake Butler

Union County Courthouse, built in 1936 by Work Projects Administration (WPA funds: $32,000, county funds: $7,000). Monumental brick structure with concrete quoins and concrete bands at window sill lines. First architect: John Pearson, Gainesville; additions in 1967 by architect Harry E. Burns, Jr., Quincy, and Vinson T. Forrester, Jr., builder.

J

30 West Main St.
Lake Butler

Permenter Brothers Building, built in 1896 as retail store, now used for storage by Rivers Hardware Store. Brick structure with entry recessed at center arch, cast iron step with original owner's name still in place.

K

10 East Main Street
Lake Butler

Bank of Lake Butler, built in 1906, now barber shop with chairs of leather and white porcelain appropriate to surroundings even though not a part of original building. Interesting architectural features: arched window, brick detail at cornice, and original metal ceiling.

L

180 South Lake Ave.
Lake Butler

York House, built in 1872 by Capt. Henry F. York. Moderate late Victorian Revival house, typical of turn-of-the-century houses in North Florida with wood frame on masonry piers, large porches on both first and second floors, sheet metal roof with standing seams, and brick chimney at each end. Clay pit in back yard from which York Pottery made.

M

235 South Lake Ave.
Lake Butler

Boarding house (now single family rental residence), built by a Mr. Futch of Hampton, Florida, in 1892. Late Victorian Revival house with little ornamentation. Originally, there was a circular gazebo at left of entry, matching one at right.

N

105 Southeast
First Ave.
Lake Butler

King House, built in 1892 by John A. King around small building on site which became kitchen of main house. L-shaped gable roof with Mansard form at intersection and projecting gable covering second floor porch,

O

210 North Lake Ave.
Lake Butler

Odum House, built by W. L. Odum in 1895, one of finest residences still in existence in county. Queen Anne style with irregular roof massing, basically hip roof with three large cross gables and a separate roof beneath to cover porch, small projecting gable defining entry. Porches on east and south intersecting at gazebo, ornamental balustrade on porch repeated at porch roof, windows in pairs, double-hung, without shutters.

BRADFORD

BERTRAM Y. KINZEY, AIA, FLORIDA NORTH CHAPTER

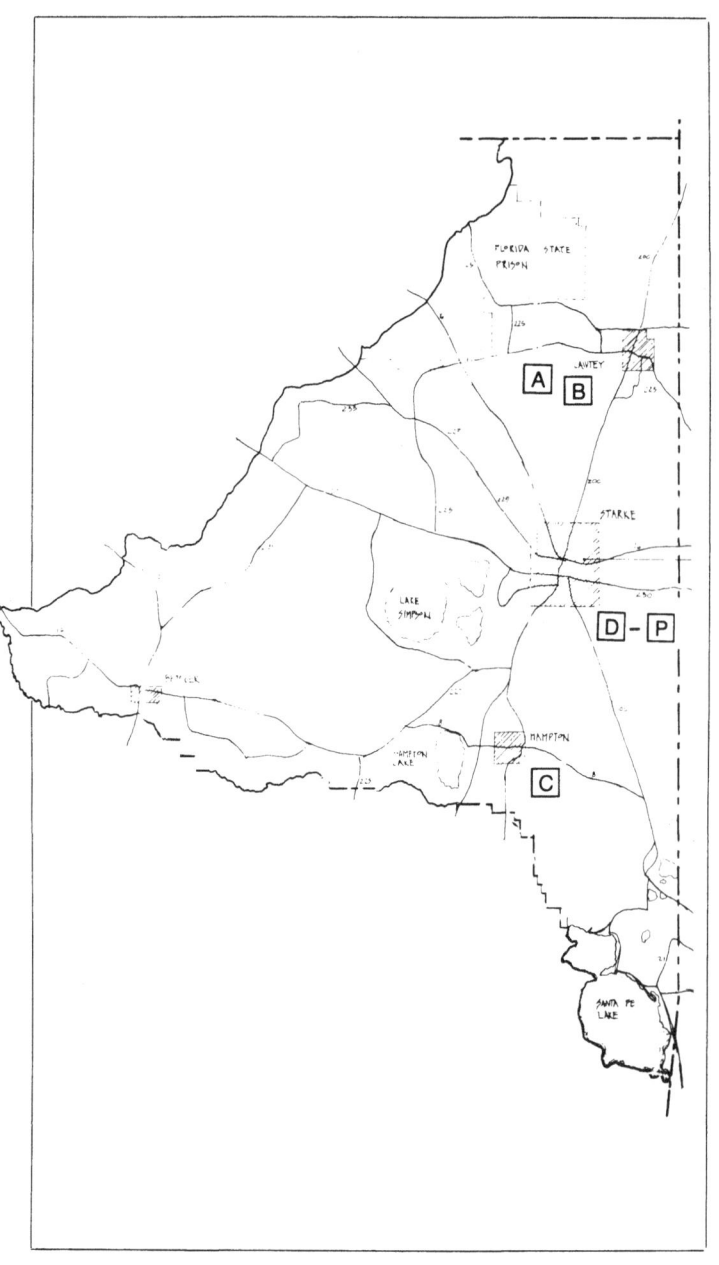

Early settlers in Bradford County, primarily farmers from Georgia and South Carolina, arrived about the time of the Second Seminole War, 1835-1842. Their principal crops were corn and cotton with some cattle production. Basically, the architecture consisted of survival structures made from on-site materials. Log houses with mud and stick chimneys were common. Fort Crabbe on the New River, Fort Hardee on the Santa Fe River, and Fort Van Cortlandt, southeast of Kingsley Lake, were built to provide protection from Indian attacks. New River Baptist Church, the oldest Baptist church in Florida, was founded in 1831.

With the coming of rail transportation through the county in 1858, linking the area with Jacksonville and Cedar Key, the agrarian economy was augmented by lumber and turpentine industries. The new prosperity and growth were interrupted by the Civil War. When post-war conditions stabilized and building resumed, standardized materials and hardware were available and buildings were decorated with the latest fancy millwork.

Bradford County, which included Union County until 1921, was named for the first Confederate officer from Florida who died in action, Captain Richard Bradford. There was much controversy over the location of the county seat. Starke, which was incorporated in 1876, wanted the seat moved from Lake Butler. With the formation of Union County in 1921, both Lake Butler and Starke became county seats. Four incorporated municipalities exist in Bradford County today – Starke, Brooker, Lawtey, and Hampton.

Freezing weather in 1894-1895 eliminated the orange groves developed in the county, and by 1920 the boll weevil destroyed cotton crops. To replace these agricultural products, strawberries were cultivated. Now Bradford County claims the title, "Berry Capital of the World." Farming is diversified with truck crops, watermelons, and pecans among the products.

During World War II, the location of Camp Blanding east of Starke brought a surge in population to the area. The camp remains as a National Guard center. Also influencing population is the location of the Florida State Prison at Raiford near Starke.

The most significant architecture in the county is in Starke where there is increasing interest in the rehabilitation of older buildings with a major contribution by the private sector. In 1970, a Board of Historic Trustees was formed to purchase buildings for restoration or renovation. One of the board's projects, the old courthouse, has been adapted to serve as a regional center for Santa Fe Junior College. The Bradford County Historical Society also fosters interest in the architectural heritage.

A
Madison St. at
S. Pine St.
Lawtey

Grace Methodist church, built 1889, excellent example of Victorian revival architecture. Addition in same style constructed within decade of original.

B
N. Grove St. at
W. Lake St.
Lawtey

Kaiser Residence, built at turn of century, typical two-story wood frame residence with original clapboard siding and windows. Later addition in rear.

C
32 S.R. 18 across
railroad tracks
Hampton

Horne Homestead, Roland Residence, built about 1830. Large frame dwelling with original barn on site, at one time a railroad boarding house. Original finishes replaced with asbestos cement siding and metal roof and large porch reduced by 1965 den addition.

D
W. Call St. and
N. Temple St.
Starke

Old Bradford County Courthouse, built 1902. Fine example of Victorian Romanesque Revival brick public building, on National Register of Historic Places. Builders: Smith and Blackburn and F. Dobson. Adapted for use by Santa Fee Community College, 1985.

E
Church St. and
Adkins St.
Starke

Comer L. Peek Residence, built at turn of century for a professor at Starke Institute. Classical Revival house on high foundation with imposing two-story hexagonal portico, originally located at 211 W. Madison St. Behind house, facing Call St., Peek's realty business office.

F
SE corner W. Call St.
and S. Walnut St.
Starke

Bradford County Bank, built 1914 at cost of $12,500. Typical Neo-Classical bank building of early twentieth century. Brick structure with limestone Ionic columns, pedimented entry, cornices, and base, now used as a jewelry store.

G
North side of 400
block of W. Call St.
Starke

Commercial Block, late nineteenth century buildings. From east to west: first-floor stable with second floor opera house and armory; 1890 building, originally housing law offices upstairs and post office on ground level, now drug store; and 1870 building on west corner, served as courthouse until 1902.

H
305 N. Walnut St.
Starke

E. M. Johns Residence, built 1920, state senator's house. Victorian Revival details simulating brick infill of timber frame and random brick patterns. Incongruous white columns supporting entry gable and porch added later.

I
315 N. Walnut St.
Starke

Sanders House, built about 1870 by Lawrence Wall. Strong asymmetrical facade with entry to right emphasized by large second-story bay and porch roof pediment, full-width porch balancing entry.

J
319 N. Walnut St.
Starke

R. A. Green House, built 1922 by Nat Sternberg. Victorian Revival with details simulating stucco infill of second story timber work, brick first story, casements, entry arch, and steep gables.

K
324-326N. Walnut St.
Starke

N. B. Hull House, built 1882 for general store owner who served as postmaster several terms. Unusual features: two-story porch and clipped gables.

L
556 N. Cherry St.
Starke

Sternberg House, built 1885 by early merchant, Sidney Sternberg of Truby and Sternburg General Store. Virtually unaltered example of large two-story frame house with full attic, high foundation, and continuous verandas at each floor on three sides.

M
N. Church St. and
Jackson St.
Starke

St. Mark's Episcopal Church, built 1880 in Fairbanks and moved to Starke in 1905, typical example Florida Victorian Revival church architecture. Rectory, originally social hall at Camp Blanding; parish house, originally cotton gin at NE corner of Madison St. and Thompson St.

N
400 S. Water St.
Starke

George Pace House, built 1880 for local merchant. Early Victorian Revival house which had surrounding first floor porch. Second-floor porch, siding, and shutters to north added later.

O
304-308 S. Water St.

Dr. J. O. Haynes Residence, built 1890 as dentist's one-story Victorian Revival house. Delicately spaced porch columns contrasting with heavy, incompatible posts of airport addition.

P
Bessent Road and
Call St.
Starke

First Presbyterian Church, built 1886, Victorian example, corner entry compatible with original location at SE corner of N. Cherry St. and Bridges St. Historic Jardine organ sold before building move.

GILCHRIST

ANTHONY J. DASTA AND ROCKE HILL, ARCHITECTS

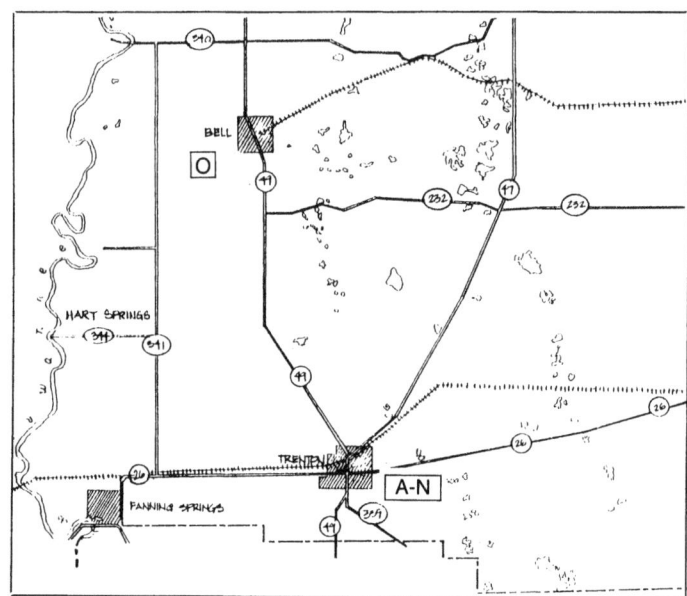

Once a part of Alachua County, Florida's newest county (Gilchrist) was created due to a dispute between area residents and the Alachua County Commission. In the mid 1920's area citizens requested that a road to be built from the Suwannee River at Fanning Springs to Gainesville to help promote economic development. When the commission would not yield to their request, the state legislature was petitioned to create a new county, and a resolution was passed in November and signed into law in December, 1925, by Governor John W. Martin. It contained one change. The name Gilchrist was substituted as the county name in honor of Albert H. Gilchrist, an ex-governor, instead of the name Melon for one of the area's abundant crops.

An election determined that Trenton would be the governmental seat of the new county. Rather than build a new courthouse, officials decided new schools and roads were more important. A new school was built in Trenton, and the old two-story frame school building was converted into the courthouse. Unfortunately this old building burned in 1932 destroying nearly all of the county's records. A new courthouse, completed in 1933, continues in use.

The area's development began about 1840 when John B. Stanley, one of the area's first settlers, moved into the region and purchased a large tract of land from the government. William F. Smith arrived in 1870 from Levy County, purchased land from Stanley, and built the Joppa Church and Post Office where mail was delivered from Gainesville. This site was located approximately a mile northeast of present day Trenton.

Railroads meant success or failure to early towns in the county. The town of Yulee was a flourishing community before Trenton or Bell existed. When the railroad reached Bell in 1902 and a depot was constructed, Yulee became a ghost town. Bell continued to thrive until area timber was depleted. Only the tenacity of some of the older settlers enabled Bell to remain a community, a town that developed into a prosperous farming center. One of the older settlements on the Suwannee River was known as Wilcox Landing. The name was changed to Wannee after the railroad from Alachua reached there in 1897. This settlement became all but forgotten when the tracks were removed between the settlement and Bell. Today Wannee exists only as a name on the map. The Atlantic Coast Line, built in 1907, ran through Tyler, Trenton and Wilcox and crossed the river north of Fanning Springs which is now known as the town of Suwannee River.

Located a short distance west of the Suwannee River and approximately 200 yards north of the present Highway 19 is an open field which was the site of Fort Fanning. Named for Major A.C.W. Fanning, this log fort was built about 1836-1837. as part of a network of North Florida forts used for defense against hostile Indians during the 1835 Seminole War. It is believed this particular site was chosen because of the high bluff and springs located nearby. Later, during the Civil War, it was used to store cotton.

Tyler, located in a phosphate belt, is a prosperous agricultural community, the first town in the county to have electric lights. After boll weevils wiped out cotton crops in 1907-1908, farmers started planting watermelons and raising hogs. Today, watermelon, corn, and soybeans are Gilchrist's major money crops.

Hart Springs, one of four major springs in the county, was used by the Creek Indians during hunting trips and was named after an Indian left near the springs in 1842 after the Seminole War. At present the springs area serves as a county park consisting of about 200 acres of forest on the Suwannee River.

The completion of the Three County Suwannee River Bridge in 1923 was the beginning of motor traffic across the Suwannee River. This partially wood bridge was replaced by the steel constructed Benjamin Chaires Bridge which opened in 1935 with a celebration, barbecue, and dance.

Today Gilchrist County, with an adequate system of roads, is seeking to attract industrial development to the region. However, the agricultural orientation, not unlike that at the turn of the century, remains with the network of quiet towns seeking to support the surrounding farmland. Even though the county lacks any type of organized architectural preservation effort in the mid 1980's, the historic residences, churches, schools, and public buildings are saved because they remain in constant use and receive the maintenance and repair necessary to preserve them.

A
E. Wade St at
NE Second St.
Trenton

First Baptist Church. Congregation established before 1890. Building constructed during 1920's. One story red brick masonry with projecting entry porch and gable roof. Two story additions at rear.

B
E. Wade St. at
NE First St.
Trenton

Residence, built in 1917. Two-story wood frame, simple Bungalow style with masonry piers and paired wood columns. Gable roof with bracketed wide overhangs.

C
E. Wade St. at
S. Main St.
Trenton

Gilchrist County Courthouse, built in 1933 and designed by Smith, Holborn, and Dozier of Jacksonville and constructed as part of Works Progress Administration. Two-story red brick with decorative corbeled courses, arched window openings with drip courses, triple arched entry porch, and 1965 additions.

D
S. Main St. at
SE First Ave.
Trenton

Trenton Church of Christ, built in 1920. One-story, Florida field limestone rubble masonry structure, brick quoins at openings, arched windows, triple-arched entry porch, gable roof. Additions to rear.

E
SW Fifth Ave. at
SW First St.
Trenton

Residence. One of the oldest residences in Trenton, an example of "Florida Cracker" vernacular style. One-story wood frame, horizontal siding, masonry piers, central brick chimney, gable roof, and wide porches.

F
NW First Ave.
at NW First St.
Trenton

Trenton Hotel, built in 1920's. Wood frame building with horizontal wood siding, hip roof with intersecting gables, sheet metal roofing. Entry porch with brick piers and wood columns. Varied occupants.

G
N. Main St. at
NE First Ave.
Trenton

Trenton City Hall, built in late 1930s. Two-story red brick facade. Side and back walls of yellow concrete block. Brick quoin decorations at front corners and window openings. Roof sheathed in metal shingles, open eaves.

H
N. Main St. at
NW Fourth Ave.
Trenton

Trenton Depot, built in 1904. One-story wood frame building with vertical siding, gable roof with wide overhangs, and an open truss ceiling. Trusses supported on wood braced columns. Several additions to the rear. Not in use in mid 1980's and in disrepair.

I
NW Third Ave.
Trenton

Mother's Soup Kitchen, behind commercial buildings on N. Main St., built in 1914. In use during economic ordeals of the early twentieth century. One-room wood frame building with horizontal wood siding, wood piers, and a roof sheathed in metal.

J
NW Second Ave. at
NW Second St.
Trenton

Residence, formerly Gilchrist County Jail. Two-story masonry building with stucco exterior finish. Flat roof, triple-arched front porch. Upper level windows retaining jail bars.

K
NE Fourth Ave. at
NE First St.
Trenton

Residence. One-and-one-half story wood frame building with horizontal siding. Gable roof with shed at the rear. Masonry piers, wide porch the length of the facade, bracketed wood columns.

L
N. Main St. at
NE Lancaster St.
Trenton

Warehouse. Probably one of the oldest commercial buildings in Gilchrist County. One-story wood frame structure, gable roof, dormer, and roof sheathed in metal. Large sliding door faces railroad tracks.

M
N. Main St.
at NW Fifth Ave.
Trenton

Coca Cola Building. Once a Coca-Cola bottling and distribution center, later Gilchrist County Chamber of Commerce, then in disrepair and not in use. One-story red brick structure with hip roof, tower, cast stone details. Several additions to the rear of the structure.

N
N. Main St.
Trenton

Trenton High School, built in 1924. Designed by Newblod L. Goin. Trenton's only high school and Gilchrist County's first high school. Two-story red brick building with flat roof, cast stone details, and arched from entry porch.

O
State Highway 49
Bell

Bell High School, constructed in 1928. Two-story light colored brick building with flat roof, cast stone coping at parapet, corbeled brick courses form panels in spandrels. Front porch and other additions.

ALACHUA

CHARLES F. MORGAN

Spanish explorers traveled through the area of Alachua County as early as 1529. After the establishment of St. Augustine in 1565, several missions were built in the northern part of the county. The wood, red clay, and thatch missions did not survive in the Florida climate. Local Indians did not readily convert to Christianity and revolted in 1656. In 1702, Creek Indians attacked and burned one mission, Santa Fe de Toloca.

The British acquired Florida in 1763 and governed until 1783. During that period, botanist William Bartram traveled in the county and studied the area south of present Gainesville, including the Indians near Micanopy and Payne's Prairie. He wrote vivid descriptions in his 1791 book, *Travels of William Bartram*. (Payne's Prairie, now one of Florida's largest state preserves, was once a lake. In the nineteenth century steamboats carried produce from the south edge of the lake to Gainesville for rail shipments.)

Spain reoccupied Florida in 1783. An 1817 land grant from the King of Spain, the Arredondo Grant, included much of present day Alachua County. The United States acquired Florida in 1821. Settlers had moved into the Alachua area in spite of intermittent resistance of the Seminole Indians which continued into the 1840s.

Alachua County was created on December 29, 1824, with territory stretching from the Georgia border to Charlotte Harbor. Subsequent land divisions, which only concluded a hundred years later, reduced Alachua to an interior county whose development was determined by land transportation. Newnansville, settled between 1823 and 1826 at the crossing of early trails, was declared Alachua's county seat in 1828. Later the community was served by the Bellamy Road, a road proposed at the first Florida Territorial Convention in 1832 to connect St. Augustine and Pensacola and built by John Bellamy.

Newnansville grew, even during the Seminole Wars period, but declined when the town was bypassed by railroads constructed in central Florida. In the 1850s settlers, particularly those some distance from Newnansville, wanted a county seat on the proposed railroad between Fernandina and Cedar Key. A small town near Payne's Prairie, Gainesville (named for Seminole War hero General Edmund P. Gaines and located on the railroad route), was designated as the new county seat in 1853. In 1860 the town had a population of 300 and eight or nine small businesses and three hotels, all clustered around the courthouse square and the 1856 two-story frame courthouse. In 1884 the Savannah, Florida, and Western Railroad reached Gainesville.

Gainesville became the region's agricultural center and the state's fourth largest city despite the end of the local citrus industry after several hard winters late in the last century. Cotton and lumber were major regional industries focused in Gainesville. During this same period, the architectural nature of Gainesville changed as several downtown fires resulted

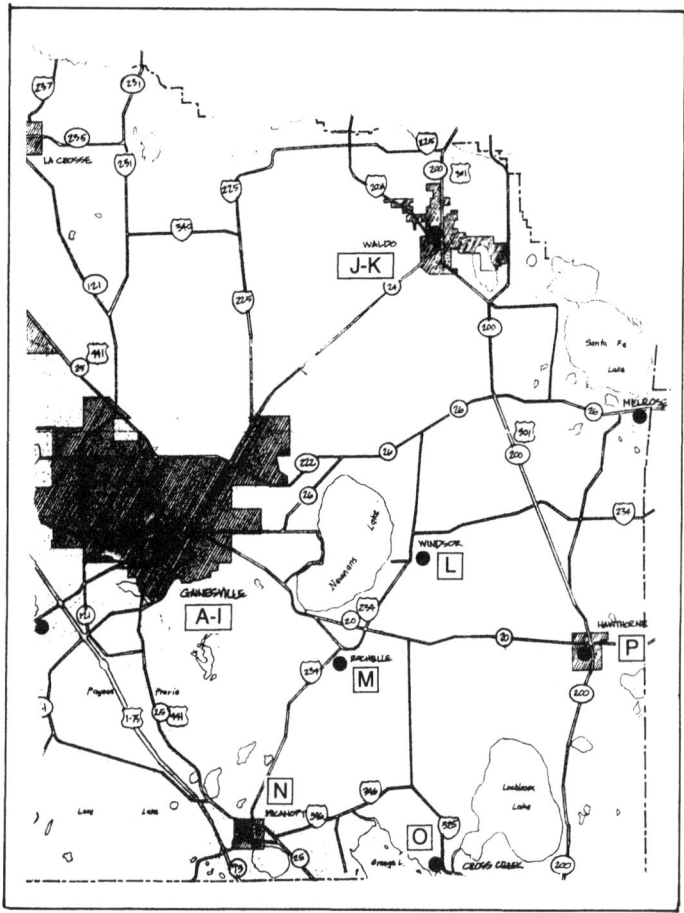

in the replacement of the wood-frame commercial buildings with masonry structures.

Education has been the chief business in Gainesville since the Buckman Act of 1905 created the University of Florida in Gainesville. The University of Florida replaced East Florida Seminary, an earlier state college, and became co-educational in 1947. In addition, Santa Fe Community College, opening in 1965, and Sunland Training Center, a state institution for the mentally handicapped, contributed to the area's reputation as an educational center. Gainesville has also evolved into a nationally known medical center with four major hospitals, including a teaching hospital, and the university's health science center which trains future doctors, nurses, pharmacists, dentists, veterinarians, and other health related professionals as well as conducting extensive research programs.

The oldest permanent settlement in the county is Micanopy, established in 1821. Micanopy, Waldo, and Melrose had populations in excess of 500 during the 1880s but failed to maintain growth after the turn of the century. Other incorporated towns in the county include Alachua, Newberry, High Springs, LaCrosse and Hawthorne.

A

University of Florida
Gainesville

Library East, built in 1925. Designed by architect William A. Edwards, who also designed most of the university's early buildings. This building with Peabody, Anderson, Floyd, Flint, and the University Auditorium, all in collegiate styles, define the Plaza of the Americas. Library East remodeled and expanded in 1949.

B

University of Florida
Gainesville

University Auditorium, built in 1924. Auditorium served for all university assemblies, including chapel. Originally intended to receive addition for university administrative functions to face the plaza. 1970 addition of reception areas.

C

1121 NW 6th St.
Gainesville

Major James Bailey House, built in 1848 to 1854 as plantation house by Major Bailey who sold portion of plantation land to county for the courthouse site. One-and-a-half story, braced frame structure built in native materials. Classical Revival style. Restored and adapted as housing for the elderly.

D

NE 6th Ave at 2nd St.
Gainesville

Hotel Thomas, begun in 1906 as a residence for C. W. Chace and completed in 1910 as residence for Major William Reuben Thomas. Additions in 1928 adapted structure to serve as a hotel. Purchased by City of Gainesville in 1974. Restored and adapted in 1979 as a cultural center and city offices, a major American Revolution Bicentennial Celebrations project.

E

2 W. University Ave.
Gainesville

Endel Brothers building, built in 1884. Site originally occupied by the Arlington Hotel which burned in the 1880's with several other wood-frame buildings located around the courthouse square. Endel Brothers Building occupied by variety of businesses including F.W. Woolworth's, a bank, and furniture, clothing and fruit stores. Rehabilitated in 1980 as Chesnut's Office Supply.

F

25 SE 2nd Place
Gainesville

U.S. Post Office, designed by federal architect Thayer Ryerson and completed in 1911. Beau-Arts Classicism style with modern innovations of the time, an elevator and steam heat. Interior significantly altered in 1980 for use as a state theater, the Hippodrome Theatre.

G

408 W University Ave.
Gainesville

John F. Seagle Building, designed by F. Lloyd Preacher and Rudolph Weaver as a hotel for W. McKee Kelley. 1926 construction interrupted by ten years of economic depression. Completed in 1937 with Works Progress Administration and Georgia Seagle contributions. Structure donated to State of Florida and used as university offices and museum. Adapted in mid-1980's as condominiums, social club, and office and retail spaces.

H

120 S. Main St.
Gainesville

Commercial Hotel, built in 1885 as Alachua Hotel. Faced Main Street and Savannah, Florida, and Western Railroad track. After 1900 housed printing companies, then Commercial Hotel in 1924. Donated to Alachua County in late 1970's. Rehabilitated in 1981 as county office building.

I

617 E. University Ave.
Gainesville

McKenzie House, one of Gainesville's most elaborate Queen Anne residences. Two-and-a-half-story structure with shingle and horizontal siding, polygonal tower, projecting gable at entry, and attached one-story gazebo. Stabilized and adapted as tourist agency in 1980.

J

SW 2nd Way and
W. Blvd.
Waldo

Schenk Hardware, built in 1913. Brick masonry building occupied and maintained since construction. Inlaid tile stoop left from long-time bank occupancy. Second floor served as meeting hall for the city council and community organizations.

K

SW 7th Way
Waldo

George Granger House. Elaborate Victorian Revival style, wood frame structure. Built in 1894 for George Granger, railroad engineer, when Waldo served as an exchange point for goods and passengers on railroads and canal to Lake Santa Fe and Melrose.

L

SR 25
Windsor

R. W. Kelly House, built in 1884 for Kelly when Windsor was an active citrus center. Town in decline after major 1890's freezes with many buildings lost to fires and neglect.

M

SE of SR 234
Rochelle

Rochelle School, quarter of a mile southeast of SR 234 and SCL tracks. Built in 1885 as Martha Perry Institute.

N

Micanopy

Feaster Building. Built in 1903 as general store and drug store on first floor, town council and dentist office on second floor, and theatrical productions on third floor. Adapted for use as art gallery and residences.

O

State Road 325
Cross Creek

Rawlings House, quarter mile south of Cross Creek, built in the late 19th century. Typical "Cracker" style farm house with open porches, cross ventilation, board and batten construction, brick foundation piers. Purchased in 1928 by Marjorie Kinnan Rawlings, famous writer of *The Yearling* (Pulitzer Price 1939), *Cross Creek*, and other books based on Cross Creek locale.

P

NW 1st Ave &
NW 2nd Ave.
Hawthorne

First United Methodist Church. Cornerstone of church laid in 1891, a year after Hawthorne incorporated. Building lot purchased for $55 from town founder, James Hawthorne. Simple Victorian Revival style, well-maintained, wood frame structure.

LEVY

GEORGE SCHEFFER, AIA, FLORIDA NORTH

Timucuan Indians lived in what is now Levy County for hundreds of years before Europeans arrived in Florida. In 1539-1540 Hernando de Soto passed through one of their villages, probably in the area of Long Pond near present day Chiefland. As the Timucuan population decreased almost to the point of extinction during Spanish rule, a few were absorbed into the Seminole groups that took their place. During the Spanish and British periods this portion of Florida was isolated. Spanish pirates are said to have visited the area, and the Louisiana pirate Jean Lafitte is supposed to have stopped briefly on one of the coastal keys at the beginning of the nineteenth century.

In 1821 Spain ceded Florida to the United States. On March 19, 1822, Florida was organized as one territory with two counties, Escambia and St. Johns. Part of St. Johns became Alachua County in 1824 and then part of Alachua County became Levy County on March 10, 1845. (Bronson, incorporated in 1884, is the present county seat.)

Before Florida became a part of the United States, General Andrew Jackson had invaded Spanish territory to fight the Seminole Indians. As conflict between the increasing settlements and Seminole Indians escalated, the U.S. Army built forts in Florida. During the Second Seminole War, which began in 1835, a military hospital and supply base were built on Atsena Otie or Depot Key across from Way Key. In the 1840's a small resort for planters developed on the same key. As the Seminole War drew to a close, both the military post and civilian buildings were destroyed by an 1842 hurricane. Further development of this area occurred on Way Key, the site of the town of Cedar Key.

Fishing and timber soon became the economic base. Resin was extracted from the extensive forests in Levy County as the production of turpentine became an important industry. Pine and cypress were cut to meet the growing national demand for lumber and other forest products. The deep water port at Cedar Key encouraged the development of a major shipping industry for fish, wood products, and cotton.

Levy County and its first county seat, Levyville, were named in honor of Florida's first senator, David Levy Yulee, who was influential in attaining statehood for Florida in 1845. Yulee (David Levy added Yulee to his name by state legislative act) was a leading promoter of a cross-Florida railroad to link the Gulf with the state's eastern seaports. In the mid 1850's he began construction of the Atlantic, Gulf and West Indies Transit Company Railroad and completed this tie between Fernandina and Cedar Key in 1860.

In 1855, at the same time Yulee was beginning to build his railroad, Eberhard Faber purchased vast tracts of timber in Levy County and built a saw mill on Atsena Otie Key to cut cedar into slats for shipment to his pencil factory in New Jersey. Faber's Cedar Key operation, which expanded its production capacity, provided a growth stimulant to the area for the next thirty years.

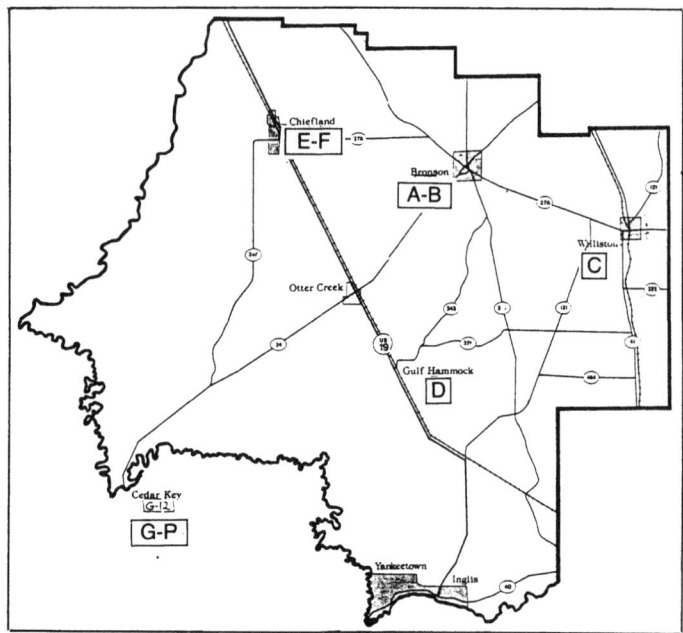

During the Civil War, the port of Cedar Key was blockaded. Union landing parties destroyed a Confederate artillery battery, the railroad depot, wharf, shops, and salt and turpentine factories.

After the Civil War, growth began again. In addition to its prewar enterprises, Cedar Key developed a shipbuilding industry, and the federal custom office was moved from St. Marks to Cedar Key to handle increased shipping. Twenty years after the war, the Cedar Key area had five lumber mills and two cedar mills owned by Faber and the Eagle Pencil companies, a successful fishing industry, newspapers, banks, and three hotels. Depletion of cedar, pine, and cypress stands and the oyster and fish beds brought an end to the successful industries which had supported the area. A powerful hurricane in 1896 destroyed many commercial and residential buildings. Population decreased from 5,000 in 1885 to 864 in 1900.

Financial depression and natural destruction paralyzed the town. Although minor developments occurred in the area, a paved road from Archer, built in 1923, provided access to other regions and improved the economy. The 1930's depression and the discontinuation of railroad service to Cedar Key stalled progress again.

Post-World-War-II tourism, attracted by fishing opportunities and the village quality of Cedar Key, has caused major changes in the economy and architecture of the town. Restaurants, hotels, condominiums, and shops have been built or housed in renovated structures. The character of the community has been maintained, and visitors still find the experience of retreat.

A
Court St.
Bronson

Levy County Courthouse, built in 1927 by O.R. Woodcock and designed by Henry L. Taylor using some material salvaged from 1906 courthouse. Classical Revival style featuring arched entry with fan light, keystone lintels above double hung windows, and cupola with copper roof.

B
235 Court St.
Bronson

United Methodist Church, built in 1866 and moved in 1920 from lot east of Bronson High School. Victorian Revival style with bell-tower clad with metal shingles and verge board trim.

C
112 SE 1st Ave.
Williston

L.C. Hester House, built in 1906 by Hester. Hip roof, two gable dormers at street elevation, shed roof porch with angled entry, and corbeled chimney decorations.

D
U.S. 19
Gulf Hammock

Old "No. 3" Locomotive, Gulf Hammock Village, constructed in 1915 with parts from 1897, 1915, and 1919. This locomotive known as "three-spot," one of five that hauled timber to Pac and Mac Sawmill near Gulf Hammock. In use until World War II.

E
City Hall Square
Chiefland

Chiefland Public Library, built in 1923 as bandstand, closed in and used as first town hall until 1938. Moved in 1959 to cemetery and used as Boy Scout meeting place. Moved in 1974 by Chiefland Women's Club for use as library.

F
NW 13th St. at
NW 16th Ave.
Chiefland

Old Hardeetown Hotel, built in 1910 as hotel to house railroad workers laying track for Seaboard Railway in 1913. Rehabilitation in 1982 as single family residence. Simple wood frame bulding, hip roof with projecting polygonal bay with gable roof.

G
Seahorse Key
Cedar Key

Seahorse Key Lighthouse and Keepers Dwelling, built in 1855 under the direction of Lt. George Meade, Corps of Engineering, US Army. Marked entrance to Cedar Key Harbor. Lens removed by US Marines from the federal gunboat Hatteras during the Civil War after skirmish with Confederate defenders. Lighthouse and quarters used as marine laboratory by University of Florida.

H
B St. at 2nd St.
Cedar Key

Parson and Hale Store-Island Hotel, built in 1850 as general store. Fragments of earlier building in rear portion of building. Parapet walls and flat roof under sheet metal hip roof. Veranda on principal elevations. Tabby masonry walls.

I
D Street
Cedar Key

Edward Champlin-Reynolds House, built in 1884. Victorian Revival style, wood frame house with bay window and porches, verge board.

J
D St. at 5th St.
Cedar Key

United Methodist Church, built in 1889. Simple Victorian Revival style, wood frame building with L plan. Tower-entry at intersection of gable roof. Damaged in 1896 hurricane and rebuilt.

K
4th Street
Cedar Key

Old School Building, built in 1880. Two-story wood frame building. Verandas at north and east elevations.

L
2nd Street
Cedar Key

John Lutterloh Residence-Cedar Key Historical Society Museum, built in 1871 for Lutterloh, Cedar Key agent for the Florida Railroad. Later used as restaurant, Women's Club, public library, service station, and shop. Historical Society's museum in mid 1980's.

M
B St. at 2nd St.
Cedar Key

Masonic Lodge, built in 1910. Served as store on first floor with meeting space above. Wood frame, hip roof with bracketed eaves, recessed corner entrance, and display window at street elevation.

N
2nd Street
Cedar Key

W. R. Hodges Residence, built in 1910 for Hodges, a wholesale fish exporter. Duplicate of house in Inglis. Victorian Revival style with two gables at street elevation, shed roof porch with gable at entrance, verge boards in gables, and bracketed porch columns.

O
2nd Street
Cedar Key

First Baptist Church, built in 1923 with James Taylor as builder. Wood frame Classical Revival style building with gable roof, four square columns at gable end, frame portico. Projecting bay behind columns at first floor providing narthex.

P
F St. at 4th St.
Cedar Key

W. H. Hale-A. W. Johnson House, built in 1880's as residence for Hale of Parsons and Hale. One-story wood frame cottage with hip roof, recessed porch with pairs of bracketed columns, turned balusters, and a front doorway with sidelights and transom.

MARION

EDWARD D'AVI, AIA & ERIC WIEDEGREEN, AIA, FLORIDA NORTH

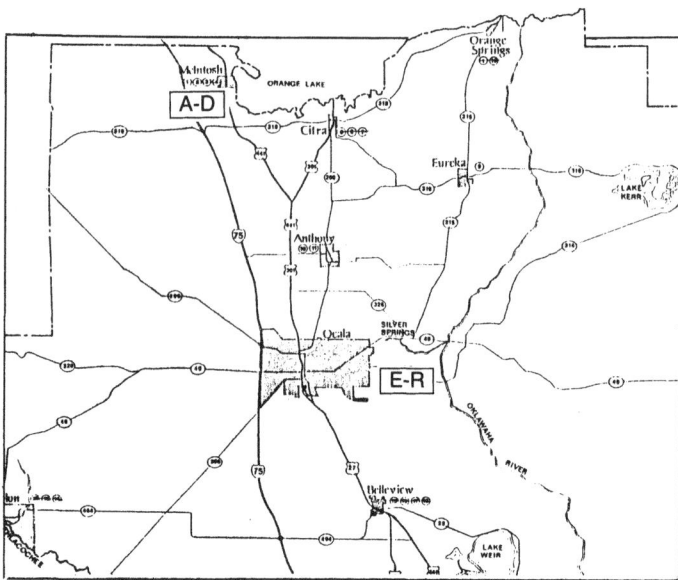

The combination of the cultivation of oranges beginning in 1870, the coming of the railroad in 1879, and the introduction of the phosphate industry encouraged rapid growth in the county. Typical of the development from this era are the towns of Citra, Anthony, Orange Springs, and McIntosh.

McIntosh was platted along the Florida Southern Railroad line in 1885 in a strict grid pattern. As with other citrus boom towns, McIntosh grew rapidly with most of the town structures dating between 1885 and 1910. The 1895 freeze ended McIntosh's most dramatic development, and vegetable production took over from citrus as the economic base until the 1960's. Most of the houses in McIntosh share many architectural features. The structures are two-story wood frame buildings with steep roof pitches, lap siding, simple ornamentation, and the ever present porches. The old depot and packing houses bear witness to the strong link to the land, and the four period churches underscore the importance of the church in small town life. Because of the concentration of significant structures, McIntosh was listed on the National Register of Historic Places as an Historic District in November 1983.

Citra, settled in the early 1800's, was a citrus town until the 1980 freezes. Several buildings remain from the early history. The Baptist Church is a Victorian Revival style building with a gridded rose window and open bell tower. The oldest, most completely documented building in Marion County is the Orange Springs Community Church which was built in 1852 as an Episcopal Church and restored in 1972.

The 1889 discovery of limestone near Dunnellon by Albertus Vogt brought prosperity to that community. The mining and shipping of phosphate and limestone rock was a leading industry in the area until 1914. "Rosebank," Vogt's house, is at Vogt Springs on SR 40. Goethe Mill, also on SR 40, is one of the few remaining steam-powered saw mills in Florida.

Ocala's history is associated with Fort King and the 1835 beginning of the Second Seminole Indian War. Following the Seminole wars, varieties of citrus were introduced to the area. In 1852, the first state-supported school, East Florida Seminary, opened classes in Ocala. East of Ocala, Silver Springs was developed as a resort by Col. W. M. Davidson and Carl Ray. (The attraction continues to draw visitors to the

locale and to stimulate real estate development between the Springs and Ocala.) Because of its proximity to the Springs and to the Oklawaha River, Ocala became a distribution point, and, with the advent of the railroad, a citrus and produce shipping center. In 1935, when work began on the Gulf-Atlantic Ship Canal, Ocala enjoyed a real estate boom until work was suspended in 1936. Eureka Dam and Locks are surviving elements of the project.

Cattle breeding (1870-1895), real estate (1890-1920's), phosphate mining (1889-1914), and tourism (after 1880) have all contributed to the city's growth. On November 29, 1883, a fire destroyed a major portion of Ocala, forcing many to rebuild in brick for permanence and fire protection. The number of structures dating from this era testifies to the prosperity of Ocala at the time. A majority of the residences constructed then by prominent citizens were located in the Caldwell's Addition, now known as the Fort King Historic District.

The county's natural beauty has always attracted tourism. With the railroad and the Dixie Highway (now US 441) and later Interstate 75, Marion County is located in a major north-south corridor. Since 1956 an important economic boost has been the horse farming industry. Marion County horses have gained international recognition and established the area as a leader in the sport with Ocala Breeders' Sales Company at its pinnacle.

Preservation efforts in Marion County have risen from crisis situations. The Friends of McIntosh, Inc., were organized in 1974 in response to the proposed demolition of the McIntosh Depot. The organization sponsors an annual 1890 Festival in the fall to generate funds for preservation. A proposed public works road project which involved the demolition of nine significant structures in Ocala helped bring the Historic Ocala Preservation Society (HOPS) into being. HOPS has been instrumental in the passage of a city preservation ordinance (1982) and an historic district designation (1984). In 1985, Ocala was chosen for the national "Main Street Program" which focuses efforts for the revitalization of the downtown area in the context of historic preservation.

A
Ave. G and Third S.
McIntosh

McIntosh Railroad Depot, built in 1890. Wood frame building constructed by the Florida Southern Railroad as a produce shipping point. Restored to 1913 appearance in 1974 by the Friends of McIntosh.

B
East Ave. G
McIntosh

McIntosh Hotel, built in 1895 to service railroad passengers with food and lodging. Two-story wood frame building with double porch and nineteen rooms including dining room.

C
Ave. F & Seventh St.
McIntosh

William Gist-W. A. Norsworthy House, built in 1890, for Gist who was one of the town's founders. Two-story, Victorian Revival style, wood frame building. Restored in 1975.

D
Ave. F & Seventh St.
McIntosh

McIntosh Presbyterian Church, built in 1907. Victorian Revival style, wood frame building with corner entry, bell tower, and art glass windows.

E
850 SE Ft. King Ave.
Ocala

Jewett House, built in 1890. One-story Victorian Revival style frame vernacular building with an unusual Y-shaped plan and entry. Renovated into offices in 1979.

F
798 SE Ft. King Ave.
Ocala

Edward Holder House, built in 1906 for Holder, one of Florida's first phosphate miners and owner of the Marion Block. Two-and-a-half story wood frame Victorian Revival style.

G
943 SE Ft. King Ave.
Ocala

R. A. Burford House, built in 1893 for Burford, prominent lawyer and counsel to the railroad. Two-story frame Victorian Revival style house with porches and tower. Iron fence around the lot from the old Ocala courthouse. Renovated in 1975 as law offices.

H
808 SE Ft. King Ave.
Ocala

W. S. Bullock House, built in 1891 for Bullock who was judge of the Fifth Circuit Court and mayor of Ocala at the turn of the century. Two-story Victorian Revival style frame building with gazebo porch.

I
416 SE Ft. King Ave.
Ocala

John E. Dunn House, built in 1888 for Dunn who was early Ocala entrepreneur and founder of the First Bank of Ocala in 1882. Two-story Victorian Revival style wood frame structure with delicate porches and tower.

J
531 NE First Ave.
Ocala

Union Station, built in 1917 to replace Union Station of 1881. Brick and shingles. Now an AMTRAK station.

K
SE First St. and Broadway
Ocala

Marion Block Building, built in 1885. Three-story brick commercial structure, one of the first buildings constructed after the 1883 fire. Incorporated opera house. Renovated in 1983 as offices and restaurant.

L
Corner Magnolia & SE Broadway
Ocala

Commercial Bank of Ocala, built in 1890. Three-story brick commercial building with corner entry, typical of many downtown commercial buildings erected after the fire of 1883. Main commercial area centered on Courthouse Square (now a public space with a fountain.)

M
623 S. Magnolia Ave.
Ocala

Mt. Zion A.M.E. Church, built in 1891. Six-hundred seat church, simplifed Victorian Revival style. Designed by Levi Alexander, Sr., architect. Congregation founded in 1861.

N
503 SE Broadway

Grace Episcopal Church. Congregation started in 1853. Original sanctuary built in 1875, moved to present site in 1905. Major additions in 1906.

O
729 NE Second St.
Ocala

United Hebrews of Ocala, Temple B'Nai Daron, built in 1888. Wood frame Victorian Revival style structure with art glass windows.

P
108 N. Magnolia Ave.
Ocala

Francis Marion Hotel, built in 1927. Seven-story complex of hotel fucntions and street level retail function. Mediterranean Revival style. Adapted for use as offices in 1983-1984 as The Sovereign Building.

Q
1205 Silver Springs Blvd.
Ocala

The Ritz Apartments, built in 1925. Complex of four two-story buildings of stucco over hollow clay tiles. Spanish Colonial Revival style. Introduced apartment living to Ocala.

R
939 N. Magnolia Ave.
Ocala

Coca-Cola Bottling Plant, built in 1939 with Courtney Stewart as architect. Cast cement and concrete block Mediterranean Revival style. Adapted as a warehouse and office supply in 1978.

BAKER

LES MAY, AIA, FLORIDA NORTH CHAPTER

Baker County, Florida's twenty-eighth county, was established at the beginning of the Civil War and named for James McNair Baker, a circuit judge and later a senator in the Confederate Congress.

Early settlement in this locale was slow. Rivers were not deep enough for commercial travel. The area had large acreages of wet and swampy land. A boundary dispute between Florida and Georgia left the land south of the Okeefenokee Swamp with little law enforcement until after the Civil War. The offical end of the Second Seminole War and the Armed Occupation Act of 1842, which gave land grants to settlers, encouraged those willing to run the risks of pioneering to come to Florida. Construction of the Main Post Road from Jacksonville to Lake City in 1857 caused some population increases.

Efficient transportation and communication between inland areas and the Florida East Coast developed when railroad construction began in 1857 with the Florida, Atlanta, and Gulf Coast Railroad. By 1858 rails reached from the east to the Gulf of Mexico.

Early architecture in Baker County reflected the basic problems of survival in a hostile environment. The James M. Burnsed Blockhouse, constructed of squared logs in the 1830's, was built with cut gun ports (apparently unused) for protection from "Coweeter" Creek Indians. Log construction, especially in isolated areas, continued until saw mills permitted milled wood construction.

During the Civil War, Baker County was the site of the 1864 Battle of Olustee which was won by Confederate forces to save vital interior agricultural resources. A monument was placed at the site in 1912 to commemorate the victory.

Growth following the war was nearly halted by an 1888 yellow fever epidemic. Almost ninety percent of the population of major settlements was lost. Darbyville, the county seat, became a ghost town until 1890. At that time a revival of development began, and the town was renamed Macclenny for Capt. Carr Bowers MacClenny, a Virginian who had moved south to cut timber for the post-war building boom in northern states.

Late nineteenth century residential building in this area used mill construction as evidenced by the 1865 Shuey-Sessions house. The popular Victorian Revival styles are reflected in carved verge boards and pendants found in the Charles F. Barber house built in Macclenny in 1881 and in the gingerbread porch columns of the Taber House built in 1893. During a spurt of building between 1905 and severe flu epidemics in 1918-1919, the Dykes Building was constructed in 1910; a Neo-Classical Revival County Courthouse built in 1908; and many residences completed in the Bungalow style. David Griffin established the Griffin All-State Nursery in 1905 which later became the Southern States Nursery, a major economic resource for the area.

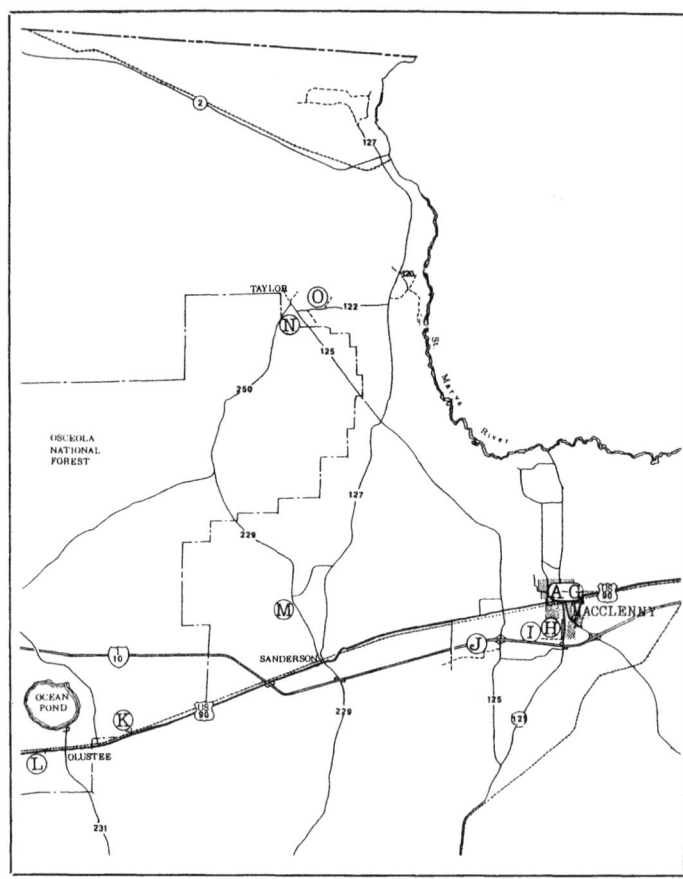

The completion of US 90 in 1924 provided the first paved east-west road across Baker County. Transportation was further enhanced with the building of the Southern Coastline Railroad Station in 1928. The 1931 Olustee Naval Stores and Experimental Station and the new courthouse, begun in 1941 and finished in 1948, were in Neo-Classical Revival styles. Interstate 10, paralleling old US 90, has stimulated the local economy through real estate action and the attraction of new businesses and modest population increases. Baker County remains primarily an agricultural area dependent on forest products, tobacco, poultry, and landscape nurseries.

Preservation in Baker County has occurred when economic conditions dictate continued use rather than demolition. The Koon-Lyle house near Taylor was moved in 1973 to the Jacksonville Museum of Arts and Sciences. The 1908 courthouse and adjacent jail were adapted for use by the Public Library and the Baker County Historical Society. Macclenny's Downtown Revitalization Committee was organized in 1979 to encourage private investment in commercial rehabilitation projects. In the mid 1980's there is tangible concern for the preservation of Baker County's architectural heritage.

A
339 E. Macclenny Av.
Macclenny

Baker County Courthouse, construction started with Works Progress Administration funds in 1941, completed in 1948. Neo-Classical Revival style typical of governmental-encouraged municipal improvements 1930-1940. Portico with four Ionic columns, corner pilasters, pediment bas relief of clock and scales of justice.

B
S. Fourth St.
Macclenny

Charles F. Barber House, built in 1881. Oldest existing house in Macclenny, referred to as "fever house" implying construction before 1888 yellow fever epidemic. Extensively modified.

C
Railroad Road

Southern Coastline Railroad Station, built in 1928. A version of H. H. Richardson's architectural style of railroad stations. Low dormer, hip roof, and wide overhang.

D
212 McIver
Macclenny

"Suits Us," Dorman House. Designed and named by Mrs. Dorman. Built in 1910 for her by her husband with Jess Rowe as builder. Queen Anne style structure with multiple dormers, north chimney penetrating dormer roof, and porch with shed and conical roofs.

E
Fifth St. & McIver
Macclenny

Old Courthouse-Baker County Public Library, built in 1908 by Arthur Lowe. Neo-Classical Revival style two-story brick building with octagonal rooms at four corners and central portion with portico and cupola. Cast-iron fireplaces and mantles and pressed metal ceilings.

F
228 S. Fifth St.
Macclenny

Merritt-Herndon House, built in 1885 for James C. Merritt, one of northern investors recruited by Carr McClenny's "Florida Investment and Colonialization Society." House purchased in 1886 by Judge John Herndon.

G
N. Sixth St.
Macclenny

Edgar Turner-Duncan Rhoden House, built from 1903-1905. Victorian Revival style, one-and-a-half story wood frame house with gable roof, projecting central bay and dormer, and board and batten siding.

H
George Hodges Rd.
Macclenny

Williams-Shuey House (west of CR 121 and south of Macclenny) built in 1865 by Rep. Samuel Neil Williams, merchant and timber buyer for Eppinger and Russell, N.Y. In 1880's purchased by Dr. George Shuey. Served as first hospital in county and used in yellow fever epidemic of 1888. Possibly oldest example of mill construction residence in county.

I
George Hodges Rd.
Macclenny

David Griffin House (west of CR 121, south of Macclenny) built in 1905 for Griffin, founder of the All-State Nursery (Southern States Nursery). Classical Revival style, two-story wood frame structure with gable roof and center bay portico. Exotic plants on site.

J
Dick Mann Road
Macclenny

George Lindley Taber House, Glen Saint Mary Nursery, built in 1893 for Taber who in 1892 established a 900-acre nursery for trees and shrubs with H. Harold Hume, horticulturist of Florida Experiment Station and University of Florida as company's vice-president. Hume's house, built in 1920, and barns and outbuildings still on site.

K
US 90
Olustee

Olustee Battlefield State Memorial, (2.45 miles east of CR 231). Battle of Olustee/Ocean Pond fought Feb. 20, 1864, in open forest with no fortifications. Site purchased by State in 1909. Monument erected in Romanesque Revival style in 1912. Interpretation site and self guided tour in 1980's.

L
US 90
Olustee

Olustee Naval Stores and Experimental Station/SCM Corporation, built in 1931. Part of the forest management complex serving Osceola National Forest (established in 1929. Reflects importance of timber industry in the county.) Office in Georgian Revival style with side wings added. Laboratories dating from the 1920s.

M
CR 229, n. of US 90
Sanderson

James "Jim" Rhoden Sr. House, built in 1864. Log house sheathed with original milled siding, cypress log piers, early brick chimney. Typical isolated mid-1800's residence.

N
CR 250
Taylor

John Taylor House, built in 1888 on part of plantation established by Gordon Stewart Taylor, Methodist minister. Two-pen with central open hall (dog trot). Original detached dining room and kitchen removed.

O
South of CR 120

James M. Burnsed-Carl Brown House, on private graded road, inaccessible. Built in 1837 by Burnsed as blockhouse-residence. Probably oldest structure in Baker County. Squared hewn logs with half-dovetail joints, logs partly cut through to permit knock-out sections to serve as gun ports, holes drilled to provide dowels for weaving warp. Trapezoidal wood piers on sleepers. Two rooms, first floor with ladder to loft. Porches front and back, connecting dining space and kitchen. Brown family in house after Civil War to 1950's.

PUTNAM

AL DOMPE, AIA, FLORIDA NORTH CHAPTER

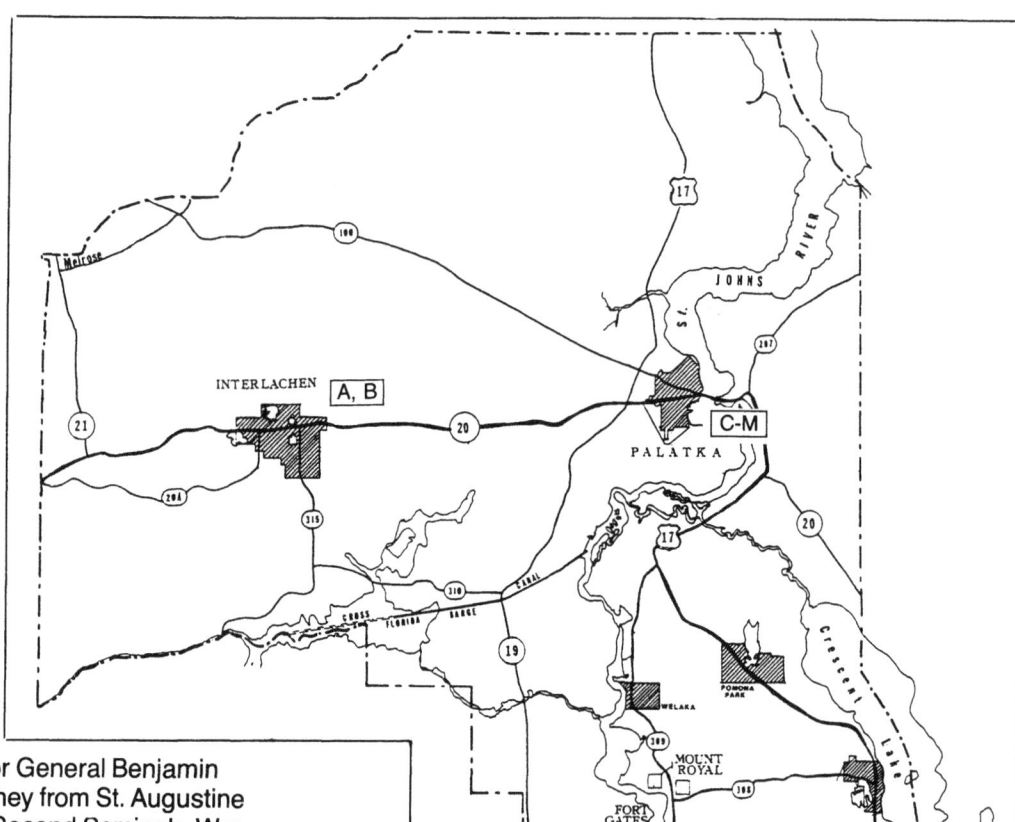

Putnam County, named for General Benjamin Putnam who was an attorney from St. Augustine and a commander during the Second Seminole War (1835-1842), was incorporated January 13, 1849, from parcels of surrounding counties. Located north of Lake George and crossed north to south by the St. Johns River, with many lakes in the west portion, the county provided bountiful fishing and hunting resources. Exploring Spanish soldiers and missionaries and later William Bartram found Indians living along the river. One settlement at an elbow bend on the St. Johns River was once known as Pilotaikata, a Seminole Creek term meaning "crossing." Palatka continues to serve as one of the few points at which to cross the river.

Although some attempts were made to establish settlements in this area during the first half of the nineteenth century, the Seminole Wars prevented much development except for the maintenance of Fort Shannon and military warehouses at Palatka. As stability returned, settlers began to arrive. Until 1860 the area prospered through lumbering and freight transport with steamship service playing a dominant role. Development stopped during the Civil War, but post-war years witnessed the county's most productive era.

From 1865-1890 the area prospered as a transportation hub. By the 1880's five railroads served the area and steamboats plied the river. Many small towns were created. Crescent City, known for its citrus, was founded in 1876. Interlachen was incorporated in 1886 after the Charlotte Harbor Railroad connected Palatka and Gainesville. Victorian Revival styles were predominately popular. Abundant lumber and mills encouraged production and use of palings, brackets, vergeboards, and other elements for houses, churches, schools, and workplaces. Although the business district of Palatka was consumed by a fire in 1884, reconstruction

began immediately. Sidewalks, brick streets, and utilities were in place by 1894. However, hard freezes in 1894-1895, diminution of rail and river traffic, and depletion of timber resources brought development to a standstill.

The twentieth century saw improvements in highway construction, the erection of the Putnam County Memorial Bridge across the St. Johns River, renewed citrus and other agricultural production, and trucking industries development. Unfortunately architectural preservation had several setbacks during this period. Many buildings were lost to thoughtless demolition, fires, and neglect.

A statewide historical survey was conducted in 1939, but no historical or architecturally significant sites were noted in Putnam County. As preservation efforts increased in the 1960s and 1970s, a few buildings and sites were nominated to the National Register of Historic Places. The Bronson-Mulholland House, St. Mark's Episcopal Church, the Hubbard House, and Mount Royal are among other sites registered in the county.

The Office of Community Development, which opened in 1975, has increased preservation efforts in the county. Local historians have helped the cause by increasing awareness. Commercial and residential preservation projects have been initiated throughout the region and have fostered revived business districts and revitalized neighborhoods.

64

A
Commonwealth at Boylston
Interlachen

Brush General Store, built in 1890. Typical of late nineteenth century small-town general store. Porch on first and second floors at street elevation. Entrance with large glass display windows on either side of recessed doorway, transoms above.

B
SR 20 at Grand Ave.
Interlachen

Interlachen Community School, built in 1880's. Oldest remaining wood frame schoolhouse in use in Florida. Classical Revival style. Restoration planned for late 1980's.

C
Corner of Main and North Twelfth St.
Palatka

Union Depot, built in 1909, owned by CSX Transportation Corp. Richardsonian style railroad depot with hip roof and bracketed eaves and hexagonal dormers. Brick masonry walls painted white. Rusticated course at water table and trim at openings.

D
Whitewater Drive
Palatka

Palatka Waterworks, constructed in 1887 by investors from Boston with Wheeler and Parks of Boston as builders when Palatka Waterworks established. Victorian Revival style with hip roof, louvered cupola, and pressed metal shingles. Brick masonry with corbeled cornice and drip course.

E
319 St John's Ave.
Palatka

East Florida Savings and Trust Company Bank-Putnam County Courthouse Annex, built 1924. Classical Revival bank building with stone veneer with granite stylobate. Symmetrical facade with six fluted Ionic columns, small pediment at entrance. Paired Ionic pilasters at side elevation.

F
121 S. Second St.
Palatka

First Presbyterian Church, constructed 1886 after the fire of 1884. Romanesque Revival style in brick masonry. Prominent landmark notable for copper-covered semi-circular portico with Doric columns, projecting tower, hipped roof, and stained glass windows.

G
260 Reid St.
Palatka

Larimer Library, designed by Henry Klutho, well-known Jacksonville architect, and constructed in 1930. Exhibits characteristics of Prairie School and Art Deco styles. Donated by James R. Mellon, Pittsburgh banker and seasonal resident of Palatka, as memorial to his wife, Rachel Hughes Larimer Mellon.

H
Corner of N. Second & Main St.
Palatka

St. Marks Episcopal Church, designed by Richard Upjohn, architect, and built in 1854. Victorian Revival style wood frame building. Latin Cross plan with elongated pointed openings glazed with stained glass, a central rose window, and elaborately detailed bell tower (not original). Used during the Civil War as a meeting house and barracks.

I
807 St. John's Ave.
Palatka

St. Mary's, constructed in 1883-1884. Small Victorian Revival style wood frame structure. Only surviving black church of the pre-1885 period in Palatka. Vertical board and batten siding, lancet windows, and curvilinear trim. Important landmark.

J
Madison St. between First & Second Sts.
Palatka

Bronson-Mulholland House. Classical Revival house built in 1845. Home of Judge Isaac Hopkins Bronson who was one of the first four circuit judges appointed after Florida was made a state and who also served as a district federal judge. Estate sold after his death in 1855. Mary Mulholland, well-known subsequent owner. House restoration begun in 1969 by the Putnam County Historical Society. Opened to the public eight years later as Palatka's historic museum.

K
603 Emmett St.
Palatka

Conant House, built in 1886 for Sherman Conant, general manager of Florida Southern Railroad and vice-president of Palatka National Bank. Queen Anne style house with dormers, gable roofs and polygonal turret with a tent roof. Encircling veranda with ornamental woodwork, turned posts, and balusters, lattice frieze work and curvilinear brackets.

L
1122 South 15th St.
Palatka

Residence, built in 1890. One of the oldest extant residences in Palatka Heights residential area near Ravine Gardens. Victorian Revival style with ornate half-timbering on front and side gable areas and applied wood ornament round the ten bay veranda.

M
407 N. First St.
Palatka

Herbert F. Wilson House, built in 1916 for Herbert Wilson, executive officer of Palatka bank, lumber company, and wood processing companies. Combination of Prairie School and Bungalow styles with wide overhangs, narrow paired windows, porches, and ornamental wood columns.

N
Central & Prospects St.
Crescent City

Bank of Crescent City, built in 1909. Served as a bank until 1952 and later housed city hall and fire department. Romanesque Revival style with rounded arch openings and barrel-vaulted corner entrance accentuated by large marble column.

O
Central St. between Cedar & M
Crescent City

Preston's Store, built from 1900-1920. Mediterranean Revival style commercial building with arched collonade, stucco finish, masonry quoins, and hip roof. Early grocery store in building sold everything from shirt buttons to buggy whips.

P
600 N. Park St.
Crescent City

Henry Hubbard House, built in 1880. Hubbard, noted entomologist who conducted independent research (particularly on citrus diseases) on property. Queen Anne style structure with traces of the later Shingle style. First story sheathed with clapboards and second story shingled. Large covered piazza extending entire length of south side of house. Turret in northeast corner next to polygonal dormer. Scrollwork and bracketing used. Hubbard botanical garden and park, once surrounding house, now gone.

Q
Park & Central
Crescent City

Morrow-Sprague House, built in 1880's. Guilford Sprague, city's first mayor and also state legislator. Bicameral plan, large central hallway with spacious dining room opposite two separate parlors. Two tiered veranda. House once served as tourist hotel.

R
Fort Gates

"Palmetto", built in 1880's. Flamboyant Victorian Revival style house, the focal point of a building complex which includes Coolidge House, G.B. Plant house, and "Palmetto" estate with house (illustrated), six-bedroom guest house over two-lane bowling alley, bridal cottage, and boat house. After the 1894 freeze, many of the houses abandoned. Private residence not accessible to public in mid 1980's.

NOTES

TRAVEL NOTES

NASSAU

GAR BARKMAN, AIA

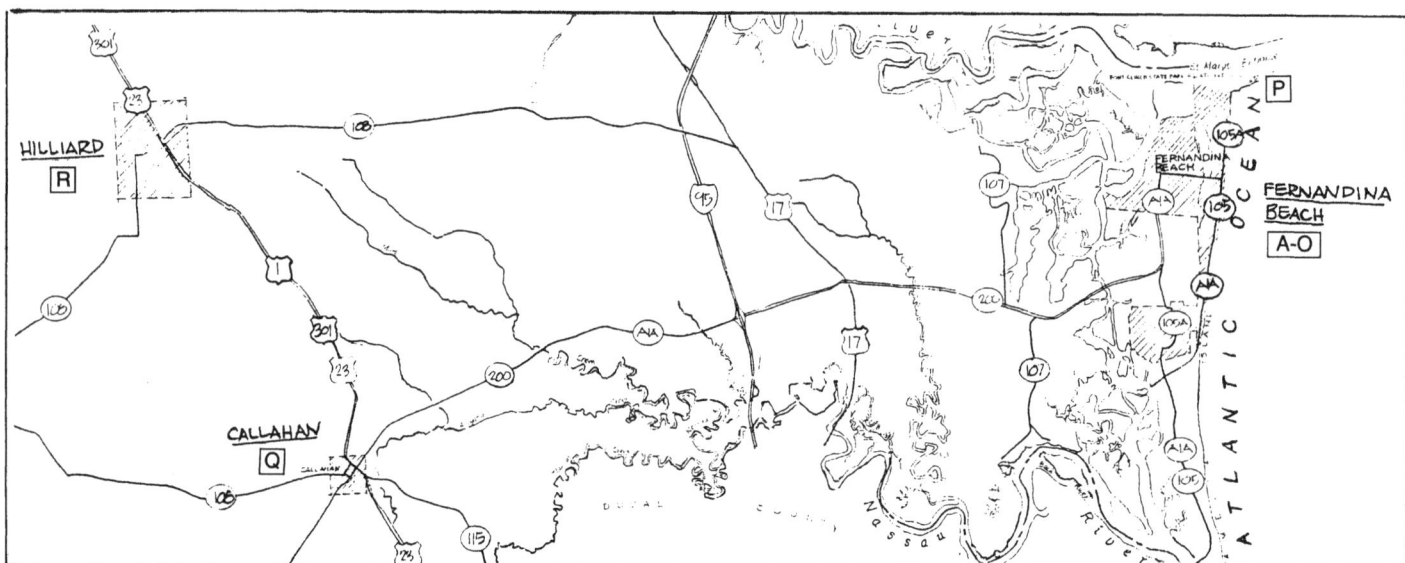

Nassau County was established on December 29, 1824, as one of Florida's early counties, located on the northeast coast of Florida, directly south of the Georgia border. The St. Mary's River forms the north and west borders of the county. Historians differ as to the origin of the county's name. Some feel it was derived from the city in the Bahamas; others feel it was named after the Duchy of Nassau, a former state in the western part of Germany.

The county seat is Fernandina Beach, consolidated with Fernandina in the 1950's. The local boast is that Fernandina Beach is the only city in the United States to have served under eight flags.

Recorded history of Nassau County began on May 8, 1562, when Jean Ribaut, leader of a French expedition, landed at the mouth of the St. Mary's River and named the island Isle De Mai. Spain claimed the island in 1567; and, approximately 100 years later, built Fort San Fernandina. A settlement, Old Town, grew around the fort.

The area changed hands again in 1735 when Governor Oglethorpe of Georgia claimed the island for England and re-named it Amelia Island after Princess Amelia, the younger sister of King George II of England. Amelia Island was con-tested by England and Spain until Spain finally gained con-trol in 1783.

During the patriot revolution on March 17, 1812, Amelia Is-land was taken and claimed as the Republic of Florida. The following day, the patriots ceded the island to the United States. In 1817 Amelia Island briefly existed under two flags. First Gregor MacGregor flew the Green Cross of Florida. Then shortly afterwards, a French privateer Luis Aury be-came the Supreme Commander of Amelia Island and, with-out authority, displayed the Mexican Flag.

On July 10, 1821, Florida was ceded to the United States

by Spain, and Nassau county was established three years later. The United States flag has flown since 1821 except in 1862 during the temporary control of the Confederacy.

A major influence in the development of Nassau County was the construction of the first cross-Florida railroad which was begun in 1853. Land was purchased by the railroad company and a new town platted, a community that is now Fernandina Beach. The railroad, completed in 1861, con-nected Fernandina to Cedar Key on the west coast of Florida. After the Civil War, the railroad provided access to the interior of the state and moved goods and passengers across the peninsula.

With its natural harbor and climate, Fernandina soon at-tracted visitors from the north. The first tourist hotel in Florida, the Egmont, was built in 1877 by the Florida Railroad Company. It was later torn down and part of its lumber was used to build four houses on the hotel's site. Another hotel, the Strathmore, was built in 1881 on the beach but later de-stroyed by a hurricane.

With its deep harbor, Fernandina became a busy port. A steamship line made weekly trips between New York and Fernandina. Many of the commercial structures, ware-houses, and homes along Centre Street and the side streets from the waterfront to Tenth Street were built during this time. Port activity was increased by the Spanish-American War when lumber, cotton, and phosphate were shipped all over the world.

Fernandina's tourist industry declined when Flagler built hotels in St. Augustine and extended rail service further south where tourists could find a sub-tropical climate. The extension of rail lines also stimulated the development of in-land towns where mills were constructed as forests became accessible. Yulee and Callahan are located where highways and railroads intersect. Much of the population of the county was directly or indirectly involved with the timber industry. The eventual depletion of natural resources contributed to the dwindling number of mills; and the county turned to shrimping, phosphate, and paper industries in the early 1900's.

The shift of the tourist industry and extensive land development to central and south Florida resulted in a period of decreased construction in Fernandina and surrounding areas. Victorian Revival style structures remained in use with little modification. Agricultural production of poultry and cattle increased. The fishing industry, especially shrimping, became important to Fernandina, as well as fish factories producing fish oil for soap, cosmetics and tempering steel and fish meal for fertilizer and stock feed. In 1937 Rayonier and Container Corporation constructed multi-million dollar plants. World War II brought the large military installations between Fernandina and Jacksonville.

Post-World War II development included the opening of the beach highway A1A which connected by ferry with Mayport and Jacksonville. US 1 and US 17 served Nassau County as north-south routes and SR 200 as the east-west road from Callahan to Fernandina Beach by way of Yulee. Interstate 95 increased the convenience of travel and made the county more accessible to visiting tourists.

The development of Amelia Island Plantation and other resort communities along the Atlantic Coast in Nassau County created population increases and demands for new services. As these growth patterns emerged, preservation of Fernandina's high concentration of Victorian Revival style architecture became a priority of many residents.

Centre Street was redeveloped in the 1970's as part of a planned project to restore the historic character of the downtown building core. In 1974 a summer field office of the Historic American Buildings Survey prepared drawings of several significant buildings. Centre Street Historic District, a thirty block area, was listed on the National Register of Historic Places. An ordinance establishing the formation of the Historic District Council to oversee construction and alterations to historic buildings was adopted in 1975, and The Amelia Island-Fernandina Restoration Foundation was organized to ensure that the character of the district would be maintained.

E
Centre Street at 5th St
Fernandina Beach
Nassau County Courthouse, built in 1891. Red brick Victorian Revival style structure with cast-iron Corinthian columns and an iron balcony and steeple. Central tower dominating the main facade.

F
NE corner 7th at Ash
Fernandina Beach
Bailey House, built in 1895 by Effingham W. Bailey, a steamship agent, with George W. Barber of Knoxville, Tenn., as architect. Queen Anne style. Adapted as bed and breakfast in 1980's.

G
27 S. 7th St.
Fernandina Beach
The Tabby House, built in 1885 for Charles W. Lewis with Robert S. Schuyler as architect. Only house in Fernandina with tabby construction using Portland cement during this era.

H
119, 123, 127 and 131
S. 7th St.
Fernandina Beach
Egmont Houses. Four houses built from lumber of Egmont Hotel on hotel site. Gable roofs with two-story galleries on east side.

I
227 S. 7th St.
Fernandina Beach
George Fairbanks House. Designed in Italianate style by architect Robert S. Schuyler for George Fairbanks, historian, citrus industry pioneer, and editor of the *Florida Mirror* from 1879 to 1885.

J
317 S. 7th St.
Fernandina Beach
Waas Home. Original structure, one of the oldest houses in the city, built in 1856. Purchased in 1901 by Dr. W. T. Waas and remodeled extensively in Queen Anne style.

A
Centre Street at
the waterfront
Fernandina Beach
Fernandina Depot, built in 1899. Rectangular brick structure with gable roof, wide overhang on ornate wooden brackets. Both gables have elaborately pierced bargeboards. In mid 1980's housed Chamber of Commerce.

C
NE corner Centre St.
at 4th St.
Fernandina Beach
Post Office and Custom House, built in 1910. Mediterranean Revival style. Constructed and maintained by the federal government.

D
415 Centre St.
Fernandina Beach
Dr. John F. Lesesne-Judge John Friend Residence, built in 1857 by Lesesne. One of oldest houes in the district. Constructed of hewn timber and wooden peg fasteners. Purchased by Friend after the Civil War and passed down on female side of family to present owners.

B
20 & 23 S. 3rd St.
Fernandina Beach
Florida House. Two structures constructed for use as tourist accommodations. Building to south built from 1857-1859. Addition closer to Cenre St. built in 1882.

K
SE corner 8th St. at Atlantic Ave.
Fernandina Beach

Hoyt House, built in 1905 by John R. Mann for Fred W. Hoyt, merchant and owner of the local bank. Said to be modeled after the Rockefeller Cottage on Jekyl Island. Adapted as attorney's office in 1970's.

L
8th St. at Atlantic Ave.
Fernandina Beach

St. Peter's Episcopal Church. Complete in 1884 and rebuilt after a fire in 1893. Gothic Revival building designed by Robert S. Schuyler. Basilica plan with a steeple at the entrance.

M
Mid-block 5th St.
Fernandina Beach

Fernandez Reserve. Burial ground for the heirs of Don Domingo Fernandez who sold the land for the new town. Chapel and Convent of the Sisters of Saint Joseph, built in 1882, nearby.

N
304 Alachua St.
Fernandina Beach

Villas Las Palmas. Elaborate mansion, built in 1910, for Nathaniel B. Borden. Heroically scaled wood frame, shingle-clad structure with clay tile roof, wide porch with masonry piers, and semi-circular parapet wall at dormers.

O
SW corner Alachua at 2nd St.
Fernandina Beach

Seydel Building. Constructed in 1877 to contain a general store and millinery store downstairs and apartments for the owners, the Seydel brothers, upstairs.

P
A1A
Fernandina Beach

Fort Clinch. Construction beginning in 1847. Pentagonal brick fort. Never completed. Named after General Duncan Lamont Clinch who was famous for activity in Second Seminole War. Restored by Florida Park Service from 1962-1971.

Q
Brandies Ave.
Callahan

Farmers Cooperative. Built in 1915 as a farmer's cooperative. Later a general store, then a garage with a silent movie house upstairs. In 1980's a hardware store.

R
301 at 3rd St.
Hilliard

First School. Built in 1882 as first school in Hilliard. One-story wood frame structure. Porch addition later.

NOTES

70

DUVAL

ROBERT C. BROWARD, AIA, JACKSONVILLE CHAPTER

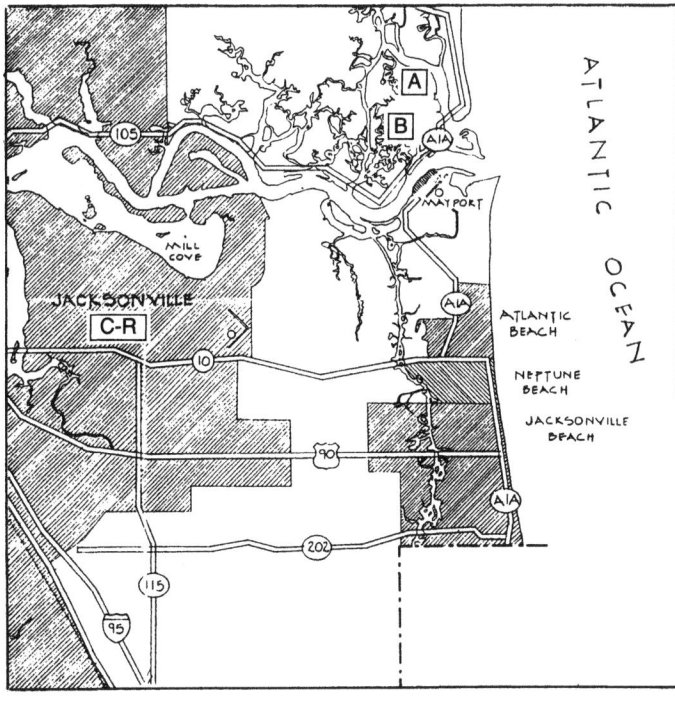

Duval County, which today forms the boundaries of the consolidated City of Jacksonville, was created on August 12, 1822, by the First Legislative Council of the Territory of Florida.

Its human history, however, reaches back approximately 5,000 years to the first known native inhabitants. This northeast section of Florida contains the largest and most important river in Florida, today bearing the English name of St. John's. Abundant oysters, fish, and game along the banks of the beautiful river made human habitation possible without extensive agriculture.

On May 1, 1562, the French explorer, Jean Ribault, landed at the mouth of the St. John's and named it Reviere de la Mai, in honor of the month discovered. Two years later a French Huguenot colony, the first settlement by Protestants in America, was established approximately four miles up the river on a high bluff and named Fort Caroline. Spanish settlers from St. Augustine destroyed the colony two years later and the Jacksonville-Duval County area remained under Spanish rule for the next 200 years. In 1763, Great Britain acquired Florida from Spain and constructed the King's Road to connect St. Augustine and British communities in Georgia. This early road, much of which is still in use known as St. Augustine Road, passed through the center of present day Jacksonville.

During British rule, a village developed at a narrow bend in the St. John's River and was called "the Cowford." In 1783, Britain ceded Florida back to Spain and in 1821 the United States acquired the territory from Spain. In 1822, Cowford was chartered as the city of Jacksonville. Before this, however, Cowford was part of one of the shortest-lived nations in history. During the four years between 1812-1816, the provisional government of the "Republic of Florida" existed with its "Patriots" organized against Spanish rule, its own president, and an army of disgruntled planters. The Republic's boundaries were the St. Mary's River on the north and the St. John's River on the south. It ended when the Spanish agreed to a more representative rule within the Republic's boundaries.

Jacksonville grew from this chaotic era of backwoods anarchy into a rather prosperous seaport at the commencement of the Civil War. The city was occupied four times during the war and burned by Federal troops.

From the postwar period until the late nineteenth century Jacksonville continued to prosper not only as a seaport, exporting local timber, naval stores, and citrus fruit, but as the center of tourism in Florida. However, when Henry Flagler extended his Florida East Coast Railway down the state's coastline, the city was by-passed for the warmer climate to the south.

By the 1890's well-developed Jacksonville was Florida's largest city. The downtown boasted many large hotels, business buildings, churches, an opera house, and a recently-completed city hall and market. The waterfront was busy with ships from along the east coast and Europe, and the streets were lined with beautiful live oak trees.

On May 3, 1901, all but a small portion of Jacksonville's downtown was destroyed by the most destructive fire ever to hit a southern city. In less than eight hours 10,000 people were left homeless, and the once-beautiful city was a memory except for its outlying residential districts and a few blocks of its pre-1901 downtown. Because of this tragedy, Jacksonville's downtown architectural heritage dates primarily from 1901 when a legion of architects and builders from other cities and states descended upon the city to profit from its reconstruction.

From 1901 through 1920, Jacksonville grew at an unprecedented rate and boasted "the newest downtown in the United States." During this period, many talented architects contributed to the city's architectural fabric. The most important of these architects was Henry John Klutho from New York City who was known as the creator of the early skyline. Deeply influenced by Louis Sullivan and Frank Lloyd Wright, Klutho designed so many Prairie School buildings in his adopted city that by 1920 Jacksonville contained more buildings influenced by Wright and Sullivan in its downtown than any other city outside of the Midwest. Fortunately, a few of the important ones still stand.

Because of its excellent rail transportation and climate during the period preceding World War I, Jacksonville was the motion-picture capital of the U.S., losing out to Hollywood in the early twenties. The city never grew at a strong pace again until recently when it entered a new period of rediscovery of its riverfront and an expansive downtown revitalization. It experienced modest growth in the twenties' boom period ending with the depression era. During the post World War II period, the outlying suburbs grew as the downtown exodus began in the manner typical of most American cities.

Jacksonville's present expansive growth was helped in part by its consolidation with Duval County in 1968 to make it the largest land area in the United States under a single city government — nearly 800 square miles. As the other urban areas of the state become overly-dense in population with dwindling water supplies and other natural amenities, Jacksonville is undoubtedly facing its greatest period of expansion as it approaches the third millennia with its natural environment still relatively intact.

The foundation of the Jacksonville Historic Landmarks Commission in 1971 has awakened the city to its architectural heritage but only after many major examples of both Classical Revival and Prairie School work were demolished. The neighborhood preservation groups, Riverside-Avondale Preservation (RAP), Springfield Preservation and Restoration (SPAR), and San Marco Preservation have been instrumental in the prevention of re-zoning which threatened the integrity of these neighborhoods as well as in the actual preservation of certain historic buildings.

Jacksonville's downtown has a number of historic buildings that have been restored and placed into adaptive use. Among these are the 1919 Union Passenger Terminal with a portion of the 1895 Flagler Terminal now used as part of the recently completed Prime Osborn Convention Center, the Florida Theatre now used as the performance hall for the Jacksonville Symphony Orchestra, and the original 1904 Carnegie Library in current use as law offices. Further restoration of other historic buildings will help create an ambiance in the downtown area which will afford creative contrast with the current glass skyscapers rising along the riverfront.

A
Ft. George Island
Kingsley Plantation, built in the early 1800's. One of Florida's oldest existing plantation houses. Related buildings, once center of a working plantation, including brick and tabby barn, a tabby house, and tabby ruins of 24 slave cabins. State historic site, guided tours.

B
9953 Heckscher Drive
Ft. George Island
Napoleon Bonaparte Broward House, built for Dr. J. Gilbert in 1878. Sold to Napoleon Bonaparte Broward, nineteenth governor of Florida, in 1897 and still owned by Broward family. Two-story wood frame buildings with two-tier veranda and widow's walk looking out to sea.

C
317 Florida Ave.
Jacksonville
St. Andrews Episcopal Church, built in 1887. Brick Gothic Revival style church designed by architect R. B. Schuyler of Fernandina. Characterized by asymetrically-placed bell tower, polychrome slate roof with clerestory, hammerbeam wood trusses, and tabby foundations. In mid 1980's abandoned and in state of decay.

D
513 W. Bay Street
Jacksonville
El Modelo Block, built in 1888. One of the oldest commercial structures in Jacksonville. Three-story, brick bearing wall structure which originally housed a drugstore and cabinet shop. In 1889 occupied by the El Modelo Cigar Co. Site of Cuban patriot Jose Marti's visit and speech before Spanish-American war. Housed hotels between 1915-1965. Renovated into law and insurance offices in mid 1980's.

E
Downtown
Jacksonville
Thomas V. Porter House, designed in 1901 by H. J. Klutho and constructed in 1902. Three-story residence moved around the corner from original site and shorn of a wrap-around veranda. House adapted for use as office for architects. Corinthian-columned entrance portico. Indication of how downtown lined with important residences after 1901 fire.

F
NE corner Duval and Laura Streets
Jacksonville
Former YMCA Building, built in 1907. Designed by architect H. J. Klutho. Seven-story reinforced concrete building, first reinforced concrete mid-rise commercial structure in Florida. Amazing structural concept for its time with ten-foot cantilevered running track encircling partially clear-spanned second floor with six-foot deep reinforced concrete girders carrying the five levels above it. Building empty in mid 1980's, awaiting rehabilitation.

G
30 W. 9th Street
North Jacksonville-Springfield
Klutho Residence, built in 1908. Designed by H. J. Klutho as personal residence. First Florida house designed in the manner of Frank Lloyd Wright's Prairie School style. Two-story house with broad overhangs and "Tree of Life" leaded glass windows, two-story vertical mullions, and belt-course at second floor sills. In process of restoration as private residence in mid 1980's.

H
51 W. Forsyth Street
Jacksonville
Bisbee Building, built in 1908 with H. J. Klutho as architect. Jacksonville's first "skyscraper," a ten-story reinforced concrete high-rise. Designed as a single-loaded corridor office building only twenty-five feet wide with clear span reinforced concrete. Identical tower attached making it a double-loaded corridor office building.

I
Downtown
Jacksonville

Morocco Temple, built in 1910 with J. H. Klutho as architect. Egyptian Revival style reinforced concrete building influenced by Frank Lloyd Wright's 1906 Unity Temple in Oak Park. Twelve-foot-high cartouches on either side of entrance, Klutho's first use of Sullivanesque ornament re-interpreted in his own manner.

J
Downtown
Jacksonville

The St. James building, entire block immediately north of Hemming Plaza, built from 1910 to 1912 with H.J. Klutho as designer and builder. (He subcontracted all work on a fast-track basis with an office on site.) His Prairie School masterpiece, a mixed-use building including Cohen Brothers Department Store and professional offices. Largest reinforced concrete mercantile building in the south, originally featuring a seventy-five-foot-wide octagonal glass skylight.

K
Laura Street
Jacksonville

Florida Life Building, center of block between Forsyth and Adams Streets, build in 1911 with H.J. Klutho as architect. Only twenty-eight feet wide, eleven stories high, with broad Chicago windows, and bursts of Sullivanesque terra-cotta ornament as capitals of pilasters rising the full eleven stories. Built of reinforced concrete with the first caisson poured concrete piling in Florida. Design related to the Chicago School and the Prairie School.

L
Broad Street
Jacksonville

Masonic Temple for the Most Worshipful Union Grand Lodge and Belize, C.A., built from 1912 to 1916 with the firm of Mark and Sheftall as architects. Both principals had trained with H. J. Klutho and were well versed in the work of Wright and Sullivan. Temple still in use.

M
2030 Main Street
Springfield

Klutho Apartments, designed and built by H. J. Klutho in 1913 adjacent to his 1908 residence. Cantilevered balconies with outdoor street overviews. Further Prairie School techniques including third-story belt-course, projecting prow-roof, and gold-leaded windows.

N
2821 Riverside Ave.
Jacksonville

L. T. Smith Residence, built in 1913. Architect unkown but design indicating knowledge of Prairie School style. House completely restored in 1976.

O
Downtown
Jacksonville

Jacksonville Terminal, built in 1919 with Kenneth M. Murchison of New York City as architect. Built at the height of Jacksonville's role as a major railroad transportation center near an earlier terminal (built from 1897-1898) which was destroyed by fire several years ago. Classic Revival building recently restored as part of Prime F. Osborne Convention Center.

P
2650 Park Street
Jacksonville

Riverside Baptist Church, built in 1925 with Addison Mizner as architect. Romanesque style in details but Byzantine in plan. Only church Mizner designed (it is said that he designed spaces for relics within this church).

Q
San Jose Residential Section
Jacksonville

Alfred I. DuPont Residence (Epping Forest), built in 1925. Mediterranean Revival style structure designed by Harold F. Saxelbye. Richly detailed residence with formal garden overlooking St. Johns River. Concrete dock encircling yacht basin. DuPont haven during Florida boom days and following depression. Currently renovated as clubhouse for residential enclave using grounds for single-family and multi-family dwellings.

R
128-134 E. Forsyth St.
Jacksonville

The Florida Theatre, built from 1926-1927 with R. E. Hall and Company as architects and Roy Benjamin as associate architect. Mediterranean Revival style theater planned as mixed-use building with office floors and roof top dancing pavilion. One of first air-conditioned buildings in Jacksonville. Recently restored as center for the performing arts, home of the Jacksonville Symphony. Owned by the City of Jacksonville and administered by the Arts Assembly of Jacksonville.

CLAY

E. WENDELL HALL, AIA

The land which is now Clay County was originally inhabited by various Indian tribes. One of the earlier tribes was the Timucuans. The first intrusion of Europeans was prior to 1560. Ft. St. Francis de Pupo, which was built by the Spanish, was begun in 1717 and later destroyed by Oglethorpe's British forces in 1740. The fort, whose only remains are earthen mounds, was located south of present day Green Cove Springs on the St. Johns River. Its purpose was to protect the route from St. Augustine to the Spanish missions in western Florida.

Spain lost Florida to Britain by the Treaty of Paris in 1763; and for the next twenty years English settlers received grants, including at least four plantations in the Doctors Lake and Black Creek areas of Clay County. Loyalists escaping from the American Revolution also came into the area, mostly as squatters, prior to the Treaty of Paris in 1783 which recognized American independence and returned Florida to Spain.

The next permanent settlement of this area occurred during the second Spanish period, after 1783. Huge land grants were given to individuals and squatters laying claims to smaller tracts.

Following the short-lived Patriots' Rebellion (1812-14) of landowners against Spain, the First Seminole Indian War and Andrew Jackson's resultant raids into Florida brought about Spain's ceding the territory to the United States in 1821.

The Second Seminole War was the catalyst for the building of Ft. Heileman in 1836. It was located near the forks of Black Creek (present day Middleburg) and acted as the Quartermaster depot for the U.S. Army of the South, as well as a major military post, arsenal, hospital, rest camp, and haven for refugees until mid-1841. The end of the war in 1842 brought additional population growth to the Florida Territory and statehood by early 1845. Life in frontier Florida was severe. Illness, weather and Indians plagued early settlers and soldiers.

In 1858, Clay County was officially created out of Duval County. The first county seat was in Webster, a town that is near Middleburg. This part of the county was flourishing as a supplier of the interior of Florida. Black Creek was navigable to the forks, so ships could bring supplies this far inland and wagon-loaded goods from the interior could be shipped out. The county seat changed to Green Cove Springs in 1872 as settlement grew in that part of the county.

Sawmills appeared in the area as early as 1816. There were several throughout the county by the Civil War. In the latter part of the 19th century the emphasis changed from lumbering industry to the naval stores industry. Brickworks, phosphate mining and camphor farming were other early industries in the county. Agriculture was also important in the area.

After the Civil War, the tourist trade had a major impact on the eastern part of the county. Steamboats from Charleston, Savannah and Jacksonville came down the St. Johns River from before 1850 until the early 1900's. The railroads, constructed in the 1880's, gradually replaced most all steamboat travel and continued to bring tourists until the 1940's.

Building styles changed with these industries. Initially, log cabins were common with some post and beam construction in the more substantial residences. Wire nails made rough sawn board and batten characteristic of this area. The tourist trade of the late 19th century brought wealth to the area and introduced frivolous, large and ornately detailed buildings.

The next major impact on the county was World War II. Camp Blanding, which occupies some 70,000 acres in the western part of the county, was developed during this period.

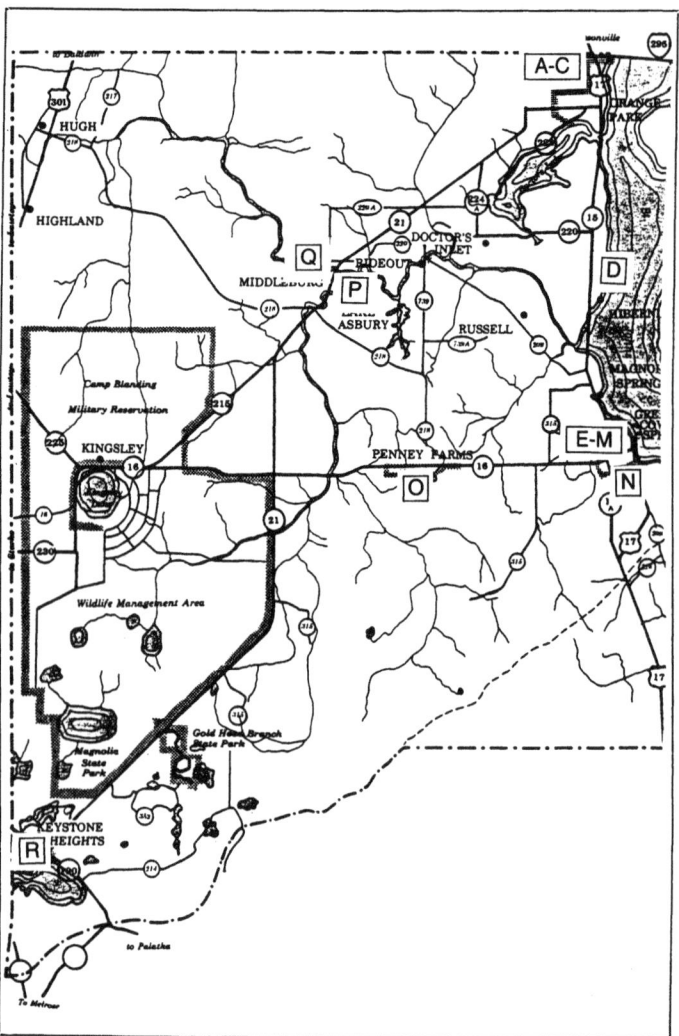

Military restrictions still prohibit development of any other nature on this property. The Navy built an auxiliary air station just south of Green Cove Springs during World War II. In the 1950s it became the home of the Atlantic Reserve Fleet, some 600 ships and 5000 men, the largest gathering of ships in Navy history. Closed in 1961, the eleven huge docks and the two air strips of the naval station are barely utilized today.

Economic hardship in the county has acted as a preservation tool. New construction has not often been feasible.

When it has been possible to build, much of the old building was torn down. Fire destroyed countless old buildings especially many hotels in the Green Cove Springs area. The Florida climate quickly deteriorates buildings left untended.

Present day architectural preservation efforts are not well organized in the county. There are some individual interests and efforts. The Clay County Historical Society is the only avenue for group preservation efforts at this time. The Society operates a small, but interesting museum on the old Clay County Courthouse. It is open Sundays from 2 p.m. to 5 p.m.

A
230 Kingsley Road
Orange Park
Grace Episcopal Church. This "river" church was designed by Robert S. Schuyler and completed in 1881. It was, supposedly, built in Jacksonville and brought down the St. Johns River on a barge. The well-maintained church retains most of its original fabric.

B
2061 Astor Street
Orange Park
"Winterbourne." Originally a small house on the river, this structure was extensively expanded and remodeled when it was purchased by Mr. B.J. Johnson in 1878. The house, with its delicate roof railing and Queen Anne type arched window lites, remains basically as it was when Mr. Johnson renovated it for his family.

C
2223 Astor Street
Orange Park
Club Continental. The son of B.J. Johnson, Caleb E. Johnson, built this residence in 1923. As president of the Palmolive Soap Company, Mr. Johnson wanted an impressive "Italian villa." This Palm Beach-style home now serves as the clubhouse for a condominium complex built on the grounds of the old estate called "Mira Rio."

D
Old Church Road
Hibernia
St. Margaret's Episcopal Church. This small but lovely board and batten chapel is located on what was once part of the Fleming plantation, "Hibernia," one of the earliest settlements in the county. Margaret Seton Fleming founded the church, which met in her home until the chapel was built in 1875. The chapel is known locally because of the books *Margaret's Story* by Eugenia Price and *Hibernia: The Unreturning Tide* by Margaret Seton Biddle. It is listed on the National Register of Historic Places

E
St. Johns Avenue
Green Cove Springs
St. Mary's Episcopal Church. This church, which is on the National Register, was designed by Lewis, Lawrence and Adams in 1878. It is a highly developed example of the Carpenter Gothic style as it was applied to many churches in North Florida.

F
401 Magnolia Avenue
Green Cove Springs
First Presbyterian Church. This is one of the finest Presbyterian churches in the State with its intricate exterior detailing. This well proportioned church which is Latin-cross in plan was supposedly designed by J.A. Wood in 1884.

G
West Walnut &
Gratio Place
Green Cove Springs
Clay County Courthouse. This is one of the few pre-1900 (1889) courthouses still standing in the State and is on the National Register. Wide bracketed eaves, entrances recessed behind arcades, pedimented gables and decorative brickwork shows this to be one of the highlights of the career of architect A.E. McClure of Jacksonville, The brickwork has since been covered with concrete and additions made on each side of the main building. The home of the Clay County Historical Museum was added in 1911 for the Clerk of Courts office.

H
Magnolia Avenue
Green Cove Springs
The Boil. Legend has it that this boil attracted pirates down the St. Johns to fill their casks. From before 1850 until 1930, the alleged medicinal qualities of these springs made the town a tourist center attracting people from all over the county.

I
Magnolia Avenue
Green Cove Springs
Qui-Si-Sana Hotel. This hotel, built in 1906 by Louis McKee of New Jersey, replaced an older hotel, the Clarendon, which was destroyed by fire in 1901. This Spanish-Mission style structure was constructed around an indoor court and built completely of coquina concrete with a red tile roof in an attempt to be fireproof. Workers had to be imported from the North as no one was familiar with this type of construction.

J
Spring Street
Green Cove Springs
Oakland Hotel. Originally the Oakland House, this structure was built as a "Swiss cottage" for Lucas Muhoberaz in 1880. In 1883 it was enlarged and changed into a hotel by Mr. Muhoberaz. It is constructed as a series of connected wooden structures averaging 2½ stories each and is one of the few hotels which remain. Other than missing verandas on the front, it remains basically unchanged and is used as a boarding house.

K
502 Magnolia Avenue
Green Cove Springs
Borden House. This house was called "Villa Cottage" when it was built by John C. Borden, son of the inventor of condensed milk, around 1880. The tower was supposedly for judging the horse races which occurred on Magnolia Avenue. It was later the first home of the Women's Club and, therefore a gathering place with concerts, and a library.

L
Corner St. Johns Ave.
& Center St.
Green Cove Springs

W.M. Hoyt House (St. Johns Terrace Apt.). Mr. Hoyt, a Chicago grocery chain magnate, was one of several wealthy Northerners to invest in real estate in Green Cove Springs in the late 19th century. This pseudo-Mediterranean style home was built some time between 1906 and 1912. Mr. Hoyt built an earlier home which is located diagonally across the street.

M
700 Walnut Street
Green Cove Springs

Kirkpatrick-Wilcox House. This Victorian house dating from the late 1800's displays both quality and quantity of exterior detail. There is evidence that this was the home of J.L. Kirkpatrick, a dry goods dealer, a saloon keeper and one of the early merchants in the area.

N
U.S. 17
just past S.R. 16
Green Cove Springs

Farmhouse (c. 1850) known as the Hankins or Talbott House though not built by either. This "fever" house is an unusual milled log construction with a slate roof and only mortise and tenon joinery. A "fever" house would be built high off the ground to avoid the malaria fumes they thought came from the earth. This house is, also, allegedly haunted and even inspired one owner to remove the second story veranda some years ago.

O
S.R. 16
Green Cove Springs

Penney Farms — Memorial Home Community. This retirement complex for ministers was founded by J.C. Penney, the founder of the department store chain, in 1926. It was designed by Alan B. Mills and Arthur E. Davis, Jr. in the Normandy style requested by Mr. Penney. Lumber was milled at Mr. Penney's nearby sawmill and then hand-hewn on the site.

P
Main Street
Middleburgh

Middleburg United Methodist Church. This building has been used for worship continuously since 1847 with the congregation dating from 1823. It remains basically as it was, both inside and out.

Q
Main Street, between
Thompson & Harvard
Middleburgh

Copp-Clark-Chalker House. This house was built by the Army in 1835. The original second story veranda has been removed, but part of the exterior siding is the original hand-worked tongue and groove pine. The star found in either eave may have been to designate that it was the headquarters of Generals W. Scott and T. Jesup in the Seminole War.

R
Lawrence Boulevard
Keystone Heights

Keystone Inn. This inn attracted Northerners and Floridians to hear arts, musicians and authors from the Chatauqua Circuit in the 1920s and 30s. A fire in 1954 destroyed much of this building and it has not been reopened since.

OTHER SITES TO SEE:

Green Cove Springs
Ferris-Jensen-Pratt House
101 Palmetto Avenue
(Corner of Spring & Palmetto St.)

Amara House
115 St. Johns Avenue
(This was originally the Hoyt House, It has been completely remodeled and very little of the original house is visible.)

Padgett House (Bentley)
627 Spring Street

Hallock Hotel (Schultz House)
15 St. Johns Avenue

W. J. Wilson House
303 North Magnolia Street
(Mr. Wilson was a merchant and politician)

Applegate House
Corner of Spring & Magnolia St.
10 S. Magnolia
Built as a "cottage" for the Clarendon Hotel in 1871.

Green Cove Springs Naval Air Station
U.S. 16

Shands Bridge
S.R. 16

Middleburg:
Mary Chalker House
106 Thompson Street

Other:
Camp Blanding
S.R. 16

ST. JOHNS

F. BLAIR REEVES, FAIA

St. Johns County, established in 1821 as Florida's first county and named for the St. Johns River, was the governmental center for all of Florida east of the Suwannee River. Presently occupying only 387,000 acres, its principal communities include Hastings, the center of a rich agricultural area which was named for the horticulturalist, Thomas Horace Hastings; Moultrie, named for a lieutenant governor of Florida during the British occupation; and St. Augustine, the first permanent European colonial settlement in the continental United States.

St. Augustine began in 1565 as a Spanish military base and continued to serve that function for nearly 250 years. This fragile outpost was established by Don Pedro Menendes de Aviles partly in response to the French construction of Fort Caroline on the St. Johns River, a direct threat to Spanish trade routes following the Gulf Stream from Central and South America. In the end France lost; their colony was destroyed. Drake of England burned St. Augustine in 1586; pirates sacked it in 1668; South Carolinians beseiged and burned it in 1702; and then in 1740 James Oglethorpe took all the outerworks but failed to capture the fort.

Its role as a small military outpost in a wilderness frontier did not justify significant architecture. Early houses were of wood and thatch, and forts were palisaded of wood. After the English established Charleston in 1670, Spain in 1672 began the construction of a masonry fort, built of coquina stone quarried on Anastasia Island. The labor force consisted of a few skilled workers, common laborers, convicts (including British prisoners), Indians paid about 20 cents a day plus corn rations, and slaves from Havana. The fort was ready for the 1740 Oglethorpe siege and was able to withstand a bombardment of twenty-seven days. Work continued on the fort after this engagement. The masonry tower-battery defense at Matanzas inlet was built in 1742 to protect the backdoor to St. Augustine. Spain's work on the forts ended in 1762 when the news arrived that Spain would give Florida to Great Britain. On July 21, 1763, the transfer was made. Spanish troops and St. Augustine's entire population departed leaving the English with an empty town.

Under British rule, St. Augustine, as the capitol of East Florida, enjoyed prosperity. Spanish buildings were modified to accommodate British living patterns and new construction used British building techniques. Plantations were established and a highway constructed to Georgia. During the American Revolution, the city became a depot for British military operations, a prison for prominent dissenters and a refuge for Tories. When, in 1783, St. Augustine received word that Spain would regain control, the British evacuated. In spite of unsettled conditions between 1783 and 1821 during the second Spanish period, several substantial houses, churches, and public buildings were constructed.

Excellent references for study of St. Augustine's colonial architecture are *The Houses of St. Augustine 1565-1821* by

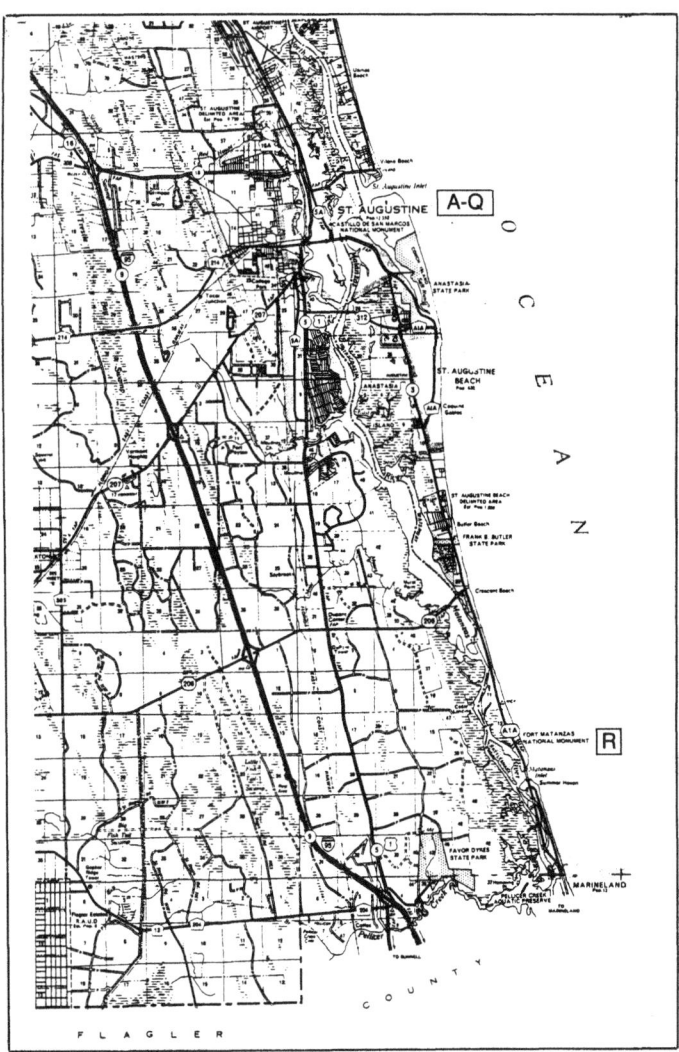

Albert Manucy, the acknowledged expert of that period, and his beautiful history of Castilo de San Marcos written with Luis Rafael Arana.

When Florida became a United States territory, there was no great exodus of Spanish subjects. Many new settlers soon arrived and prospered in spite of yellow fever epidemics and relative isolation. While never threatened by the Seminole Indian Wars from 1835-1842, the city figured in national news and attracted visitors and refugees from interior settlements.

While the Civil War wreaked its havoc throughout the South, St. Augustine played an unwilling and uncontested host to Union troops from 1862 until the end of the war. There was no battle destruction of town buildings.

St. Augustine continued to be isolated from the rest of Florida except for coastal traffic until the arrival of the first railroad in 1874. Until then, river boats reached Picolata on the St. Johns, and passengers and freight moved overland forty-eight miles by stage, later in mule-drawn rail cars.

With improved transportation, St. Augustine soon attracted tourists. The most influential of these was Henry Flagler who established St. Augustine as a winter resort. His presence, from an architectural viewpoint at least, is more obvious than most colonial work since disastrous fires, modern improvements, and even preservation efforts all but erased evidence of earlier habitations. Flagler's hotels, churches, and railroad created a new St. Augustine. However, wars, depressions, epidemics, and climatic disasters continued to take their toll. The Ponce de Leon Hotel began to run at a loss in 1924, was occupied by the US Coast Guard from 1942-1945, reopened in 1946, but finally closed its doors in 1967. The Alcazar was purchased in 1947 by O.C. Lightner of Chicago for use as a museum, but only a few rooms were used and maintenance was poor. The Cordova Hotel had only a few shops on the ground floor.

When architectural landmarks begn to deteriorate, many of St. Augustine's citizens and its friends elsewhere began efforts to save the city's treasures. The Castillo de San Marcos and the Matanzas Blockhouse were declared national monuments in 1924 and were preserved by the National Park Service. Local concern resulted in 1949 state action to establish St. Augustine's historic district. In 1961 the St. Johns County Commission began turning the Cordova Hotel into a court house, and the City Commission remodeled part of the Alcazar as a city building in 1974. In 1968 the Ponce de Leon Hotel became home to Flagler College.

To visitors in St. Augustine the most obvious evidences of preservation interest are around the plaza and north to the fort. St. George Street has been developed to portray the different colonial periods of the city's history and has become, with the Castillo, a major tourist attraction. St. Augustine continues to be preserved through the efforts of many individuals and organizations, public and private, at local, state, and national levels. As in all creative processes based on independent thought (St. Augustine has a reputation for that), there are and have been many differences of opinion about preservation policy and technique. What is vital to contemporary St. Augustine is that preservation has become an integral element in the city's architectural heritage.

A
St. Augustine
Castillo de San Marco, built from 1672 to 1756. Constructed of coquina stone. Derived from sixteenth-century Italian-Spanish military designs with a symmetrical plan of four bastions. Preserved by the National Park Service

B
St. Augustine
City Gate, built in 1806. Two piers, sentry box, and a short segment of covered way built into the city wall west of the Castillo.

C
St. George Street
St. Augustine
Main street of the restored historic area which dates from 1740. Collection of eighteenth and nineteenth century colonial architecture. Restoration begun in 1959.

D
St. Augustine
The Plaza, laid out in 1598 by the Spanish governor, Mendez de Canzo. Bordered by Cathedral Place, King Street, Cordova Street, and Charlotte Street and featuring the Monument to the Spanish Constitution of 1812, the Public Market, and memorials to heroes of U.S wars.

E
King Street
St. Augustine
Ponce de Leon Hotel-Flagler College, built from 1887-1888 for Henry M. Flagler. Designed by Carrere and Hastings. Constructed of coquina shell aggregate and Portland cement poured-in-place concrete. Spanish Renaissance Revival style. After 1967 closing of the hotel, structures adapted for use as Flagler College. In 1980's in process of careful restoration and adaptive use. Public areas accessible.

F
King Street
St. Augustine
Hotel Alcazar and Hotel Cordova. Alcazar built in 1887-1888 for Henry Flagler, designed by Carrere and Hastings. In 1980's housed Lightner Museum and St. Augustine City Hall (illustrated). Cordova built in 1887 as the Casa Monica for Franklin W. Smith, purchased in 1888 by Flagler. Adapted as St. Johns County Courthouse in 1961.

G
102 King Street
St. Augustine
Villa Zorayda, built in 1885 by Franklin W. Smith in a Spanish-Moorish Revival style using poured-in-place concrete mix, iron rods, and railroad track iron for reinforcement.

H
King Street
St. Augustine
"Markland" (part of Flagler College campus), built in 1839. Classical Revival style residence of Dr. Andrew Anderson who persuaded Flagler to build his hotels. Twentieth-century additions.

I
8 Carrera St.
St. Augustine
Grace Methodist Church, built in 1887, designed by Carrere and Hastings. Renaissance Revival style structure of coquina shell and Portland cement poured-in-place concrete with terra cotta decorative elements.

J

Valencia St. at
Sevilla St.
St. Augustine

Flagler Memorial Presbyterian Church. Built by
McGuire and McDonald in 1890 for Henry Flagler as a
memorial to his daughter, Jennie Louise Bennedict.
Venetian Renaissance Revival style with elaborate
terra cotta decoration, Tiffany glass, mahogany screens
and paneling, and an Aeolian-Skinner organ.

K

King Street
St. Augustine

Florida East Coast Railroad Office (at Sebastian
River), built from 1923-1924. Office complex located in
westernmost section of Henry Flagler Model Land Company Subdivision.

L

20 Aviles St.
St. Augustine

Ximenez-Fatio House, built in 1798 for Andres
Ximenez. Modified from 1834-1840. Occupied from
1855-1875 by Louise Fatio. Bought in 1939 by the National Society of the Colonial Dames of America in the
State of Florida and restored as house museum.

M

14 St. Francis St.
St Augustine

"Oldest House," built in 1700's. Purchased by St.
Augustine Historical Society and operated as house
museum.

N

90-96 Marine St.
St. Augustine

Dade Monument, U.S. National Cemetery. Three stone
pyramids marking tombs of Major Francis Dade and
104 men massacred in 1835 by Seminole Indians.

O

Cathedral Place
St. Augustine

First National Bank of Florida, built in 1927. Designed
by F. A. Hollingsworth, architect, and constructed by
San Marco Construction Co. Rehabilitated in 1986 as
offices and residential condominium.

P

Anastasia Island
St. Augustine

Octagon House, Lighthouse Park. Built in 1900 for
Rollin N. Clapp. Part of first residential subdivision on
Anastasia Island.

Q

Old Beach Road
St. Augustine

St. Augustine Light. Built in 1847 to replace a Spanish
lighthouse and watchtower. Now in adaptive reuse.

R

Highway A1A
Near Matanzas Inlet

Matanzas National Monument. Fort Matanzas built in
1742 to protect backdoor entry to St. Augustine. Restored by National Park Service. Visitor's Center built
by Works Progress Administration in January, 1937 (illustrated).

NOTES

FLAGLER

SIDNEY D. CORHERN, AIA

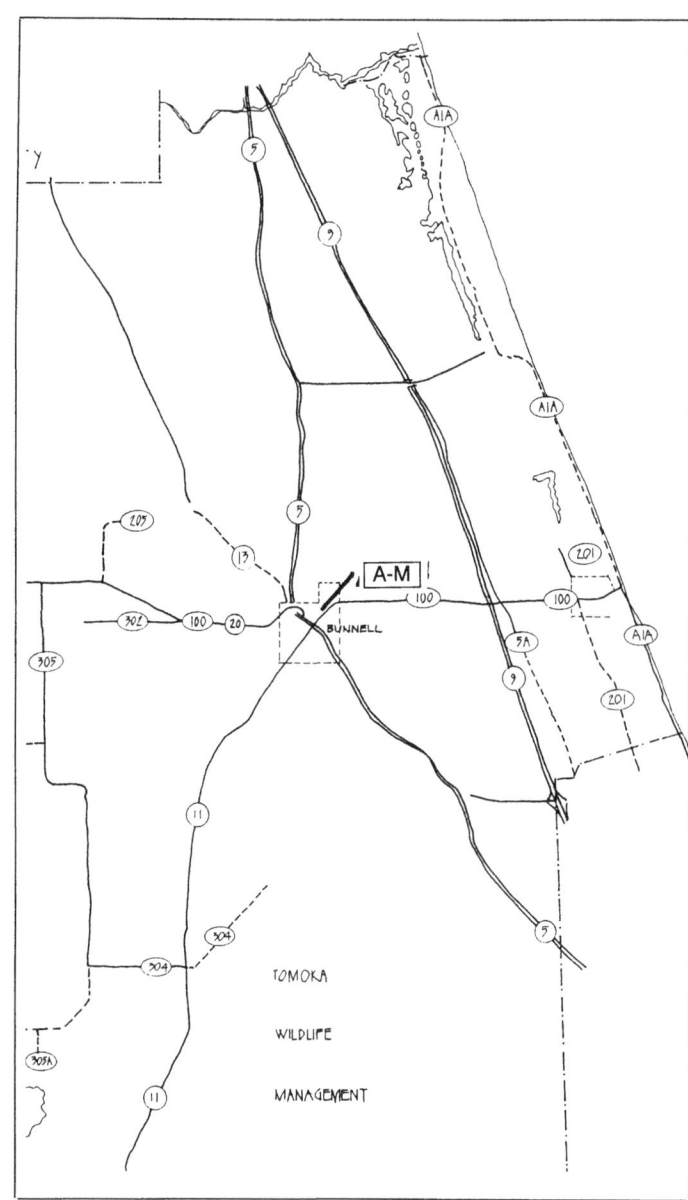

Flagler County was established in 1917, having been taken from part of St. John's and Volusia counties. The county was named for Henry Morrison Flagler, founder of the Florida East Coast Railroad and the major developer of Florida's East Coast between 1880 and 1920. Bunnell, the county seat and main population center, was named for Alvah A. Bunnell, the city's first settler.

Flagler County's earliest settlers lived on plantations located along the main transportation routes, the King's Road, built in the 1770's, and the Matansas River. John Bulow, Orlando Rees and Joseph Hernandez owned the three major plantations in Flagler county producing sugar cane, indigo, cotton and oranges. Hernandez gave one of his plantations, Mala Compra, to his daughter Luisa. Luisa later married George Washington, a relative of the president. Washington Oaks State Park on Highway A 1 A is the site of Mala Compra plantation.

In the 1880's, Henry Cutting, a wealthy New England sportsman, built a large hunting camp in the northeast corner of the county near the Matansas Inlet. Cutting built a pool, stables and tennis courts and created a resort center for Northern and Mid-western tourists. After his death, Cutting's wife married an exiled Russian prince and inspired the renaming of the camp, the Princess Estate. The building is still standing and is considered the most architecturally significant building in Flagler county.

In the 1880's and 1890's, the introduction of the railroad by U. J. White and Henry Flagler and the connecting of the Halifax and Matansas Rivers improved transportation in the county. In November, 1886, White routed a rail line through Bunnell. Henry Flagler brought his railroad to Daytona Beach in 1892, providing an additional catalyst for population and economic growth. Railroad spurs from White's lines on the west side of the county created the communities of Haw Creek, Tipparary, St. John's Park and Dead Lake.

Alvah A. Bunnell established a cypress shingle mill along White's rail line in what is now Bunnell. In 1898, Issac I. Moody moved to Bunnell, and along with J. F. Lambert bought 30,000 acres and formed the Bunnell Development Company. Many of the early residential and commercial buildings in Bunnell were built by Moody's company, and in 1913 Bunnell was incorporated.

The Dixie Highway, built in 1913, connected Bunnell to Hastings. By 1915, it linked Bunnell to Jacksonville, St. Augustine and Flagler Beach. An original section of this brick highway still exists between Espanola and Hastings. Flagler county's early railroads helped create the new communities of Flagler City, Espanola and Korona, which was settled by Polish immigrants and is famous for its shrine to St. Christopher, the traveler's patron saint. In 1938, on the East coast near Matansas Inlet, Marineland was built as the first underwater motion picture studio and oceanarium.

In the late 1960's, ITT Corporation bought large tracts of land along the East coast and the central part of Flagler county, and I-95 was completed from Jacksonville to Vero Beach. I-95 has become the main traffic artery used by tourists from the north. In the early 1970's, ITT started to develop Palm Coast, a major housing and commercial development in Flagler county, making it the prime economic base for the county.

A
East Moody Blvd.
Bunnell

Flagler County Courthouse, built in 1924, Wilbur Talley architect and O.P. Woodcock builder. Neo-classical style, two-story brick building.

B
204 East Moody Blvd.
Bunnell

Holden House, built in 1918, by S.M. Bortree for his daughter and son-in-law. Thomas Holden was the town pharmacist. Bungalow style house with coquina pedestals and piers was part of the planned housing envisioned by the Bunnell Development Company.

C
106 Bay Street
Bunnell

Tribune building, built in 1914, two-story Masonry Vernacular style. The Tribune Building housed the *St. Johns Tribune* which became the *Flagler Tribune* in 1917.

D
101-107 Bay Street
Bunnell

Bunnell State Bank, built in 1918, two-story Masonry Vernacular. One of the best examples of commercial architecture in Flagler County.

E
102 Railroad
Bunnell

Moody Residence was built in 1909 for Isaac Moody, the president of the Bunnell Development Company. One of the best examples of frame vernacular architecture in Flagler County.

F
201 Bay Street
Bunnell

Hardesty House, built 1909, one-story frame vernacular residence, was the third house built in Bunnell after the town was laid out in 1909.

G
202 N. Railroad
Bunnell

Cochran House, built in 1909, is a massive two story, frame vernacular residence. W. H. Cochran was one of the first members of the Bunnell City Council.

H
200 N. Railroad
Bunnell

Lambert House, built in 1909, is a two story frame vernacular, and the oldest existing building in Bunnell. Home of J.F. Lambert, who with Isaac Moody started the Bunnell Development Company.

I
E. Lambert
Bunnell

George Moody House, built in 1916, two story frame vernacular building. George Moody was prominent in the development of Flagler Beach where he was the first mayor.

J
Church Street
Bunnell

Bunnell City Hall, built in 1937, by Z.D. Holland. One-story governmental building, Masonry Vernacular style with coquina exterior. A federal works projects completed the Works Progress Administration (W.P.A.).

K
1000 Moody Blvd.
Bunnell

George Moody House, built in 1917, is George Moody's second house in Bunnell. A one-and-one-half story Bungalow style residence.

L
805 Moody Blvd.
Bunnell

Dr. W. H. Deen House, built in 1918, is a two story, Neo-Classical style residence. Dr. Deen was the Department of Agriculture & Farm Demonstrator for Flagler County.

M
802 Moody Blvd.
Bunnell

Hendricks House, built in 1918, by the Bunnell Development Company. Bungalow style, one-and-one-half story wood building.

N
220 State 11
Haw Creek

Cody House, built in 1909, by V. J. White. Carpenter Gothic Style, 2-story frame residence.

O
King's Road

Princess Estate, built in 1887, frame vernacular style, modeled on an Adirondack Hunting Lodge by original owner, Henry Cutting. The estate is considered to be most architecturally and historically significant building in Flagler County.

VOLUSIA

SIDNEY D. CORHERN, AIA

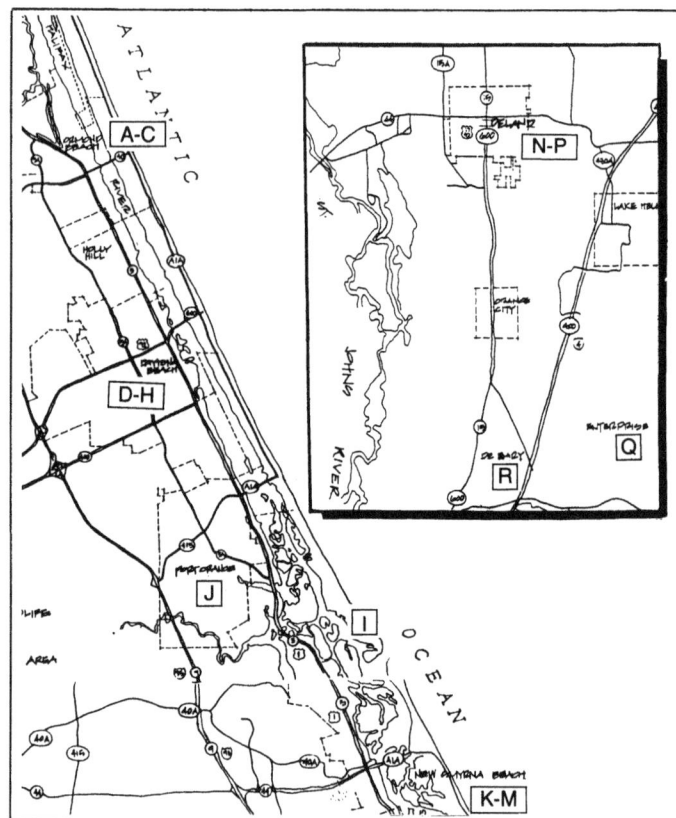

V Volusia County's first inhabitants were the Timucuan Indians who lived in the area eight to ten
thousand years ago. The only remaining evidences
of their culture are the large refuse mounds containing
shells, broken pottery, and bones along the waterways on
both county borders. This area contains an old Indian mound
called Turtle Mound, said to be the first Florida land sighted
by Ponce de Leon. Early attempts to explore the locale were
unsuccessful, but Franciscan friars established missions on
the east coast of Volusia in 1587.

After the British gained control of Florida, Dr. Andrew
Turnbull established a settlement at New Smyrna in 1767
and named it after his wife's hometown, Smyrna, Turkey.
Turnbull's dream of producing cash crops, especially indigo,
was hindered by adverse living conditions. When granted
permission to leave New Smyrna after the American Revolution, many of the settlers moved to St. Augustine in 1777.
From 1763 to 1783 British sugar plantations developed along
the Kings Highway from New Smyrna north to Bulow Plantation in what is now Flagler County. The plantations, whose
buildings were constructed of coquina stone, thrived until the
Seminole Wars when parties of Indians raided and burned
the mills. All that remains of the plantations today are
coquina block walls and some machinery parts. "Dun-Law-
ton" at Port Orange, "Mount Oswald" in Tomoka State Park,
and "Carrick Fergus" on the west bank of the Tomoka River
are a few of the plantation sites.

During the 1800's, the rivers and ocean were the main
transportation routes. Enterprise and Volusia Landing became early steamboat landings on the St. John's River for
west Volusia. Enterprise became a winter resort and later the
first county seat when Volusia County was established in
1854. Mathias Day, a developer from Mansfield, Ohio, settled
thirteen families on 2,142 acres to begin the creation of Daytona. Bridges were built in 1887 and 1899 across the Halifax
River. DeLand (named after Henry DeLand, a retired manufacturer from New York) became the permanent county
seat in 1888.

Railroads were introduced to Volusia County in the 1880's.
The St. Johns and Halifax River Railroad served the east
side of the county and the Jacksonville, Tampa, Key West
Railroad the west. Ormond Beach became a winter resort
area for the wealthy when Henry Flagler brought his passenger train service to the area. Mild weather, wide sandy
beaches, and passenger trains helped Daytona Beach and
Ormond Beach develop a tourist trade that is still one of the
main sources of economy for the area. John D. Rockefeller
was a frequent visitor.

US Highway 1, built along the old Kings Highway, and A1A,
built near the coast, brought the first automobiles to east
Volusia. Interstate 4, built in the late 1950's, connected central Florida to Daytona. In the late 1960's, Interstate 95, constructed through Volusia County, provided access to northern states and south Florida.

State highways 44 and 17-92 intersect in downtown De-
Land. Location of the highways, the citrus industry, Stetson
University, and the county seat has allowed steady growth
for DeLand while other west Volusia communities have stag-
nated since the steamboat era.

Auto racing was introduced to the Daytona Beach area in
1903. The earliest races were held on the beaches, first in
Ormond Beach then later on Daytona Beach. Beach racing
continued until the 1950's when Bill France moved to Daytona Beach and built the Daytona International Speedway.

The opening of Disney World and an improved highway
system increased tourism along the east coast of Volusia in
the 1970's. Steady growth throughout the county turned into
a surge of development for coastal communities such as
New Smyrna, Daytona Beach, and Ormond Beach and
caused a major planning problem.

During the 1980's, residents and government officials have
become inccreasingly aware of the need to preserve historic
architecture in Volusia County and of the development pressures that threaten. Both public and private individuals and
groups have begun to take appropriate measures to preserve the tangible record of Volusia County's long and diverse history.

A
Granada Avenue
Ormond Beach

Ormond Hotel, built in 1887 for John Anderson and Joseph D. Price, purchased by Henry Flagler in 1890. Frame vernacular hotel enlarged and landscaped by Flagler. Mecca for tourists and early automobile racing fans.

B
Granada Avenue and John Anderson Drive
Ormond Beach

The Casements, built in 1890's by Dr. Harwood Huntington and purchased by John D. Rockefeller for a winter residence in 1918. Architectural style representative of resort cottages at turn of the century.

C
501 N. Wild Olive Av.
Daytona Beach

Seabreeze United Church, built in 1895 with Harry Griffin as architect. Unusual example of Spanish Mission style with the typical features of red clay tile roofs, dormers and roof parapets. Wall of field stone or bag rock.

D
Daytona Beach

Daytona Beach Bandshell, built in 1936 as a Works Progress Administration project that included the boardwalk along the ocean. Moorish style structure of coquina stone. Served as outdoor entertainment center for beauty pageants, plays, and concerts since its construction.

E
Bethune-Cookman College Campus
Daytona Beach

Mary McLeod Bethune House, built in the 1920's as home of the founder of Bethune-Cookman College and the National Council for Negro Women who advised presidents and spoke for the black American community.

F
220 N. Beach St.
Daytona Beach

Daytona Beach Post Office, built in 1933 with Harry Griffin as architect. Design inspired by Havana hotel. Red clay roof tiles imported from Cuba and wall made of coral shipped from Key Largo.

G
140 S. Beach St.
Daytona Beach

S&H Kress Building, built in 1933. Art Deco building with ornate facade, built on a series of pilings.

H
South Beach St.
Daytona Beach

Merchant Bank Building, built in 1910 with Barn and Hall as contractors and W. B. Talley as architect. Beaux Arts style.

I
Ponce Inlet

Ponce de Leon Inlet Lighthouse, constructed in 1887 under the direction of General Orville Babcock, a friend of Ulysses S. Grant, activated in 1888. Originally fueled by kerosene until the 1920's when lighthouse converted to electric power. Small museum located on the lighthouse grounds.

J
4110 Ridgewood Ave.
Port Orange

Grace Episcopal Chruch, built in 1895. Victorian Revival style with original stained glass by Tiffany Studio and Willet Studio glass installed in early 1970's.

K
Riverside Drive and Washington Street
New Smyrna Beach

Turnbull Ruins. Coquina rock foundation for incomplete house intended for Dr. Andrew Turnbull, British founder of New Smyrna. Hotel and home built by the pioneer Sheldon family on the foundation. Union ships bombed and burned the building during Civil War.

L
103 Flagler Ave.
New Smyrna Beach

Riverview Hotel, built in 1896 on Indian River as hunting and fishing lodge. Originally two-story structure called Barber House after the builder, S.T. Barber, who was also the bridge-tender at the time of construction. Frame vernacular building with many additions. Name changed to Riverview Hotel in 1936.

M
Mission Drive
New Smyrna Beach

New Smyrna Sugar Mill Ruins, southernmost sugar plantation built along the old Kings Highway. Destroyed in 1830's by Seminole Indians. Walls of native coquina stone and some mill machinery fragments remaining.

N
Downtown Area
DeLand

DeLand Downtown Area, one of the best collections of late nineteenth century buildings in Florida. In 1984 became state's first Main Street Project. Since then many existing brick buildings restored.

O
Woodland Blvd.
DeLand

DeLand Hall, Stetson University Campus, built in 1884. Oldest building in continuous use for higher education in Florida. First building at Stetson University. Victorian Revival style structure which originally housed library, chapel, classrooms, gyms, and offices.

P
1031 Camphor Lane
DeLand

Stetson Mansion, built in 1886. Designed by George T. Pearson as the winter residence of John B. Stetson, hat manufacturer, who wintered in DeLand for 20 years and became involved with the community and the university named for him.

Q
Debary Av. & Clark St.
Enterprise

All Saints Episcopal Church, built in 1883, one of the oldest original Episcopal missions in Central Florida. One of finer examples of small Victorian Revival style churches. At time of construction, Enterprise was the county seat.

R
DeBary Mansion State Park
DeBary

DeBary Hall, built in 1871 as winter residence of Baron Frederick DeBary, a prominent wine importer. House remained in DeBary family until 1959 when it became property of the state.

LAKE

MICHAEL GORDON, AIA, MID-FLORIDA

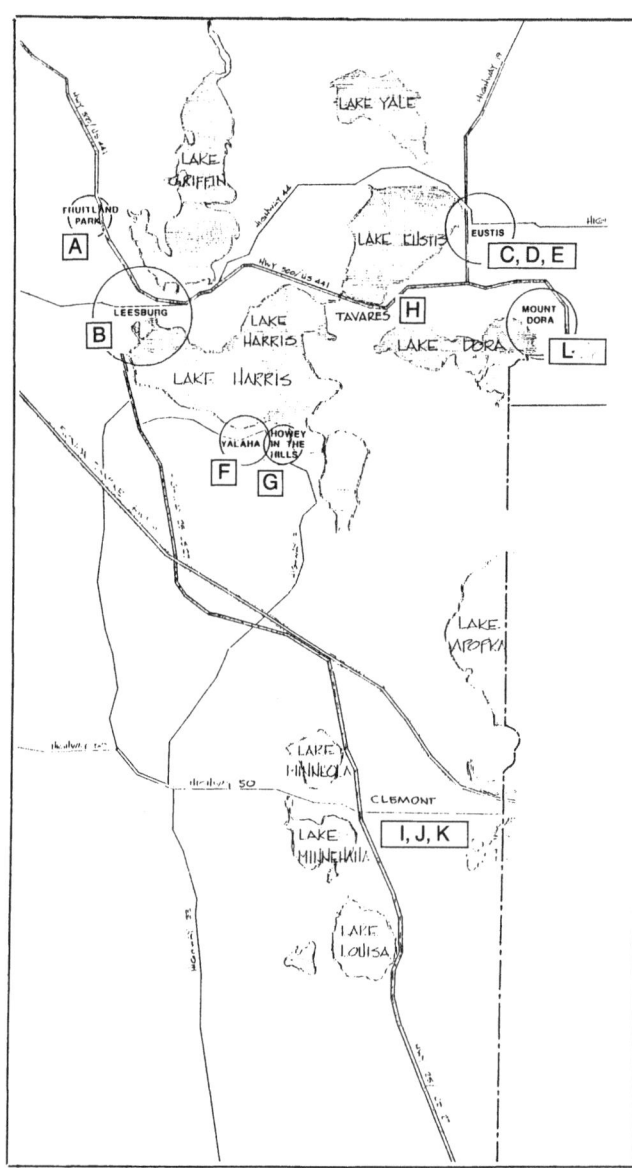

Lake County was established May 27, 1887, from portions of Sumter and Orange counties. Named for the large number of lakes in the area, the county is bordered by Marion, Sumter, Polk, Orange, Seminole, Volusia, and Putnam counties.

Settlers first came to the area in the 1840's, but the principal county communities (with the exception of Leesburg) developed in the last quarter of the past century. Leesburg, largest and oldest town in the county, was founded in 1856 by the Lee family from New York. The favorable climate, abundant lakes, and soil conditions of the Leesburg area and other Lake County regions encouraged the development of extensive citrus groves, commercial nurseries, watermelon farms, and even vineyards. The lake environment also attracted seasonal residents and drew those interested in recreational activities. Citrus and truck crop production and mineral and lake resources influenced the county's population growth.

Tavares, the county seat, was established in 1875 by Alexander St. Clair Abrams who named the town for a Spanish ancestor and planned development first as a tourist community and then as an industrial and governmental center. Abrams spent more than $500,000 in building stores, lumber mills, a hotel, and the first courthouse. An 1888 fire, followed by destructive freezes, almost destroyed the town; but development and growth returned to the area.

Eustis and Lake Eustis were named for General Abram Eustis of Seminole War fame. The town, first known as Pendryville, honored A. S. Pendry who homesteaded the area in 1876, planted an orange grove, and established the Oklawaha Hotel. Before railroads arrived, the town was a port for lake steamers. Mount Dora on Lake Dora, founded in 1882, has the appearance of a New England village, even though a southern accent can be discerned. The town was a rendezvous for boat enthusiasts and had one of Florida's first yacht clubs.

Howey-in-the-Hills was founded in 1916 as a center of a vast citrus industry occupying over 60,000 acres and providing harvesting, shipping, and marketing services. Devastated by freezes in the 1980's, the area presently caters to the tourist trade.

Lake County, once a center for the citrus industry, is now in transition because of climatic and population changes. Recreation facilities are important to the economy. Tourists, delighted with watersports, are also finding pleasure in the Victorian Revival buildings and early twentieth century business districts.

Preservation and conservation are active ingredients in contemporary Lake County. A portion of Ocala National Forest, dotted with various springs and streams, is located in the northeast portion of the county. Mount Dora's Lakeside Inn, which opened in 1893 as the Alexander House, was restored and began operating again in the mid 1980's. Royellou Museum, sponsored by the Mount Dora Historical Society, features Mount Dora memorabilia to educate the visitor. Walking tours are available for those interested in architectural preservation.

A
Spring Lake Road
Fruitland Park

Holy Trinity Church. Designed by J. J. Nevitt and built in 1888 for $12,150 by E. Thompson. Victorian Revival style wood frame structure with gable roof, three entry porches with clustered columns, decorated pediments, and verge boards. Minor modifications.

B
1021 N. Main St.
Leesburg

E. H. Mote House. Built in 1892 for $9,000 for E. H. Mote, pioneer developer of Leesburg who served eight terms as mayor and one in the Florida House of Representatives. Victorian Revival style. Projecting bays, balconies, and tower with intersecting gable roof.

C
536 North Bay St.
Eustis

G. D. Clifford House, built in 1910 by L. N. Herrick for Guilford D. Clifford, who arrived in area in 1875 as first merchant in Eustis. Designed by New York firm sixteen years before construction which was delayed by 1894-1895 freezes. Classic Revival style house with projecting two-story porch and bays.

D
Ferran Park
Eustis

McClelland Open Air Theater, built in 1926 to celebrate city's pride in local music. Moved and modified to improve acoustics in 1935. Style modified to reflect Mediterranean Revival style with stucco decorations, towers, arches, and clay tile roof.

E
305 S. Mary St.
Eustis

St. Thomas Episcopal Church, built in 1882 as first church building in Eustis. Enlarged in 1921 by sawing building in two and adding six feet to chancel allowing organ installation. Extensive modifications.

NO PHOTO AVAILABLE

F
Lake Shore Drive
Yalaha

Andrew Jackson Phares House (Howey-in-the-Hills vicinity). Built in 1874 for Phares, founder of Yalaha who worked with early mining and citrus industries. Characters in Will Allen Dromgade's *Three Little Crackers from Down in Dixie* said to be based on Phares family. Building extensively modified.

G
Citrus Street
Howey-in-the-Hills

William J. Howey House, designed by Katherine Cotheal Budd and built in 1926 for W. J. Howey, founder of Howey-in-the-Hills who served two terms as mayor and was an unsuccessful candidate for governor. Mediterranean Revival style, two-story stucco structure with arched windows, hip roof with wide bracketed eaves, and clay roof tiles. Projecting entry bay with elaborate frontispiece of spiraled engaged columns, bas relief panels, and heraldic devices. Low crenellated tower at northeast corner.

H
Alfred St. at St. Clair
Tavares

Union Congregational Church. First church in Tavares built in 1885 to house Methodist and Baptist congregations until early 1900's when each group built their own churches. Victorian Revival style with gable roof with verge board, bell cupola, and unusual front porch with paling balustrade.

I
Clermont

Lakeview Hotel, built in 1884 for L. H. Todd associated with the Clermont Improvement Company. Marked beginning of town's development.

J
Clermont

Orange Belt Railroad Depot, built in 1887 and moved from original site. In 1885 the Orange Belt Railroad and the Tavares-Apopka and Gulf Railroad, later the Tavares and Gulf (T&G known as "Tug and Grunt") provided rapid and safe local transportation.

K
Mineola at Fifth St.
Clermont

"The Gables," built in 1885 for M. E. Wilson who established the Baptist congregation and built Grace Baptist Church in 1884. House extensively modified and used for commercial functions.

L
Connelly Ave.
Mount Dora

John Phillip Donnelly House, built in 1893 for Donnelly, the early developer and two-term mayor of Mount Dora, originally from Pittsburgh. Possibly designed by George F. Barber of Knoxville, Tenn. Flamboyant combination of Victorian Revival styles. Masonic Temple Lodge since 1930.

M
Donnelly at
Seventh Ave.
Mount Dora

Community Congregational Church. Congregation organized in 1883. Church built in 1887 with additions in 1916-1917 and 1935. Victorian Revival style, wood frame, entry tower, octagonal bell cupola with elongated steeple.

N
347 S. Clayton
Mount Dora

Gilbert House. Built in 1883 as the home of Dr. Gilbert who operated the first steamboat on Lake Dora, one of the few early means of transportation in Lake County to Jacksonville via the Oklawaha River.

O
100 N. Alexander
Mount Dora

Lakeside Inn. Opened in 1893 as The Alexander House, a resort hotel for fishing, birding, and snake hunting. Purchased in 1924 by a group of investors and Charles Edgerton whose son Dick managed the hotel during many winter seasons. Additions constructed in 1930. Continuous operation except for 1985. Rehabilitated by new owners and reopened as full-service hotel in 1986.

ORANGE

MICHAEL CLARY, AIA, MID FLORIDA CHAPTER

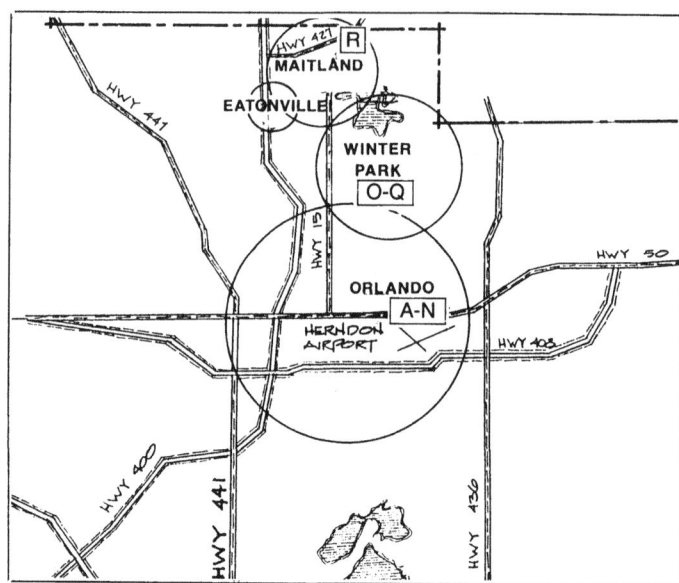

Originally part of Mosquito County, Orange County was founded in 1845. The settling of Orange County, like that of the neighboring counties of Seminole, Brevard, Osceola, Lake, and Polk, was an aftermath of the Seminole Wars. Under protection of military garrisons, settlers drifted into the area to establish towns near the forts. One of the first settlers was Aaron Jernigan, a cattleman from Georgia who moved into the Orlando area in 1842. A stockade which he built and the community which settled around it on the shores of Lake Holden became the seat of Orange County in 1856. First known as Jernigan, the town was renamed Orlando either to recognize a Shakespearean hero or to honor Orlando Reeves, a night sentry killed by raiding Indians, or to remember Orlando Rees, a wealthy planter who was plagued and finally killed by Indians stealing his slaves.

The numerous lakes and favorable climate encouraged development of commercial citrus groves in the county. One of the first was planted in 1865-1866 by W. H. Holden. Transportation problems prompted rail service which was provided by an 1880 extension of the South Florida Railroad from Mellonville to Orlando. Growth of the citrus industry drove cattle ranges further south. Maitland, a settlement on the site of Fort Maitland, attracted a group of Union veterans who incorporated the town in 1884. Nearby Eatonville was established in 1886, one of the first towns incorporated by blacks in the United States. Winter Park, first known as Lakeview and later Osceola, was incorporated in 1881 when a town site of 600 acres was laid out. Rollins College, established in 1885 by the General Congregational Association was named to honor Alonzo W. Rollins of Chicago. Apopka, Winter Garden, and Oakland in the western part of the county were settled in the 1950's. Lake Apopka, one of Florida's largest lakes, was surrounded by citrus groves and resort facilities. Oakland, settled by South Carolinians, was an early industrial center with saw mills, cotton gins, and sugar mills.

With state and railroad interests offering land at a dollar an acre to English buyers, large numbers of Englishmen immigrated to Orange County in the 1890s. The Rogers Building was club headquarters for Orlando's early British settlers. Development continued until the winter of 1894-1985 when citrus groves were frozen to the ground.

Another surge of development came to Orange County during the 1920's Florida land boom with real estate speculations, building of thousands of residences, and the introduction of new architectural styles. Downtown areas were first composed of two-story brick commercial buildings with corbeled cornices, cast stone window and door surrounds, and sometimes clad with sheet metal simulating carved stone. Canopies above sidewalks protected pedestrians against rain and sun. Residential areas presented Victorian Revival, Classical Revival, and Mediterranean Revival styles and examples of bungalow and Prairie School designs.

The financial crash of 1929, a depression lasting until the late 1930's, and then World War II slowed commercial and residential building. The post-war years included a new national phenomenon, a mobile population which revitalized the tourist industry. The perennial tourist of the late nineteenth and early twentieth century who arrived by train became the two-week vacationer driving his own automobile. Middle-aged and retired families arrived in mobile homes and set up housekeeping. Orlando, with its 47 city parks and recreation areas and 54 lakes within the city limits, became the tourist hub of Central Florida. The 1967 arrival of the Walt Disney enterprises to the area caused rapid and extensive changes in both the natural and man-made environments.

Fortunately criteria and procedures for architectural preservation have become part of planning decisions shaping the future of this dynamic locale. In 1976 the City of Orlando created an ordinance specifying a citizen advisory board to protect the architectural history of the city. There are now three historic districts in Orlando and nearly one thousand buildings noted for their value to the community. A 1984 publication, sponsored by the advisory board, *Orlando, History in Architecture,* presents an excellent record of the community's architectural heritage. Preservation efforts in other parts of Orange County have been less spectacular but through individual and group preservation efforts, there is a future for the county's most significant architecture.

A
100-102 W. Church St.
Orlando
Bumby Block, built in 1884 for Joseph Bumby, Sr. as hardware store, one of the oldest commercial structures in Orlando and a major business enterprise through 1966. Two story brick masonry construction with segmental arched display windows at first floor, corbeled cornice. Victorian Revival style features.

B
37-39 S. Magnolia Av.
Orlando
Rogers Building-English Club, built in 1886-1887. Important social gathering place for the English colony. Commercial Victorian Revival style building clad in sheet metal with polygonal window at second floor, bracketed cornice with triangular insert bearing building name and decoration. Decorative belt courses on side elevation.

C
76-78 W. Church St.
Orlando
Old Orlando Railroad Depot (Southern and Coastal Railroad), built in 1889. Unique example of Victorian Revival style railroad architecture similar to designs of H. H. Richardson; brick masonry construction, decorative shingle hip roof, eyebrow dormers, cylindrical tower with conical roof. Complex of three structures: office and baggage building, passenger station, and warehouse, connected by means of a covered loading platform. Constructed with load-bearing brick walls, a wood frame roof.

D
135 Lucerne Cir. NE
Orlando
Peleg Peckman House-Dr. P. Phillips House. Designed by L. Percival Hutton of Philadelphia and built in 1893 by L. N. Boykin for Col. Peleg Peckman, prominent seasonal resident. Bought in 1912 by Dr. P. Phillips, one of Central Florida's most successful citrus producers. Victorian Revival style, wood frame, two-story shingled residence with cylindrical tower and other Queen Anne features. Extensively modified with Classical Revival portico with Ionic columns.

E
15-17 W. Pine St.
Orlando
Elijah Hand Building, built in 1905 as a furniture store. Later used for undertaking establishment and office building. Victorian Revival style, two-story brick building with corbeled belt course between first and second floor, two-tiered corbeled denticular cornice and parapet wall with raised central portion.

F
36 W. Pine St.
Orlando
Carey Hand Funeral Home, built in 1919 with F.H. Trimble as architect. Carey Hand Funeral Home in continuous operation at this location since 1920. Renaissance Revival style featuring eight arches in street facade (one as automobile entrance, three in recessed entry, and others in wall screening parking area).

G
Orange Avenue
Orlando
Angebilt Hotel, designed by Murray S. King and opened in 1923 as Orlando's largest leading commercial hotel. Simplified Renaissance Revival style. Cut stone finish at ground and mezzanine levels; pairs of windows in brick masonry wall expressing rental room; and three-part rectangular and circular arched windows at top floors below heavy bracketed cornice.

H
239 E. Copeland Dr.
Orlando
S. J. Sligh House, built in 1925 for citrus magnate S. J. Sligh at cost of $25,000. Colonial Revival style, two-story brick building with gable roof and gable roof dormers, two-story portico with pairs of Corinthian columns, and fan light in pediment.

I
18 W. Pine St.
Orlando
Tinker Building, built in 1925 by H. C. Construction Co. for Joe Tinker of baseball fame. Two-story masonry commercial building. Street facade featuring glazed tiles, cut and pressed stone, stained glass, and wood trim. Projecting trim at first and second floor ceiling lines.

J
525 S. Eola Ave.
Orlando
Cherokee School, built in 1926. Mediterranean Revival style, two-story masonry building with stucco finish, two square towers with pyramid clay tile roofs flanking entry porch. Polychromatic glazed tile inserts on window surrounds, decorative bas reliefs.

K
1400 Sligh Blvd.
Orlando
Seaboard Coast Line Station, built in 1926. Spanish Mission Revival style with arcade curvilinear parapet and flanking bell towers, three arches at porch, and tile roof.

L
24 N. Rosalind Ave.
Orlando
First Church of Christ Scientist-St. George Orthodox Church, built in 1928 with George Foote Dunham as architect. Neo-Classical Revival style structure with Greek cross plan, intersecting gable roofs with dome at intersection. Two-story portico at street entrance.

M
578 N. Orange Ave.
Orlando
Firestone Tire and Rubber Building, built in 1930 for Firestone Tire and Rubber Co. Anchored northern limits of Orlando's commercial development. One of few commercial structures constructed in the 1930's. Brick and concrete masonry building with covered service area, two-story sales and office area, decorative tower with lantern.

N
15-17 W. Church St
Orlando
Kress Building, built in 1935 with Edward F. Siebart of New York as architect. One of few Art Deco style structures in Orange County. Stone veneer over reinforced concrete, granite veneer, and polychromatic terra cotta ornament.

O
Eastern Shore of Lake Osceola
Winter Park
The Palms, built in 1899 as winter cottage for Edward Hill Brewer. Remodeled in 1924 to duplicate Brewer's residence in Cortland, N.Y. Originally clapboard exterior with wood shingle roof and spindle balustraded veranda. Colonial Revival style facade with Ionic pedimented portico and paired columns.

SEMINOLE

JERRY MILLS, FLORIDA CENTRAL CHAPTER

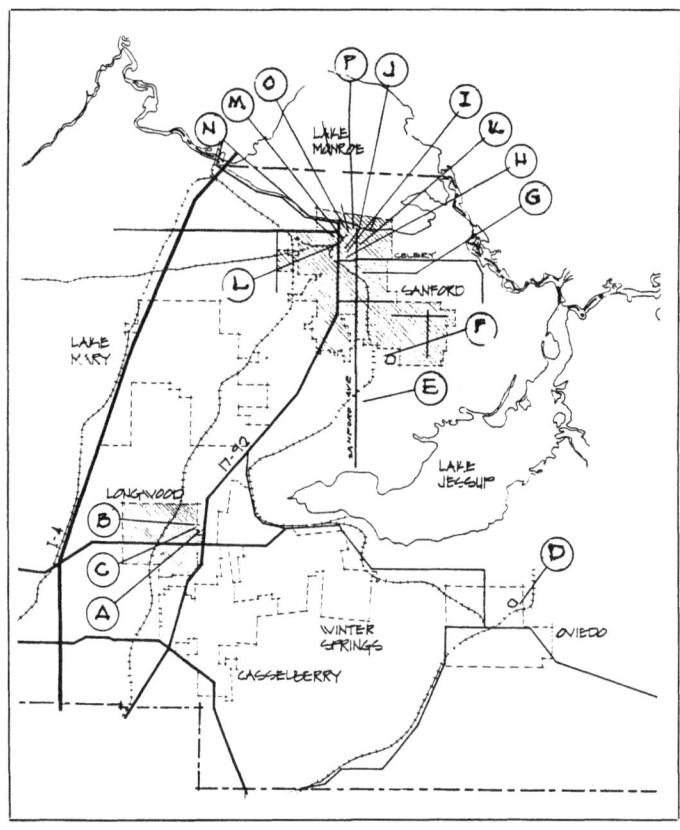

One of Florida's smaller counties, Seminole County is defined by the St. Johns River and Volusia County to the north and east and by Orange County to the south. During the area's early history, when the British occupied Florida (1763-1783), land near Mosquito Inlet was developed into sugar cane and indigo plantations. These fell into ruins following British withdrawal, and settlements were limited to coastal locations.

After Florida was transferred to the United States, East Florida was subdivided into several counties. One of these was Mosquito County, established in December 29, 1824, with New Smyrna as the county seat. Due to Indian hostilities around Lake Munroe during the Second Seminole War, Fort Mellon was erected on the lake's south shore in 1837. Roads were constructed to provide communication with other forts including Fort Brook (Tampa), Fort Gatlin (Orlando), and Fort Meade. During a period of relative calm, the settlement around Fort Mellon became known as Mellonville. In 1843 the county seat was moved from New Smyrna to Enterprise on the north shore of Lake Munroe. Then, on January 30, 1845, a law was enacted to change the name of Mosquito County to that of Orange County with Mellonville as the county seat. Because of its location at the headwaters of the St. Johns River, Mellonville was the natural gateway for supplies to the growing population of South Florida. In 1854 Volusia County was formed from the north end of Orange County. In 1856 Orlando became the new county seat for Orange County.

By 1866 new settlers began to arrive in this locale to establish wharves, packing houses, and groves. Gen. Henry S. Sanford purchased 12,535 acres of the Levy Grant at Lake Monroe on the St. Johns River. The town of Sanford was incorporated seven years later and gradually grew to absorb Mellonville. In 1871 Sanford settled a colony of immigrants from Sweden on a tract of land west of Sanford which he named St. Gertrude. The 1870's were years of building commercial, institutional, and residential structures. In 1879 a charter established the South Florida Railroad from Sanford to Tampa, and in 1884 the J.T. and K.W. Railroad came into Sanford from Jacksonville. The South Florida Railroad was purchased by Henry B. Plant in 1883, and Sanford served as headquarters for his company and the railroad. Longwood, a community southwest of Sanford, developed as a railroad stop. Mellonville, by-passed by the railroads and eclipsed by Sanford, disappeared by the late 1880's. On Sept. 20, 1887,

a fire destroyed four blocks of Sanford's commercial district, after which buildings in this area had to be of masonry construction. In 1913 the northeastern third of Orange County became Seminole County with Sanford as the county seat. After severe freezes of 1895, some business interests turned from fragile citrus to the security of vegetable production, food processing, and fertilizer and crate manufacture.

Rapid population growth in neighboring Orange County and the construction of Interstate Highway 4 made Seminole County attractive to modern land speculators, especially in the Altamonte Springs locale. Several historic buildings, threatened by changes in land use, were moved to Longwood in 1973 to provide a focus for local preservation efforts. To protect its heritage of late nineteenth century architecture, Sanford has established an architectural district including twenty-six buildings. Preservation organizations include the Central Florida Society for Historic Preservation, Inc., and the Seminole County Historical Society.

A
130 Warren Ave.
Longwood

Bradlee-McIntyre House, built in 1885 in Altamonte Springs and moved to Longwood in 1973. Queen Anne style building which Ulysses S. Grant's widow and children visited shortly after his death.

B
141 West Church Ave.
Longwood

"Inside-Outside" House. Fabricated in Boston for a ship's captain, transported in disassembled state by steamer to Sanford and by mules to Altamonte Springs, reassembled in 1883. Unusual vertical stud framing exposed on exterior with plaster over tongue and groove, horizontal siding on interior. Recorded by Historic American Building Survey, moved to Longwood in 1973.

C
150 Lake St.
Longwood

Longwood Hotel, built in 1883. Wood frame, three stories, once known as "The Orange and Black," one of Central Florida's finest gambling establishments. Adapted in 1985 as restaurant and retail office spaces.

D
6297 Lake Charm Circle
Oviedo

Calvin Whitney-Wyatt House, built in 1886- 87 for Whitney who owned the Chase Piano Co. of Ohio. Victorian Revival style with west elevation porch at both floors extending half bay beyond width of house to north.

E
South Sanford Ave.
Sanford

James E. Ingraham House, built for Ingraham who was agent for Gen. Henry S. Sanford when the new town of Sanford was developed (Ingraham also president of South Florida Railway in 1881 and president of Henry Flagler's Model Land Company which supervised construction of West Palm Beach in 1983.) Two-story wood shingle Victorian Revival style structure.

F
Silver Lake
Sanford

Phelps-Burton House, built in 1898. Wood frame, two-and-a-half-story building with basement, ornate verge boards, and engaged four-story tower with steep hip roof.

G
1719 S. Sanford Ave.
Sanford

Ginn Brothers House (Jarvis Farm), built from 1904-1908. Raised cottage, wood frame, two and a half story with full basement, rough-cut cypress siding, engaged hexagonal turret. Victorian Revival style.

H
1201 Magnolia
Sanford

Dyson House, built before 1924 with Elton Moughton as architect. Probably the best example of Arts and Crafts Bungalow style in Seminole County. Wood frame sheathed with sawn cypress shingles.

I
918 South Magnolia
Sanford

W. J. Thigpen House, built in 1910. Cross plan with Palladian windows in each gable. Sheathed with aluminum siding in 1978, lightning rods and pressed metal roof shingles remain.

J
801 Park Avenue
Sanford

Thigpen House, built in 1905. Queen Anne style building with ornamental shingle pattern in gables, a cylindrical turret on northwest corner sheathed in vertical tongue and groove beaded boards, and curved sash and glazing.

K
Cypress at Ninth St.
Sanford

St. James African Methodist Episcopal Church, built in mid 1880's. Oldest black ecclesiastic structure in Sanford. Brick exterior, wood frame, and pressed metal roof shingles.

L
301 West Seventh St.
Sanford

Sanford High School-Grammar School-The Margaret K. Reynolds Building. Main structure built in 1902, wings added in 1916 with E. J. Moughton as architect. Adapted as Seminole County School Board's Student Museum.

M
500 South Oak Ave.
Sanford

George Fernald House-Fernald-Laughton Memorial Hospital-Florida Hotel, built in 1910. Additions constructed in 1919 when house converted to hospital.

N
701 West Third St.
Sanford

Wilton Miller-George Fernald House, built in 1887. Ornate wood Victorian Revival building in Sanford. Restored as bed and breakfast inn in mid 1980's.

O
209 North Oak Ave.
Sanford

PICO (Plant Investment Company) building, built in 1886 with H.M. Papworth as builder and William T. Cotter as architect. Ornate brick building in Romanesque Revival style. Originaly designed as hotel to accommodate rail and steamship passengers. Adapted in 1966 as attorneys' offices.

P
301 East First St.
Sanford

Bishop Block, built immediately after the 1887 fire by Capt. J.O. Northesag for J.N. Bishop. Romanesque Revival style using brick and pressed metal.

BREVARD

SANDY JOHNSON

The history of Brevard County is remarkably diverse, encompassing periods from prehistoric times to European colonization and finally to the most technologically advanced achievements of space exploration.

The Colonial Period began in Brevard County in 1513 when Ponce de Leon landed just south of Cape Canaveral. The Cape was a landmark for Spanish explorers using the Gulf Stream as the principal return route to Spain. The Spanish initiated the cultivation of citrus in Florida which was to have a significant impact on the landscape and economy of the area.

Aside from early exploration, little settlement occurred for the next 300 years. The outbreak of the Seminole Indian War in 1835 stimulated the first significant development. Land was cleared, trails were built and a fortification was constructed on Merritt Island. The Armed Occupation Act brought soldier-settlers, such as Captain Douglas Dummitt and Captain John Houston, to the area. Dummitt chose a site on Merritt Island and planted a citrus grove which was producing 60,000 barrels of fruit of year by 1859. Dummitt became known as the Father of the now-famous Indian River citrus. Brevard County continued to produce enormous amounts of citrus until the disastrous freeze of 1895 which devastated the industry statewide.

In 1892, work was begun on the Cape Canaveral Lighthouse. Settlers continued to trickle in, but it was not until the last half of the 19th century that a real influx of settlers occurred. This was a direct result of the Homestead Act of 1862 offering free land for farmers and speculators. The Indian River and its environs offered fish, game and an easy means of local transportation for the settlers. The first homes in the county were palmetto shacks which were later replaced by rustic log cabins. Simple frame construction did not appear until the early 1880's. The hardwood hammocks along the shore of the Indian River and the groves of pinewood on Merritt Island were used in this early construction. The lumber was milled in Titusville, the county seat, and rafted up and down the river for construction of homes in the communities situated on the banks such as Cocoa, Eau Gallie and Melbourne.

The railroad had an immediate impact on the economy of the county. It allowed for the rapid entry of both tourists and permanent settlers, while facilitating the export of products, particularly fish and fruit, to northern markets. The businesses associated with these two products, such as ice plants, packing houses and canneries, developed at this time.

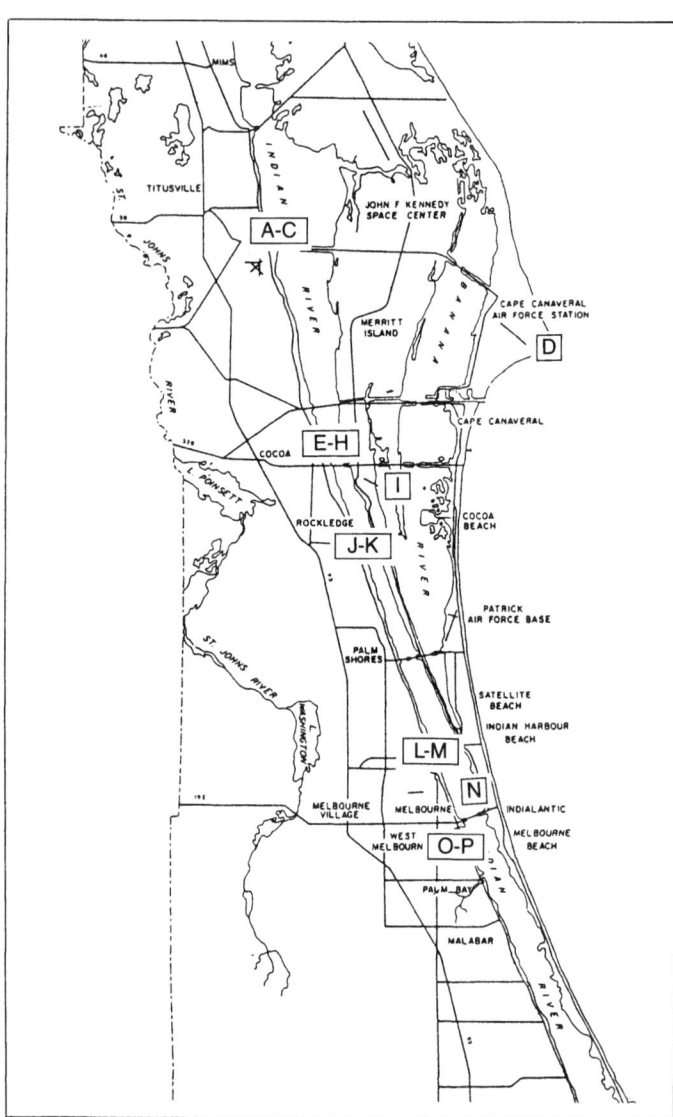

Improvements in transportation continued to be important to the development of Brevard County. The Dixie Highway, winding along the length of the Indian River, brought travelers and tourists by automobile to discover Brevard's climate and beaches. Florida's land boom of the 1920's also stimulated growth and the stylistic models for the architecture of this period, the Mediterranean Revival and Spanish Colonial, can be seen throughout the county. Building construction was accompanied by a lot of subdivision development at this same time.

After World War II, rapid growth was stimulated by the Federal Space Complex at Cape Canaveral and its main support system at Patrick Air Force Base. As a direct result of the building of these two facilities, Brevard County became a tourist center in the 1960s, as thousands of visitors witnessed the space launches.

A
506 Palm Avenue
Titusville
Brevard County Courthouse. This Classic Revival structure was built in 1912 on property donated to the county by Col. Henry Titus for whom the county seat of Titusville was named.

B
414 Pine Avenue
Titusville
St. Gabriel's Episcopal Church. St. Gabriel's is listed on the National Register of Historic Places and is a fine example of the Neo-Gothic style of architecture. It was constructed in 1887 on a large lot which was given to the congregation by the widow of Col. John Titus.

C
424 Washington Ave.
South Titusville
Pritchard House. James Pritchard, a decorated captain in the Confederate army, built this Queen Anne-style house in 1891. Pritchard played prominently in the economic development of Titusville and the house has remained in his family to this day.

D
Cape Canaveral
Cape Canaveral Lighthouse. The present lighthouse is only a mile-and-a- half from the site of Brevard's first lighthouse built prior to 1842. The light's first keeper, Capt. Olcott Mills Burnham, was one of group of Brevard pioneers known as "The Indian River Colony." Burnham served as lighthouse keeper until his death in 1886.

E
844 Indian River Dr.
Cocoa
Cannon-Kupper House. This Bungalow-style residence was built in 1910. It is sited on a bluff overlooking the Indian River and was built by Henry W. Cannon, Comptroller of the Currency under President James A. Arthur, as his winter residence.

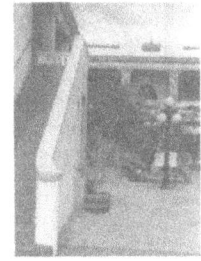

F
Brevard Avenue
near State Rd. 520
Cocoa Village
Bel Aire Arcade. This commercial arcade is typical of the Mediterranean Revival style of architecture which was so common in Florida during the 1920's.

G
300 Brevard Avenue
Cocoa Village
Cocoa Village Playhouse. Built in 1924, this old vaudeville theatre has been restored and is one of the few theatres to have survived from the 1920s.

H
434 Delannoy Ave.
Cocoa Village
Porcher House. This Classic Revival house was built in 1916 of coquina limestone and it is listed on the National Register of Historic Places. Its builder, E.P. Porcher, was a pioneer citrus grower who invented a washing machine for citrus and was instrumental in forming a commission to guarantee standards for fruit shipped from Florida. This became the now-powerful Florida Citrus Commission.

I
1609 Rockledge Dr.
Rockledge
Magruder-Waley House. This 1879 house is an example of a form of construction called an I-house. It was one of the dominant forms of building in the rural South. This house is an expansion of a log structure built in 1869 which is still visible underneath.

J
2275 U.S. Highway 1
Rockledge
Victory Groves Packing House. Sorting, washing and packing of citrus has been done in this huge warehouse since its construction in 1930. Constructed of heart pine, known locally as "Merritt Island Mahogany," whole timbers can be seen in the exposed trusses of the packing area.

K
So. Tropical Trail
Merritt Island
Georgiana First Methodist Church. This example of Gothic Vernacular architecture was built in 1886 and is known as "The Little Church in the Wildwood." It is one of the oldest Methodist church buildings in Florida.

L
Highland Street
Melbourne
Houston-Rossetter House, south of the Eau Gallie Causeway. This house was built in 1907 by carpenters who were boat builders who did very interesting finish work on the interior.

M
1115 Hyde Park Lane
Eau Gallie/Melbourne
Fowler Boathouse. In 1904, the Kentucky Military Institute built its winter headquarters in Eau Gallie. The headmaster, Col. Fowler, built his boathouse on the Eau Gallie River. This building is all cypress which was milled nearby.

N
1604 S. Harbor Blvd.
Melbourne
Florida Power and Light Company Ice Plant. This 1927 building is listed on the National Register of Historic Places. The masonry building was of great commercial importance to the community, serving households, businesses and the local fishermen.

O
1218 E. New Haven Av.
Melbourne
Lee House (Strawberry Mansion Restaurant). This Queen Anne-style residence was build in 1905 by John Lee as a winter residence. Claude Beaujean, a boat builder and carpenter, contributed to the beautiful interior details.

OSCEOLA

BILL BAUER, ARCHITECT

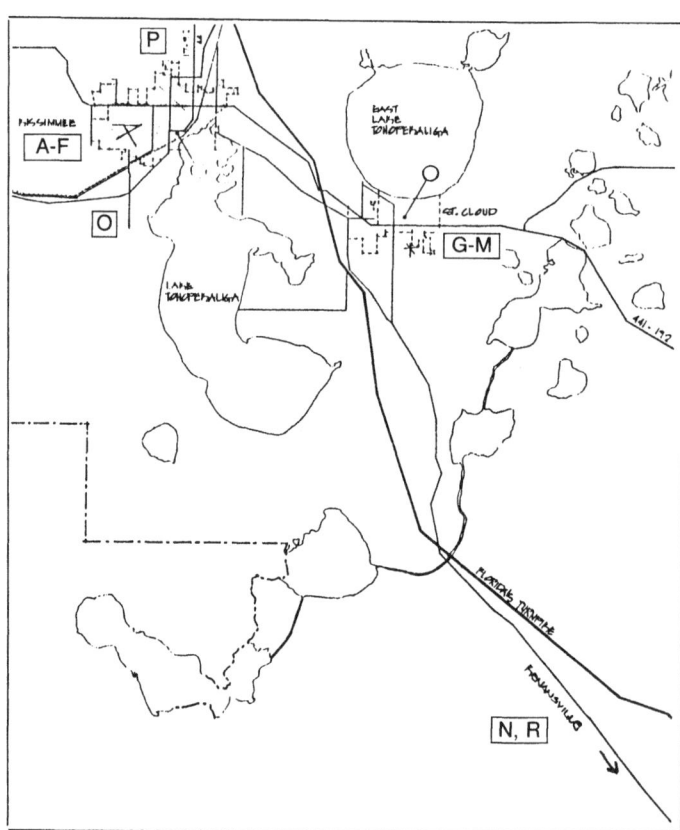

Osceola County encompasses 1,467 square miles, the sixth largest of Florida's counties, but the 1980 population of 49,287 made the county the thirty-fourth most populous. Since that census, growth has been phenomenal in and around the cities of Kissimmee and St. Cloud. The county was formed from portions of Orange and Brevard Counties in 1887.

Habitation of the region can be traced to the Ais-Calusa, possibly Timucuan, and later Seminole Indians. With the exception of place names, village sites, and numerous mounds, little evidence remains of their earlier presence. This area of Central Florida was surveyed in 1845, soon after the state was admitted to the United States, but it was not until after the Third Seminole War and the removal of the Indians that extensive settlement of white families began. Some of the first settlements were in the Shingle Creek area, a midway point for mail carriers between Orlando and Bartow. The temperate climate, large lakes, creeks, and prairie lands of the region attracted those interested in citrus and cattle, and large tracts devoted to these industries were amassed. Before the Civil War, there were a number of small communities and trading centers, such as Allendale and Whittier, and family settlements near the lakes and creeks. Log and simple frame structures were constructed using native pine and cypress timbers.

The nature of the area's development changed in 1881 when Hamilton Disston, a Philadelphia industrialist, and several of his associates agreed to purchase four million acres across the state from Ocala south to Lake Okeechobee for a million dollars, the largest single, private land purchase in U.S. history. In order to exploit his holdings, Disston believed that interconnecting canals betweeen lakes had to be dredged and investors attracted to the newly drained and accessible lands. Allendale, on the north shore of Lake Tohopekaliga, was chosen as the base for shipbuilding, drainage, and land sales and renamed Kissimmee City after the primary river of the region.

Growth was rapid with a Kissimmee post office being established in 1883. The year also marked the official arrival of the South Florida Line from Sanford and the construction by the railroad of a three-story hotel. The Tropical was described as the most spacious hotel south of Jacksonville. (The hotel had many important guests including Chester A. Arthur and John Jacob Astor.) By 1884, dredges had created a navigable waterway linking Kissimmee with the Gulf of Mexico by way of Lake Okeechobee. Publicity and promotion for the Kissimmee Valley region extended overseas and attracted foreign investment. An English settlement, centered around the Runneymede Hotel, was begun at Narcoossee.

After the creation of the new Osceola County in May, 1887, one of the first measures taken was construction of a three-story courthouse from locally made red brick. Large homes around the courthouse reflected area prosperity. This was also the period for new agricultural ventures, principally sugar cane production. Disston invested in the St. Cloud Plantation east of Kissimmee on the canal he had dug between East Lake and Lake Tohopekaliga. The $350,000 cost, the three to four hundred workers, the capacity of 372 tons of cane a day, and the construction of the Sugarbelt Railroad from Kissimmee to Narcoossee to serve the mill brought national recognition. The financial panic of 1893, coupled with natural disasters of freezes and worm infestations, brought an end to the plantation by 1897, one year after Disston's suicide. Over seven thousand acres of Disston lands around Alligator Lake were purchased by the Shakers. The community of seven or eight member-residents existed for twenty years and successfully grew pineapples and bananas. No structures of this southernmost Shaker effort survive.

The freezes which contributed to Disston's plantation disaster also were responsible for the exodus of many county residents, especially citrus growers. A measure of prosperity was to return to the area during the Spanish-American War years when Kissimmee cattle were in demand. The population of Kissimmee in 1905 was 1,530, a decrease of 500 from a decade earlier when Kissimmee was the nineteenth largest Florida city. During this period there were several major fires. One in 1905 destroyed the grand Hotel Kissimmee (The Tropical). Four years later an even larger fire burned most of the commercial district along Broadway.

In 1909 The Grand Army of the Republic, a national organization of Union veterans of the Civil War, decided to locate a community for its members east of the old sugar plantation, St. Cloud. The town, named St. Cloud, attracted new residents from nearly every state and many foreign countries. Within five years St. Cloud could boast of 4,000 residents, one of the largest G.A.R. posts in the country, the only national bank in the county, and an electric plant and telephone company. Although a majority of the homes were small-scaled frame structures, a number of residences were built of rusticated cement block produced in St. Cloud plants.

Trading heavily with county newcomers, Kissimmee businesses were rebuilt in brick. A road was built from Kissimmee through St. Cloud to Melbourne. The southern part of the county began to develop with the construction of a Florida East Coast Railroad branch line from New Smyrna to Okeechobee. Kenansville, named in honor of Henry Flagler's wife, developed near the older settlement of Whittier. Sawmill and turpentine operations also brought growth.

In 1917 a St. Cloud business district fire destroyed eighteen buildings along Pennsylvania Avenue. Rebuilding was slow. Even in Florida's 1920's boom years, construction in Osceola County never reached the level of other state areas. Several new town and subdivison developments were attempted, but none fulfilled their developers' hopes. With the end of the boom and the beginnings of the 1930's depression, private investment in the county was limited. Construction was essentially undertaken only in governmental projects. A fighter squadron was stationed in Kissimmee during the Second World War, but the county experienced little wartime development. The post-war era brought new growth as tourist courts and ranch-style residences were built in subdivisions.

Throughout the 1950's and 1960's, Osceola maintained an image as a retirement area and the center of Florida's cattle industry. Then, in the 1970's, the development of an immense Disney World complex in Osceola and Orange counties (preceded by transportation improvements, particularly the construction of the Florida Turnpike and Interstate 4) brought major investment and building activity. The region became a tourist mecca of international fame. Disney projects were constructed; motels and restaurants were built; service and construction employment expanded, and an unprecedented number of new homes and apartments were developed.

Although Osceola County continues a period of rapid growth (one of the highest in the country), the area has been able to maintain much of its earlier character. Many of the historic commercial blocks remain, as do the historic neighborhoods in both Kissimmeee and St. Cloud. Cattle and citrus productions continue as predominate land uses in all but the northwest quadrant of the county. Efforts undertaken as part of the county's centennial celebration focused upon this rich heritage and the local action required to preserve the best of Osceola's past for future generations.

A
12 S. Vernon Ave.
Kissimmee
Osceola County Courthouse, built in 1889 with F.C. Johnson as architect and George H. Frost as builder. Three-story Romanesque Revival style constructed from locally made red brick.

B
404 S. Vernon Ave.
Kissimmee
Captain Clay Johnson-Steffee House, built in 1894. Story-and-a-half Queen Anne style designed and contracted by Captain Johnson and son, Amory. Built by ship's carpenters using locally milled lumber. Design duplicated in Bearden House across from courthouse.

C
113 N. Stewart Ave.
Kissimmee
Kissimmee Valley Gazette-Jordon Norris Building, built in 1912. Two-story brick, flat-iron building fronting on three streets. First floor (glass storefronts between square brick columns) housed newspaper offices and printing operation. Upper floor (corner masonry quoins) designed for three apartments.

D
15 Church St.
Kissimmee
First Presbyterian Church, completed in April, 1886, under direction of Rev. Caleb Jones. Victorian Revival style with mixture of Gothic and Classical style detailing. Corner "stone" buttresses and "rose window" translated in wood.

E
215 N. Orlando Dr.
Kissimmee
Winn-Hunter House, built in 1900 and moved in 1920 from adjoining corner lot for construction of massive brick Makinson House. Outstanding porch-balcony detailing. Excellent restoration.

F
104 Monument St.
Kissimmee
I.M. Mabbette House-Lakeview Lodge, built in 1886. Structure enlarged and two-story balcony added when converted to hotel and rooming house in 1907.

G
1101 Massachusetts Avenue
St. Cloud
G.A.R. Memorial Hall, built in 1914 with M.V. Cheesman as architect and contractor. Auditorium on first floor and meetings rooms on second floor for Post No. 34, Grand Army of the Republic. Signed brick panels behind front entrance gates. Served as Masonic Hall. Preserved by the SCEEE Services Corp. in 1980's.

H
1200 New York Ave.
St. Cloud
First National Bank Building-Golden Age Club, built in 1910. Narrow, two-story buff brick structure. Originally two massive concrete columns at entrance. Only national bank in county when constructed. After 1918 headquarters for a variety of veteran and senior citizens organizations.

I
1004 New York Ave.
St. Cloud

St. Cloud Hotel, built in 1910. Three-story, masonry hotel with 72 rooms built for Massachusetts developer-investor Frederick Merrill. Originally double verandas wrapping around the front and north side. Center of early St. Cloud's social life.

J
915 New York Ave.
St. Cloud

St. Cloud Railroad Station, built in 1924. Dutch-bonded brick with masonry belt course and water table and bracketed broad roof overhang. Replaced earlier frame structure. Occupied in mid-1970's by VFW Post No. 3227.

K
1025 Tenth St.
St. Cloud

Livingstone Memorial Church-First United Methodist Church, built in 1911. Red brick church building with bell tower, twelve-inch thick walls, beautiful interior wood-work, and stained glass. Parsonage with shingled second story and matching brick first story, completed soon after church.

L
813 Tenth St.
St. Cloud

St. Luke and St. Peter's Episcopal Church, designed by F.J. Kinnard. Construction begun in 1892 for the English colony at Narcoossee and finished in 1898. Victorian Revival style with seventy-two foot tower. Building moved to St. Cloud in 1930 in numbered pieces. Nave and transcept enlarged when moved again. Beautiful wood interior details.

M
711 Lakeshore Blvd.
St. Cloud

Sam L. Lupfer-Davidson House, built in 1887 as one-story residence. Enlarged to two-and-a-half story shingled home by B.L. Steen in the 1920's. Enormous oak in front yard planted in 1888 by Mrs. Lupfer.

N
SR 523
Kenansville

Kenansville Bank, built in 1914. Symbol of prosperity when lumbering and railroad extension created town. fine brickwork in semi-circular arched openings, pilas-ters, and corbeled cornice. Forty-five degree corner entrance.

O
1964 Ham Brown Rd.
S.W. Kissimmee
Rd. 17-92

Lanier House, built in late 1890's. Dog-trot house built of local tank grade cypress. Exterior walls supported entirely by board and batten construction. Originally painted red, white, and blue.

P
Old Orlando Hwy.
North of Kissimmee

Tucker-Ivey Estate, built in 1917. Classical Revival style, two-story residence with Ionic columned portico. Originally over fifteen acres of grounds with golf course and tennis court. Center of area society life.

Q
Off Highway 441
St. Cloud

St. Cloud Plantation, East Bank, St. Cloud Canal, built in 1888 for Hamilton Disston. Sugar cane mill (most advanced for its time) and commissary. Except for two-story frame commissary, only brick foundations and granite slabs remain.

R
SR 523
Kenansville

Piney Woods Inn-Heartbreak Hotel, built in 1915 by the Phillips Brothers when Florida East Coast Railroad constructed through area. Later changed name after Elvis Presley's hit. Became south county landmark.

NOTES

TRAVEL NOTES

CITRUS

SUSAN TURNER, AIA, FLORIDA CENTRAL CHAPTER

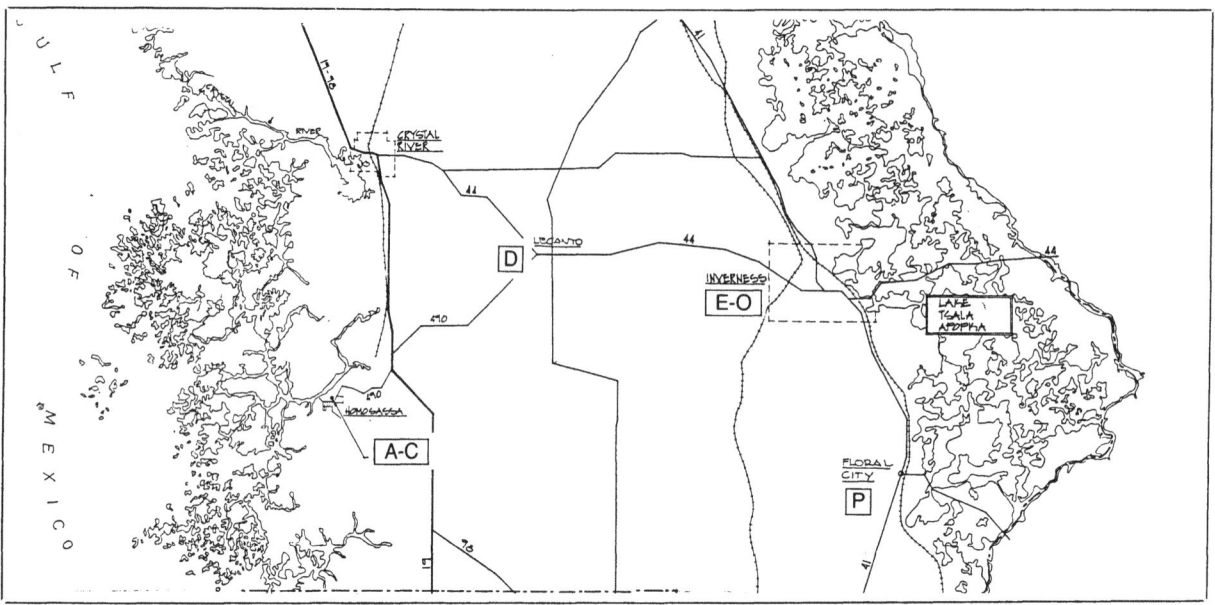

The settlement of Citrus County began in the early 1820's with Red Level as the first community. The first settler, William Turner, built his house, *Cedar Grove,* near this area in 1820. Settlements were sparse and skirmishes with the Indians frequent. After the outbreak of the Second Seminole War in neighboring Sumter County, several battles were fought in Citrus County along the Withlacoochee River. Fort Cooper, near Inverness, was erected in 1836 as part of a campaign to remove Indians from the Withlacoochee area. The Homosassa and Crystal River areas were settled at this time. The county's first post office was established in Crystal River in the 1850's.

One prominent early resident of Citrus County was David Levy Yulee, a member of Florida's first territorial legislature and part of the group that drafted Florida's constitution. After Florida attained statehood, he became the state's first U.S. senator. Yulee established a sugar and citrus plantation near Homosassa and in 1851 created the railroad from Cedar Key to Fernandina Beach. During the Civil War Yulee's plantation, which supplied sugar for Confederate troops, was burned.

Development increased in the Citrus County area after the Civil War. A.D. Tompkins founded Tompkinsville in 1868, a town later sold to a Jacksonville firm that changed the name to Inverness. Francis M. Dampier, who surveyed the town and became its first merchant, established a sawmill and built the first house in the county to be constructed of sawed lumber. Hernando was established in 1881 and Floral City in 1883. Mannfield, founded in 1884 and named for A.S. Mann, a state senator, became the county seat when Citrus County was established in 1887 and served as the county seat until 1891 when the government was moved to Inverness.

Citrus County had several successful industries during the late 1800's. Cedar trees were harvested and slats of cedar shipped to the Dixon Pencil Company in Crystal River to be manufactured into pencils. When natural resources were depleted, this part of the county became famous as a sportsman's paradise. In 1880 Grover Cleveland built a lodge in Homosassa. MacRae's Homosassa Inn and the Atlanta Fishing Club attracted fishermen. The area was visited and painted by Winslow Homer and George Innes. Sugar cane, vegetables, citrus, and Sea Island cotton were the major crops in the county. Between 1880 and 1890 many acres were planted with citrus. Although the freeze of 1894-1895 forced many growers to move farther south, the county still maintains a steady citrus crop. In 1889 phosphate was found in the county by Albertus Vogt. The wild speculation following the discovery eventually produced a stable industry which exists today.

In the mid-1880's the principle form of transportation was by boat on the Withlacoochee River to a railroad shipping point or to Yankeetown where products were put on boats bound for the Mississippi River. In 1884 the Orange State Canal was dug by the Florida Orange Canal and Transit Company to allow vessels to reach Floral City from the Withlacoochee River. Railroad lines extended into Citrus County and, by the 1890's, had replaced shipping as the major form of transportation. During the first ten years of the twentieth century, the first automobiles began to appear in the area. In 1909 the first paved road was built between Inverness and Dunnellon. In 1910 a hydro-electric dam was built at the mouth of the Withlacoochee River. Most of the county's towns had electricity by 1912. A lumber industry was developed around Inverness, and many new public buildings were constructed.

Architectural preservation occurs mostly through continued use. Many buildings are still serving their original purpose, some inhabited by original owners. The Citrus County Historical Society maintains a listing of the county's historic structures and Hampton Dunn, historian and author born in Citrus County, has written a county history. In the mid-1980's there were no organized architectural preservation programs despite Citrus County's abundant architectural resources worthy of preservation.

A

2½ miles west of
US 19-98 via
County Road 490A
Old Homosassa

Yulee Sugar Mill Ruins State Historic Site, built in 1849 on David Levy Yulee's plantation grounds. Constructed of limestone, nine-foot-square chimney and forty-foot-long structure housing boiler. Boiler, steam engine, and kettles brought by sailing vessel from New York. Partially restored with interpretive signs.

B

End of State Road 90-
Highway 490 at
Homosassa River
Old Homosassa

Dunn House-Homosassa Inn, built in 1882 as four-bedroom home of John F. Dunn, land agent credited with subdividing Homosassa. Wood frame two-story structure with porch on three sides of each floor, several additions. Converted to sportsman's lodge, Homosassa Inn, and visited by John Jacob Astor and Thomas Edison. In mid-1980's a small inn and restaurant.

C

Halls River Road
Old Homosassa

Atlanta Fishing Club, across Homosassa River from Yardarm Restaurant. Built in 1903 as club for sportsmen from Atlanta. Two-story wood frame house with Victorian Revival decorative gable ends, many alterations and additions.

D

State Road 44
Lecanto

Barnes House-Country Oaks Inn, built in 1911 as two-story wood frame structure, home of George Oscar Barnes (surrounding lands used by Barnes to raise sugar cane). Wide porch extending across the front and side of the first floor and connecting with out-building. Interior bead board paneling retained. In mid 1980's used as restaurant.

E

110 N. Apopka Ave.
Inverness

Citrus County Courthouse, built in 1911 with J.R. MacEachron-W.R. Biggers as architects and Read-Parker Construction Co. as builder. Modeled after Polk County courthouse and sited on small town square.

F

SE corner of
Main Street-US 41
and Pine Street
Inverness

Masonic Temple, built in 1910 with W.B. Talley as architect. Brick commercial building with stores on first floor offices on second floor, and Masonic lodge room on third floor. Neo-Classical details with round-arch entrance, rectangular wood window frames with keystones, and cast stone cornice.

G

109 N. Seminole Ave.
Inverness

Orange Hotel-Colonial Hotel-Crown Hotel. Orange Hotel built before 1900 by Frank M. Dampier as first store in Inverness, then moved and converted to hotel around 1900. In 1926 moved for second time and enlarged to present size, a three-story rambling wood frame structure. In mid 1980's a hotel with two restaurants.

H

SE corner of
Main St.-US 41 and
Osceola St.
Inverness

Inverness Women's Club, built in 1922 on site originally intended for the public library. Single-story wood frame structure. Club established in 1917.

I

N. Apopka Avenue
Inverness

Seaboard Air Line-Seaboard Coast Line Railroad Station, built in 1900. First railroad station in Inverness, wood frame structure with vertical board siding and a small bay window.

J

410 Tompkins St.
Inverness

R. O. Hicks House, built at turn of century. Wood frame one-story irregular octagonal house with highly pitched roof, small dormer window at front.

K

410 W. Main St.-
US 41
Inverness

Kelley House, built before 1910. Two-story wood frame structure, porch on first floor, porte-cochere and Palladian window in front gabled end. One of a series of three similar structures in neighborhood.

L

301 West Main St.-
US 41
Inverness

Scott House, built between 1900-1910. Single story Victorian Revival style frame residence characterized by long porch ending in an octagonal corner turret.

M

Corner of Bay St. and
Line St.
Inverness

Dampier House, built in 1880 by Francis Marion Dampier who is credited with surveying town and owning first store.

N

414 Lake Street
Inverness

Morrison House-Biance House, built in 1904. Two-story wood frame Victorian Revival style structure with porch extending across the front of first floor and curving to wrap around the side. House restored in 1985.

O

8480 Marvin St.
Floral City

Floral City United Methodist Church, constructed in 1876 with George Higgins as builder. Wood frame, gabled-roofed church with square bell tower vestibule at corner. Ony existing pioneer church in county.

P

North Museum Point
Off US 19 and
W. State Park St.
Crystal River

Crystal River Indian Mounds Museum and State Park. Pre-Columbian mound complex, about 500 B.C., used for civic and religious center, constructed of oyster shells. Now with museum-visitor's center and self-guided marked trail on site.

SUMTER

SUSAN TURNER, AIA, FLORIDA CENTRAL CHAPTER

Established in 1853 as Florida's twenty-ninth county, Sumter County was named for Gen. Thomas Sumter of Revolutionary War fame by settlers from Sumter, S.C. The county was very sparsely populated in the early 1850's since most settlement of the area had not begun until 1842, the official end of the Second Seminole War.

At the end of the Seminole Indian War, the Armed Occupation Act provided land grants which encouraged settlement, and Sumter County began to develop. Early population centers were Adamsville, Center Hill, Indian Wahoo, and Webster. Adamsville became the county seat, and the first courthouse was built of log construction. In 1858, the county seat was moved to Sumterville by popular vote and then moved three more times before Bushnell became the permanent county seat in 1911.

Sumter County was affected only slightly by the Civil War. Pro-secession residents joined the war effort by forming local militia to protect citizens and by providing cattle for the army. After the war, the Homestead Act of 1866 offered 80-acre farms to freed slaves and to whites loyal to the Union, but this encouraged only a few settlers.

Most of the early settlers farmed the land, raised citrus, and grazed cattle. Their crops and cattle were primarily for their own or local use before the arrival of the railroad. Supplies from Jacksonville were delivered by boat to Silver Springs and carried overland to Citrus County. The early settlers built one or two room houses of rough-hewn unpainted cypress or pine boards with detached kitchens. "Breezeway houses" usually had rooms opening off both sides of a long straight center hall that permitted a constant flow of air throughout the house. In 1857, Granville Bevill installed the first horse-powered grist mill near Shady Brook and in 1866 opened a mercantile business near Center Hill which sold supplies to farmers on credit.

In the 1880's railroad development brought new settlers and a method of exporting citrus and other produce. The present county seat, Bushnell, was established in 1885 as a stop on the railroad. It was named for J. W. Bushnell, a railroad surveyor, and was incorporated as a city in 1913. With the development of the railroad, citrus and farming industries expanded. Sumter County was among the leading vegetable producing counties in the country until 1926. The town of Coleman was settled in 1882 by farmers who wished to live near their farmland. The town developed rapidly and by 1923 was known as the "cabbage capital of the world." In 1925 its streets were paved and electric lights installed. D.W. Swicord built a hotel in Coleman in 1910 to serve businessmen who came to purchase crops. Each hotel room was equipped with its own phone as the town had become so prosperous that it owned its own telephone system. In the mid 1920's the Seaboard Air Line built a railroad line from Coleman to West Palm Beach. The town of Center Hill had prospered as a string bean farming area and boasted the county's only telegraph service.

Sumter County continued to develop as a major agricultural and cattle producing area until the 1930's depression. The area experienced some development from the real estate boom of the 1920's, including Moreland Park, north of Wildwood, developed by Joseph F. Moreland as the county's first planned subdivision with electric lights, city water, parks, and playgrounds.

Since the 1930's growth in Sumter County has been slow. The Florida turnpike and I-75, two major highway systems which meet in Wildwood, have done little to change the face of Wildwood or Sumter County. US 301 (which passes through Bushnell, Coleman, and Wildwood) has promoted little development. Today Sumter County is still a farming, cattle grazing, hunting, and fishing area.

Preservation in Sumter County exists through continued uses of historic structures, largely for their original function and often by descendants of original owners. The Sumter County Historical Society was formed in 1977 and has published a pictorial county history.

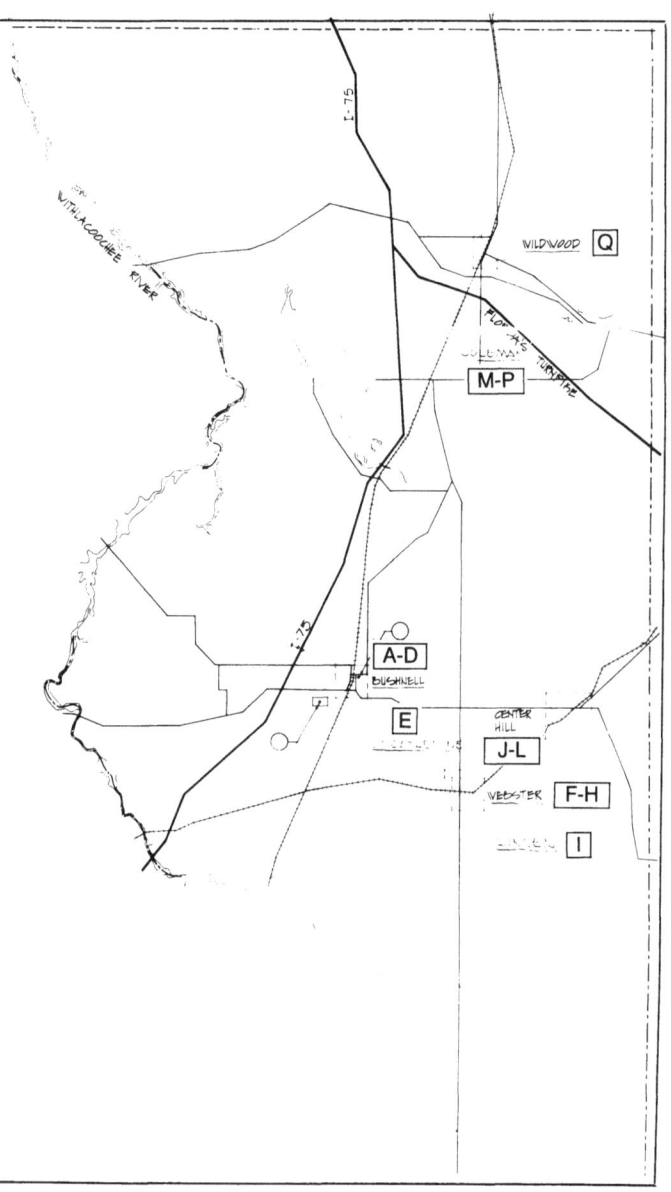

A
Florida St. and
Bushnell Plaza
Bushnell

Sumter County Courthouse, built in 1913-14 with James Nairn, builder. Three-story Neo-Classical Revival style with entry colonnade of Ionic columns flanked by a pair of towers with octagonal windows. Light-colored brick walls with decorative corbeling.

B
West Noble Ave.
Bushnell

Pierce Hotel-Beville House, built in 1895 by T. R. Pierce. Two-story wood frame structure with front porch on each floor and two-story octagonal bay at one side. Later home of Mrs. Anna L. Beville.

C
323 E. Noble Ave.
Bushnell

Bilby House. Victorian Revival style wood frame house with original stained glass in front windows. Tobacco barn in rear built of lumber shipped by barge.

D
End of CR 542
Bushnell

Towns House-Franklin House, built in 1905 as hotel in Lake Panasoffkee. Large wood-frame structure with Victorian Revival details. Building dismantled and moved by mule team to present site for reconstruction.

E
CR 738B
St. Catherine

St. Catherine United Methodist Church, built in 1913 on land given by the Fussell family. Wood-frame church with altar rail and other woodwork constructed by A.T.S. Atkins, an area pioneer. Corner bell-tower remodeled. One of few remaining structures of what was once a thriving town.

F
SE Third St.
Webster

United Methodist Parsonage, originally built as first Methodist Church in Sumter County on site of Stewart's Chapel, the first church in the county. Wood frame building with central bell-tower. In 1910 moved to Webster. Used in mid 1980's as parsonage.

G
11 E. First Ave.
Webster

Sumter County State Bank, built in 1900. Small brick storefront building with large single arched brick entrance leading to a wooden storefront which has been altered. Facade detailed with brick corbeling at cornice.

H
Corner NE Third Ave.
and NE Second St.
Webster

Wilbur Fussell House, built in 1910. Two-story wood house with porches supported by Doric columns across front of each floor. Three-sided bay window on first floor, second floor porch with balustrade, gable ends ornamented in shingle patterns. House surrounded by decorative iron fence.

I
CR 772B
Linden

Linden United Methodist Church. Wood frame structure built of heart pine with corner bell-tower and steeply pitched roof. Only remaining original church building in Linden.

NO PHOTO AVAILABLE
J
SR 48
Center Hill

Daniel Smith House, built in 1914 by Daniel Smith, descendant of Sumter County pioneer family. Two-story wood frame house with characteristics of Queen Anne style. Roof covering of pressed metal shingles, two prominent gables with a lunette window in each gable end and a window below, and curving porch extending across the front and side of the house.

K
Virginia Ave.
Center Hill

Center Hill Presbyterian Church, built in 1888 with volunteer labor and $600 worth of materials. First church in Center Hill. L-shaped building plan that originally had bell tower at foot of the "L." Now tower removed and relocated in front of building. Facade ornamented with shingle patterns.

NO PHOTO AVAILABLE
L
SR 48
Center Hill

Center Hill High School, built in 1925 as fourth high school in community. Stuccoed building in Mediterranean Revival style. Separate entries for boys and girls. Use as high school discontinued in 1929 when population decreased. In mid-1980's used as adult recreation center.

M
Corner Central Ave.
and Martin St.
Coleman

Coleman Baptist Chruch, constructed in 1908 by local citizens with C.A. Hooks of Oxford laying masonry and Ed Laws as carpenter. One of the few masonry churches in county. Simple rectangular plan and corner bell tower which was originaly capped with a steeply pitched roof of wooden shingles.

N
Corner Central Ave.
and Hubbs St.
Coleman

John Nicks House. Simple one-story pioneer house with vertical board siding, small vertical spindles at porch frieze matching spindles of porch handrail, and a roof originally shingled.

O
Corner Central Ave.
and Church St.
Coleman

Jim Caruthers House, built in 1910. Two-story wood frame house with wide L-shaped porch on first floor and decorative millwork in gable ends.

P
Highway 44A
Orange Home

Baker Homestead, built in 1896 by David Hume Baker, state senator. Two-story wood frame house wrapped with porches deorated with ornate millwork. Mansard roof, unusual for early Central Florida home.

Q
Barwick St.
Wildwood

Wildwood Presbyterian Church, built in 1884. Simple L-shaped wood frame building, typical of early Central Florida church buildings. Oldest Church building in county.

HERNANDO

REED BLACK, FLORIDA CENTRAL CHAPTER

Indians, Spanish explorers, and early settlers left little evidence of their presence in the Gulf Coast highlands section of West Central Florida. The Second Seminole War, 1835-1842, saw the first permanent impact of man with the construction of four wood palisade forts built by the United States Army. Roads built to enhance the movement of troops and the Armed Occupation Act (federal legislation encouraging homesteading on land formerly occupied by Seminole Indians) attracted settlers to the area. This aided in defeating the remaining Seminole Indians and encouraged economic development.

Development of the area continued until 1843 when Hernando County was subdivided from Alachua County. Hernando County took its name from Hernando de Soto, a sixteenth-century Spanish explorer who passed through the area.

Early settlers built wooden structures of logs or band sawn lumber, possibly similar to the Homestead House on Citrus Highway. Several larger plantation houses were also constructed, but details about their design and materials are sketchy. One of the largest circular sawmills in the state, constructed at the mouth of the Withlacoochee River, encouraged the timber industry and provided better building material for local construction. The keys to economic and architectural development were the 1885 building of a railway to Brooksville, the county seat of Hernando County, and the development of easier access to Tampa, a deep-water port. Agricultural and timber products and phosphate could quickly reach northern markets, and large quantities of brick and other building materials could be imported. The population growth resulting from the arrival of the railroad caused a subdivision of the original Hernando County in 1887. The state

legislature created Citrus County to the north and Pasco County to the south.

Early growth in Hernando County and its varied economic factors are reflected in local architecture. Residential housing developed as a simple frame vernacular of symmetrical forms and few details. Wealthier citizens (particularly successful citrus growers, business men, and professionals) built larger, more elaborate homes in the Victorian or Neo-Classical Revival styles. Frame packing houses and barns were constructed to support the agricultural industry. The railroad built passenger stations, depots, warehouses, and office buildings. A brick storefront business district began developing in Brooksville during the 1880's. However, fires in 1899, 1914, and 1917 destroyed most of these early structures. A monumental building that symbolized early area growth and prosperity, the Hernando County Courthouse, survived.

Two areas along Hernando County's coast developed differently from the agricultural inland areas. Aripeka grew into a fishing camp that played host to several famous sports figures and remained a favorite retreat for fishermen. Weeki Wachee Springs, the fifth largest spring in Florida and once a popular swimming hole, became a multi-million dollar mecca for tourists after World War II and also served as location of several movies.

At present Hernando County is one of Florida's less populated, more rural counties. However, the movement of population from south to central and north Florida is increasing development rapidly in areas around Weeki Wachee and Spring Hill. The mid-1980s are a critical time for preservation of natural and manmade environments in this county.

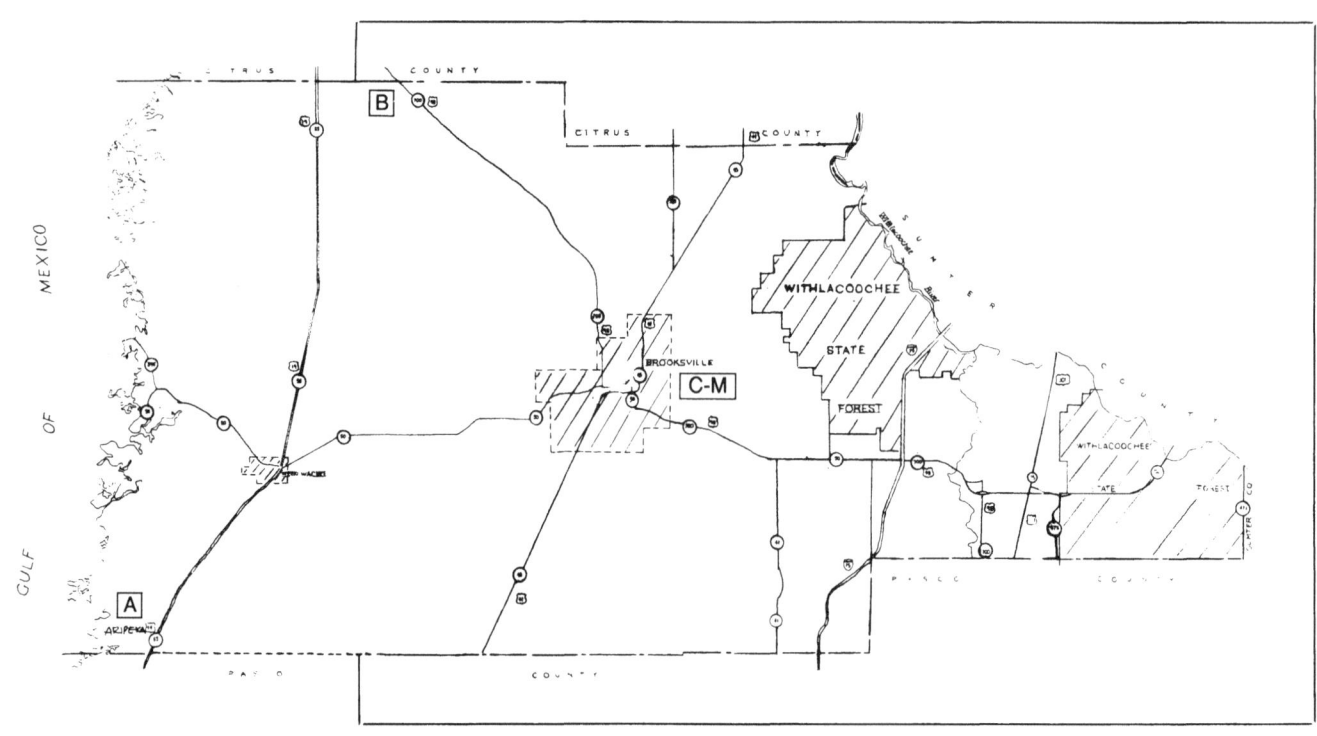

A
SR 595 at Hernando
County Line
Aripeka

General Store and Fish Camp, built in 1918. Small village consisting of a cabin, general store, house, and blacksmith shop. Only existing early fishing village in county.

B
One mile south of
Citrus County Line
Citrus Highway

Homestead House, date unknown. Farmstead with house, detached kitchen, and small barn. Similar to many homesteads built in North Florida.

C
48 Olive Street
Brooksville

Roer's House, built in 1880. Three-story wood frame structure with gable roof, decorative wood shingles and lattice work, and bay window with octagonal roof. Once lived in by William Sherman Jennings, governor of Florida.

D
235 Howel Avenue
Brooksville

Mackenzie House, built in 1880. Two-story wood frame house with gable roof. Two-story veranda with elaborate paling pattern in second floor balustrade.

E
7 Orange Avenue
Brooksville

Hale House, built in 1882 for John J. Hale, Hernando County pioneer Three-story wood frame structure with gable roof with dormers. Originally two-story veranda on front and back and a separate kitchen. Rear veranda and breezeway between house and kitchen now enclosed.

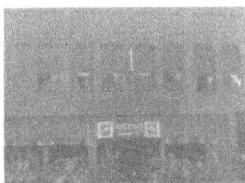

F
115 N. Main
Brooksville

Weeks Hardware, built in 1913. Typical mercantile architecture of period. Cast iron columns supporting a brick facade stuccoed in 1930. Second floor originally office space. Original cast iron columns, pressed metal ceiling, and freight elevator in interior. One of few survivors of downtown Brooksville fire.

G
1 Main Street
Brooksville

First National Bank Building, built in 1910. Originally two-story building with simple brick walls and flat arched window openings. In 1927 Classical Revival style additions of columns, pediment, and stucco. Previously used as bank and post office.

H
SE corner of US 41
and Main St
Brooksville

J. A. Jennings Building, built in 1915. Two-story brick mercantile building. Cast iron columns supporting brick facade, simply detailed windows, and a corbeled brick cornice. Canopy hanging from steel bars. Typical storefront building.

I
US 41
Brooksville

Hernando County Courthouse, built in 1913. Classical Revival style brick building with cast concrete details, massive Ionic columns, a symmetrical facade, latticed windows, elevated base, and a simple rectangular plan.

J
133 Brooksville Ave.
Brooksville

Coogler House, built in 1910. Two-story wood frame Greek Revival style structure with paired Ionic columns supporting pediment over two-story porch.

K
Sw corner of
Brooksville Ave and
Russel Street
Brooksville

Railroad Station, date unknown. One-story building with loading platform at one end, wide overhang supported on brackets, vertical board and batten siding, and post and beam construction.

L
600 West Jefferson
Brooksville

Stringer House-Heritage Museum, built 1850. Three-story Queen Anne style structure with four story tower over entry, two-story veranda, decorative balustrades, crown molding over windows, and stained glass. Restored as county historical museum.

M
US 41
Brooksville

Chinsegut Hill House, built for Col. Byrd Pearson. Greek Revival style two-story house framed with twelve-inch hewn cypress posts and beams, a gable roof, wood lapsiding, two-story veranda on all four sides supported on Doric columns. Oldest known building in the county.

NOTES

PASCO

REED BLACK, FLORIDA CENTRAL CHAPTER

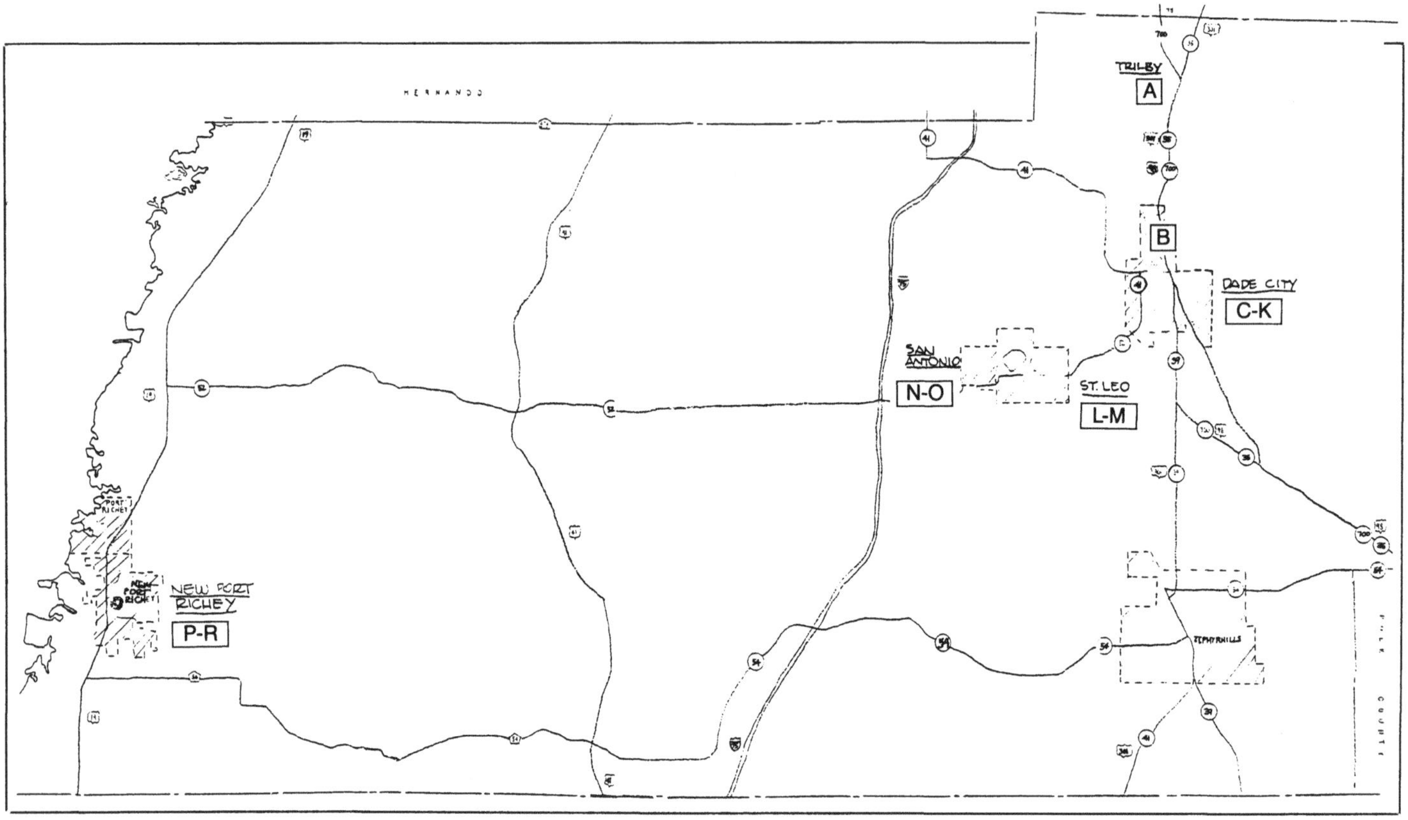

Pasco County's architectural history began in 1836, during the Second Seminole War, with the construction of the log palisade Ford Dade near present-day Dade City. This Indian war also resulted in the building and improving of roads and the passage of the Armed Occupation Act, the federal legislation which encouraged settlers to homestead on land formerly occupied by the Seminoles. Early buildings of these settlers were probably simple wood-frame structures in combinations of hewn logs or band-sawed lumber.

Little changed in this sparsely populated agricultural community until the mid 1880's when the Florida Southern Railroad arrived and stimulated development. After the arrival of the railroad, the Hernando County area which existed in 1887 was divided into three counties, one of which was Pasco County. Named for Samuel Pasco, speaker of the Florida House of Representatives, the county selected Dade City, a railroad town, as county seat.

Early residential construction in developing Dade City was in simple frame vernacular. Wealthier citizens, such as successful citrus growers, built more elaborate homes, many in Victorian or Classical Revival styles. Citrus growers also constructed packing houses and barns as the railroad built passenger stations and depots and the religious denomina- tions their churches, usually Victorian Revival styles. Examples of these early houses and churches remain on West Church Street, a historic district in Dade City. The Pasco County Courthouse, an impressive brick and marble building in Classical Revival style, was built as a symbol of the county's prosperity at the beginning of World War I.

The Florida Pioneer Musuem off US 301 north of Dade City has several early buildings that have been salvaged from around the county and moved to this museum site. Another fine architectural example is St. Leo Hall at St. Leo College near San Antonio. Begun in 1906 and completed in 1918, this was the first concrete block building in the county. Brother Anthony Poiger designed the structure and supervised the manufacture of the concrete blocks and building construction.

Pasco County's coastal area developed after World War I in a pattern distinct from the eastern agricultural regions. During the state's 1920's land boom, Port Richey and New Port Richey attracted many seasonal visitors and permanent residents who wanted to escape northern winters. With this development came Mediterranean Revival style architecture with asymmetrical plans, stucco walls, clay tile roofs, and vertical emphasis of a chimney or tower.

Today major growth in Pasco is occurring along US 19 as the urban sprawl of Pinellas County moves up the coast. Large housing developments and regional shopping centers are changing this once rural scale to urban and commercial streetscapes.

A
Corner of CR 575 and
Old Trilby Road
Trilby

Trilby United Methodist Church, built in 1898 by the
congregation. Simple Victorian Revival wood frame
structure, bevel-edged siding, central entry below bell
tower. Moved from original site near railroad tracks
about 1920, new additions to south and west.

B
U.S. 301
Dade City

Trilby Depot-Pioneer Florida Museum, built in 1925.
Moved from Trilby in 1976. One-story frame structure
with covered walks on either side. Typical of small town
Florida railroad station.

C
111 Edwinola Way
Dade City

Edwinola Inn, built in 1912. Two-story rusticated concrete block building with third story Mansard roof clad
with metal fish scale shingles, porches on first and
second floors. Originally an inn. In mid 1980s a social
and administration center for elderly housing.

D
103 West Meridian
Avenue
Dade City

Lock House, built in 1906. Two-story Dutch Colonial
Revival style wood frame house. Gambrel roof and
dormer. Unique casement windows with many panes.

E
Magnolia Avenue and
11th Street
Dade City

St. Mary's Episcopal Church, built in 1892. Wood frame
Victorian Revival with pointed windows, beveled siding,
wood roof trusses exposed on interior, choir loft and
altar as later additions. Moved from original site in
Pasadena, Florida in 1909.

F
North 12th and
Main Street
Dade City

Rodney B. Cox Elementary School, built in 1922 as
Dade City Grammar School. Two-story brick building
with U-shaped plan and elaborate white glazed terra
cotta details around windows and at entry which is
flanked by two towers.

G
10th Street and
Robinson
Dade City

Old County Jail, built 1892. Two-story brick structure
with two-story windows with flat arch and addition on
west side. Mid-1980's adapted use as law offices and
rental office space.

H
418 Church Street
Dade City

Grace Lock House, Church Street Historic District,
built 1890. Late Victorian Revival style one-story house
with stucco on wood frame, hip roof with gable dormer,
wide verandas, and decorative paling pattern in
balustrade.

I
516 West Church St.
Dade City

First Presbyterian Church, built in 1880. Victorian
Revival style with wood frame and siding, corner bell
tower and entry, pointed arch windows with intersecting
tracery, interior diagonal double beaded siding and
exposed roof trusses.

J
707 Church Street
Dade City

Miller House, built in 1890. Two-story wood frame
Victorian Revival style structure with beveled siding,
decorative barge board, and metal roof. One-story front
porch supported by turned columns with brackets.

K
US 301 and Meridian
Dade City

Pasco County Courthouse, built in 1914 with Artemus
Roberts as architect and builder. Two-story Beaux Arts
Classical Revival style brick structure with massive
columns supporting pediment, a symmetrical plan,
domed clock tower.

L
St. Leo College
Campus
St. Leo

St. Leo Hall, built in 1915, with Brother Anthony Poiger
as architect and builder. Four-story rusticated concrete
block building with decorative block over paired
windows, brackets supporting cornice, and a pierced
parapet.

M
St. Leo College
Campus
St. Leo

Abby Church, designed and built in 1936 by Brothers of
St. Leo. Romanesque Revival style brick structure with
carved Indiana sandstone around doors and windows
and at corners, a bell tower, crucifix plan, trussed roof,
arched door, and double arched windows.

N
219 North Main Street
San Antonio

Arnado House, built in 1885. Two-story wood frame
home with two-story veranda. Gable roof with central
dormer. Victorian Revival details include balustrade,
brackets, and decorative barge board.

O
Pampanic Street and
Jesse Jones Avenue
San Antonio

Old Brown House, built in 1907. Two-story Victorian
Neo-Classic Revival style wood frame structure with
shiplap siding and columns with Ionic capitals supporting roof of curved porch.

P
West Main and
Bank Street
New Port Richey

Hacienda Hotel, built in 1927 for a corporation of
Hollywood celebrities. Mediterranean Revival style
stucco building with U-shaped plan around courtyard,
arched doors, and corner towers with pyramidal roofs.

Q
South Boulevard and
Nebraska Avenue
New Port Richey

Thomas Meighan Theater, built in 1925 as a movie
house and named for a silent film star. Mediterranean
Revival style building with a large arched entry flanked
by twisted columns, stucco walls, red clay tile roof,
decorative cornice, and a central silver dome. Used as
live theater in mid 1980's.

R
South Boulevard and
Nebraska Avenue
New Port Richey

Pasco Building, built in 1921. Two-story commercial
building of Mediterranean Revival style with an octagonal corner tower, round transom windows, ceramic tile
and stucco, arched doorway, and clay tile shed roofs
over wooden brackets.

HILLSBOROUGH

KEITH SILAS, FLORIDA CENTRAL CHAPTER

Hillsborough County's history encompasses several of the earliest explorations of the New World. The sixteenth century Spanish explorers, Narvaez, DeSoto, and DeAviles, landed near Tampa Bay. The Timucuan Indians occupied the Gulf Coast of Florida when these first Europeans arrived; but they left little evidence of their sojourn after their extinction due to the introduction of new diseases and Spanish civilization. The area was not occupied by new settlers for two hundred years.

In the eighteenth century, the English explored this region during their Florida occupancy and gave the name "Hillsborough" to the river and the bay. When the United States acquired Florida in 1821, settlement of the Tampa Bay area increased. Fort Brooke was built near the mouth of the Hillsborough River to guard against the Seminoles, and the town of Tampa began to develop around the fortification. The Seminole Wars slowed settlement until their end in 1842 when pioneer families moved inland and farms began to produce cattle, oranges and strawberries.

Hillsborough County seceded from Alachua County in 1834 and established Tampa as the county seat. At that time Hillsborough County included areas which would be eight future counties. The first courthouse was built in Tampa in 1848. The city of Tampa was incorporated in 1849 and chartered in 1855.

When Henry Plant brought the railroad to Tampa Bay in 1884, prosperity came with it. The village of Itchepucksassa changed its name to Plant City and incorporated in 1884. Vincente Martinez Ybor founded his cigar industry in Tampa in 1886. Plant opened the magnificent Tampa Bay Hotel in 1891. During the Spanish-American War, Tampa became a debarkation point for soldiers bound for Cuba. This national service spurred further growth.

The Florida real estate boom of the 1920's brought rapid development to the county. The city of Temple Terrace was incorporated in 1925. Davis Island was developed, and the Gandy Bridge was built to connect Tampa to the Pinellas Peninsula. Little development occurred during the 1930's financial depression, but the Works Progress Administration did undertake several projects in the area, including the construction of Peter O. Knight Airport on Davis Island.

Hillsborough County has grown rapidly since World War II. High rise buildings were built in downtown Tampa, and the suburbs developed in areas that had been orange groves and pastures. The construction of interstate highways through the county and the building of causeways and bridges strengthened ties to the rest of the state. An award-winning regional airport stimulated national and international travel and tourism.

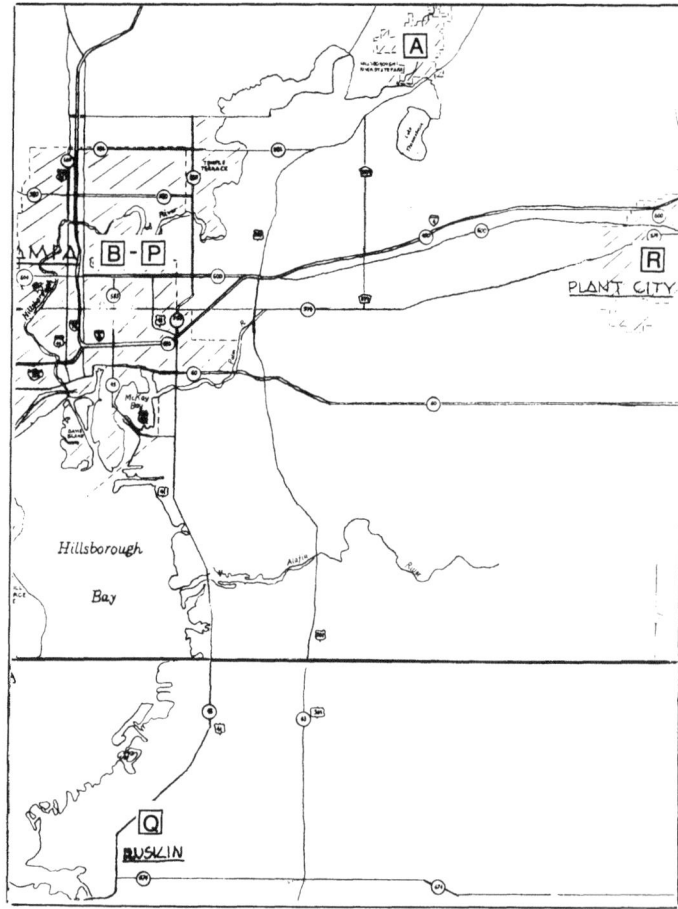

Urban renewal projects in the 1950's destroyed the unique character of Ybor City by leaving only a strip of commercial architecture along Seventh Avenue and a few isolated pockets of residential, commercial, and institutional buildings. In the 1970's preservation concern for this area and the rest of the county culminated in the chartering of the Historic Tampa Hillsborough County Preservation Board, an agency of the state. The Barrio Latino Commission, an agency of the city of Tampa, was formed to oversee the architectural and physical environment of Ybor City. Several private, non-profit groups, such as Tampa Preservation, Inc., and Tampa Historical Society, contribute to preservation of the area's architectural heritage. There are three National Register districts in Tampa. Plant City was selected as a National Trust for Historic Preservation Main Street City. Architectural preservation is now included in Hillsborough County's planning for the future.

A

U.S. 301
Zephyrhills

Fort Foster, (approximately nine miles south of Zephyrhills), Hillsborough River State Park, log stockade built in 1836 during the Second Seminole War. Supply depot and guard post for the Hillsborough River. Not in full service after 1849. Rebuilt in 1978. Interpretative program and guided tour for visitors.

B

401 W. Kennedy Blvd.
Tampa

Tampa Bay Hotel. Built in 1888-1891 by railroad tycoon Henry B. Plant to provide accommodations for patrons of his railroad line. One of finest examples of Moorish Revival architecture in United States. Designed by Plant's personal architect, J. A. Wood.

C

601 N. Nebraska Ave.
Tampa

Union Railroad Station, designed by J.F. Leitner and built by two railroads, Atlantic Coast Line and Seaboard Air Line. Italian Renaissance style of building with locally manufactured brick, terra cotta, and stone trim used. Owned and operated by Amtrak.

D

315 E. Kennedy Blvd.
Tampa

Tampa City Hall. Designed by the architectural firm of Bonfoey and Elliot and built in 1915. Successful blend of architectural styles. In continuous use by city, recently restored and rehabilitated.

E

709 Franklin St.
Tampa

Tampa Theatre Building. Excellent example of the "atmospheric theatre," designed by John Eberson, originator of this theater design concept. Italian and Spanish Renaissance Revival style. Recently restored, still operating as film theater.

F

811 N. Franklin St.
Tampa

S.H. Kress building. Designed by G.F. McKay, New York architect, and built in 1929. One of last major structures erected in Tampa before depression of 1930's. Four story Renaissance Revival brick building, significant use of glazed and polychrome terra cotta on two major facades.

G

508 E. Kennedy Blvd.
Tampa

Masonic Lodge, designed by M. Leo Elliot in 1928. Excellent example of boom-time Florida Mediterranean Revival style. Built of brick with glazed terra cotta trim. Exterior slightly altered but major interior spaces completely intact. Gilt and gesso coffered ceiling.

H

7th Avenue Area
Tampa

Ybor City Historic District, built between 1903 and 1917. Originally an independent city founded by Vincente Martinez Ybor. National Register district centering on 7th Avenue comprised primarily of brick storefront buildings. Local historic district covering larger area which includes cigar factories and workers' housing. Significant buildings: Ybor factory complex (now Ybor Square), El Pasaje Hotel, Ferlita Bakery (now a state historic museum), Circulo Cubano de Tampa, and El Centro Espanol.

I

Howard and Amenia Ave. Area
Tampa

West Tampa Historic District, built from turn of century to 1920. From 1895 to 1925 an independent city, founded as cigar manufacturing community. Largely intact with large brick factory buildings and many wood frame houses for workers.

J

2306 N. Howard Ave.
Tampa

El Centro Espanol de West Tampa. Built in 1912 to serve West Tampa members of El Centro Espanol, oldest of Tampa's Latin Clubs, after original building in Ybor City burned. Victorian Revival building with details in red and yellow brick, a gable and hip tile roof, a wrought iron balcony, arched windows, and a terra cotta and brick cornice.

K

Hillsborough Bay
Tampa

Hyde Park Historic District, constructed between 1886 and 1929 in area originally known as Spanish Town. Established as neighborhood and renamed by O.H. Platt in 1886. Steady development after opening of Tampa Bay Hotel and Lafayette Street, now Kennedy Blvd. bridge. Southern portion of district developed during 1920's boom. District notable for variety of architectural styles, including many bungalows.

L

349 Plant Avenue
Tampa

Anderson-Frank House. Built in 1898 for James B. Anderson. Impressive brick structure designed by Francis J. Kennard, architect.

M

802 S. Delaware Ave.
Tampa

Himes House, built in 1911 for James F. Himes, Tampa lawyer. Symmetrical massing, stone and brick detailing, and Palladian dormer window.

N

304 S. Plant Ave
Tampa

Hutcheson House, built in 1908. Second Empire style. Adapted for use as office building by Tampa Preservation, Inc.

O

716 Newport Ave.
Tampa

Leiman House, designed by M. Leo Elliot, architect, and built for Henry Leiman in 1916. Excellent example of Prairie School style.

P

6823 S. DeSoto St.
Tampa

Johnson-Wolfe House, (Port Tampa). Built in 1885 with a flat roof, a second story balcony, and traces of Latin influence in the ornamentation. Altered in 1893 with the removal of the balcony and the addition of a porch and a hipped roof with cross gable.

PINELLAS

SUSAN TURNER, AIA, FLORIDA CENTRAL CHAPTER

Pinellas County, the only county on the Florida peninsula to occupy its own sub-peninsula, derived its name from the Spanish "Punta Pinal" meaning Point of Pines. The area was discovered in 1528 by Panfilo de Narvaez while he was searching for Apalachen, a mythical golden city. When the Spanish found that the inhabitants (later known as the Timucuan Indians) had no gold, they searched elsewhere. The peninsula's Indian population had deserted the area by the time of the Seminole Indian Wars. Fort Harrison was established in the area which is now Clearwater but, since there were no battles in the region, was abandoned within six months.

The first permanent settler to enter the county was Count Odet Philippe, a former surgeon general of the French Navy under Napoleon Bonaparte. He brought his family to the area in 1823 and introduced citrus by planting a small grove. The Armed Occupation Act of 1842 had encouraged settlement by offering land grants but had attracted little interest in this area. By the time of the Civil War, only fifty families lived in the county. In 1859 the first post office was established in Clearwater. Dunedin beame the first trading post.

Major development began in 1882 when Hamilton Disston, a Philadelphia land speculator, bought four million acres of Florida land. Disston platted the town of Tarpon Springs and several years later Disston City (now Gulfport). In 1888 the peninsula was made accessible by railroad. Peter Demens, a native of Russia, created the Orange Belt Railroad Company which began in Sanford and terminated in Pinellas County. St. Petersburg was developed as the terminus of the railroad as a joint venture between Demens and Gen. John C. Williams who owned much of the land which is now St. Petersburg. The city was named after Demen's Russian native city, St. Petersburg. The first hotel erected, the Detroit, was named after William's native city.

In 1885 a report by Dr. W. C. Van Bibber to the American Medical Society stated that the peninsula was "the healthiest spot on earth" and set the stage for the development of the tourist industry. The citrus industry flourished in the northern part of the county, and the sponge industry began to develop in Tarpon Springs with John K. Cheyney establishing the Anclote and Rock Island Sponge Company in 1890.

During the first years of the Twentieth Century, rapid growth and changes occurred when electricity, telephones, and automobiles were introduced to Pinellas County. In 1904 the Peninsula Company established telephone operations in Clearwater, Tarpon Springs, and St. Petersburg. F. A. Davis, a Philadelphia entrepreneur, brought electric service to St. Petersburg in 1897 and opened an electric street car line in 1904. An attempt to make St. Petersburg a deep water port proved unsuccessful when Henry B. Plant purchased the Orange Belt Railroad and prohibited St. Petersburg from competing with the port of Tampa. Plant aided the development of Clearwater by building the Belleview Biltmore Hotel at a railroad stop near that city.

Pinellas County was officially created in 1911 when it seceded from Hillsborough County because of problems in obtaining services, and Clearwater was established as the county seat. The first courthouse, a two-story wood frame structure, was built in 1912.

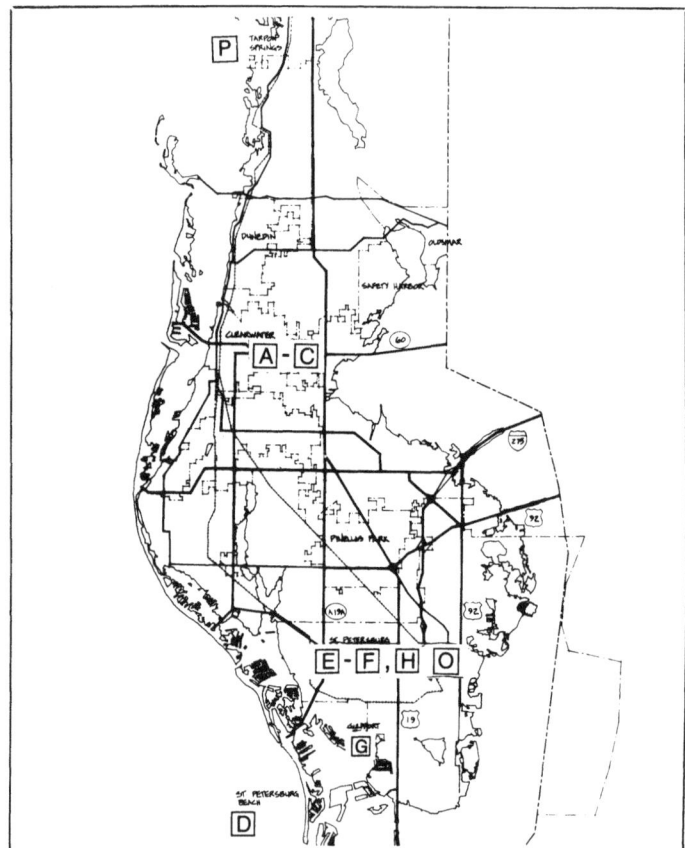

The building boom of the 1920's brought a period of wild speculation to the county with many investors developing large subdivisions, commercial areas, and hotels. In 1924 the Gandy Bridge, connecting St. Petersburg with Tampa, was completed in the same year ferries began carrying cars and passengers from the southern tip of the county to Manatee County. In St. Petersburg most property was available for development until 1905 when the City Council purchased the majority of downtown land fronting on the bay and preserved the city's waterfront.

After World War II, Pinellas County's tourist industry thrived. Light industry also came to the area in the 1950's. Several large electronics-aerospace firms opened. Agriculture began to decline as light industry and urban construction developed. In 1954 the Sunshine Skyway Bridge replaced ferry service to the south. In the 1960's the railroad's prominent role in county growth ended. Interstates, I-75 extending east to west and I-275 north to south, aided development but destroyed many acres of property.

Today Pinellas County is supported primarily by tourism and light industry. St. Petersburg and Clearwater have developed into metropolitan areas. Even though development consumed many county landmarks, much of the county's architectural resources survive. Many individual structures have been restored or adapted for continued use, and St. Petersburg has continued to preserve its waterfront park land. Pinellas County retains a rich architectural heritage worthy of preservation.

A
650 Cleveland St.
Clearwater

Cleveland Street Post Office, built in 1932 with Theodore H. Skinner as architect and Walt and Sinclair of Florida, Inc., as builder. Mediterranean Revival style structure representative of 1929-1939 federal public works program which reflected regional design influence and commissioned local professionals and industries.

B
700 Orange Ave.
Clearwater

Donald Roebling Mansion, "Spottis Woode," built in 1929 with Roy W. Wakeling as architect, A.D. Taylor as landscape architect, and John Phillipoff as builder. Residence and workshop of Donald Roebling (1908-1958), inventor, and local philanthropist and descendant of one of America's most important engineering families. Tudor Revival style structure containing carved likenesses of the building's designers and craftsmen on staircase newel posts. Estate subdivided, only mansion remaining.

C
Bellair Section
Clearwater

Belleview-Biltmore Hotel (end of Detroit Street at the bay), built in 1896 with Francis J. Kennard as architect and Michael J. Miller as builder for Henry B. Plant as part of his railroad and hotel system. In 1919 sold to Biltmore Corp. and operated as a winter season hotel since then except for 1943-1944 when building leased for auxiliary army barracks. Largest wood frame building in the state. Shingle Style characteristics with moderately pitched roof with intersecting gables, broad verandas, and clear division of stories.

D
3400 Gulf Blvd.
St. Petersburg Beach

Don Ce Sar Hotel, built in 1928 as conceived by Thomas J. Rowe, developer, at height of Florida land boom with Henry Dupont, architect. Mediterranean Revival style luxury resort hotel constructed of Belgian concrete and stucco, painted pink and called "Pink Palace." Housed many famous guests including F. Scott Fitzgerald, Clarence Darrow, Babe Ruth, Lou Gehrig, Faith Baldwin, Dr. Walter Mayo, and New York's Macy family. Restored in 1973.

E
510 Park St. North
St. Petersburg

Casa Coe Da Sol-Williams House, built in 1931 with Addison Mizner as architect and Oscar J. Steinert as builder. Designed as winter residence for the Williams family of the Cincinnati-based Western Southern Life Insurance Co. Mediterranean Revival style building featuring many products from Mizner Industries. Last building designed by Mizner to be built and only Mizner building on Florida's West Coast.

F
501 Park Street North
St. Petersburg

Jungle Country Club-Florida Military Academy, built in 1925 with Henry Taylor as architect for Walter Fuller who originally developed and operated the project for four years as the Jungle Country Club Hotel, adjacent to the Jungle Country Club Golf Course. Mediterranean Revival style building adapted for use as an educational facility.

G
1401 61st St. South
Gulfport

Hotel Roylat-Stetson University Law School, built in 1925 with Paul Reed as architect for Jack Taylor, the developer credited with the development of the Pasadena section of St. Petersburg, who named the hotel by combining letters in his last name. Mediterranean Revival style structure that includes materials imported from around the world including a reproduction of El Greco's studio fireplace in the lounge and a reproduction of Seville's octagonal tower, "Torro Del Oro."

H
3747 34th St., South
St. Petersburg

St. Bartholomew's Episcopal Church, built in 1887 of pine by the newly organized congregation on a donated acre of land. Oldest church in Pinellas County. Original building enlarged five times and moved to new site in 1970.

I
SW corner of
First Avenue North
and Fourth St. North
St. Petersburg

United States Post Office-Open-Air Post Office, built 1916-1917 with George W. Stuart as architect, M.C. Holliday as builder, and Roy S. Hanna, postmaster. Renaissance Revival style structure designed as open loggia on three sides to meet demands of Florida's climate and of the public for access to a post office.

J
405 Central Avenue
St. Petersburg

Snell Building-Snell Arcade, built in 1925 with Krehnel and Elliott as architect, C. Perry Snell as developer and designer, and E.B. Rang as builder. Mediterranean Revival style commercial building which was praised in 1926 as "the most artistic building in Florida." Arcade, originally filled with statues and building tiles collected in Europe by Snell, connecting building to southern entrance of Open Air Office. Structure restored in 1983.

K
515 Fourth St., South
St. Petersburg

St. Mary's Roman Catholic Church, built in 1925 with Henry L. Taylor as architect. Romanesque Revival style. Public Comfort Station at NE corner of Second Ave. and Bayshore Drive North, St. Petersburg, small Romanesque Revival Style building which resembles St. Mary's, also designed by Taylor.

L
300 Fifth St. North
St. Petersburg

Mirror Lake Public Library, built in 1915 with Henry Whitfield as Carnegie Fund architect and Walter C. Henry as builder with a donation of $17,500 from the Carnegie Corporation. Neo-Classical structure, first public library in St. Petersburg and only one of the ten Carnegie-funded libraries in Florida which still retains original facades.

M
501 Beach Drive
St. Petersburg

Vinoy Park Hotel, built in 1925 with Henry L. Taylor as architect and George A. Miller as builder and developed by Aymer Vinoy Laughner as a luxury resort hotel, one of St. Petersburg's earliest and largest. Mediterranean Revival style with an exterior of stucco over hollow tile and an interior including large dining and ballroom spaces, cypress ceiling beams, and murals.

N
375 Brightwaters
Blvd. Northeast
St. Petersburg

Snell Residence, build in 1928 as residence for C. Perry Snell, whose career in real estate resulted in development of more St. Petersburg property than any other person or group, with the owner as designer and Maynard Welch as builder. Mediterranean Revival style.

O
2505 Fifth Ave. North
St. Petersburg

St. Petersburg High School, built in 1926 through the efforts of Capt. George Lynch, superintendent of public schools, with William B. Ittner as architect. Mediterranean Revival style structure, known as "the million dollar high school."

P
Tarpon Springs

Tarpon Springs Sponge Dock Exchange District (from US 19A west along Anclote River, southeast along Tarpon Bayou, and east on Park St. to US 19 A), built from 1890 to 1896.

POLK

ROBERT RAY, AIA, FLORIDA CENTRAL CHAPTER

D During the sixteenth century the Spanish, who introduced citrus to Florida, established small missions in the area now known as Polk County. This section of Florida remained wilderness with only a few settlers until forts were built during the Seminole Wars. Fort Meade, built on the banks of the Peace River in 1849, provided security for a trading post. A settlement of planters and their slaves developed around the site of Fort Blount in 1851. (The town was named Bartow in 1867 after a Confederate officer, General Francis Bartow.) When Indian wars ended, the forts were gradually abandoned. Small log cabin homesteads and farms were built in the wilderness, and small settlements grew around these and developed into communities.

In 1861 Polk County was named for President James Knox Polk, the first president to hold office after Florida became a state. In 1867 Bartow was named the county seat after other locations proved unsatisfactory. A wood frame weather board courthouse was built for $3,800 to replace several earlier log structures. During these years small settlements developed around one-room schools, churches, and stores. A real estate boom occurred in Polk County after 1883 when H. B. Plant built the railroad from Tampa to Kissimmee. Towns developed along the line, and communities too distant from the track dwindled in population. Railroad depots handling passengers and citrus cargo became focal points of towns. As the tourist and citrus industries expanded, elaborate Mediterranean Revival style masonry buildings were constructed.

Phosphate was discovered in Polk County in 1894 and, with the help of the railroads, the region soon led the nation in phosphate production. During the early 1900's, stimulated by land and population booms, cities were planned and roads built and electrical and telephone service installed. From 1900 to the 1930's depression, the county experienced tremendous growth. City planners took advantage of the natural beauty in Central Florida and created promenades and parks surrounding the many lakes found within the communities. Munn Park around Mirror Lake in downtown Lakeland remains a testament to the foresight of early developers such as Abraham G. Munn, who helped plan much of present-day Lakeland's center in 1884. The planning of Auburndale, Winter Haven, Haines City, Davenport, and Lake Alfred soon followed. Lake Wales, located on the highest point of land in peninsular Florida, was planned as a model city in 1911, one year before the railroad came to that area.

By 1926 seven hundred miles of roads were built connecting communities. During this time, paved streets, municipal sewage systems, fire and police protection, and newspapers became common. Wealthy citizens built substantial homes which still stand. Large Classical Revival mansions, Mediterranean Revival villas, Victorian Revival houses, and many bungalows remain in Central Florida cities. Specific types of

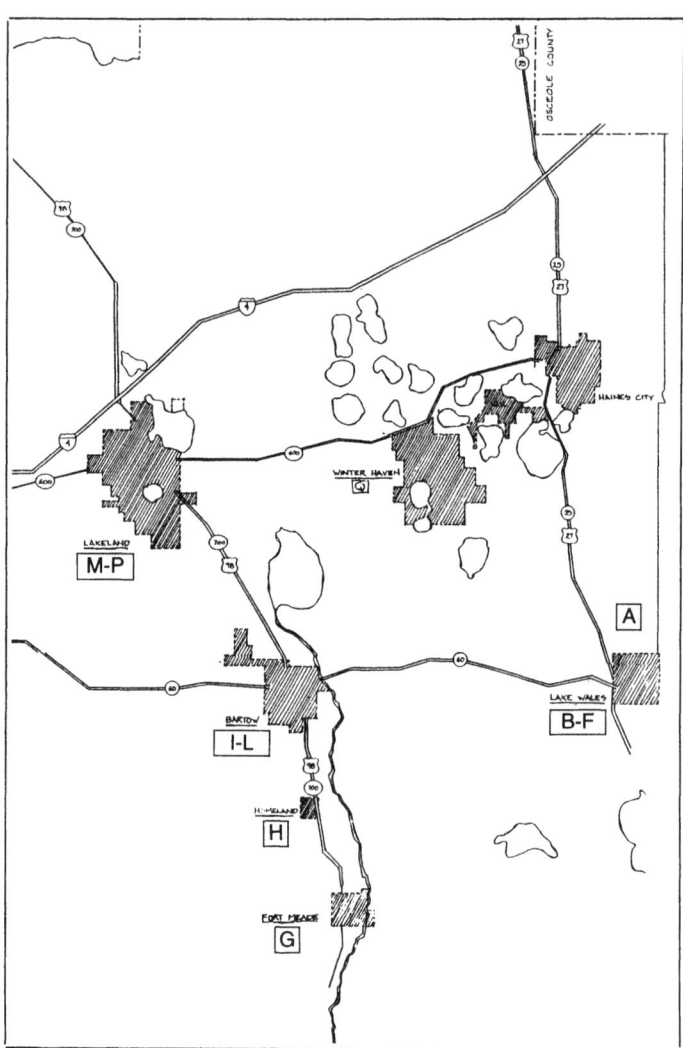

buildings were associated with specific styles. Typically, multi-story hotels, railroad stations, and early movie theaters were designed with Mediterranean Revival elements to inspire vacation or entertainment moods. Banks, government buildings, churches, schools and academies were usually Classical Revival in style to symbolize strength and integrity. The present Classical Revival county courthouse in Bartow was built in 1909 with wings added in 1926 to make the large building more impressive.

Probably the most internationally important architecture in Florida is the portion of the Florida Southern College campus, eight buildings and covered esplanades, designed by Frank Lloyd Wright during an extended period from the mid 1930's to the mid 1950's. These buildings by the American architectural genius, his largest collection in one location, are focal points for Florida architectural tours. The campus has continued to grow with buildings designed by other well-known architects, including one of Wright's students.

A

Tower Boulevard
Lake Wales

Bok Tower and Mountain Lake Sanctuary, 2 miles north of Lake Wales. Developed in 1929 by Edward Bok as wildlife sanctuary for public with Milton B. Medary as architect, Horace H. Burrell and Son as builder, and Frederick Law Olmstead, Jr. as landscape architect. Located on 130 acres at top of Iron Mountain, highest point of land on peninsular Florida, with focal point of 205 foot high singing tower with 53 bell carrillon.

B

First Street
Lake Wales

Hotel Walesbilt, between Park Ave. and Stuart Ave., built in 1912. Mediterranean Revival style with tall arched windows, two-story lobby, ornate mezzanine handrails, interior shopping arcade from Park Ave. to Stuart Ave., and ornamented parapet.

C

Park Av. to Stuart Av.
Bet. 1st & 2nd St.
Lake Wales

Rhodesbilt Arcade, built in 1920s. Open-air, two-story shopping arcade with entrance under ornate brick facade and cast iron canopy and a skylight running length of the building to provide light and ventilation. Second level containing office space with perimeter balconies and bridges.

D

Central Ave. & 4th St.
Lake Wales

Central Avenue Baptist Church, built in 1923. Classical Revival building with Greek cross plan, dome at octagonal crossing, classical pediments and Ionic columns marking entry, and Palladian-style stained glass windows.

E

325 S. Scenic Hwy.
Lake Wales

Lake Wales Museum-The Depot, built as a passenger station by the Atlantic Coast Line Railroad in 1928. Mediterranean Revival style structure with pink stucco and red tile roof, a symbol of post-boom era in Lake Wales. Opened as musuem in 1976. A historical resource center for the area.

F

Central Avenue
Lake Wales

Lake Wales City Hall. Mediterranean Revival style two-story brick building with cast-stone decorative quoining, lintels, keystones, frieze, three brick arches at entry, and red tile roof.

G

East Broadway
Fort Meade

Christ Episcopal Church, built in 1899 with J. H. Weddell as architect and Thomas A. Atkins as builder. One-room rectangular Victorian Revival style wood-frame building with pointed arch windows and three-story bell tower. Probably the oldest church building in Polk County.

H

On the Green
Homeland

Homeland School, built in 1855. Oldest public building in Polk County, used as school until 1956. Converted to workshop. Notable rural town architecture of small church and houses surrounding building in center of town.

I

1075 Mann Road
Bartow

Conrad Schuck House, construction begun in 1925 with Conrad Schuck as architect-builder. Unique 24-room country villa. Two-story house with dormers and basement. Concrete workmanship accented by medium size aggregate at surface, inset colored tiles, colored glass, and curving forms. Extensive lawn and garden with concrete-lined ponds and bridges.

J

1100 blk. S. Broadway
Bartow

South Florida Military College, built in 1895 as one of several buildings housing pioneer education programs established by Major General McInver Law. Two-story wood frame building with two-story bay on north side.

K

590 E. Stanford St.
Bartow

Benjamin Franklin Holland House, "The Gables," designed and built in 1895 by E. R. Wharton. Shingle style house. Boyhood home of Sen. Spessard L. Holland whose father, Benjamin F. Holland, established the first abstract company in the county and worked in citrus culture.

L

Main St. & Broadway
Bartow

Polk County Courthouse, built in 1909 by Mutual Construction Co. of Louisville, KY, with identical east and west wings added in 1926. Classical Revival style with Corinthian columns at north and south porticos and central dome-rotunda.

M

S. Massachusetts Ave.
Lakeland

Lakeland City Hall. Mediterranean Revival style with red tile roofs, tower, stucco exterior, and ornate entrance.

N

McDonald Street
Lakeland

Florida Southern College Architectural District, Frank Lloyd Wright buildings, Florida Southern College. Eight campus buildings and covered esplanades constructed between 1938 to 1955. Largest concentration of buildings designed by Frank Lloyd Wright. Site plan reflects Wright's planning concepts. Annie Pfieffer Chapel, 1938-1941 (building illustrated).

O

West of Mirror Lake
Lakeland

Munn Park Historic District-Frances Langford Promenade. District of commercial and public buildings with focal point of Mirror Lake which is surrounded by a sidewalk promenade named after Frances Langford, actress and Lakeland native. Grand staircases descending from downtown to promenade over bathhouses and Corinthian columnns constructed to frame a downtown and lake view also part of design.

DE SOTO

RICHARD GARFINKEL, AIA, FLORIDA GULF CHAPTER

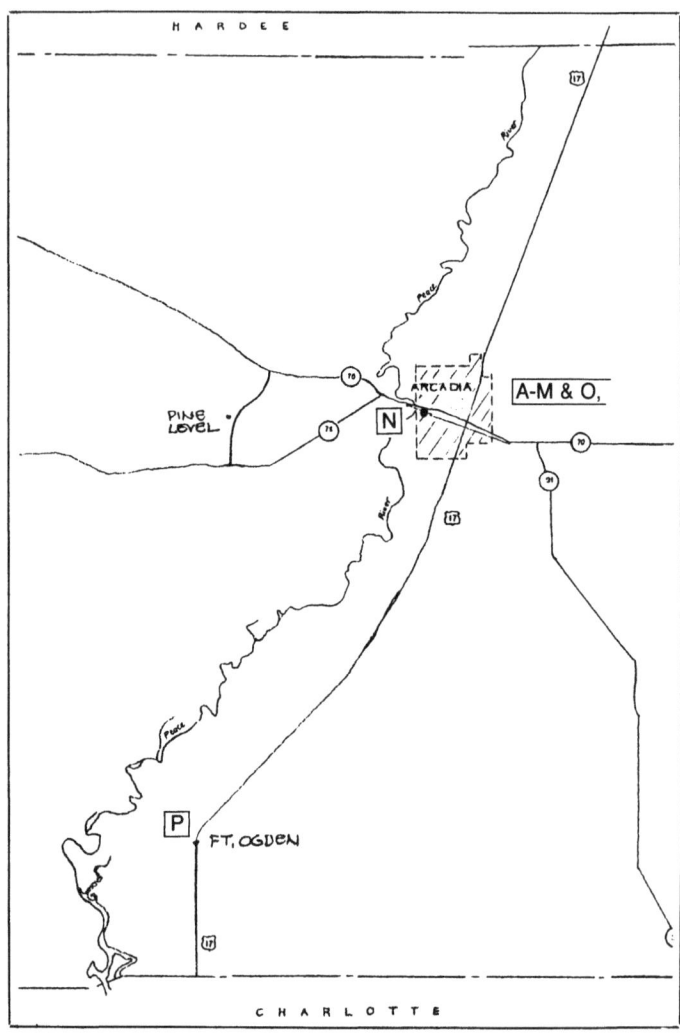

Even though the county was named for Spanish explorer Hernando de Soto, it is doubtful that sixteenth-century expeditions reached inland as far as De Soto County. Prehistorically, the area fell within the sphere of settlement of the Calusa Indians from Charlotte Harbor. However, it was not until the mid-nineteenth century, when the "Rio de Paz" served as the boundary of Seminole Indian lands, that human inhabitants came to stay in this region.

The Seminole Wars brought soldiers and surveyors, and the Armed Occupation Act of 1842 brought permanent settlers. Ft. Ogden, the area's oldest community, developed around the 1840's site of a Second Seminole War army post, Camp Ogden. Settlements spread to the land adjacent to the Peace River, and small communities were started throughout the river valley and adjacent prairie.

These communities became part of Manatee County in 1855 with the partition of Hillsborough County. Rough hewn timber and log structures served the needs of the frontier population when the county seat was moved to Pine Level in 1866. Across the river, a trading post at "Tater Hill Bluff" grew into the community of Arcadia where a post office was established in 1884.

A construction boom in the late 1880's was directly spurred by the coming of the railroad and the opening of a sawmill in 1886. Shifting population again caused a county split. De Soto County was created in 1887 from Manatee. Arcadia became the county seat in 1888, offering the new county both a railroad and a new courthouse. Pine Level, once a thriving community, gradually disappeared leaving only the United Methodist Church and a few houses a hundred years later.

The discovery of phosphate in the river added mining to cattle, timber, and citrus industries as the county's economic base even though range wars raged throughout the 1890's. Religious congregations built the county's first significant structures in frame Victorian Revival style.

The first masonry structures appeared in the 1890's, but frame construction dominated until the Great Fire of 1905 destroyed Arcadia's business district. Laws were then passed limiting downtown construction to masonry. Brick and decorative cast concrete block, such as "Miracle Pressed Stone," served as the basic material in the massive rebuilding that followed the fire. Concurrently, the areas surrounding the downtown expanded with a multitude of massive frame revival style residences. Renewed civic pride and economic growth spurred this boom which culminated with the construction of the new courthouse in 1912.

World War I slowed economic growth and brought Carlstrom and Dorr Airfields to the county. Used as training facilities for both World Wars, Carlstrom now serves as G. Pierce Wood Memorial Hospital and Dorr is the De Soto Correctional Institute.

The 1920's brought the Florida land boom, Mediterranean Revival architecture, and the partition of De Soto County in 1921. Four counties, including Hardee, Highlands, Glades, and Charlotte, were severed from De Soto as growing population again required localized governments. A severe hurricane in 1928 caused extensive damage to the agricultural business of the county only to be followed in 1929 by an infestation of the Mediterranean fruit fly and the stock market crash. The combined effect stopped development for over thirty years. However, the Arcadia Rodeo, established in 1929, remains the area's largest attraction.

Extremely slow but steady growth in population and local industry (cattle, citrus, and phosphate) has helped preserve both the physical and environmental quality of the area. A growing awareness of the significance of the county's historic built environment seems to insure that De Soto County's architectural legacy will survive.

A
31 N. Polk Ave.
Arcadia

First Baptist Church, built in 1907 with Francis Kennard as architect and Peyton Read as builder. Romanesque Revival style brick structure, one of several major buildings constructed of masonry following fire of 1905. Currently owned by the city and leased to Heritage Baptist Church.

B
121 W. Hickory St.
Arcadia

City Hall, built in 1926 with Ralph Cannon, builder. Mediterranean Revival style structure with stucco finish, a symbol of civic prosperity.

C
101 E. Oak St.
Arcadia

De Soto County Courthouse, built in 1913 with Bonfoey and Elliot of Tampa as architects and Read-Parker Co. as builder. Masonry Neo-Classical Revival style, restored as a Bicentennial project. Arcadia's most important building, a symbol of county growth that cemented Arcadia's claim to the county seat.

D
101 S. De Soto Ave.
Arcadia

Atlantic Coastline Railroad Depot, built from 1914-1919. Brick masonry building which occupied a significant location in community that once had four rail lines. Acquired by city of Arcadia to prevent demolition. Scheduled for sale and restoration by private enterprise in mid 1980's.

E
10-14 N. De Soto Ave.
Arcadia

J. L. Jones Building, constructed in 1926 by J. L. Jones who founded the De Soto Abstract Company, Arcadia's oldest business, in 1889 and later served as mayor when the city was incorporated. Brick masonry commercial building.

F
17 S. De Soto Ave.
Arcadia

Chesterfield Smith House, built in 1892. Wood frame building, one of the oldest in Arcadia. Former residence of Chesterfield Smith who served as Arcadia mayor and the American Bar Association president.

G
201 E. Oak Street
Arcadia

Courthouse Annex, built in 1909 as residence for George R. Parker. Queen Anne style structure with wood frame and novelty siding.

H
102-112 W. Oak St.
Arcadia

J. J. Heard Opera House Block, built in 1906 after downtown fire with Francis J. Kennard as architect. Masonry construction of Miracle Pressed Stone rusticated block. Second floor opera house which was later Arcadia's first movie theater. Variety of stores in building including department store owned by family of Gen. James Dozier.

I
101-115 W. Oak St.
Arcadia

The Arcade-Koch Building, built in 1927 for Simon Rosin to house Arcadia's post office and to use for commercial purposes. Mediterranean Revival style with intricate cast stucco ornament. Final major building of boom period.

J
2-8 W. Oak St.
Arcadia

Daniel T. Carlton Block, built in 1905, one of three business district buildings to survive 1905 fire. Masonry vernacular with Italianate Revival style overtones.

K
10 W. Oak St.
Arcadia

William H. Seward Building, built in 1900 with J. A. Crist as builder. Brick structure, one of first masonry buildings in Arcadia and one of three buildings surviving 1905 fire. Addition to building during the rebuilding of the commercial district after fire.

L
20-24 W. Oak St.
Arcadia

W. E. Daniel Buildings, built in 1906 for pioneer merchant, William E. Daniel. Masonry rusticated block. Typical of immediate post-fire construction.

M
W. Hickory St. and
Manatee Ave.
Arcadia

Old St. Edmund's Church, built in 1897. Wood frame Victorian Revival style, earliest Episcopal church in Arcadia. Relocated in 1935 to present location for use as parish hall.

N
W. Hickory St. and
Peace River
Arcadia

The Old Peace River Bridge, built in 1925 with Luten Bridge Co. as builder. Three-span arched bridge, 18 feet wide, first concrete bridge across Peace River. Still in use in mid 1980's.

O
Orange Avenue
Arcadia

De Soto County High School, built in 1914. Three-story brick masonry construction. County's second high school, abandoned in 1978. On same campus as West Elementary School (1925) and a portion of the original high school (1906) designed by Frances Kennard.

P
Ziba King Memorial
Recreation Park
Ft. Ogden

Ziba King Family Cemetery, established in 1870's. Family cemetery for a De Soto County cattle baron, merchant, realtor, and state representative (1898-99). Located in large grove of live oaks.

HIGHLANDS

MIKE KELLY & TOM VAN CLEAVE, FLORIDA GULF CHAPTER

In contrast to beach-seeking Sunshine State travelers of today, many early Florida settlers gravitated toward the central region of the state. It was in the area now known as Highlands County that early pioneer cattlemen took advantage of vast grazing pastures.

In 1909 Congress declared land originally set aside for the Seminole Indian nation as an area for homesteading. Some settlers had been in the region for years. The opportunity to homestead brought many more inhabitants who fashioned shelters out of the plentiful timber in the area. Small communities, typically two or three log cabins, began to develop. Construction of a sawmill at Avon Park was a major boon to building. Wood plank sidewalks were built, new houses, a church, and another sawmill. Development of surrounding communities followed.

Transportation between the new towns was difficult, particularly with the introduction of automobiles. The sandy, wagon-rutted roads were inadequate for the new vehicles until palmetto fans were laid on existing roads to fill ruts and to give substance. Citizens argued for smaller counties and county seats that would not require one or two days of travel from rural areas. In 1921, Highlands County was created with Sebring named as county seat. Poor transportation continued to be the major obstacle to the development of Highlands County. The arrival of the Atlantic Coastline Railroad provided the first dependable link to other areas of the state and ended the isolation of the county. The railroad brought building supplies, along with developers, land speculators, and more homesteaders.

Highlands, along with the rest of Florida, enjoyed the boom years of the 1920's. Citrus became a major industry, along with land development and real estate. Melvil Dewey, creator of the Dewey Decimal System and an advocate of a simplified spelling system of the English language, played a major part in the development of the Lake Placid area.

Florida felt the depression years of the 1930's, but less extensively than the rest of the country. In this period Highlands Hammock State Park near Sebring was developed as a public works project. During World War II, Hendricks Field became a major military training base with many pilots receiving flight lessons there. The 1950's saw continued growth in Highlands County. In 1950, the first twenty-four hour Sebring auto race was held, and a major sporting event was established.

Highlands County continued to grow through the 1960's and 1970's with new commerce, schools, light industry, and housing developing in the area. Typical of many other areas of Florida, the major industry remained citrus production.

Preservation efforts in Highlands County have been the result of the work of several organizations. Sebring and Avon Park have active historical societies. The Avon Park Chamber of Commerce has a Mall and City Beautification Committee which focuses its efforts on maintaining Avon Park's mile long grass mall, a major feature of the city's downtown.

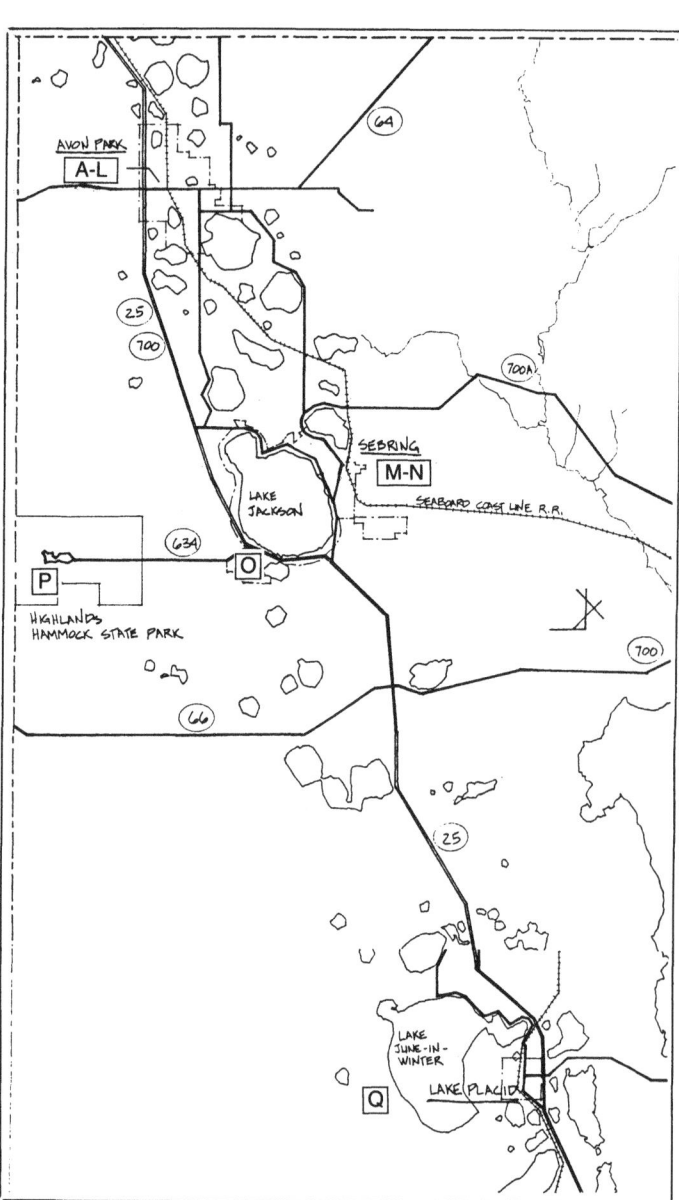

The restoration of Avon Park's Bandstand, a site of civic events built in 1897, was accomplished through the combined efforts of the Old Settlers Association and the Avon Park Bicentennial Commission. It was designated as the Avon Park's Bicentennial Project. The Historical Society of the Old Settlers Association of Avon Park restored the Seaboard Airline Railroad Station and adapted it for use as a museum. Individuals have also undertaken preservation projects. Two hotels, the Jacaranda in Avon Park and Harder Hall near Sebring, have been restored and several residences have been renovated.

A
Main St. Mall
Avon Park

Bandstand, built in 1897 on the shore of Lake Verona as site for community events. Moved to downtown mall in 1912 to serve as community's focal point. Restored in mid 1970's.

B
Corner of W. Main St. and N. Michigan Ave.
Avon Park

Seaboard Airline Railroad Station-Historical Society Museum, built in 1925. Mediterranean Revival style building, typical of Florida's 1920's real estate boom. Bought and converted to museum in 1979 by Historical Society of the Old Settlers Association after railroad abandoned it.

C
E. Main St.
Avon Park

Jacaranda Hotel, built in 1926 by John Raab and Harry Winters of Michigan. Brick masonry vernacular style typical of the fine hotels built during the Florida real estate boom. Named for a 150 year old jacaranda tree removed for construction.

D
105 N. Forest Ave.
Avon Park

Union Evangelical-Union Congregational Church, built in 1892 on land donated by Mr. and Mrs. O.M. Crosby, founders of Avon Park. Original wood-frame structure renovated by having the crenellated bell tower replaced by a steeple, interior walls plastered, and siding added to exterior walls.

E
20 E. Pleasant St.
Avon Park

Episcopal Church, built in 1894. Simple wood frame structure in Victorian Revival style.

F
Shockley Rd.-
Lake Pythias
Avon Park

Bunbury-Shockley Residence, designed in 1889 for Lord and Lady Bunbury of England by J.H. Nettleton, architect of Avon Park's first hotel, Hotel Verona. Combination of English farm house and hunting lodge. Kitchen section on foundation of large tree stumps. Sold in 1908 to Shockley family. Attic dormers added.

G
Lake Lotela Drive
Avon Park

Hollyhurst, built in 1895 for Dr. Augustine Gandler of Quebec, Canada, and named for the many varieties of holly trees on the property. Sold to Col. and Mrs. R. P. Davidson who rebuilt house and then remodeled it again in 1926.

H
Lake Byrd Blvd.
Avon Park

Lake Byrd Lodge-Florida Congregational Church Headquarters, built in 1919 by D. B. Farnell, builder, as a club house for the Florida Pittsburgh Co. Unique wood vernacular structure built of bay logs which were hewn smooth, sized, and fitted together. Remodeled extensively. Now state headquarters for Florida Congregaional churches.

I
Lake Lotela Dr.
Avon Park

Pinecrest Lakes Hotel-Florida Capital of the Age of Enlightenment, built in 1925 as a private club with membership of people who came only for the winter months. Mediterranean Revival style.

J
Lake Isis Drive
Avon Park

Red Top Ranch-Lillydale Farm, built in 1893 for Mr. and Mrs. Charles Perkins. Two-story frame structure. In early 1920's operated as health resort, Dr. Mary's Health Villa, by Mary E. Coffin, M.D., and Ida B. Peffers, M.D. Purchased by Norton T. Smith and known as "Red Top Inn" or "Red Top Ranch."

K
Main St.
Avon Park

Brickel Building, built in 1919 with John Hood as architect. One of few Main Street buildings retaining original appearance. Large pediment on central portion and several large oriel windows on second floor. Second floor auditorium that was once used for town council, lodge meetings, and public dances altered in 1966 to provide temporary space for South Florida Junior College.

L
West Pleasant St.
Avon Park

Blue Goose Packing Co.-American Fruit Growers Association, built in 1926 by Seaboard Air Line Railroad. Only remaining original citrus packing house. Corrugated metal siding and vaulted roof.

M
Commerce Ave.
Sebring

Highlands County Courthouse, built in 1927. Original exterior unchanged. Several interior rearrangements and improvements. Additional annexes on lots near main structure.

N
309 S. Circle Ave.
Sebring

Chamber of Commerce, built in 1916 by volunteer labor to house the Board of Trade, precursor to the Chamber of Commerce. At different times location for city hall, town recreation center, Red Cross headquarters, city planning board, and Chamber of Commerce in mid 1980s. One of few downtown Sebring structures retaining original characteristics.

O
Golf View Dr. and
US 27
Sebring

Harder Hall, built in 1925 and named for corporation's principals, Lewis Hardee and Vincent Hall, who started building's construction during land boom and stopped construction after land boom collapse. In 1929 building completed in Mediterranean Revival style as plush hotel by new corporation.

HARDEE

MATTHEW PLOUCHA, AIA, FLORIDA GULF CHAPTER

Located in South Central Florida and bisected by the Peace River, Hardee County is a land of flatwoods and rolling countryside devoted mostly to farming. Its settlement began when military roads were built during the Seminole Wars and U.S. forts were constructed at strategic points along these roads. Fort Chokonikla was established on the west bank of the Peace River about a mile south of Bowling Green in 1849.

Owing to the Seminole Wars, frequent conflicts with Indians, and hazardous travel conditions, few settlers attempted to penetrate into Central Florida. By the middle of the nineteenth century less than a dozen families lived in the Hardee County area. Between 1843 and 1855, the county was surveyed and divided into plats. In 1851 Fort Hartsuff was established in the area which would later become Wauchula, the first permanent settlement in the county. The final battle with Indians in the Hardee County area occurred on June 14 to 16, 1856, when soldiers from Fort Meade drove the Seminoles permanently to the east side of the Peace River.

Shortly after the 1856 battle with the Indians, Daniel Carlton settled at Troublesome Creek between what is now Wauchula and Ona. In 1867 he built the first school in the county. The first church, founded by Rev. John Hendry in 1867, was called Maple Branch and later the New Zion Church. In following years Rev. Hendry, along with Rev. W. P. McEwen, traveled in the region establishing numerous churches. Cattle and oranges, the chief products of the area, were hauled to Punta Gorda, Fort Myers, or Tampa, a seven-day trip.

With the close of the Civil War, settlers began to enter the area in greater numbers. In 1874 Eli English settled in the area of old Fort Hartsuff and opened the only store south of Fort Meade. The settlement, called English Post Office, later became Wauchula. Development continued slowly until 1881 when Gov. William D. Bloxham offered to sell Hamilton Disston, a Philadelphia businessman, and his associates 13 million acres of central Florida which were released from government control. Disston secured four million acres and sold the land to prospective settlers. Growth began, large sums of money were invested within the state, and taxable income increased.

In 1885 the Florida Southern Railroad, now the Atlantic Coast Line, constructed tracks south into the county and by 1886 reached English Post Office which the railroad company renamed Wauchula. As the railroad continued south in the early 1890's, the towns of Zolfo Springs, Charlie Apopka, and Bowling Green developed along its route.

After the railroad arrived, the region developed rapidly. By 1895 four schools had been established. By 1901 large-scale vegetable and citrus farming provided a large portion of the area's income. A seedless orange tree was discovered in Albert Carlton's grove, and "Carlton's Seedless Orange" became famous.

At this time the area which is now Hardee County was part

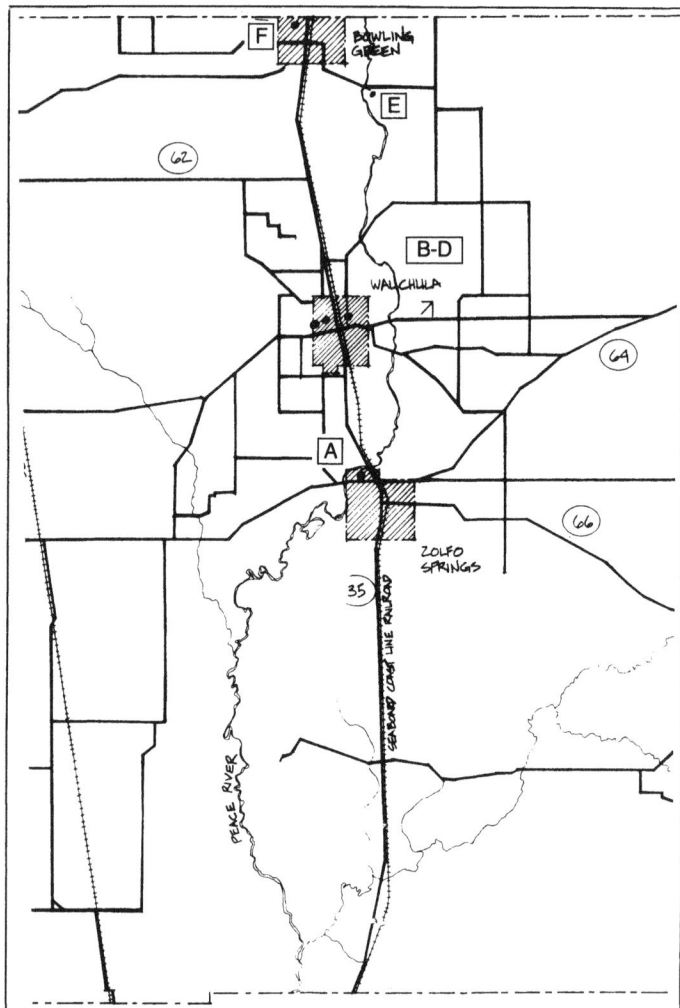

of De Soto County. As the area developed, many began to see the need to divide the county into a number of smaller counties. On April 23, 1921, after a fourteen year fight for division, the county division bill creating the counties of Hardee, Highlands, Glade, De Soto, and Charlotte passed the legislature. Hardee County was named after Cary Hardee, the governor of Florida at that time. In 1921 Wauchula was selected as county seat.

Aside from agriculture, the largest industry to locate in Hardee County was the Wauchula Manufacturing and Timber Co., a manufacturer of crates, boxes, and other wood products. This company is credited with bringing more settlers to the area than any other single industry. In 1911 the company organized the Wauchula Development Company to survey and sell over 54,000 acres of land. The prosperity of the company suffered when portions of its factory were destroyed by fire in 1924.

After World War I, development occurred on a larger scale. In 1923 funds were appropriated for construction of hard surfaced roads, and by 1927 the county had over 150 miles of such roads. Newspapers publicized the county's "combination soil" which allowed farmers to produce citrus and vegetables on the same land, and the county attracted more population.

The real estate boom can be traced to the summer of 1924 when developer Harry E. Prettyman located in the area. In 1927 the market crashed and Prettyman and other real estate men left. Since farming was the basis of the region's economy, the boom did not have as much effect as in other sections of the state. However, from 1924 to 1927, a new jail, county high school, and courthouse were built.

Hardee County continued its development. The Florida Public Service Co. built power lines covering a large part of the county. The Wauchula Truck Growers Association, later the Hardee County Growers Inc., opened one of the largest vegetable packing houses in the state. The cattle industry declined slightly, but the citrus and vegetable industries made Hardee County famous.

A
Rt. 64 & Oak St.
Bowling Green
Green Hotel, built in 1925. Served as city hotel when Bowling Green was county seat. Later served as train station.

B
Wauchula
Hardee County Courthouse, built in 1927. Constructed by Robertson Construction Co. with H. G. Little of Wauchula as architect.

NO PHOTO AVAILABLE   **C**
SR 664-A, south of Rt.64
Bowling Green
Paynes Creek State Historic Site. Site where Fort Chokonikla and the Kennedy-Darling store once stood, important site during third war with Seminole Indians. Store built to give Indians a place to trade and to limit contact between Indians and white settlers. Fort one of several built to prevent the Seminoles from traveling north and later to force them south.

D
Wauchula
Wauchula County Jail. Constructed in 1924 with H. G. Little as architect.

E
S. Fourth Ave.
Wauchula
Wauchula City Hall, near Route 64, built in 1926. Designed by M. Leo Elliot of Tampa and constructed by Paul H. Smith.

F
Rt. 17 & Sixth Ave.
Zolfo Springs
Pioneer Park, site of one of last battles fought by the Seminole Nation. Indians defeated by soldiers from Fort Meade. (In park antique locomotive provides focal point and commemorates history of Florida Southern Railroad-Atlantic Coastline. Zolfo Springs named by Italian railroad workers.)

NOTES

MANATEE

LINDA STEVENSON, AIA, FLORIDA GULF CHAPTER

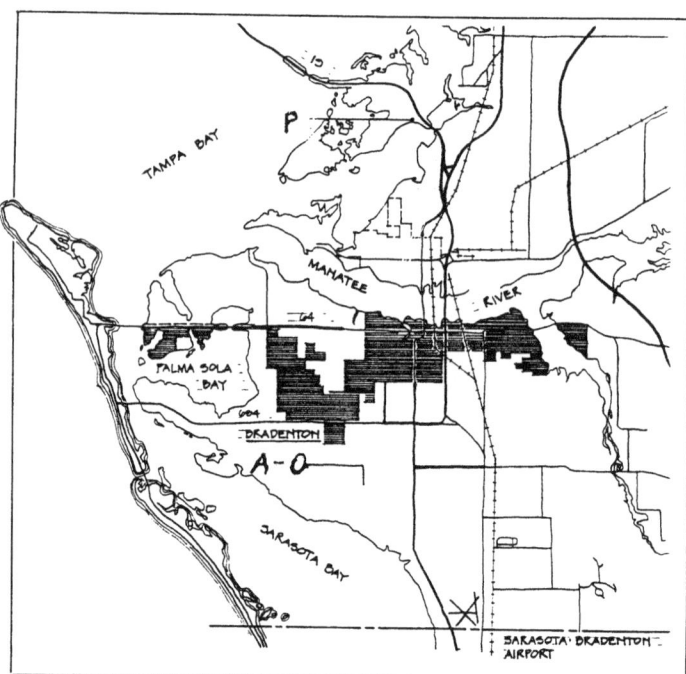

In 1539 when Hernando de Soto discovered the Manatee River (the geographical feature that was to determine the area's socio-economic and architectural development), the Spanish found sea cows which were called "manati" in their language. These unique animals became the source of the river's and then the county's name. The indigenous area dwellers, the Timucuan Indians who had depended on nearby waters to exist, left many traces of their shell mound culture. One site, the Madira Bickel Mounds on Terra Ceia Island, is on the National Register of Historic Places.

Three hundred years passed from the time of the Spanish discovery to the settler's acquisition of the lands of the Manatee. Enticed by the 1842 Armed Occupation Act, the homesteaders were promised ownership of 160 acres of land upon five years residence. Josiah Gates, the first settler, founded the village of Manatee in 1842. Most of these early settlers were farmers or tradesmen who supplied services to the fledgling community. A few were former plantation owners who established sugar plantations on the Manatee River as a way to recoup wealth. The Braden brothers' "Castle" and mill were on the south shore and Maj. Robert Gamble's house and vast plantation on the north.

Manatee County, formed in 1855, encompassed over 5,000 square miles from the Gulf of Mexico to Lake Okeechobee. The first county seat was in the village of Manatee. The 1860 census showed a sparse population of 601 settlers and 253 slaves.

The early structures of the pioneers used simple materials, hand-hewn pine logs or sabal palmetto fans laced onto a wooden frame. Timbers were mortised on site, but window sash and dressed lumber had to be imported. In 1866 the first saw mill in Manatee provided milled pine boards. When placed vertically, the cracks between boards were covered with battens, as seen in the old Settler's House. Wealthier settlers desired more substantial structures and built their houses of poured tabby, a cement-like mixture of shells, sand, burned shell lime, and water.

During the Civil War, Union blockades undermined the region's economy. Post-war recovery came as a result of the cattle industry. Developed on large inland tracts, herds were driven to the river for export.

The county seat was moved to "Braidentown" in 1887, spurring this community's growth with the region's economic livelihood still centered on the river. Improvements in transportation, such as steamers and railroads in the 1880's and 1890's, encouraged the growth of the citrus industry and increased the flow of people and goods.

Buildings of this period reflected the styles and materials popular throughout the country. In towns commercial buildings were constructed of brick or locally quarried stone or wood. The revival styles of Second Empire and Classical or loose adaptations of Italianate Revival style were used.

Wood was still the preferred residential material with the Classical Revival styles giving way to the Craftsman Bungalow style after 1910.

Further development along the shoreline was stimulated by land speculation and tourism in the 1920's. The automobile, boon to the middle class, further aided in accessibility to the area. These "Tin Can Tourists" created an early planned community on the site of Braden Castle. The architecture of this boom period is best exemplified in the fanciful Mediterranean Revival style as seen in the Manatee River Hotel and the Memorial Pier.

This trend of development has continued to the present with the river as a focus of activity. Current architecture ranges from picturesque adaptations of local vernacular forms to modern statements that sometimes bear little in common with the charm of old downtown or the vistas of the Manatee River.

The major preservation effort in Manatee County has been the creation of the Manatee Village Historical Park in 1975. Several significant structures have been moved to the site in what was the old Village of Manatee. The Old Settlers House received an award from the Florida Trust for Historic Preservation for its restoration work.

An architectural survey of Bradenton's historic structures was conducted, and Palmetto received a state grant to make a survey of significant structures on the north side of the Manatee River. The city of Bradenton created several historic districts, the Manatee Village Historical Park and the Braden Castle Park Historic District. An architectural review board was created by the city of Bradenton to represent the interests of the preservation community.

Unfortunately, despite these efforts, a number of structures were lost in the mid-1980's, including the Garr House and Le Chalet.

A
604 15th St., East
Bradenton

First Manatee County Courthouse, Manatee Village Historical Park, built in 1860 with Ezekiel Glazier as builder. Oldest existing courthouse in Florida, simple Classical Revival style. After county seat relocated in 1866, building used by Methodist Church first as sanctuary, then parsonage, and finally social hall. Donated by church to park and moved in 1975. Restored with much interior woodwork replaced.

B
604 15th St., East
Bradenton

Old Meeting House — Old Methodist Church, Manatee Village Historical Park, built in 1887-1889. Third structure occupied by the oldest Christian group south of Tampa. Moved to the park and restored in 1975. Typical of late nineteenth-century ecclesiastical architecture with small pediments over doors and windows, vaulted ceiling, and "Star of Creation" window.

C
604 15th St., East
Bradenton

Old Settler's House, Manatee Village Historical Park, built in 1912 by Will Stephens. Third house built on the original 1894 homestead of the Stephens family. Typical of warm-humid climate construction with a central hall, pier foundation, broad eaves, porches, and board and batten siding. Building donated to County Historical Commission in 1982 and moved to present site. Recognized by the Florida Trust for Historic Preservation in 1984 as outstanding example of residential restoration.

D
1577 Fourth Av. East
Bradenton

Josiah Gates, Jr. House, built in 1881 by one of the first settlers along the Manatee River. Simple Classical Revival style with recessed porches and raised floors on masonry piers. One of best preserved early residences in area.

E
210 15th St., East
Bradenton

Ella Hamilton House, built between 1906 and 1910 with John Glazier as builder. Two-story wood frame house combining elements of Classical Revival and Victorian Revival styles with carved verge board and decorative railing on balcony above front porch. Rear porch added in 1917.

F
420 Manatee Ave., West
Bradenton

Atlantic Coastline Railroad Depot – Fulmore House Site. Mediterranean Revival style depot built in 1920 with curvilinear parapet walls and semicircular arches. Fulmore House, built in 1867, reputed to have been remodeled into train station but no physical evidence to support story.

G
309 10th St., West
Bradenton

Manatee River Hotel, built in 1926 by Van Sweringer Interests of Cleveland, Ohio, at cost of $850,000. Well-preserved example of Mediterranean Revival style popular during Bradenton's 1920 period of development. Originally contained 285 rooms and featured projecting bays, red tile roof, and pyramidal roofed towers at each corner. Most of interior original and some of furniture original.

H
603 11th St. West
Bradenton

First Methodist Church, built in 1922. Classical Revival style with pedimented portico featuring Ionic columns, pedimented window heads, and leaded windows. Large addition constructed in 1956.

I
Manatee Ave. and 12th St. West
Bradenton

Manatee County Courthouse, built in 1913 with McGucken and Hyer Engineers of Tampa as builder. Classical Revival style with brick walls, Doric columns, and pedimented portico. Undergoing renovation of interior and restoration of ceramic cornice and pediment in mid 1980's.

J
530 12th St. West
Bradenton

Iron Block Building, built in 1896. Originally occupied southwest corner of Manatee Ave. and Main St. (12th St.) as Reed's Cash Store. Restored with preserved pressed metal facades on three sides.

K
1206 Manatee Ave. West
Bradenton

Fuller Block, built in 1905 by W. D. Fuller using yellow stone from his quarry on the Manatee River. Commercial structure containing Mediterranean Revival style elements, red-tiled roofs, and mosaic frieze added before 1925. Building housed Manatee River Bank and Trust Co. for many years.

L
430 13th St. West
Bradenton

First Baptist Church, built in 1912. Building combines elements of several eclectic styles. Corner towers with steep pyramidal roofs and round-arched openings recalling French and Italian Romanesque tradition of ecclesiastical architecture. Several alterations.

M
12th St. and Manatee River
Bradenton

Memorial Pier, completed in 1927 and dedicated to veterans of World War I. Mediterranean Revival style structure including tile roof, corner tower, spiral column mullions in round-arched windows and entrance arcade.

N
104 15th St. West
Bradenton

Hough-Stuart House, built by T.W. Hullinger in 1912. Bungalow style with functional floorplan, expression of construction materials, ornament based on expression of structural members, broad overhangs, deep porches, bands of casement windows, projecting side bays, and supporting brackets.

O
1405 Fourth Ave. West
Bradenton

Manatee County Historical Records Library – Carnegie Library, built in 1918 by T. W. Hullinger. Original portion of building constructed as library with $10,000 grant from Carnegie Foundation. Classical Revival style with elevated entrance, Tuscan pedimented entrance. Excellent example of adaptive use as county archives.

P
US 301
Ellerton

Gamble Plantation, built in 1846 with slave labor by Major Robert Gamble, one area's earliest settlers.

SARASOTA

RICHARD M. GARFINKEL, AIA, FLORIDA GULF

Sarasota County's archaeological evidence of man's habitation more than 10,000 years ago indicates early recognition of natural geophysical features which attracted generations of Indians, Europeans and most recently North Americans.

Possibly explored by Hernando de Soto in 1539 and mapped by military expeditions during the Second Seminole War, Sarasota did not have its first U.S. settler until 1842. William H. Whitaker homesteaded a tract of land along the bayfront at Yellow Bluffs (now 13th Street) and built the area's first structure, a log cabin later burned by Seminole Indians.

It was more than two decades after Whitaker's arrival before there was a major increase in population in the area. The Homestead Act of 1862 attracted pioneering farmers, fishermen, and cattlemen, and small pockets of growth sprang up along a shoreline which was accessible only by boat or ox cart along unmarked trails. Safe haven from Union soldiers along the inaccessible Myakka River initiated the development of a cattle community (Old Myakka) in the east county.

Slow, but steady, homesteading growth came to a halt in 1881 when the Florida Legislature, taking advantage of a loophole in the Homestead Act of 1862 and the Swamp and Overflowed Lands Act, reclaimed and then sold 700,000 acres around Sarasota (some already homesteaded) to land speculation companies. Of the land speculation companies, the Florida Mortgage and Investment Company, headed by Sir John Gillespie of Scotland, influenced the area's development most.

The fishing village lifestyle of Sarasota County was shattered when Mrs. Potter Palmer, a well-known Chicago socialite, visited the area in 1910 and purchased 80,000 acres. The publicity attending her move to Sarasota catapulted land values and Sarasota soon was known as a winter resort.

Among other influential figures moving to Sarasota at this time were Andrew McAnsh and Owen Burns, developers, and John and Charles Ringling, circus magnates. McAnsh built Sarasota's first major Mediterranean Revival structure, the MiraMar Apartment and Hotel, designed by William Kreig, a Chicago architect. Burns was the area's first significant developer-builder of small and large scale projects. The Ringling brothers began purchasing and developing large portions of real estate in 1912. In 1927, they made Sarasota the winter home of the Ringling Brothers and Barnum and Bailey Circus.

In 1921, a 526-square-mile portion of southern Manatee County seceded and formed Sarasota County with the city of Sarasota as county seat. Dwight James Baum, commissioned to design the new county courthouse, became the area's most influential architect. Many of his Mediterranean Revival designs remain in use today. His local office was directed by Ralph Twitchell who later established the modern direction which guided Sarasota's architectural development

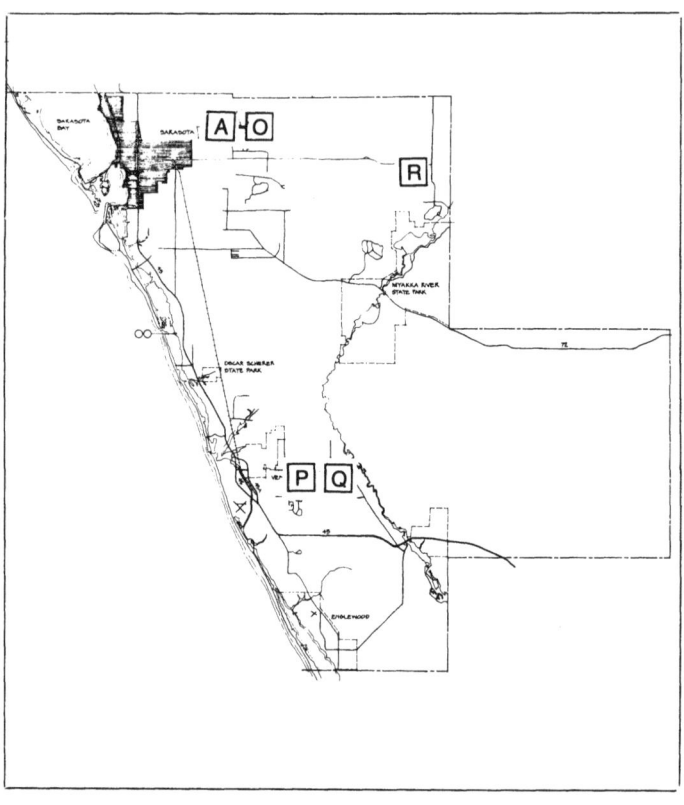

after World War II. Planner John Nolan also had a significant impact on the 1920's boom by directing growth patterns in Sarasota and formulating the city plan for Venice.

As the tourists, wealthy retirees, and winter visitors returned after World War II, the cultural legacy of the Palmers and Ringlings led to a strong revitalized economy and the "Sarasota School" of architecture. Starting with small guest houses for the weathy, such notable architects as Twitchell, Paul Rudolph, Victor Lundy, and others established a contemporary and environmentally oriented style of architecture which still pervades the best local work.

A steady growth pattern throughout the county during the 1950s and '60s accelerated to boom proportions by the mid-1970s and continues with tremendous growth in outlying communities such as Venice, Englewood and North Port. While attracting growth was one of early Sarasota's major problems, controlling growth has now become the first planning priority.

The tourist and retirement trade is clearly the largest income producer in the county, but construction and agriculture also are important industries with celery and oranges being the major crops. In addition to the Ringling museums and structures, major attractions in the area include Sarasota Jungle Gardens, Selby Botanical Gardens, the Oscar Scherer Park, and the Myakka River State Park.

A
1700 Seminole Drive
Sarasota

McClellan Park School, built 1915-16 as clubhouse for early subdivision adjacent to Indian mound. Two-story vernacular with fancy cut board on board cypress, partially altered in 1933 to adapt to private school use.

B
900 Euclid Ave.
Sarasota

Bidwell-Wood House, built 1882, oldest extant residence in Sarasota. One-and-a-half story wood frame vernacular (Victorian Revival) with attached kitchen.

C
1001 S. Tamiami Trail
Sarasota

Sarasota (Bay Haven) High School, built 1925-26, with M. Leo Elliot as architect, when Sarasota constructed three schools in one year at the recommendation of John Nolan, planner (all three still in active use).

D
1001 S. Tamiami Trail
Sarasota

Sarasota High School Addition, built 1956 with Paul Rudolph as architect, one of two Rudolph-designed high schools in Sarasota. Innovative design concept with use of planes and passive design.

E
Main St. and
Washington Blvd.
(U.S. 301)
Sarasota

Sarasota County Courthouse, built 1927 with Dwight James Baum, architect, and Stevenson and Cameron, Inc., builder. Mediterranean Revival style, stucco finish.

F
111 S. Orange Ave.
Sarasota

Federal Building — U.S. Post Office, built 1934 as post office with George Albree Freeman, architect, and Harold N. Hall, local architect. Classic Revival style.

G
424 N. Osprey Ave.
Sarasota

Art Rowe Residences, built 1933 with Rowe as designer and Oliver Blackburn as builder, (Rowe served as yacht captain for John Ringling, circus magnate, and William Selby, philanthropist).

H
330 S. Pineapple Ave.
Sarasota

United States Garage, built 1924 for Calvin Payne and W. L. Pearsall to provide seasonal storage of automobiles.

I
Off 300 Block,
Pineapple Ave.
Sarasota

Burns Court Subdivision, built 1924-25 with Thomas Reed Martin, architect, developed by Owen Burns, Sarasota's first significant developer-builder.

J
1218 1st
Sarasota

Sarasota Times Building, built 1925-26 with Dwight James Baum, architect, and Ricket and Haworth, builder, for L.D. Reagin to house offices and plant for his newspaper.

K
308 Coconut St.
Sarasota

Dr. Joseph Halton Residence, built 1909 with Joseph S. Maus, designer-builder, for one of Sarasota's first physicians. Two story masonry Queen Anne structure of blocks cast by Maus using the "Miracle Pressed Stone" machine.

L
5700 Bayshore Dr.
Sarasota

Charles and Edith Ringling Residence, University of South Florida campus (west), built 1925 Alfred Clas of Clas, Shepherd and Clas, architect, and Eisenbery of Wisconsin, builder, on property adjacent to the mansion of Ringling's brother, John. Classical Revival structure.

M
5401 Bayshore Dr.
Sarasota

Ca'd' Zan, John and Mable Ringling Residence, built 1926 with Dwight James Baum as architect by circus magnate for his wife. Mediterranean Revival mansion modeled after Doge's Palace in Venice.

N
5401 Bayshore Dr.
Sarasota

John and Mable Ringling Museum of Art, built 1930 with J.H. Phillips, architect, to house collections of Baroque Art (particularly Rubens). Italian Renaissance style,

O
Spanish Point at Oaks
Osprey

Frank Guptill House (The Hill Cottage), built 1901 by Frank Guptill, son-in-law of John Webb, one of Sarasota's first homesteaders. Sited on a shell midden dating to pre-2000 B.C. overlooking Little Sarasota Bay.

P
200 Block,
N. Nassau St.
Venice

Hotel Venice, built 1927 Italian Renaissance Revival style with D.M. Plumb of Walker and Gillette, architect, and George A Fuller Co., builder. One of two major hotels built by the Brotherhood of Locomotive Engineers to anchor their ideal city.

Q
Harbor Drive and
Venice Ave.
Venice

City Plan of Venice, Fla., Commemorative Plaque and Memorial Garden, 1925, John Nolan, Massachusetts planner, and Brotherhood of Locomotive Engineers, developers. Contracted by Dr. Fred Albee.

R
Wilson Rd.
Old Myakka

Old Myakka School, built 1917. Vernacular schoolhouse, frame construction, drop-lap siding with cornerboards, gabled roof and entry porch, open belfry.

CHARLOTTE

ROBERT E. FORSYTHE, AIA

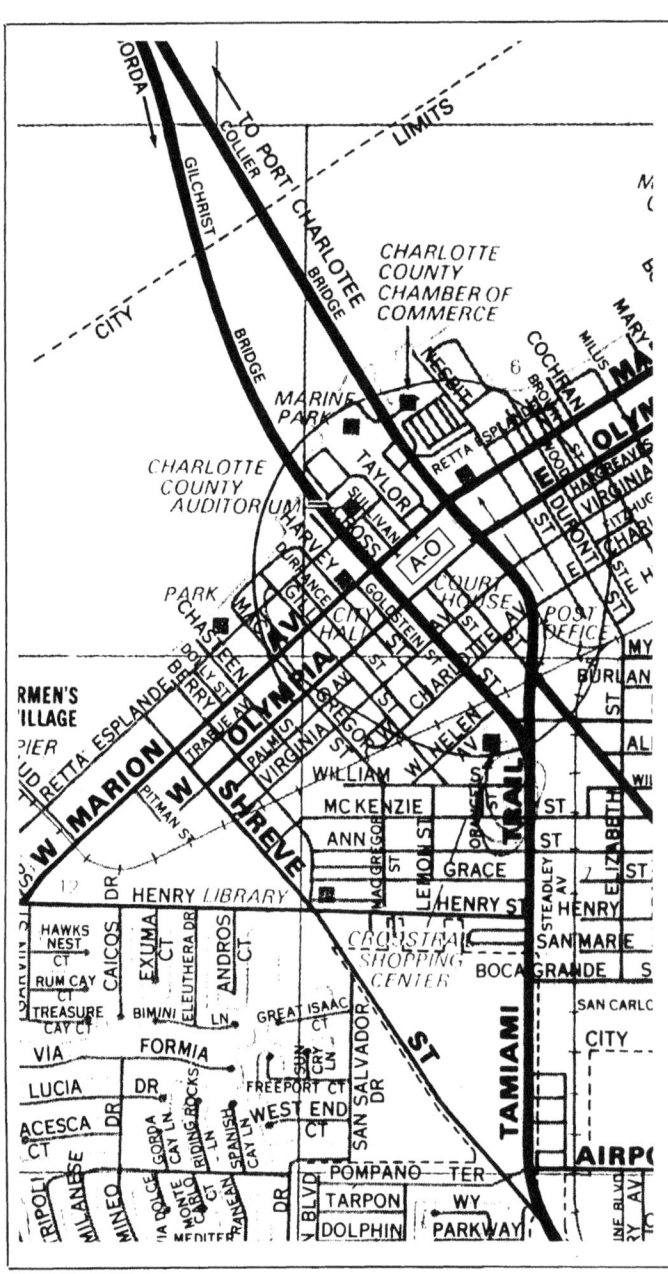

A At the time of the Civil War, settlement in southwest Florida was sparse, although this was the area that supplied beef to the Armies of Tennessee and Northern Virginia. There were regular cattle drives from the region of what is now Charlotte County to the railhead at Savannah, Georgia. Federal forces, determined to stop the cattle drives, blockaded Charlotte Harbor and occupied Fort Myers. Although Floridians ran the blockade and were able to continue getting supplies to the Confederacy, there were few structures left standing between Fort Myers and Fort Meade by the end of the War.

When Congress passed the Swamp and Overflow Land Act of 1850, it made huge tracts of land available for homesteading and with Hamilton Disston's purchase of four million acres in 1881, peninsular Florida was opened for development. The state offered large land grants to railroads to expand their systems, and as a result, Henry B. Plant built a line to Tampa in 1883, and the Florida Southern Railway brought the first train to Punta Gorda in 1886. New towns including Arcadia, Nocatee, Fort Ogden and Punta Gorda sprang up along the railroad right-of-way and in 1887 Charlotte County was created from Manatee County and the town of Punta Gorda was incorporated.

The railroad was extended to Fort Myers in 1904, and the Charlotte Harbor and Northern Railroad was built to Boca Grande in 1907. In 1908, Punta Gorda's favorite citizen, Albert W. Gilchrist, was elected Governor of Florida.

During the 1920's, the Tamiami Trail moved forward dramatically and with the construction of the Charlotte Harbor Bridge this major highway was routed through Punta Gorda. Three major hurricanes in 1921, 1926 and 1928 left a trail of damage, but did not prepare anyone for the crash of 1929. The land boom had permeated the economy of Charlotte County. Punta Gorda had three operating banks during the 1920's. Subdivisions sprang up and homesite sales skyrocketed. When the stock market crashed in 1929, prosperity ended abruptly.

The 1930's brought two more hurricanes, freezes, a major fire and the WPA. Prior to the exodus of young men at the beginning of World War II, many of Charlotte County's fishermen and farmers were happy to work for the Federal government's WPA for one dollar a day. During the post-World War II period, Punta Gorda and Charlotte County experienced continuous growth and change. Charlotte County grew from 4,000 people in 1940 to 60,000 people in 1980. It is one of the fastest growing areas in the nation and its citizens, many of whom came as tourists, have the highest median age of any county in the United States.

A
West Marian Avenue
Punta Gorda

City Hall, built 1927 with an addition built in 1986, is an example of Neo-Classical Architecture as are several public building in Punta Gorda. Characterized by parapet roof with a central pediment and a combination of Greek and Roman orders.

B
Taylor Street
Punta Gorda

Charlotte County Courthouse, built 1928, Neo-classical Style accented by parapet wall with central pediment. Brick exterior with brick pilasters. Clock was removed from center of pediment.

C
103 Cross Street
Punta Gorda

Maxwell Butler Residence, built circa 1900, Late Victorian Style with gable front and wing plan. Shotgun plan with board and batten vertical wood siding.

D
401 Retta Esplanade
Punta Gorda

Built 1893, this late Victorian Gothic Style house is characterized by a steeply pitched side gable with a central cross gable. Jig-saw cut thin wood trim is found at end of gables. A belvedere is located on the roof top.

E
108 Gill Street
Punta Gorda

Residence, built in 1900, Late Victorian Gothic Style, depicted by steep roof pitch, wrap-around porches and two story structure. Detailed wood trim is hung from porch roof and gable ends. Built on piers with lattice infill.

F
321 Retta Esplanade
Punta Gorda

Everett Barnhill Residence, built 1925, Prairie School Style with a low hip roof and dormers. One story porches with low hip roof. Windows are paired in two bay arrangements.

G
551 Retta Esplanade
Punta Gorda

Residence, built c. 1914, Frame Vernacular Style. Two story structure with gable roof front and one-story porch.

H
565 Retta Esplanade
Punta Gorda

Residence built 1887, Queen Ann Style with wrap-around porches and steeply pitched roofs. Unique tower and dormers. Originally more simple in form, building has been enlarged.

I
233 Taylor Street
Punta Gorda

Hector House, built 1895, characterized by being one room deep with a central hall, two stories and a side gable roof. Fronted by a veranda at each level the structure is of wood frame with balloon construction.

J
Cross Street
Punta Gorda

First Baptist Church, built c. 1909, Gothic Style with lancet windows, metal roof with gable ends. Tower at street corner becomes the dominant element.

K
507 W. Marion Ave.
Punta Gorda

Methodist Church, built 1917, late Gothic Revival, facade is common brick and rusticated concrete block with lancet windows. Latin Cross plan type.

L
133 West Marion Ave.
Punta Gorda

Mercantile Bank, built in early 20th Century, Classic Revival with columns and large pediment to create entryway. Brick and stucco facade with continuous brick foundation.

M
100 blk. E. Marion Ave.
Punta Gorda

King Arcade, built 1926, Mission Style, parapet roof with tile coping. Smooth stucco finish. Two large shops front the building with smaller shops along the arcade in the rear. One of the oldest interior malls.

N
Copper Street
Punta Gorda

Charlotte High School, built 1925, Neo-Classical Style with a straight parapet roof with a central pediment. Pediments and columns create an impressive entrance.

O
1009 Taylor Street
Punta Gorda

Atlantic Coast Line, built 1926, Mission Spanish Colonial Revival structure with flat roof and built-up parapet with tile coping. The chimney is capped with clay tile. The exterior is brick with stucco finish. At the southern end of the building is the freight section.

LEE

ROBERT E. FORSYTHE, AIA

Lee County was founded by an act of the Florida Legislature on May 9, 1887. At that time, 2,000 people lived in Lee County, 550 of them in Fort Myers. The others lived in an area of 4,752 square miles including what is now Collier County. All of this was previously the northern part of Monroe County and citizens living there with business in the county seat had to make the arduous trip to Key West by schooner.

When the county was founded, Fort Myers was a fairly old city, having been established as a settlement nineteen years earlier. The weekly Fort Myers Press was the qualified medium for legal notices, having been founded in 1884.

Early history, collected from accounts in the Press and an article written by Dr. L.C. Washburn described the city as having "Six general stores, one jewelry store, one barber shop, one saloon which was poorly patronized, one billiard hall, one weekly paper, one large commodious church, Methodist, one blacksmith, one lawyer, six physicians, six or eight hotels and boarding houses, two telegraph lines and two railroads." The city exported ten to twelve thousand head of beef yearly at $18 a piece, plus numerous hogs.

The town of Fort Myers was first founded as Fort Harvie on November 4, 1841, and was named after Lt. John M. Harvie,

a young officer who was killed in the Seminole War. That post was abandoned on March 21, 1842, on the assumption that the Seminoles had been conquered.

A new post named Fort Myers was set up on the site by Major Ridgely of the Tampa Bay command on February 20, 1850. The post was garrisoned by two companies of one of America's oldest regiments, the Fourth Artillery. Troops remained here until December of 1858 when Chief Billie Bowlegs and his warriors attacked the camp on what is now Billie's Creek. The name Fort Myers was in honor of Col. Abraham C. Myers, chief quartermaster of Florida and a North Carolina native who later became a Confederate general.

The area that is now Fort Myers was homesteaded by James Evans of Virginia and by 1878 a settlement began to spring up in the vicinity. Growth was steady and after a town had been organized, the movement for making it the county seat of the new county was started.

The first Lee County Courthouse, built in 1895 at a cost of $3,640 was a three-story frame building with a square tower. In 1915, following a heated controversy over the need for and cost of a new, more elaborate courthouse, construction began on the new building which still stands today.

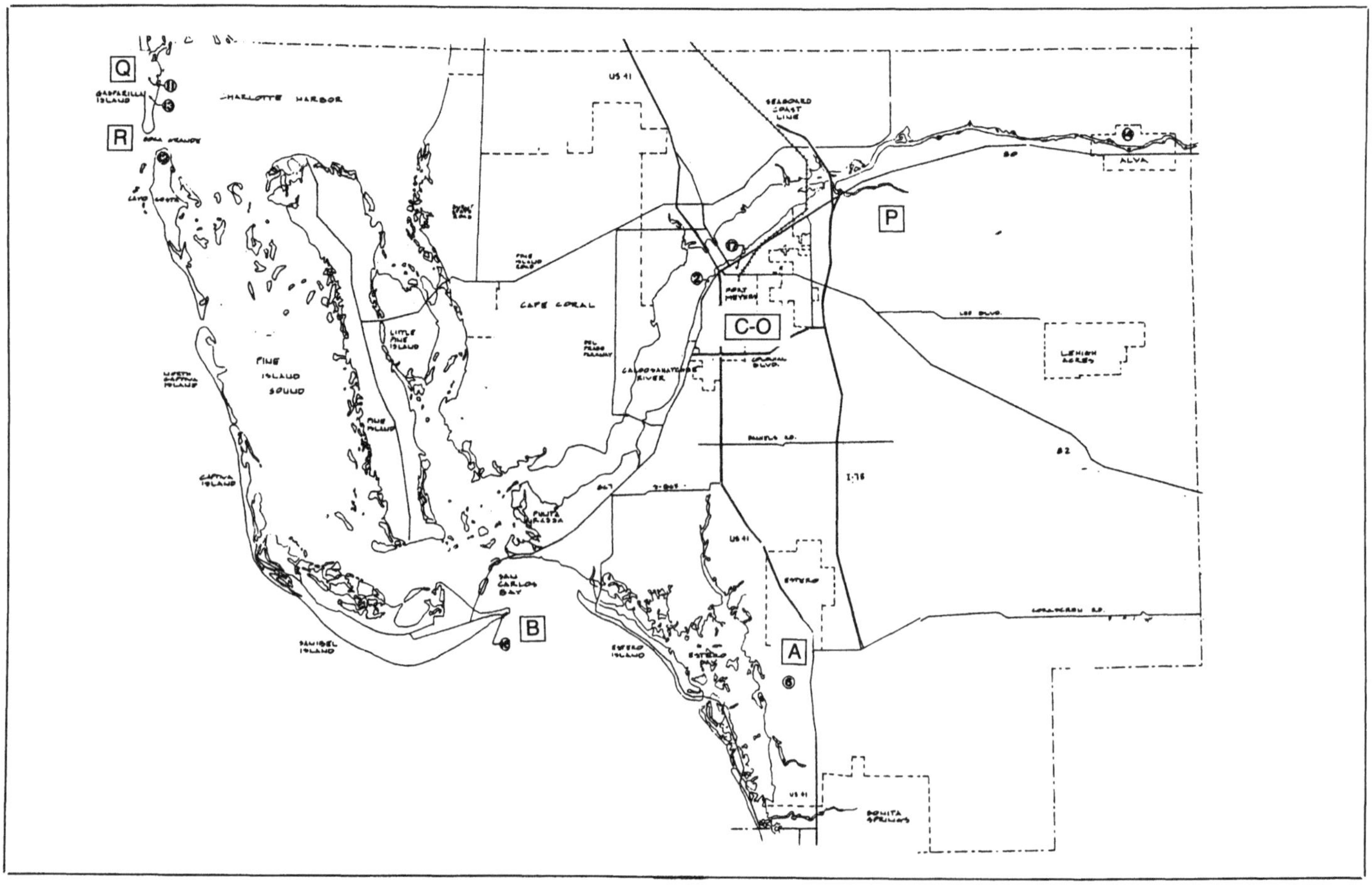

A
US 41
Estero

Koreshan State Historic Site contains seven of thirteen existing buildings from a Utopian Commune established in 1894 by Cyrus R. Teed. The buildings were constructed from native materials and some represent Florida Cracker style construction.

B
Point Ybel
Sanibel Island

Sanibel Lighthouse and keepers quarters, built 1884, large overhangs and low pitched roof adapts these structures to the climate. Light is still in use as an automatic electric light.

C
1249 Osceola Drive
Ft. Myers

Burdette-Roberts House, built 1924, Bungalow style frame house with low-pitched gable roof and heavy brick piers. Upswept wood trim and western patio. Constructed of locally milled heart-pine.

D
2400 McGregor Blvd.
Ft. Myers

Henry Ford — Biggar Home, built 1896, Bungalow style home with low roof lines, dormers, stone chimneys and large verandas. Made of Lee County Pine. Twice the size of the average bungalow.

E
2350 McGregor Blvd.
Ft. Myers

Thomas Alva Edison Residence, built 1886, Victorian style home was prefabricated in sections at Fairfield, Maine and brought by boat to Ft. Myers. A veranda wraps the home. Detailed wood work is suspended from the hipped roof.

F
2505 First Street
Ft. Myers

Murphy-Burroughs Home, built 1892 by John T. Murphy, Victorian house is largest and most ornate 19th Century residence in Ft. Myers. A veranda with detailed woodwork extends for three sides of the house. A widow walk, two chimneys, and ten dormers top the structure.

G
2581 First Street
Ft. Myers

Heitman House, built 1908. The roof shape and building mass is of the Queen Ann Style. Brick piers flanking the entry are of the Bungalow style. Circular veranda with upper story topped with a widow's walk.

H
2466 First Street
Ft. Myers

Langford-Kingston Home, built 1919 by Walter G. Langford. Bungalow style with red brick and white masonry. Modeled after home in Jacksonville. Two hip dormers, four full story dormers, and two chimneys.

I
2120 Main Street
Ft. Myers

Lee County Courthouse, built 1915, Neo-Classical Revival building having a two-story columned portico on the northwest side. The yellow brick complimented by the stone work create the exterior.

J
2248 First Street
Ft. Myers

First National Bank, built in 1914 in the Neoclassic Revival style, is one of two of its kind in Ft. Myers. The granite building is accented by four two-story columns and Palladian windows with brass frames.

K
2258 First Street
Ft. Myers

Earnhardt Building, built 1915, commercial architecture with brick facade complimented by trim work. At the cornice are spiral scrolls between green borders.

L
1534 Hendry Street
Ft. Myers

Old Lee County Bank, built 1911 by James A. Hendry, Neo-Classical Revival influence best seen in the entryway. Mosaic of Robert E. Lee recessed on the Hendry Street side. The red brick was stuccoed when the Lee County Bank moved in, in 1927.

M
1615 Hendry Street
Ft. Myers

Richards Building, built 1924 by Architect Fred J. James, brick exterior with stepped pilasters that create three vertical sections. Above each pilaster is a folliated bracket that pierces the frieze. The building was primarily used as the headquarters for the local chapter of the Knights of Pythias.

N
1625 Hendry Street
Ft. Myers

Robby and Stucky Building, built 1924, Neoclassic Revival industrial architecture with four pilasters slightly protruding from the brick exterior. A plain brick parapet capped with terra cotta crowns the building. A penthouse set back from the front becomes unnoticeable from street level. Important to economic growth of the downtown.

O
2300 Peck Street
Ft. Myers

Atlantic Coast Line Railroad Station, built 1924, Mediterranean Revival style with arched openings creating an arcade and curvilinear parapets. Rafters pierce the stucco finished facade to expose structure.

P
Buckingham Road
Buckingham

Buckingham School, built 1895, wood frame with metal roof. Simplicity of detail in the belfry is of interest. Used now as a community center.

Q
Fourth Street
Boca Grande

Charlotte Harbor and Northern Railway Depot, built 1910, Mediterranean Revival Style. A symbol to the railway's contribution to the growth of the area.

R
Southern tip of
Gasparilla Island

Boca Grande Lighthouse, built 1890 to open Boca Grande Harbor. Unique in the fact the light did not require much elevation due to its service as a harbor beacon.

HENDRY

FRANK COMARATI, FLORIDA SOUTH WEST

The earliest settlers in the area now known as Hendry County, came in the early 1800's as trappers and hunters. These pioneers traveled the Caloosahatchee River and traded with Indian inhabitants. During the Second Seminole War (1835-1842), the United States Army constructed several forts along the river, including two in Hendry County, Fort Denaud and Fort Thompson.

In 1854, the founding father of Hendry County, Francis A. Hendry, became a scout and dispatch rider for the army and was sent to the Labelle area, where he remained until the Third Seminole War ended in 1858. When the Seminole Wars finally ended, settlers from many section of the United States moved into southern Florida. As the population of southwest Florida grew, more and more cattlemen were attracted to the area, and ranching became one of the region's largest industries.

By 1889, Francis A. Hendry had founded the city of Labelle on the Caloosahatchee River, and by 1890, the area had its first school, an Indian Chickee. By the early 1900's, steamboats were traveling the Caloosahatchee bringing more settlers and visitors. Some of the famous frequent visitors included Harvey Firestone who experimented in the Labelle area with the planting of goldenrod as a sythetic rubber, Henry Ford who planted rubber trees, and Thomas Edison who searched for an inexpensive filament material.

In 1911, the city of Labelle was incorporated into what was then Lee County. By the 1920's, citizens of what is now Hendry County, felt they were not fairly represented and demanded their own government center. In 1923, the State of Florida divided Lee County into Lee, Henry and Collier counties. By 1926, Hendry County had its new county courthouse.

The 1930's saw a surge of population in Hendry County when the Army Corps of Engineers undertook the task of deepening and widening the Caloosahatchee River to improve drainage and to prevent the floods that had plagued the area. The Caloosahatchee, which had previously meandered in a snakelike path to the Gulf of Mexico, was dredged into a straight canal with locks to control water levels.

The major economic base of Hendry County during the 1930's and 1940's remained dependent upon cattle and ranching. Open range prevailed in Hendry County until the late 1930s, and cattle roamed almost anywhere. In later years, rangeland was slowly converted into citrus groves. Spurred by devastating freezes in central and north Florida, citrus growers found a frost-free climate in Hendry County ideal for groves. In the late 1980's, over 100,000 acres were used for citrus production in the Labelle area alone. Additional acreage in Hendry County was also under active citrus development.

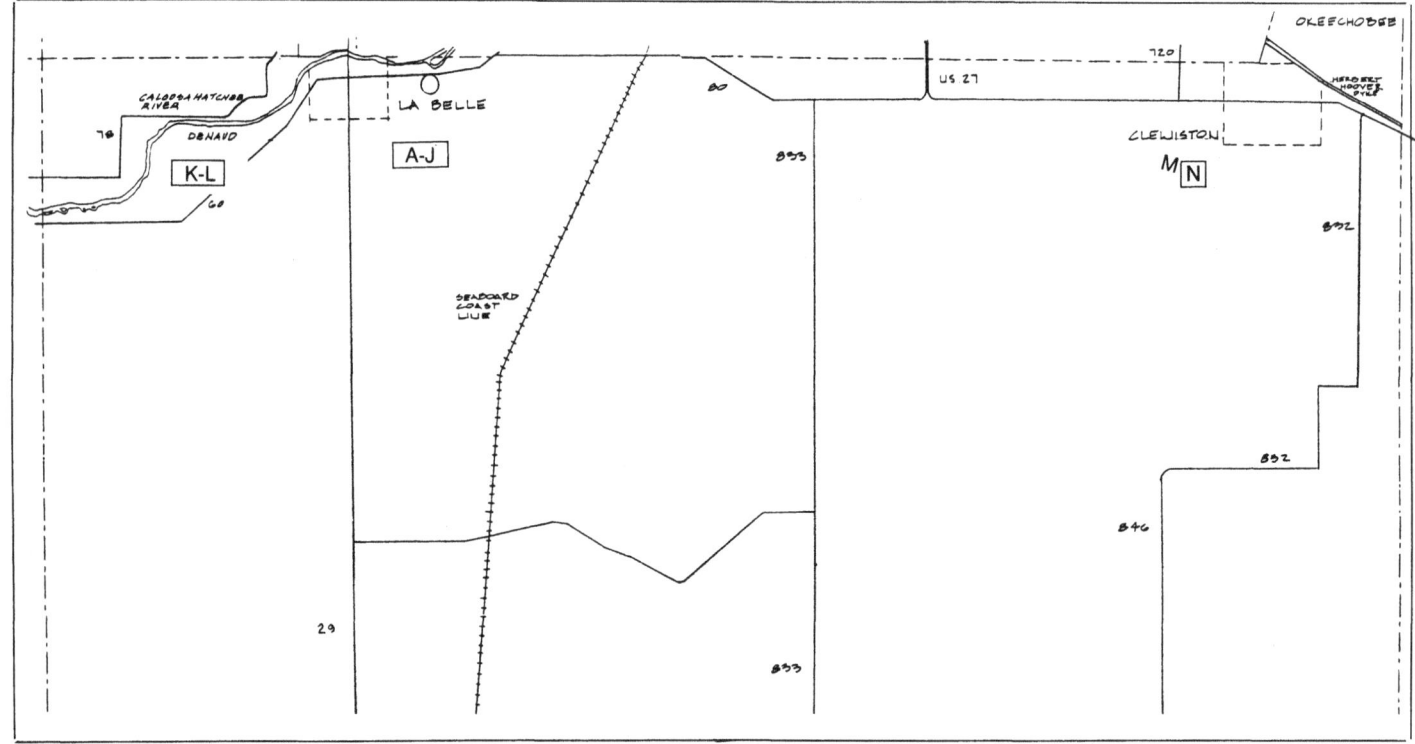

A
SR 29 & SR 80
Labelle

Hendry County Courthouse, built in 1926 with E. C. Hosford as architect. Italian Renaissance Revival brick structure, still in active use in the 1980's, with limestone-columnized entry arcade and imposing four-story corner clock tower.

B
Bridge Street &
Ft. Thompson
Labelle

Forrey Building, built in 1928. Masonry and stucco building with clay tile roof, attached buttresses, second story loggia, unique arched corner entry. First floor used, at different times, by Labelle post office, a bus station, a Western Union office, and (from 1942 to late 1980's) a popular local restaurant with second story as owner's residence.

C
Bridge Street
Labelle

Commercial Building, constructed in 1926 in Sears, a small sawmill town 12 miles south of Labelle, and moved to present location in early 1940's. Florida vernacular, two-story, wood-frame structure with metal roof, original twenty-foot-long, heart pine, board and batten siding.

D
Bridge Street &
Park Avenue
Labelle

Commercial Building, built in early 1920's of masonry with stucco finish and wood windows. Once owned by Henry Ford and occupied by the First Bank of Labelle. In late 1980's, structure occupied by two commercial spaces below two apartments and central stair.

E
160 Riverview St.
Labelle

Residence constructed in 1925 in Sears, a sawmill town, and moved to present location in 1940's. Two-story, wood-frame structure raised above grade, wood windows, and side porch addition. Symmetrical composition.

F
14 Washington Ave.
Labelle

Ollie Hampton House, built in Sears and moved to present site in 1930 after sawmill closed. Two-story, wood frame structure raised above grade, wood windows, large continuous overhang and operable wood shutters. Good example of early twentieth century vernacular architecture.

G
Bridge St. &
Washington Ave.
Labelle

One-story, wood-frame, hip-roofed structure, constructed in early 1920's. Excellent example of Florida construction with board and batten siding, raised above grade, and porch along front facade.

H
SR 29
Labelle

Warehouse, west of courthouse complex, constructed in 1920's as commissary in town of Sears. Building with metal roof, bracketed overhangs, wooden louvered vents, interior and original beaded panel ceiling and walls with exposed columns and beams and cuts resulting from moving structure to its present site.

I
West end Fraser St.
Labelle

Capt. F. A. Hendry House, constructed in 1914. Two-story, wood-frame structure, metal-shingled, steeply pitched roof, board and batten siding, and continuous veranda around first floor. Example of Florida vernacular style with bracketed columns, wood railings, and wood lattice surround on elevated veranda.

J
Curry Street
Labelle

Caldwell House, constructed in 1900's and initially used as hunting lodge. Said to be oldest house in Hendry County and visited by Thomas Edison and Henry Ford. Wood-frame structure with metal roof, board and batten siding, and elevated veranda with wood rails and lattice work. Excellent example of early Florida architecture.

K
South of SR 78
Denaud

Roan House, Caloosahatchee River, constructed on river bank as small store, post office, and telegraph office soon after Civil War. Constructed of wood frame with heart-pine board and batten siding and veranda later enclosed. In 1980's used as a residence.

L
South of SR 78
Denaud

State Historic Site of Fort Denaud, south bank of the Caloosahatchee River. Fort established in 1838 to serve as supply depot for troops in the Lake Okeechobee area during Seminole Wars with company quarters, hospital, guardhouse, store, and stables. Fort burned and abandoned in 1858.

M
729 N. Francisco Ct.
Clewiston

Commercial Building, believed to have been constructed in 1930's. Masonry and stucco with ornate parapet and detailing. Major alteration.

COLLIER

FREDERICK CALE

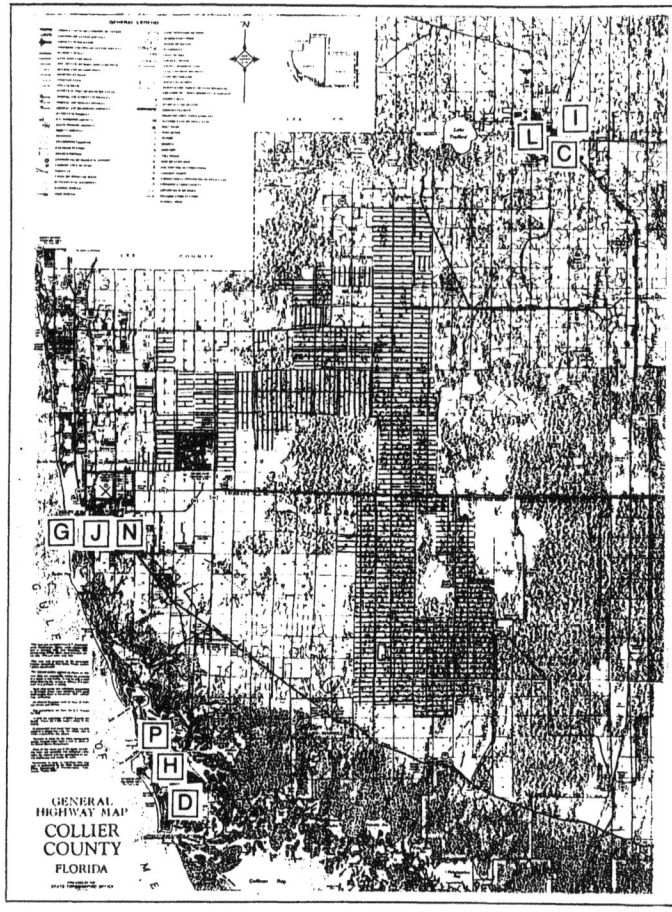

General Highway Map
COLLIER COUNTY
FLORIDA

O Of all Florida's 67 counties, Collier is perhaps the least known. With the exception of the cities of Naples and Immokalee, the communities are widely scattered in sparsely populated pockets located along the coast and on the interior of the county in an area larger than the state of Delaware. Only the extensive development of Marco Island in recent years has altered the established pattern of growth which has evolved in the rural and island settlements over the last century.

The first serious exploration of the region occurred during the closing years of the Second Seminole War, when combined service units of the U.S. Army and Navy converged on present day Collier County in a joint effort to seal off the southern portion of the Florida peninsula and pursue a more active strategy against the scattered bands of Seminoles still in the Everglades. Four forts were known to have been built in the area at the time.

Although Collier County was virtually untouched by the destruction of the Civil War, a number of Confederate blockade runners are known to have been active in this area between 1862 and 1864. An event that is worth noting was the flight of Confederate Secretary of State Judah P. Benjamin, along the Ten Thousand Islands at the conclusion of the war. To elude Federal patrols in the Gulf of Mexico, Benjamin skirted the maze of islands by boat in June, 1865, and made a landing on Cape Romano to resupply his party with bananas and coconut milk, before continuing on to Nassau and eventually, to England.

Modern day settlement of the County evolved slowly and in isolated pockets during the 1870's, while the region was still part of Monroe County. In 1887, it became part of newly-created Lee County and remained such for 36 years until July 7, 1923, when Collier County was formed.

The state's 62nd county is named for Barron Gift Collier, a Memphis-born businessman who spurred on the region's development and the completion of the Tamiami Trail with his personal fortune from streetcar advertising.

The arrival of modern communications, road and railroads eventually opened up the area's enormous agricultural and resort potential, but modest signs of growth were abruptly blunted by the onset of the Great Depression. The county's economy and population remained at a virtual standstill until the end of World War II, when a new wave of national prosperity sent thousands of businessmen and prospective home-buyers south. In the short span of thirty years, the number of permanent County residents swelled from 6,488 in 1950 to a phenomenal 85,000 in 1980.

The rapid and sustained expansion has led Collier County toward modernization on a vast and impressive scale in a remarkably short period of time. Fortunately, a surprisingly large number of historic sites and properties still survive to remind us of Collier County's pioneer origins and its early days as an untamed and self-reliant part of the southwest Florida frontier.

A
Everglades City
Collier County Courthouse. Built in 1926, this concrete and stucco building has a classical portico that is atypical for the area.

B
Everglades City
Community Church. This simple frame building is classically treated with a centrally placed tower over the main entrance.

C
Immokalee
Baptist Church. The entrance to this simple frame building is angled into the corner, giving the facade a unique appearance.

D
Marco Island
Church of Christ. Simple frame building with wide eaves on exposed rafters typical of churches in this area that are suited to the climate.

E
Everglades City
Bank of Everglades. Built in 1926, classic revival concrete and stucco building.

F
Chokoloskee
Smallwood Store. Built in 1917, and enlarged and raised onto its present pilings in 1925, the building is nearly in original condition.

G
Third Street South
Naples
Naples Mercantile Building. Built in 1919, this 2-story frame building is covered with stucco.

H
Collier Road
Marco Island
W. D. Collier House. Built around 1873, the house is a vernacular building with porches wrapped around it and abundant Victorian bric-a-brac trim.

I
2 Roberts Road
Immokalee
Roberts Ranch. This complex, established in the 1920's, consists of a homestead, bunkhouse, privy, tannery, kitchen and barn. The main house is a two-story bungalow.

J
Twelfth Avenue South
Naples
The Palm Cottage. The cottage was built about 1895 by Walter N. Halderman. It is constructed of tabby and is the only such building left in southwest Florida. It is the second oldest home in Naples.

K
US 41
East of **Ochopee**
Monroe Station. The Monroe Station was built in 1929 for the use of the Florida Mounted Police to help stranded travelers in the Everglades. The building has a low hipped roof with the first floor used as a store and the second floor as a residence.

L
US 41
Palm Hammock
Royal Palm Hammock Station. This station was built in the late 1920's as a refuge for stranded travelers. The building is somewhat Italianate in style with low hipped roof and wide eaves carried on ornamental brackets.

M
Everglades Blvd.
Everglades City
Everglades Depot. This Mission-style depot was built in the 1920's. It is stucco with a barrel tile roof.

N
East US 41
Naples
Naples Depot. This Mission-style depot was built in 1927. The depot, which connected Naples with the rest of the country, is one of the county's most historically significant buildings.

O
Everglades Blvd.
Everglades City
The Rod and Gun Club. Built in the 1890's. By the 1920's the building had been enlarged several times. The east end was the original house from which the club evolved.

P
Collier Road
Marco Island
Marco Inn. Built in the late 19th century, the building has undergone extensive alterations, yet maintained its original character.

GLADES

FREDERICK CALE

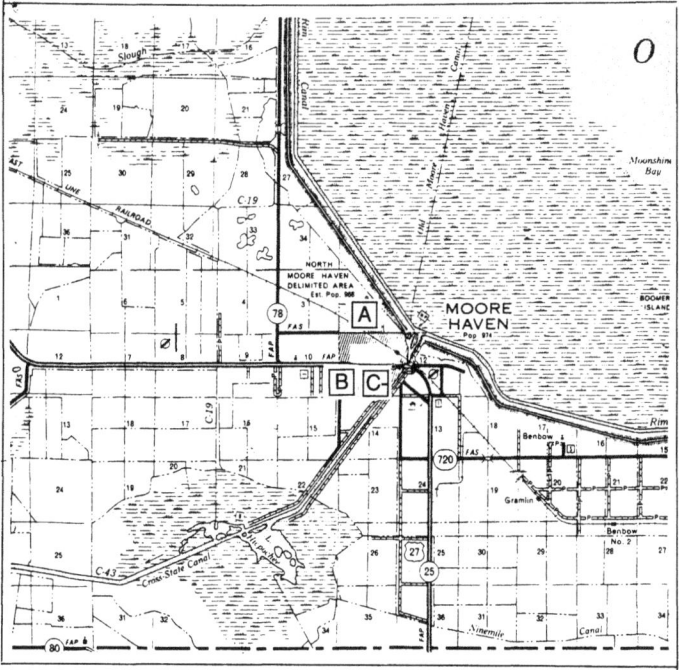

Despite the lush beauty of the land lying west and south of Lake Okeechobee, it was not until the last two decades of the nineteenth century that white settlers ventured into that area which would become Glades County. Generally designated as swampland, the territory was considered worthless and unfit for habitation. In 1839, however, U.S. soldiers began making forays up the Caloosahatchee River and along Fisheating Creek to locate and round up Indians for their relocation west of the Mississippi. Consequently, the first community of mention was Fort Center, erected on the site of a former Caloosa Indian Village on the banks of Fisheating Creek.

The potential for development of this Florida heartland was made manifest by events occurring in the 1840's. The provisions for homesteading were already in effect when the territory of Florida became a state in 1845. The passage of the Armed Occupation Act of 1842 gave 160 acres to anyone who occupied the land for five years and undertook their own defense.

A Senate bill introduced in 1848 granted Florida twenty million acres of land, mostly around Lake Okeechobee, on condition that drainage projects be financed by the sale of public lands at $1.25 an acre. The bill, known as the Swamp Land Act passed into law in 1850. Even so, homesteaders did not immediately begin flocking into the Okeechobee area. They were no doubt deterred by the subtropical heat, the swampy terrain and the abundance of snakes and insects. Notwithstanding these hardships, it was assumed that it was the presence of the Indians which discouraged homesteaders and thus began the Indian roundups of the 1850's, a campaign which did not end until 1858 with the removal of the intrepid Seminole leader, Billy Bowlegs.

The origin of cattle in southwest Florida is not known. Many historians refute legends that scrub cattle are descended from strays left during 16th century explorations along Florida's Gulf Coast. It is more commonly believed that the hardy, but non-pedigreed animals had their origins in herds brought south by the fleeing Seminoles.

Long before the first commercial fishing boats appeared on Lake Okeechobee, the cowboys were skirting the shores of the lake as they drove herds toward Punta Rassa. Yet, while the commercial fishing industry thrived and diminished over a 30-year period, the cattle industry has continued to expand.

In 1982, the cattle industry consisted of 70,000 head grazing over 400,000 acres. Some of the best pasturelands in Florida can be found along the Kissimmee and Caloosahatchee Rivers and the west shore of Lake Okeechobee.

In 1921, at the request of the DeSoto County Commissioners who were anxious to get out of long distance government, Glades County was created. It was Florida's 58th county and would eventually encompass 484,000 acres of land. Within Glades County is a 2,500 acre tract of land lying northwest of Lake Okeechobee that was acquired for the Seminole Indians as a reservation. It became known as Brighton Reservation and the Seminoles who occupy it branch from the Creek Indians of southern Georgia and Alabama. The change from a nomadic life was slow and difficult for these Indians, but after a few years Seminole children began to attend public school in Moore Haven and other towns lying near their reservations. As a generation of children became adults, the assimilation of Indians into the mainstream of life in Glades County became an accomplished fact of life.

A
Moore Haven
Glades County Courthouse. Designed by architect E.C. Hosford and built in 1928, the building is a well-proportioned Neo-classical structure of buff brick.

B
Moore Haven
Bungalow. In 1920, builder Wilson Langley Brown built a number of typical Florida bungalows which were placed on piers of higher than average height. Because of this, all of the bungalows in Moore Haven survived the devastating hurricane of 1926 which destroyed much of Glades County.

C
Moore Haven
Gram Building. In 1921, architect Victor Gram built the first post office in Glades County. The building survived the hurricanes of 1926 and 1928.

128

ST. LUCIE

FREDERICK CALE

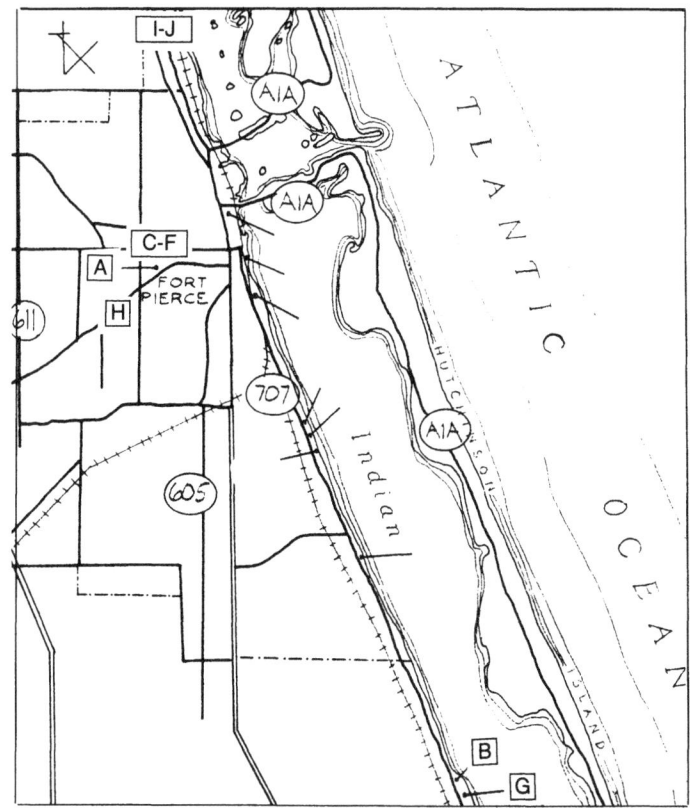

St. Lucie County has a long history of division and subdivision. In 1844, St. Lucie was created from Mosquito county. In 1855, the name was changed from St. Lucie to Brevard. By 1905, the county was once again named St. Lucie, but it was reorganized and portions of it were taken away to create Okeechobee in 1917 and Indian River and Martin in 1925. Fort Pierce, the county seat, is located approximately two-thirds of the way down the Florida peninsula.

In 1565, Pedro Menendez led 270 soldiers from St. Augustine and built a stockade near St. Lucie Inlet. By 1568, Indians, dysentery and hunger had reduced the original 270 to thirteen who fled back to St. Augustine. The Indians dominated the area until the Second Seminole War brought Lt. Col. Benjamin Kendrick Pierce in 1837. He established the Fort Pierce, which was one of a chain of forts that included Fort Capron, Fort Mellon and Fort Vinton.

The Fort Pierce area began to flourish in the 1860's and by 1866, it had a post office and general store. Fort Pierce was incorporated in 1901.

A
303 S. Indian River Dr.
Ft. Pierce

McCarty House. Built in 1905, this is the home of former governor Dan McCarty.

D
2507 S. Indian River Drive
Ft. Pierce

Hugh West Home. A 1920's example of Spanish or Mediterranean Revival architecture.

G
12387 S. Indian River Drive
Ankona

Capt. John Miller House. Sea captain John Miller built this home in 1884 of heart pine. It is presently being restored.

B
13055 S. Indian River Drive
Ankona

Eden House. Built in 1880, this building housed the pineapple business begun by Capt. Thomas E. Richardson, who brought the first pineapple ships to the area. This house is built mainly of cypress wood from wrecked ships.

E
2513 S. Indian River Drive
Ft. Pierce

Padrick House. A 1920's example of Spanish or Mediterranean Revival architecture.

H
100 Avenue A
Ft. Pierce

Pitts Furniture Co. Built in 1882 and known as Cobb's Store, it was operated 1933. It is completely restored.

C
2501 S. Indian River Drive
Ft. Pierce

Adams House. A 1920's example of Spanish or Mediterranean Revival architecture.

F
1100 Delaware Ave.
Ft. Pierce

Ft. Pierce Elementary School. Built in 1914 and in continuous use as a school ever since.

I
2515 N. Indian River Drive
St. Lucie Village

Senator Quay House. Senator Quay of Pennsylvania built this house in 1895 for use as his winter home. There are many interesting original details on the interior such as marble sinks and claw-footed bathtub.

OKEECHOBEE

PETER JEFFERSON, FAIA, INDIAN RIVER CHAPTER

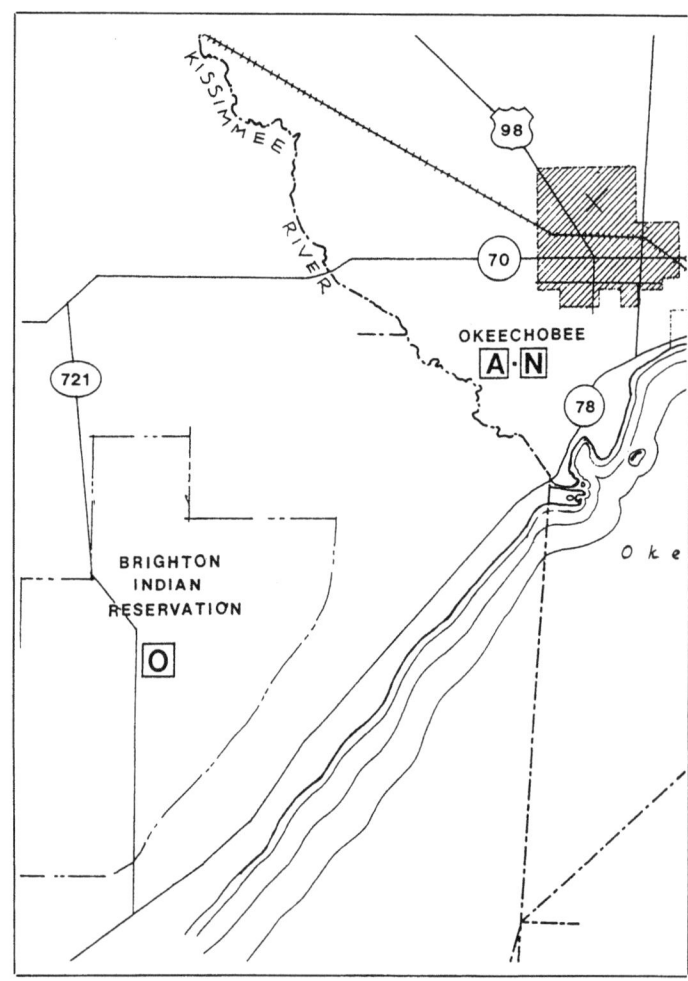

Okeechobee County is comprised of 575,360 acres bordered by the Kissimmee River and Lake Okeechobee. The name is Indian, "oki" meaning water and "chobi" meaning big. Lake Okeechobee is the second largest fresh water lake in the United States.

The first inhabitants of this area were aboriginal Florida Indians. The Seminoles appeared in the region after 1710 and were a mixture of Alachua or lower Creeks from Central Georgia and the 25 separate aboriginal tribes existing in Florida prior to 1600.

The first recorded history of the county was the Battle of Okeechobee during the Seminole War. Under the leadership of Col. Zachary Taylor, about 1,000 U.S. soldiers fought an indecisive battle on Christmas Day. Left alone in the vast Everglades into which they'd been pushed, the Seminoles made a swift and successful adaptation to a water environment. The elevated, thatched-roof, open-sided "chickee" provided housing that was easily built from native materials. To provide a cash income, the Indians hunted and trapped the abundant wildlife. They also brought fresh venison, pumpkins and bananas, arrowroot and some livestock to sell to storekeepers. Many of the traders' wives taught Seminole men and women how to use sewing machines that became so popular in developing the unique pattern of Indian dress.

Over the years, the Seminoles became an accepted part of life in the little communities that grew up near trading posts. Although they attended local churches, few showed any interest in converting to Christianity until recently.

White friends of the Seminoles took the lead in having Federal and State Reservations established in Florida as a permanent home for the Indians. This was quite different from the western U.S. where tribes were driven onto vast tracts of useless land where they were virtually prisoners on reservations.

About 1896, Peter Raulerson came from Polk County looking for more cattle range. He built a cabin on the west side of Taylor Creek at what was to become the town of Okeechobee. The Florida East Coast Railroad planned for Okeechobee to be a major transportation center, the "Chicago of the South." The railroad abandoned its plans during the 1930's, competition being a primary factor. In 1917, Okeechobee County was formed from parts of Osceola, St. Lucie and Palm Beach, with the town of Okeechobee as county seat. The hurricane of 1928 caused extensive flooding from Lake Okeechobee. Only two buildings were left standing in Belle Glade, ninety-three percent of Pahokee was destroyed and the town of Moore Haven was demolished. Damage to property and crops was estimated at $50 million.

Okeechobee County is one of Florida's largest livestock markets and dairy producers. Dozens of recreational fishing camps and parks are located on the north and east shores of Lake Okeechobee. A ratio of nineteen acres for every person in the county makes it one of the least populated counties in the state.

A
304 N.W. 2nd St.
Okeechobee

Courthouse — built 1926. The breezeway leading into courtyard has been enclosed. Open stairways to the courtroom on the second floor. Contractors — Rogers and Duncanson. Architect — George Gaynor Hyde. Southern Colonial Revival.

B
Park St. at 3rd Ave.
Okeechobee

City Hall — built 1926. A formal, elegant building. Mediterranean revival.

C
SW 2nd Av. &
SW 7th St.
Okeechobee

Okeechobee Public School — built 1916. Hanner Brothers, contractor. F.H. Trimble, Architect. A well-preserved red brick building. Colonial Revival.

D
SW 2nd Ave.
& SW 7th St.
Okeechobee

Okeechobee High School — built 1925. Rogers and Duncanson — Contractor. Wm. Hatcher and Lawrence Funke, Architects. Next to the public school in a park-like setting, the red brick building is marred by external air-conditioning units. Colonial Revival.

E
SW 5th Ave. &
SW 4th St.
Okeechobee

First Baptist Church — built 1915. A well preserved white stuccoed building.

F
NW 2nd Ave. &
NW 2nd St.
Okeechobee

Methodist Episcopal Church — built 1924. A red brick building with window detail derived from Gothic design.

G
Park St. at NW 9th Av.
Okeechobee

Bank Building and Commercial Block — built circa 1926. Yellow/buff brick and classic detail. Unoccupied.

H
Park St. & SW 5th Av.
Okeechobee

Raulerson Building — circa 1925. Continuous canopy at both streets has been removed. Red brick, two stories.

I
2 miles from town
NW on Rt. 98
Okeechobee

Elementary School House — built 1909 by Sam Matthews of Stuart. Moved from 410 S. Parrott Ave. to present location in historical park. Frame vernacular.

J
600 S. Parrott Ave.
Okeechobee

Freedman/Raulerson House — built 1923. The original structure was built by Mr. Hough in 1923. The "El" addition in 1925 was done by Mr. Zaender. The house was owned by prominent families of Okeechobee, including the Florida Speaker of the House Peter Tomasello, during the early thirties. Masonry stuccoed structure. Recently relocated. Craftsman vernacular. Listed on the National Register of Historic Places.

K
SE 3rd Ave. &
SE 2nd St.
Okeechobee

Houses, typical of neighborhood, circa 1925. Frame vernacular.

L
SE 3rd Ave. &
SE 2nd St.
Okeechobee

House, typical, circa 1925.

M
Sw 2nd Ave. &
SW 4th St.
Okeechobee

Houses, typical of a neighborhood, circa 1920.

N
NW 3rd Ave. &
NW 5th St.
Okeechobee

Jail — built circa 1916. Now used as Civil Defense Headquarters. The first woman sheriff in Florida had offices in this building.

O
Brighton Indian
Reservation
West of Okeechobee

Typical Chickee. The hut is usually thatched with palmetto fronds but occasionally with slabs of cypress bark. The cooking hut is different from the dwellings, being floorless and having a fire area in the center. Dwellings may have a raised platform. The frame is made of cypress poles.

Seminole Indians lived within the city limits in camps as recently as the twenties, and in villages nearby; still in the traditional chickee. Today, except in remote areas, the chickee is no longer utilized for dwellings.

PALM BEACH

EUGENE PANDULA, AIA, PALM BEACH CHAPTER

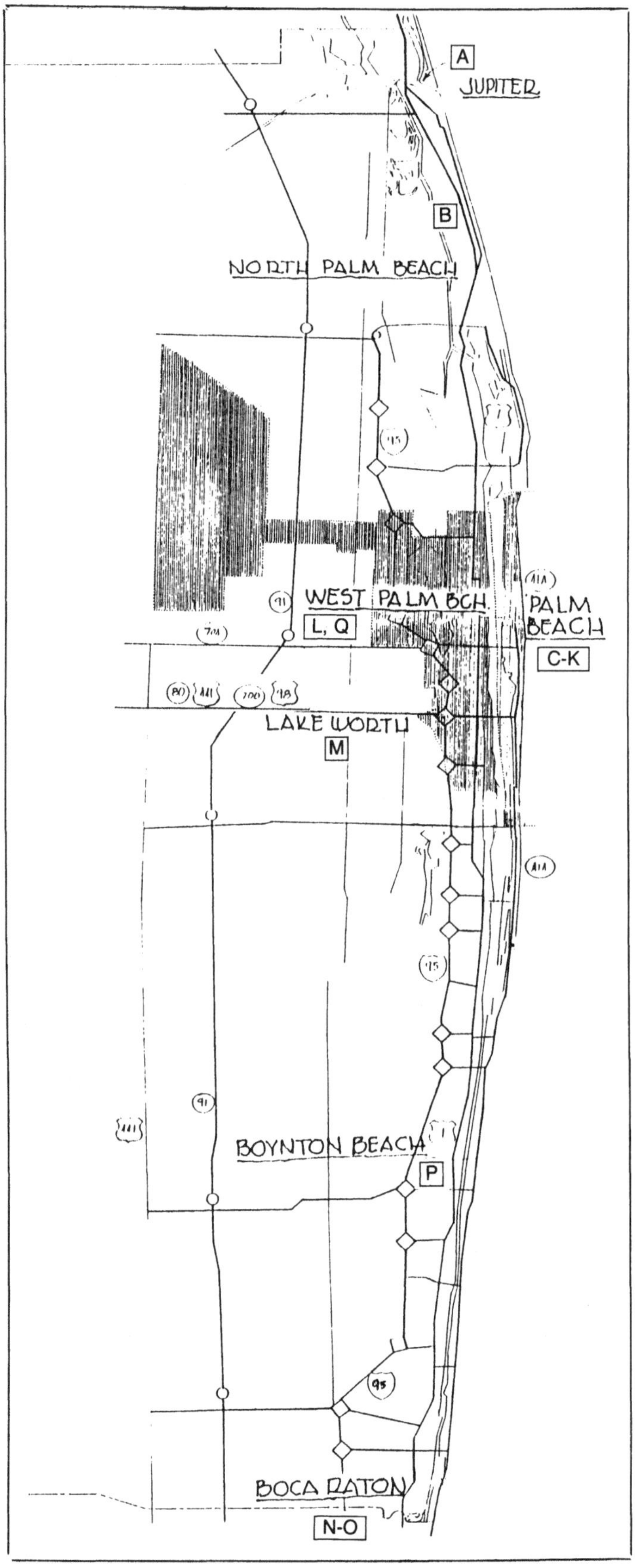

Palm Beach County was established in April 1907. Covering a total of 2,578 square miles, the county incorporates plush resorts on its Atlantic Coast and farms harvesting vegetables four times a year on its western edge. Henry Morrison Flagler saw the potential of the area and contributed much to the development of the county which attracts thousands of tourists to its communities.

Historians do not agree on who were the first settlers in Palm Beach County or where they settled. Some abandoned sites and old orange groves suggest they might have been shipwrecked Spaniards who set up remote settlements near where they happened to run aground, or they could have been Englishmen from the New Smyrna area who wandered down the Florida coast during the British period of Florida history.

Little settlement took place in this coastal area until the late 1830's. Americans built Fort Jupiter at Jupiter Inlet from 1838 to 1842. Contruction of Jupiter Lighthouse began at this site in 1853. It was not until the 1870's that many families began to arrive. Captain Elisha Newton Dimick, known as the founder of Palm Beach, came to the island in 1876 and built his house in the vicinity of the present Whitehall. In 1880 Irving R. Henry homesteaded 130 acres of land where West Palm Beach is today. One of the earliest settlers, a German horticulturalist named A.O. Lang, planted limes, oranges, mangos, pineapples, and other fruit.

The Spanish Ship "La Providencia," wrecked on the coast in 1878, carried a cargo of wine and coconuts. Though the wine might have contributed to the quality of seamanship which grounded the ship, it was the coconuts which left their mark by planting the seeds, literally, for the area's later name of Palm Beach. (In 1880 settlers were granted a post office listed as Palm City, but they discovered another Florida town had that name. The area was renamed Palm Beach.)

By 1893 Henry Flagler's East Coast Railway had reached as far south as Rockledge, a town almost halfway between St. Augustine and Palm Beach. Attracted by the beauty of the Palm Beach island, Flagler purchased property on both sides of Lake Worth and began construction of the Royal Poinciana Hotel with building materials shipped down the Indian River, cross country on the Jupiter and Lake Worth Railroad, and by boat across Lake Worth. Flagler envisioned Palm Beach as an exclusive winter resort with commercial and other services located in West Palm Beach. Passengers arriving by rail were ferried across Lake Worth to his Palm Beach hotels until a bridge was built in 1895. (This bridge was replaced by the Flagler Memorial Bridge in 1938.) Palm Beach soon became regarded as the winter counterpart of Newport. After World War I, the designer Addison Mizner transformed the prevailing architectural trend of gable-roofed frame houses with cupolas and intricate ornamentation to palatial estates constructed in a style now known as Mediterranean Revival. Following the popularity of his design for the stucco Everglades Club building with its red tile roof, medieval turrets, and wrought-iron grille work, Mizner's many commissions were built with courtyards, arcades and galleries, pools, beamed ceilings, and decorative elements of materials produced by his own factories. Architectural firms such as Joseph Urban, Shultz and Weaver, Carrere and Hastings, Hiss and Wickes, and Maurice Fatio added to the building heritage of this unusual locality.

The 1920's land boom established an attractive Florida image. Palm Beach was a major beneficiary of this development until economic distress and the devastating 1928 hurricane brought building to a halt. The storm, which hovered over the area for eight hours and killed more than 2,000 people, brought about the construction of the Herbert Hoover Dike to control the waters of Lake Okeechobee and permitted inland areas to expand production of winter vegetables, mainly tomatoes and string beans. This agricultural production is still the mainstay of the Everglades area. Belle Glade is known as the winter vegetable capital of the nation.

World War II saw Morrison Field established at West Palm Beach as a flight training school and the embarkation point for Army Air Force bomber crews. As elsewhere in Florida, many of the men trained in the area returned to establish careers and homes after the war. In new residential developments, one popular construction style reflected West Indian and Bermudian precedents.

Although highrise residential and office buildings, shopping centers, and urban sprawl sometimes dominate, the visitor can still sense the unique quality of this area and the architectural contrasts existing between the luxury of Worth Avenue, the highrise businesses of West Palm Beach, and the rural isolation of the adjoining Lake Okeechobee area.

E
Worth Avenue
Palm Beach
Worth Avenue, four block east-west street as southern extremity of shopping area. Everglades Club at west end, Memorial Fountain and Plaza at east. Via Mizner and Via Parigi, typical Addison Mizner designs in Mediterranean Revival style.

F
356 Worth Avenue
Palm Beach
Everglades Club, built in 1918-1919 with Addison Mizner as architect. Mizner's first building which was intended as a convalescent center for war veterans but emerged as an exclusive club. Venetian Gothic windows, a bell tower in the style of a California Spanish mission church, latticed balconies, and an arcade with tile spandrels, tinted stucco, barrel tiled roofs, and striped awnings.

A
Juncture of
Loxahatchee River
and Jupiter Sound
Jupiter Inlet Lighthouse. Construction beginning in 1853, designed by John W. Nystram, activated in 1860. Light not used during Civil War at order of Confederacy. Dominant landmark in Palm Beach County with post-Civil War activities, such as the life saving station, typifying the value of a coastal station to transportation and commerce.

C
561 North Lake Trail
Palm Beach
Duck's Nest, built in 1891 with Henry Maddock as assembler and Long Island Portable Housing Company as builder. Oldest house extant in Palm Beach. Two shingled gabled sections allegedly prefabricated in New York and shipped by barge to site. Central false gable added at later date. Board and batten walls. Porch roof and eaves with barge boards. Additions of two-story octagonal south wing with scalloped shingles and glass enclosure of porch. House name derived from birds attracted to fresh water lake at east side of house (now filled in).

G
255 S. County Road
Palm Beach
First National Bank, built in 1920 with Maurice Fatio as architect. Commercial building accented by Italian Mannerist and Spanish Renaissance details with elaborate grillework door set within a rusticated arch with a broken arch pediment. A shield ornament crowning the overscaled keystone, rustication repeated by quoins. Variety of materials incorporated in building with stucco balconies and pilasters, iron grilles, wood fascia, and stone cornice.

D
1100 S. Ocean Blvd.
Palm Beach
Mar-A-Lago, built in 1928 with Joseph Urban as architect, Walter and Franz Barwig as sculptors, and Lewis and Valentine as landscape architects. Seasonal residence of Mrs. Marjorie Merriweather Post. Designed for family and guests with isolated apartments, entertainment center, and service functions built around a semi-circular patio facing Lake Worth. Mediterranean Renaissance Revival style. Horizontal mass dominated by massive tower and chimneys, bas relief plants, birds and animals on walls, antique tile roof, decorative tiles and exceptional interior details.

B
951 US Highway 1
North Palm Beach
Palm Beach Winter Club, built in 1926 with Louis De Puyseger of Paris, France, as architect and Arnold Brothers, Inc., as builders at cost of $500,000. Mediterranean Revival style four-story building.

H
145 N. County Road
Palm Beach
Paramount Theatre and Shops, built in 1926-1927 with Joseph Urban as architect. Mediterranean Revival style building designed as a complete cultural center originally with cinema theater, restaurants, residences, commercial shops, and offices (in mid 1980's containing offices and shops only). Performers such as George Gershwin, Al Jolson, and Billie Burke once on Paramount stage.

133

I
South County Road
Palm Beach

Breakers Hotel Complex (hotel and cottages), built in 1925 with Schulze and Weaver as architecture firm. Mediterranean Revival style, one of the most prestigious American resort hotels. Guest lists like pages from the social register. Contemporary with the Royal Poinciana, the first hotel on island. Epitomizes the Florida boom years. Fourteen cottages built in the shingle style. One cottage (Seagull) moved behind Royal Poinciana Chapel and completely restored.

J
Whitehall Way
Palm Beach

Whitehall (Henry Morrison Flagler Museum), built in 1900-1901. Designed by Carrere and Hastings for third wife (Mary Lily Kenan) of Henry Morrison Flagler, founding partner of Standard Oil Company and creator of late nineteenth-century railroad and hotel empire on Florida's east and south coasts. Eighteen months of craftsmen's work on this architectural landmark of Neo-Classical style. Open as house museum.

K
549 North Lake Way
Palm Beach

Episcopal Church Bethesda by the Sea, built in 1894. Palm Beach's first church which originally had to be accessed by boat. Shingle style structure with wood shake gabled roof. Exposed rafters projecting under deep eaves, shingled walls, deep arched veranda across front, and Palladian window in chancel wall. Three-story frame bell tower with metal filigree numeral clock and large louvers at bell area. Last service on April 12, 1925.

L
Palm Beach

Phipps Plaza or Circle Plaza, built in 1925 as development venture by John S. Phipps. Workable alternate to linear and grid urban development. Commercial and residential cul-de-sac with automobile parking around the circuit and the circle serving as landscaped public parking.

M
Tamarind Ave. at
Datura St.
West Palm Beach

Seaboard Coastline Railroad Station, built in 1924-1925. Spanish Baroque influence similar to Cloister Hotel at Boca Raton.

N
1702 Lake Worth Rd.
Lake Worth

Coconut Tree House, built in 1910. Believed to be oldest frame building in Lake Worth. Excellent example of pioneer house built during the period when saw mills were established enabling anyone to purchase lumber. One-story frame structure with gambrel roof and second story in the gambrel.

O
West of intersection
of Old Dixie Hwy. &
SE 8th St.
Boca Raton

Boca Raton Florida East Coast Railway Passenger Station, built in 1929 with Chester G. Henninger or Addison Mizner as architect and Johnson Finance and Construction Co. of Jacksonville as builder. Mediterranean Revival Style building associated with developments initiated by Clarence H. Geist who donated the land for the station and bought railway bonds to have the station built to his specifications. Boca Raton Historical Society planning restoration in mid 1980's.

P
71 N. Federal Hwy.
Boca Raton

Boca Raton City Hall, built in 1926 with Addison Mizner and William E. Alsmeyer as architects and F.H. Link and J.E. Cramer as builders. Significant as one of the few planned buildings actually constructed in Addison Mizner's dream city, a planned Spanish-styled city on banks of Lake Boca Raton. Served as center of Boca Raton's municipal government until 1963. Still used for city offices and the Boca Raton Historical Society and Preservation Board office.

Q
Boynton Beach

Boynton Woman's Club, built in 1925 with Addison Mizner as architect. Known for Addison Mizner's distinctive adaptation of Spanish elements which created a style that greatly influenced Florida's architecture in the 1920's and 1930's.

R
105 S. Flagler Drive
West Palm Beach

Woman's Club of West Palm Beach, built in 1917 with W.B. Eckler as architect and A.C. Nelson as builder. Deeded to Woman's Club for 99 years in 1916 by the city. Original structure two-story concrete construction in modified mission style with Spanish style red roof and wide verandas on the east and south. Verandas eliminated in renovations and roof replaced twice due to hurricane damage. Current restoration completed in 1976 with Colonial style entrances.

MARTIN

PETER JEFFERSON, FAIA, INDIAN RIVER CHAPTER

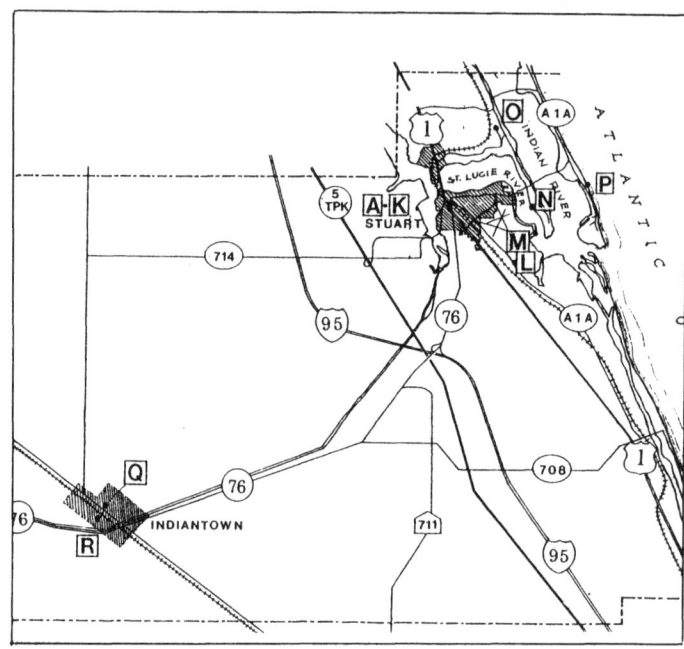

Martin County lies just north of Palm Beach County in the midst of the lower east coast winter resort section of Florida. Its coastal area consists of a succession of small resorts with Stuart, the county seat, Jupiter Island and Port Salerno as the outstanding points of interest. Linking Stuart to the west is the Okeechobee Waterway which connects the St. Lucie River to Lake Okeechobee and the Caloosahatchee River and further on to the Gulf of Mexico at Fort Myers.

The section of Florida comprised by Martin County was one of the earliest to be discovered. In Jonathan Dickinson's book, *Gods Protecting Providence,* which was published in 1720, he gave an account of a party of Quakers who were shipwrecked near Hobe Sound in 1796.

Martin County was originally part of Dade County. Originally, the only habitable part of the county lay along the Indian River, which is actually a great lagoon fed by numerous fresh water streams. The Seminoles, driven from Georgia, also settled along the river at Indiantown in the early 19th century. In 1835, the Seminole War broke out and the last battle of that war was fought fourteen miles northwest of the present site of Indiantown. During World War 1, the U.S. Army once again returned to Indiantown to dig the St. Lucie Canal as part of the Everglades Drainage System.

In 1924, S. Davies Warfield arrived with his Seaboard Airline Railway and began buying land. Warfield looked forward to the construction of a large city with the railroad as the focal point, but he died before his dream was realized.

Martin County was created in 1925 from parts of Palm Beach and St. Lucie counties. The area which became Martin county was settled in the 1870's and around 1882, the first permanent home was built at Stuart, then called Potsdam. From 1890 to 1910, the principle crop was pineapple. In 1902, Stuart was the largest shipping port of Red Spanish pineapples in the world. The thriving pineapple trade in Martin county was one of the things that persuaded Henry Flagler to extend his railroad down the eastern coast of Florida. However, the bottom dropped out of the pineapple business, along with the citrus industry, when the Great Freeze of 1895 occurred. The real estate boom of the 1920's once again brought prosperity which was only to disappear with the stock market crash of 1929 and two major hurricanes, one in 1928 and one in 1933.

During the 1930's, Martin county began attracting national attention. The fabulous fishing grounds became a magnet to sportsmen and the county's fishing villages survived and prospered while the rest of the country suffered the Great Depression. Now, in an effort to preserve the tranquility of former times, Stuart is seeking to control growth with a density cap of 15 or less units per acre and a 4-story limit on buildings.

A
101 W. Flagler Ave.
Stuart
Stuart Feed Store — Geo. W. Parks Grocery and Gen. Merchandise Store — built 1905, with living quarters above, between the railroad and St. Lucie River. Frame vernacular.

B
73 W. Flagler Ave.
Stuart
Harry E. Feroe Building — built 1913, by Sam Matthews. It housed a drug store and the post office. Built of "rock-face" concrete block and cast iron front columns.

C
216 Flagler Ave.
Stuart
Lyric Theatre — built 1926 for John C. Hancock, the third "Lyric Theatre" in Stuart. Mediterranean Revival. Architect — John M. Sherwood, Stuart; Contractor, F.M. Walton. Sherwood also designed the Atlantic Court Apartments, E. Ocean Blvd.

D
Akron Ave. at 3rd St.
Stuart
Woodmen Hall — built 1913-14. Built as the Christian Endeavour Hall by the Methodist Church. Used by Woodmen of the World fraternal and insurance organization, for the first city commission meetings, by Woman's Club, Odd Fellows, and was the first telephone exchange. Builder — Sam Matthews. Frame vernacular.

E
100 E. Ocean Blvd.
Stuart
Court House — addition built in 1937 to the front of the 1915 high school. L. Phillips Clarke of West Palm Beach, Architect. Masonry & stucco, art-deco, cast ornament.

F
524 St. Lucie Crescent
Stuart
The France — Apartment house, built 1927, garage below, common lounge areas with fireplaces, linking the two apartment wings, u-shaped with fountain in the entrance court. Mediterranean Revival.

G
210 SW Atlanta Ave.
Stuart
Walter and Emma J. Kitching House — built 1894, with large acreage of pineapples. The front faces the river. Frame vernacular.

H
110 SW Atlanta Ave.
Stuart
Dudley/Bessey House — built 1909. A dogtrot plan, the front faces the river. Alterations and additions to streetside. Colonial Revival.

I
204 SE Atlanta Ave.
Stuart
John E. Taylor House — built 1914, first floor porches and second floor added 1925 in craftsman bungalow style. The original two-story garage has been replaced.

J
1005 SW St. Lucie Crescent
Stuart
D. Harry Dyer Homestead — built 1904, with extensive pineapple fields. The front faces the river. In almost original condition. Frame vernacualr.

K
1170 E. Ocean Blvd.
Stuart
Albert R. Krueger Homestead, named "Burnbare" — built 1894, a pineapple plantation. A packing house remains on the site. Land purchased from President Harrison for $1.25/acre. Frame vernacular.

L
3231 SE Dixie Hwy.
A.1.A.
South of Stuart
Golden Gate Building — built in 1925. A real estate development company's office during the boom. Vacant, in disrepair. Mediterranean revival.

M
Old St. Lucie Blvd.
Port Sewall
Sunrise Inn — Circa 1925, near the St. Lucie Inlet, replacing early inns, used as a resort hotel, oriented to river and ocean fishing. Mediterranean revival.

N
143 S. Sewall's Pt. Rd.
Sewall's Point
Bay Tree Lodge — built 1909 for James Viles by Sam Matthews. Cypress shingle walls (and original roof), extensive veranda, boat house at river, 1909, is similar. Now owned by Kiplinger Washington editors.

O
2303 NE Seaview Dr.
Jensen Beach
All Saints Episcopal Church (originally known as All Saints, Waveland) — built 1898-99, moved a few hundred feet in 1963; the portion west of the tower was added and the original entrance at the tower base was closed. Frame vernacular.

P
301 SE McArthur Causeway
Hutchinson Island
Gilbert's Bar House of Refuge — built in 1875 — operated by U.S. Life Savings Service. Contractor Blaisdale, Boston, who built five similar houses. One of ten houses of refuge spaced 20 miles apart along the East Florida Coast, the house contained downstairs living quarters for the keeper and his family; a single room upstairs served as a dormitory for those who sought refuge there. No rescue service was provided, but aid, food, clothing and medicine were available. The building was moved about 25' back from the ocean early this century. Cost $2,900. Now a historical museum. It is the only remaining house of refuge.

Most of the original materials remain in place. New buildings have both been added or replaced — original outbuildings.

Listed National Register of Historic Places.

Q
Warfield Blvd.
Indiantown
Seminole Inn — built 1925-26 by S. Davies Warfield, president of the Seaboard Airline Railroad. Built at the same time were the Warfield School, houses and apartment houses. His niece, Wallis Warfield Simpson, became the Dutchess of Windsor. Mediterranean Revival.

INDIAN RIVER

VINCENT NICOTRA, AIA

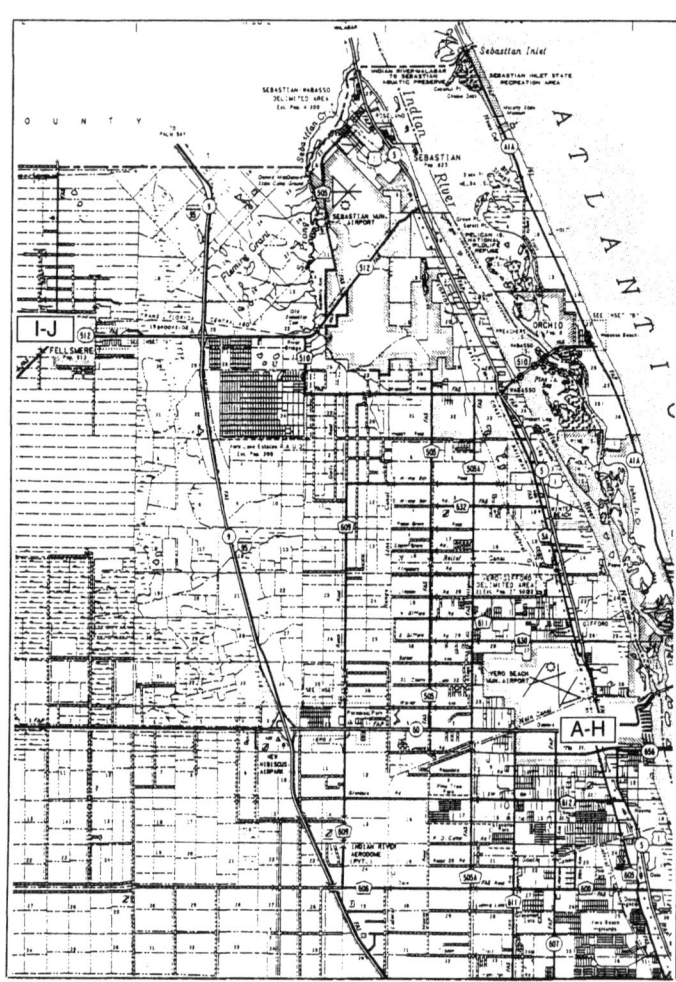

In the 1880's, the early settlers were attracted to the area by the lush vegetation, the abundance of fish, oysters and game and the government's offer of 160 acres of high land for $50. In 1887, Henry Gifford built the first log cabin and palmetto shack, and in 1889, five people petitioned for a local post office. Two names, "Venice" and "Vero" were submitted to the Postmaster General for consideration of a post office name. Vero, which means "truth" was selected and the post office was established in 1891.

The first telephone line was ordered from Montgomery Ward & Co. and put into H.T. Gifford's home in 1889. Six families were given service on this line. The first road was built by H.T. Gifford and S.T.Hughes and it extended from Sebastian to Fort Pierce.

Captain Frank Foster took a land grant in the 1880's near Wabasso and was the first person to grow citrus in this part of Florida. Other crops grown by the early settlers were pineapple, coconut and bananas, but these crops gradually gave way to the more profitable citrus culture.

In 1905, St. Lucie County was formed from Brevard. In 1910, the City of Vero Beach was incorporated while still part of St. Lucie County and in 1925, Indian River County was established as a separate entity.

Along with the rest of the Florida east coast, Vero Beach, the county seat, experienced the real estate boom days of the mid-1920's. The population grew to 2,266 in 1930, but the subsequent years of depression slowed the rate of progress. Citrus and agriculture continued expanding, however, to become the number one industry in the area. Tourism is number two, with light industry being third. The 1984 population of the City of Vero Beach was 17,031 and Indian River County 74,162.

A

1805-1815 19th Place
Vero Beach

Boarding Houses. 1915 Mediterranean-style twin buildings still in use.

B

1519 19th Place
Vero Beach

Graves House. Built in 1924 by J. Hudson Baker, a contractor, for his daughter. Ornate Mediterranean-style residence.

C

Intersection of
Railroad tracks and
19th Place
Vero Beach

Vero Beach Power Plant. Built 1926, typical brick utilitarian structure of the period.

D

1423 20th Street
Vero Beach

Illinois Hotel. Mediterranean-style commercial building with arcade at first floor level, probably built during the 1920's.

E

2004 14th Ave
Vero Beach

King's Cabaret. This 1920's commercial building has some Spanish and Moorish overtones in the ornate exterior detail.

F

2036 14th Ave
Vero Beach

Florida Theater. Built in the 1920's, this building is typical of many of the ornate Spanish-style movie houses built in Florida.

G

NW corner of
14th Ave and 21st St.
Vero Beach

Pocohontas Apartments. This 1926 apartment building occupies a corner site and is Mediterranean Revival in style.

H

NE corner of
25th St and 14th Ave
Vero Beach

Vero Beach Railroad Station. This small frame depot with wide bracketed eaves probably dates from the 1880's.

I

Corner of
Rt. 512 & Orange St.
Fellsmere

Fellsmere Public School. Built in 1915-16 with F.H. Trimble as architect. Brick, central pavilion with engaged pilasters.

J

N. Broadway and
Oregon St.
Fellsmere

Fellsmere Estates Corporation. Mission-style parapet atop this 1920's low stucco building with arcade inset.

NOTES

BROWARD

RUSSELL HOPE, AIA, BROWARD CHAPTER

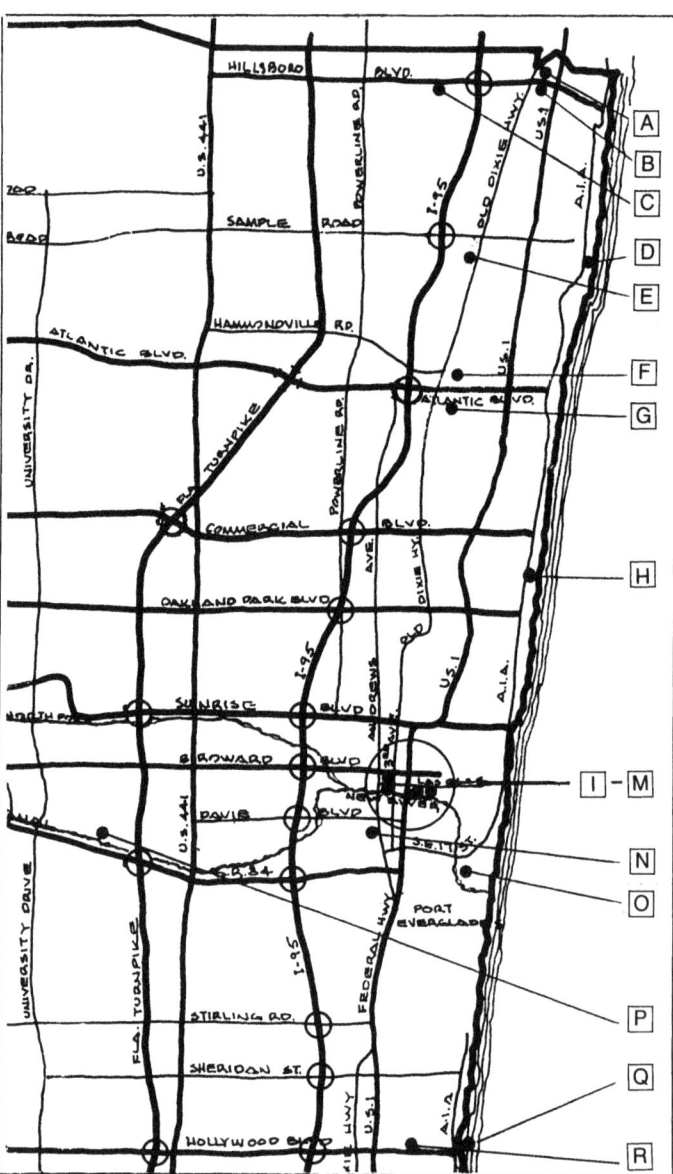

Broward County, carved out of portions of Dade and Palm Beach counties, was established in 1915 and named after the governor at that time, Napoleon Bonaparte Broward, who sponsored the project of draining the Everglades to create millions of acres of fertile soil for growing products that could feed the world.

Early Broward County was oriented more toward agriculture than tourism and construction. Around the turn of the century, the Florida East Coast Railroad was extended from Hypoluxo to Miami. This extension gave the area the ability to export fruit and winter vegetables and to import tourists.

Developer cities were started soon after the county was incorporated. The grandest of these was Hollywood, developed by Joseph W. Young and incorporated in the 1920's. The entire community was master-planned, had utilities installed, and streets paved and lighted before building sites were sold. Tourists, retirees, and land speculators flocked to the county to spark the first land boom which disintegrated before the 1930's financial depression.

During the Second World War, Broward County was used by the military as a seaport and a training area for pilots and other military personnel. During that time thousands of young men were processed in the area and, at the same time, introduced to South Florida living. After the war, many returned to set up permanent residence in the county.

Since 1950 Broward County's growth has been nothing short of phenomenal. Construction has been barely able to keep up with demand. Agriculture, while still strong, has largely been supplanted by tourism and hi-tech industry. Some of the planning mistakes made in the past are slowly being corrected, and Broward is looking forward to its third land boom.

Broward County's architectural heritage dates to the turn of this century. Even though agriculturally oriented for the first few deades, the area has only a few of the agricultural buildings remaining. Some early commercial hotels are still standing, and some of these are still in use in the major cities.

Francis Abreau, a successful 1920's boom-time architect, designed Mediterranean Revival style residences and public buildings in and around the Fort Lauderdale area. Some of his best structures (including the Fort Lauderdale Country Club and the Hall of Fame Pool) have been torn down. However, examples of boom-time architecture can be viewed on Hollywood Boulevard and parallel streets east of U.S. 1.

Much of Broward County's architecture of the 1950's and early 1960's could be characterized as developer oriented. Population increased so quickly and shelter was at such a premium that buildings could be sold then resold in a year at a handsome profit. Good design suffered in many instances. The 1970's and 1980's brought a more mature attitude toward design and land planning with a revitalized interest in landscaping. The tree canopy, which was missing for so long (even in the early days), is gradually being restored.

The Fort Lauderdale Downtown Development Authority has been instrumental in inspiring public interest in architecture and planning by rebuilding most of the downtown area and creating urban spaces which increase city pride. Fort Lauderdale's historic district encompassed only a few square blocks in the mid 1980's, but favorable public reaction to the historic buildings could insure an expansion of the area and a guarantee of the permanence of this link with the past.

A
150 NE 2nd Ave.
Deerfield Beach

Deerfield Beach School, City Hall Complex, built in 1920 by H. T. Tubbs, school board member. Two-room stucco schoolhouse used as city hall from 1926 to 1975. Restored in 1976 by Bicentennial Commission. In mid 1980's housed memorabilia from the 1920's.

B
380 Hillsboro Blvd.
Deerfield Beach

Butler House, built in 1923. Two-story stucco house built from stock plan in *Ladies Home Journal* by Butler family who held one of county's largest farms.

C
1300 W. Hillsboro Blvd.
Deerfield Beach

S.C.L. Railroad Depot, built in 1926. Single-story Spanish style stucco structure.

D
North of
Pompano Beach

Hillsboro Lighthouse, north of Pompano Beach on Atlantic Ocean, built in 1907. Second most powerful navigational beam in U.S. All steel structure 170 feet high.

E
3161 N. Dixie Hwy.
Pompano Beach

Sample-McDougald House, built in 1917 on what was the only passable north-south road at the time. Two-story, wood frame Classical Revival style house with 17 rooms, 11-foot high ceilings, and wrap-around porches.

F
First St. and First
Ave. and Flagler Ave.
Pompano Beach

Pompano Beach Historical District. Encompassing two city blocks and containing many vintage 1920 buildings including 1925 commercial Walton Hotel which originally had three stories, 34-rooms, and roof-top solar space heating.

G
Atlantic Blvd. near
Cypress Road
Pompano Beach

Kester Cottage-Pompano Beach Historical Museum. Built in 1930 by James Kester as one of a hundred tourist cabins he constructed on Pompano Beach at cost of $900 to $1200 each to rent for $25 a week. Cabins now relocated as vacation homes from the Carolinas to the Florida Keys.

H
Ocean to Federal Hwy
Oakland Park Blvd. to
Commercial Blvd.
Fort Lauderdale

Galt Ocean Mile. Eight thousand acres, including mile of beachfront, purchased at price of $19.4 million from A. T. Galt in 1953. Largest land transaction representing glitz and glitter of Fort Lauderdale.

I
Under New River at
Federal Highway
Fort Lauderdale

New River Tunnel. Four-lane, 864-foot long tunnel completed in 1960 for $6.4 million. Unique because held to bottom with tie rods into rock riverbed rather than a thick hold-down slab. Only tunnel in Florida.

J
833 N. Rio Vista Blvd.
Fort Lauderdale

Curtis House, built in 1920's with Francis Abreau as architect. Two-story Mediterranean Revival style residence of reinforced concrete built for Sperry, developer of the Sperry gyroscope.

K
SW 1st Ave.
Fort Lauderdale

Andrews and Brickell Avenue District, just north of New River. Fort Lauderdale's first main street before fire in 1912 demolished most of the wood frame structures. Pictured is the former Broward State Bank, a Neoclassic Revival building constructed in 1915. Other buildings of note in district.

L
North bank
of New River
Fort Lauderdale

Frank Stranahan House, built in 1902. Wood frame two-and-a-half-story house built on site of first trading post by Stranahan for his wife, Ivy, Broward's first school teacher and active suffrage crusader. Restored in 1984.

M
Historical District
Fort Lauderdale

New River Inn, built in 1905 by Edwin T. King, prolific contractor in area who developed hollow concrete block and used it in this construction. Two-and-a-half story hotel originally. Adapted for use as Children's Museum. Next door King-Cromartie House, built in 1907. Used to display pioneer inventions and exhibitions in mid 1980's.

N
Atlantic Ocean at
17th St. Causeway
Fort Lauderdale

Port Everglades. Construction started in 1928 by Joseph W. Young, developer of Hollywood, Florida, with George Goethals of Panama Canal fame as technical advisor. Large petroleum storage facility which was strategic during World War II. Deepest port in south at 42 feet deep.

O
SR 84 at Davie Rd.
Fort Lauderdale

Lock #1 on North New River Canal, built to prevent saltwater intrusion. Completion in 1912 signaled the beginning of access to the Everglades and to the promise of agricultural development of that area. Located on passage of barges and sternwheelers to Lake Okeechobee.

P
On Atlantic Ocean at
Hollywood Blvd.
Hollywood

Hollywood Beach Hotel, built in 1925. Early tourist-oriented resort. One of the last original resorts still left on Hollywood beach. Extensively remodeled with most of early decoration gone.

Q
1055 Hollywood Blvd.
Hollywood

John Wesley Young House, constructed in 1923 by the city's founder, planner, and prime developer. Mediterranean Revival style residence in the Hollywood Boulevard area which has several outstanding houses built in the Spanish vernacular.

R
900 N. Birch Road
Fort Lauderdale

Bonnet House, designed and built in 1920-1921 by artist Frederic Clay Bartlett on a 30-acre site between the Atlantic Ocean and the Intercoastal Waterway.

MONROE

MICHAEL MAXWELL, AIA, FLORIDA SOUTH CHAPTER

Monroe County, established July 3, 1823, soon after Florida was acquired from Spain, included all of the peninsula south of Lake Okeechobee. After Florida became a state, six other counties were created leaving only the southwest tip of the peninsula and the keys as Monroe County with Key West as its seat.

The Florida Keys, first populated by the Calusa Indians, were named "Los Martitres" (The Martyrs) by Ponce de Leon in 1513. After they came under British rule, the keys began to change when woodcutters from the Bahamas began to harvest trees for shipbuilding. Later turtlers and fishermen worked the area. Spain never settled the area, but Key West was given to Juan Salas for services rendered the government. John W. Simonton bought the island from Salas and with others soon began a settlement.

From the 1820's until the Civil War, Key West experienced a housing shortage, building boom, and increases in military activities. The U. S. Naval Station was enlarged during the Mexican War (1846-1848), and the construction of Fort Taylor and Fort Jefferson followed. At the beginning of the Civil War, Federal forces occupied Key West, built the Martello Towers, and continued construction at Fort Taylor and Fort Jefferson.

By 1868 Key West had become a large cigar manufacturing center, boosted by Cuban refugees which increased the city's population to nearly 10,000. Even though an 1886 fire destroyed nearly half of Key West's buildings, the city continued to grow. Regular steamship service to New York and Galveston became available in 1873 and continued until 1900. Railroads had been planned from the early 1830's, but none were developed until Henry Flagler's Overseas Extension of the Florida East Coast Railroad arrived in 1912.

The Spanish American War vitally affected the island as military facilities were improved and community construction increased. Visual reminders today include a memorial in the city cemetery honoring the victims of the sinking of the Battleship Maine and naval waterfront improvements which include a wharf, coal shed, machine shop, and officers quarters. Following the war, the Naval Station expanded its holdings to include former parts of the city and constructed submarine pens, a marine railway, and a coastal air patrol station.

During World War I, the Navy became more important, especially through the installation of air stations on Trumbo Point and later at Meacham Field, now the Key West International Airport. World War I brought economic growth to Key West. After the armistice, however, trade with Cuba decreased; cigar factories moved away; and military garrisons were transferred elsewhere. While, in the 1880's, Key West was considered the richest city per capita in the United States, by 1934 the city was bankrupt with 80 per cent of its inhabitants on relief rolls. The community was declared in a state of emergency, and programs were established to revive the area economy. When financial recovery seemed possible, a severe hurricane struck in 1935 and spared Key West but destroyed the railroad. Then in 1938, utilizing sections of Flagler's railroad bed and bridges, a highway was built. Key West was once again connected to the mainland.

Through the efforts of both the private and public sectors, Key West has maintained its unique architectural character. In 1962 a small group of citizens organized Old Island Restoration Foundation which began a trend to preserve the best of Key West. An annual celebration of Old Island Days was established and a summer field office of the Historic American Buildings Survey was sponsored in 1967. An historic district established in 1983 includes 190 blocks with a collection of 2,000 buildings dating from 1886 to 1912. The Historic Florida Keys Preservation Board and the City's Historic Architectural Review Commission have established strict standards for adaptive use, compatible design, and rehabilitation. Key West, while under great pressure, continues to serve as a fine architectural preservation example for all of Florida.

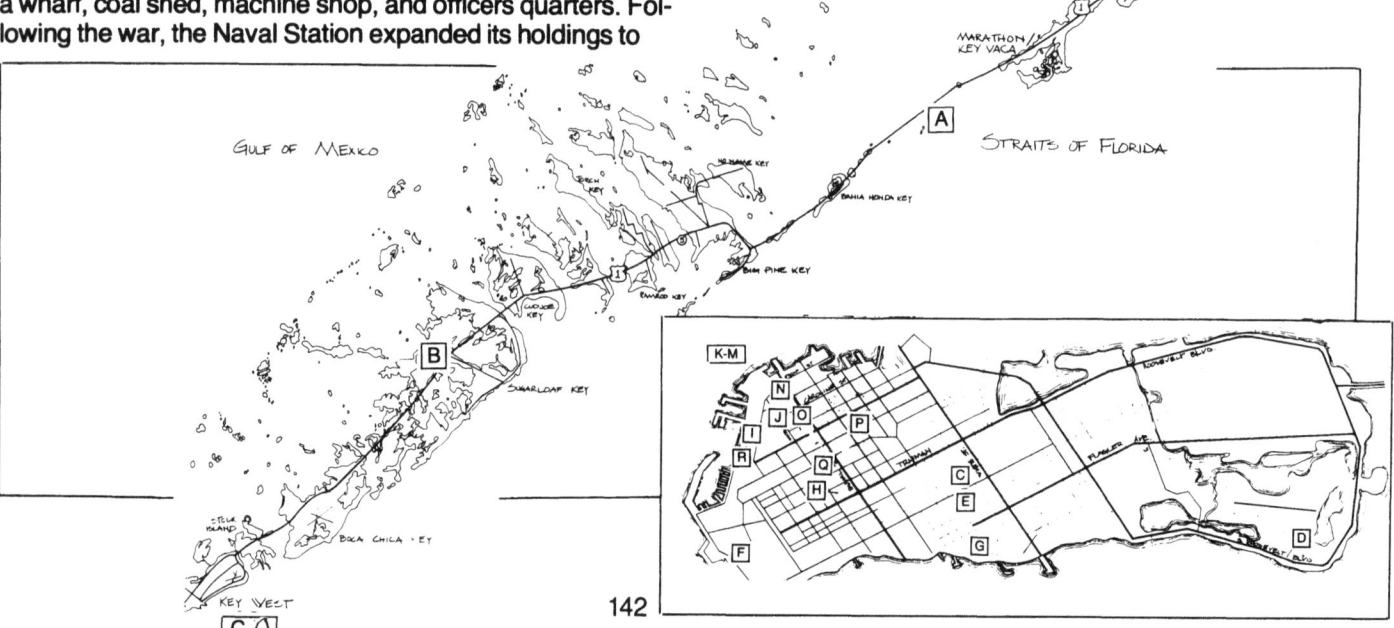

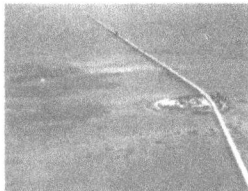

A
Connecting Key Vaca
with Bahia Honda
Key West

Seven Mile Bridge, built in 1912 for the Overseas Extension of the Florida East Coast Railroad. Reconstructed as part of US Highway 1 in 1938 after hurricane damage in 1935.

B
60 miles east of
Key West
Sugarloaf Key

Bat Tower, built in 1925 by R. C. Perkey. Intended to house bats for control of mosquitos and production of guano. Project not successful since bats deserted tower.

C
600 White St.
Key West

The Armory, designed by T.F. Russell and built in 1901 by John T. Sawyer to house arms and men for Monroe County and Key West. Two-story wood frame building with cupola at each end of partial third floor.

D
S. Roosevelt Blvd.
Key West

Fort Taylor Outerworks-East Martello Gallery and Historical Museum, built in 1862. Name derived from a type of fortified tower. Brick masonry structure with vaulted casements for gun batteries facing the sea.

E
Virginia Street off
White Street
Key West

Eduardo H. Gato House, built in 1876 as two story residence around a center patio, two-story porch on street elevation, cupolas at four roof intersections, and round arched windows. Donated in 1911 as Mercedes Hospital to benefit cigar workers.

F
Navy Base
Key West

Fort Taylor (southwest tip of Key West), contruction beginning in 1845. Named for Zachary Taylor, Mexican War hero elected president in 1848.

G
S. Roosevelt Blvd.
Key West

Marriott's Casa Marina Resort Hotel, built in 1921 to accommodate tourists arriving on the Overseas Railroad. Used as officers quarters during World War II. Rehabilitated in 1979-1980.

H
907 Whitehead St.
Key West

Tift-Hemingway House, built 1854 by Asa Forsyth Tift, a commissioner of ordinance to the Secession Convention of 1861. Purchased by Ernest Hemingway in 1935. Two-story masonry, stucco finish, verandas on all sides at both floors.

I
Naval Station
Key West

Quarters "A"-Little White House, built in 1890 by the Navy as two-family dwelling. Adapted to single family dwelling in 1946 for President Harry S. Truman who referred to it as "The Little White House." Symmetrical gables on main facade, two-story wood frame, closed porches.

J
Whitehead St. at
Greene Street
Key West

Capt. John H. Geiger-Audubon House, built in 1830 as two-and-one-half story wood frame house. In 1960 restored and furnished as house museum displaying works of John James Audubon who visited Key West in 1832.

K
Front Street at
Greene Street
Key West

Old Post Office and Custom House, completed in 1891. Designed by William Kerr, architect, in Romanesque Revival style. Three-and-a-half-story brick masonry building with center block and two wings.

L
Front Street at
Whitehead Street
Key West

U.S. Navy Coal Depot and Storehouse, built from 1856 to 1861 as supply depot and coaling station. Served the East Coast Blockading Squadron during the Civil War. Brick masonry building with stucco finish, buttressed piers, deeply recessed arched windows and doorways, gable roof, and cupola.

M
Mallory Square
Key West

Mallory Steamship Line Ticket Office, built in 1873. Restored by the city in 1961 after a successful campaign by the Old Island Restoration Foundation. Used as a tourist information center.

N
322 Duval Street
Key West

Captain Frances Watlington House, built in 1829. Moved to present location in 1832. Known as Key West's oldest house. One-and-a-half-story raised wood frame cottage. Adapted as a house museum.

O
429 Caroline Street
Key West

Dr. Joseph Y. Porter House, built in 1838 by Porter, Florida's first public health officer from 1887-1917. Two-story wood frame house with porches at both floors on the west elevation. Mansard roof added in 1896.

P
Eaton Street at
William Street
Key West

John Bartlum House and Captain Richard Roberts House, brought from the Bahamas in 1830 to relieve local housing shortage. Excellent examples of Bahamian or "Conch" architecture.

Q
Duval Street
Key West

San Carlos, built in 1924 to house an educational and social organization which was formed in 1871 to serve Key West's Cuban population. Preceding club buildings burned in 1886 fire. Replacement destroyed by 1919 hurricane. Existing Classical Revival style concrete building funded by private funds and Cuban government.

DADE

IVAN A. RODRIGUEZ, AIA, FLORIDA SOUTH CHAPTER

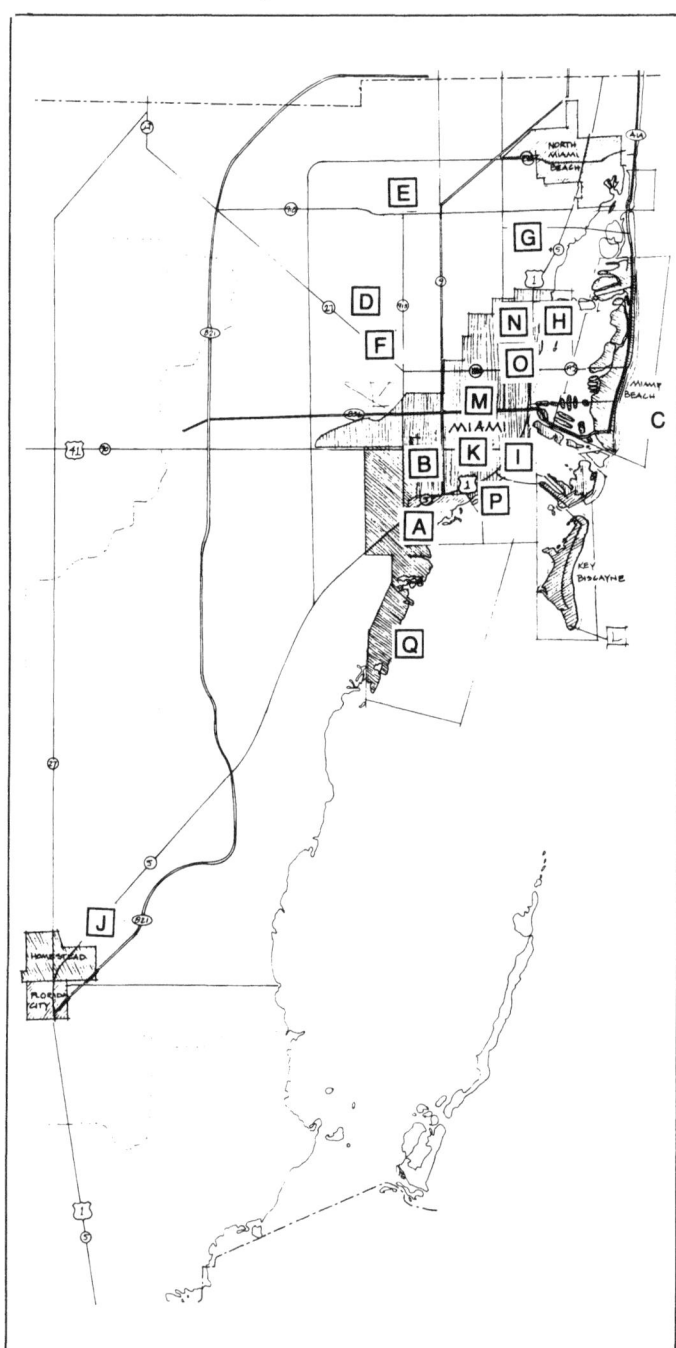

Dade County's history begins with its creation in 1836 when the designated area included present-day Dade, Broward, and Palm Beach counties. The county's more active historical period, that of continuous development, started around the turn of the century. The two major events promoting the county's development occurred in 1896. Both were associated with Henry M. Flagler. The Florida East Coast Railway was extended to Miami, and the Royal Palm Hotel was constructed as the first large scale, luxury tourist destination in South Florida. Repercussions were almost instant as Flagler donated lands for churches, public buildings, and schools and provided the new city with modern utilities. Soon a number of satellite hotels absorbed the spill-over business. Housing and commercial building accommodated the needs of those associated with either the railroad or the hotel. A living, bustling community emerged. As growth continued, suburbs surrounded the original city limits. By 1922 a new numbering system, still in use today, was approved which allowed the city of Miami and Dade County unlimited growth capabilities.

The real estate boom the area experienced from 1921 to 1926 was not equalled for years to come. Land sales reached unprecedented figures with property sometimes changing hands several times a day, each time at an inflated profit. Tourism continued to increase in South Florida, and new residents arrived by train and bus loads. Planned communities featuring buildings in eclectic styles, especially Mediterranean Revival, were designed to satisfy automotive traffic and other new living patterns. The devastation of the 1926 hurricane put an end to the wild years of the boom and sank South Florida into a depression three years before the national financial collapse.

Dade County began to recover from the Depression by the mid-thirties, partly because of a renewed interest in tourism as the country started to emerge from the depths of the disastrous economic slump. Tourists had less money to spend than during the previous decade, but the positive impact was still visible in the construction industry in Miami Beach. Hundreds of new mid-size hotels and apartment buildings were built during this more moderate boom from 1935 to 1939. This was the height of the Art Deco era in Miami Beach.

In the 1940's Miami and Miami Beach were involved fully in World War II. Most hotels and public buildings were converted to barracks, training centers, and hospital facilities. Little construction took place during these years since all energy was directed toward the war effort. A post-war economic boom acquired a different character from previous periods of active development. The tract housing typical of post-war years filled most of the demands of the new residents, many of whom had visited the area during the war and returned to settle.

With the refugee arrivals to Dade County during the 1960's and 1970's the area acquired a multi-facted image, that of a sophisticated, international metropolis with its share of beauty and problems. Amid the old Miami rises a new city, the product of the latest boom cycle and the never-ending pattern of luring new visitors through the beauty of climate, people, and shores.

A
Coconut Grove

Coconut Grove, one of Dade County's earliest settlements and a major cultural attraction with the bay, lush vegetation, and relaxed ambiance providing a tropical setting. Among important historic sites: The Barnacle, 1891, (illustrated, on Avenue Barnacle and Main Highway); Plymouth Church, 1917; and Coconut Grove State Theater, 1925.

B
Coral Gables

Coral Gables, real estate development planned in detail by George Merrick during the 1920's boom era, inspired by Mediterranean architectural styles which are incorporated into buildings, city entrances and plazas. Among important sites: Biltmore Hotel (illustrated, 1200 Anastasia), Douglas Entrance, Coral Gables City Hall, Venetian Pool, De Soto Fountain, and thematic villages.

C
Miami Beach

Miami Beach, site of Art Deco District, first and largest twentieth century historic district in the country. Includes 800 buildings of Mediterranean Revival, Art Deco, and Streamline Moderne styles built between 1920's and 1940's. Among important sites: Carlyle Hotel (illustrated, 1300 Ocean Drive), beach-front hotels along Ocean Drive, commercial artery of Washington Avenue, and European-styled architectural charm along Espanola Way.

D
Hialeah

Hialeah, 1921 development by Glen Curtiss and James Bright on their cattle ranch in northwest Dade County. Development inspired by Mission architectural style, once included Curtiss aviation school and film studios. Among important existing sites: Racetrack (illustrated, East 25th St.), Waterworks, Train Station, and Deer Park Residential Area.

E
Opa-locka

Opa-locka, planned city developed by Glen Curtiss. Based on a Moorish theme with a crescent moon plan and domes, minarets, and horseshoe arches as architectural elements. Among important sites: City Hall (illustrated, 777 Sharazad Blvd.), Hotel, and Train Depot.

F
Miami Springs

Miami Springs, Curtiss-Bright 1920's development inspired by American Southwest Pueblo architecture. Constructed with concrete block and stucco instead of adobe. Featuring courtyards, flat roofs, and soft molded parapet shapes. Among important sites: Glen Curtiss House (illustrated, 500 Deer Run), Pueblo Hotel (Fairhavens), and Stadnik's Pharmacy.

G
Miami Shores

Miami Shores, one of several bedroom communities started in northeast Dade County during 1920's boom. Original elaborate development scheme on shores of Biscayne Bay not completed because of Depression and 1926 hurricane. Among important sites: Miami Shores Elementary School (illustrated, NE 105th St. and 5th Ave.), Grand Concourse Apartments, and the Old Pump House.

H
Morningside

Morningside, east of Biscayne Boulevard between NE 54th to 60th toward the bay. Planned in 1922 as the development of Bayshore with Mediterranean Revival style architecture and underground utilities, paved sidewalks, and street lights. Among important sites: residence at NE 56th St. (illustrated) and other homes in Mediterranean Revival and Art Deco styles.

I
Miami

Downtown Miami, original boundaries of Miami dating from arrival of Henry Flagler's railroad in 1896 and forming downtown core. Early hotels and public buildings destroyed, 1920's highrise buildings remaining. Among important sites: Dade County Courthouse (illustrated, 75 W. Flagler St.), Daily News-Freedom Tower, Ingraham Building, and 1930's Alfred I. Dupont Building.

J
Florida City

Homestead-Florida City, southern-most cities in Dade County. Thriving agricultural market centers after Flagler's railroad to Key West reached Homestead in 1904. Among important sites: Florida Pioneer Museum in Florida City, one of last remaining station houses from the railroad era (illustrated, Krom Ave.), and Neva King Cooper School and Redland Hotel in Homestead.

K
Little Havana

Little Havana, composed of a series of 1910's and 1920's western Miami suburbs such as Riverside, Lawrence Estates and Shenandoah, all west of Miami River. New identity and culture for area during 1960's when thousands of Cuban refugees arrived. Among important sites: Bungalow (illustrated, 1375 NW 1st St.), Firestone Garage, Plummer Funeral Home, Domino Park, and Jose Marti Park.

L
Key Biscayne

Key Biscayne, coconut plantation at turn of the century owned by the Matheson family who, in the 1940's, donated land to Dade County in exchange for construction of a causeway to the mainland which opened key for development. Land gift now Crandon Park. Site of oldest standing structure in South Florida, Cape Florida Lighthouse, built in 1825 (illustrated, now part of Bill Baggs State Park).

M
Overtown

Overtown, black community established when Miami founded in 1896. Many buildings influenced by Bahamian style. Scheduled for redevelopment in 1986 as part of Southeast Overtown-Park West project. Among important sites of black pioneers in Miami: Chapman House (illustrated, NW 13th St.), Lyric Theater, community churches, and Overtown Historic Village.

N
Lemon City-Little Haiti

Lemon City-Little Haiti, one of earliest Dade County settlements, founded in 1888 as fishing and agricultural village and made railroad stop in 1896. Assimulated by northward expansion of City of Miami, now known as Little Haiti, home of thousands of recently arrived Haitian refugees. Among important sites: Dr. Dupuis Office (illustrated, NE 2nd Ave. and 62nd St.), Miami Edison High School, and NW 54th St. storefronts.

O
Miami

Biscayne Boulevard, palm-lined boulevard built in 1920's to link Miami with points north. Commercial artery stretching from downtown Miami highrises, the Freedom Tower, Sears Roebuck, the Omni Hotel to an array of Mediterranean Revival and Art Deco commercial buildings into Broward County. Boulevard shops (illustrated, 1401 Biscayne Blvd.).

P
Miami

Vizcaya, villa and gardens built in 1913 by James Deering. Italian Renaissance Revival extravaganza, a stone palace with gardens, fountains, gazebos, and a free-standing stone barge in Biscayne Bay. House furnished in priceless antiques (illustrated, 3251 South Miami Ave.).

Q
Miami

Charles Deering Estate, mansion built 1922 (illustrated, Old Cutler Road and 168th St.). Property encompassing 358 acres of hardwood hammocks, mangroves, virgin pinelands, rare and endangered floral and faunal species, and unexplored prehistoric fossil and Indian village sites. Also 1896 pioneer dwelling and 1900 country inn.

NOTES

RECOMMENDED READING

While a guidebook is not a place for lengthy reading lists, it is helpful to have sources of additional information while preparing for a tour. The authors of this guide were dependent on local sources: people, newspapers, publications in limited editions, and books long out of print. Some of the references listed here may not be available to the first-time visitor, but most of the Florida history and architectural references are available at bookstores. Publications available through the National Trust for Historic Preservation and the American Association for State and Local History will enrich any library shelf. Sometimes letters to historical societies and sites open to the public make planning an itinerary more efficient. Many such organizations have up-to-date histories and walking or driving tours. The Department of Tourism, Florida Department of Commerce, 126 Van Buren Street in Tallahassee provides general tourist information.

Do your homework and enjoy your trip through Florida's architectural history!

FLORIDA HISTORY

Mahon, John. *History of the Second Seminole War.* Gainesville: University of Florida Press, 1967.

Federal Writers' Project. *Florida, a Guide to the Southernmost State.* New York: Oxford Press, 1947. A splendid reference with a good section on architecture, now available in paperback.

Patrick, Rembert W. and Morris, Allen. *Florida Under Five Flags.* Gainesville: University of Florida Press, 1967. A brief and interpretative history of the state.

Tebeau, Carlton W. *A History of Florida.* Coral Gables: University of Miami Press, 1971. A basic primer.

The Florida Bicentennial Trail: A Heritage Revisited. Bicentennial Commission of Florida.

Morris, Allen. *The Florida Handbook, 1947,* Tallahassee, Peninsula Publishing Co.

Bicentennial Guide To Florida, Florida Times Union, Jacksonville, Florida 1976.

ARCHITECTURE

Harris, C.M. *Historic Architecture Source Book.* New York: McGraw Hill, 1977. Illustrated architectural glossary.

Poppeliers, John. *What Style Is It?* Washington, D.C.: The Preservation Press of the National Trust for Historic Preservation, 1977. Illustrated descriptions of American architectural styles, pocket-sized paperback.

Rifkind, Carole. *A Field Guide to American Architecture.* New York: New American Library, 1980. Drawings and brief descriptions of American architecture.

Saylor, Henry H. *Dictionary of Architecture.* New York: John Wiley & Sons, Inc., 1952. Easy-to-use paperback volume of concise definitions of architectural terms.

Blumenson, John J.G. *Identifying American Architecture.* American Association of State and Local History, 1979.

ALACHUA

Alachua County Florida Historical Tour Series published by Alachua County Historical Commission

Historic Gainesville — A Walking and Windshield Tour, Historic Gainesville, Inc.

A Walking Tour of the Historic Area on the University of Florida Campus, University of Florida.

Alachua County: A Sesquicentennial Tribute. Updyke, John B. editor; The Alachua County Historical Commission, 1974.

BROWARD

Fort Lauderdale, Self-Guided Tour. Ruth Doran, City of Fort Lauderdale.

CITRUS

Dunn, Hampton. *Back Home Citrus County — A History of Citrus County, Florida.* Citrus County Bicentennial Committee, 1965, Inverness, Florida.

Federal Writers Project American Guide, Citrus County, published in Orlando, 1936.

DADE

Florida South Chapter, American Institute of Architects; *Guide to the Architecture of Miami.* 1963. An out-of-print pamphlet featuring architecture of the 1950s.

Junior League of Miami, Inc. *Historic Downtown Miami.* 1963. Self-guided tour pamphlet.

Metropolitan Dade County, Office of Community and Economic Development. *From Wilderness to Metropolis, The History and Architecture of Dade County, Florida.* Printed by Franklin Press, 1982. A thorough and fully illustrated source for history and architecture including graphics and definitions of local styles.

Muir, Helen. *Miami, USA.* Coconut Grove: Hurricane House Publishers, 1963. In the author's own words, "a kaleidoscope of Miami's past."

DESOTO

Lane, George. *Pictorial History of Arcadia & DeSoto County.* Byron Kennedy & Co., St. Petersburg.

Lane, George. *Brief Histories of DeSoto County.* DeSoto Co. Histories, Arcadia.

DUVAL

Hallman, George. *Riverside Revisited.* Drummond Press, Jacksonville, FL, 1976.

Snodgrass, Dena. *Jacksonville, A Brief History.* The Florida Times Union, September 25-31, 1968. Jacksonville, FL, 1978.

Davis, T. Fredrick. *History of Jacksonville and Vicinity.*

Gold, P.D. *History of Duval County, Florida.*

ESCAMBIA

Pensacola Historical Landmarks. Pensacola Historic Preservation Society, 1983. *Pensacola's Navy Yard 1528-1911.* Pensacola Home and Savings Association.

FRANKLIN

"Franklin: Oysters and Tupelo Honey," Mari Moran, *Bicentennial Guide to Florida,* Florida Times-Union, Jacksonville, 1976.

HAMILTON

Hinton, Cora. *A Brief History of Hamilton County, Florida.* 1976.

HARDEE

Frisbee, Louise K. *Peace River Pioneers.* E.A. Seeman Publishing Co. Inc. Miami, 1974.

HILLSBOROUGH

Mormino, Greg and Pizzo, A. *Tampa: The Treasure City.* Continental Heritage Press, Tulsa, 1985.

Bane, M. and Moore, M.E. *Tampa: Yesterday, Today, and Tomorrow.* Mischler & King, Tampa, 1981.

The Cultural Resources of the Unincorporated Portion of Hillsborough County: An Inventory of the Built Environment. 1981. Historic Tampa, Hillsborough County Preservation Board, Tampa.

LAFAYETTE

Melton, Holmes, Jr. *Lafayette, Florida County History, 1949,* 1960.

LAKE

Mount Dora Historic Tour, Mt. Dora Chamber of Commerce and Mt. Dora Rotary Club.

LEON

Miller, Sam. *Capitol. A Guide for Visitors.* Historic Tallahassee Preservation Board. 1982.

LEVY

Romantic and Historic Levy County. Search for Yesterday, A History of Levy County.

Brier, Scott. *Levy: A Rural Retreat.*

MADISON

Sims, Elizabeth H. *The History of Madison County,* 1986. Madison County Historical Society.

MANATEE

McDuffee, Lillie Brown. *The Lures of Manatee,* 2nd edition, Bradenton, Florida, A.K. Whitaker, 1961.

Sheppard, W.L. & Moore, Margaret A. *A Walking Tour: Downtown Bradenton's Historic District,* 1983.

Schofield, Arthur. *Yesterday's Bradenton.* Lindsay Curtis, 1984.

Abel, R.D. *100 Years in Palmetto.* Palmetto Centennial Association, 1967.

MONROE

Key West in Perspective, Sesquicentennial Program. January 21, 1972.

Stevenson, George B. *Key Guide 1966,* George B. Stevenson, Publisher, Tavernier, FL.

England, Howard S. and Barron, Ida. *Fort Zachary Taylor.* January, 1977.

NASSAU

Johannes, Jan H. *Yesterday's Reflections: Nassau County, Centre Street, Fernandina Historic District.* Amelia Island Restoration Foundation, 1926.

ORANGE

Blackman, William. *History of Orange County, Florida.* Chulnota, Florida; Mickler House, 1973.

Orlando Historic Preservation Board. *Orlando, History in Architecture.* Rollins Press, Inc., 1984.

Historic Winter Park: A Driving Tour. Junior League of Orlando/Winter Park, Inc., Orlando, 1980.

OSCEOLA

Dodson, Pat. *Hamilton Disston's St. Cloud Sugar Plantation, 1887-1901.* Florida Historical Quarterly, 1971.

Metzger, Betty, Editor. *Kissimmee, A Pictoral History.* Byron Kennedy and Company.

PALM BEACH

Hoffstot, Barbara D. *Landmark Architecture of Palm Beach.* Pittsburgh: Ober Park Associates, Inc., 1974.

McIver, Stuart B. *Yesterday's Palm Beach.* 1976.

PINELLAS

Bethell, John A. *Pinellas — A Brief History of the Lower Point.* St. Petersburg: Press of the Independent Job Dept., 1911.

Fuller, Walter P. *St. Petersburg and Its People*. St. Petersburg: Great Outdoors Publishing Co., 1972.

Dunn, Hampton. *Yesterday's Clearwater*. Miami: E.A. Seeman Publishing Co., 1973.

Self-guided Tour of Pinellas County's Historic Sites. Pinellas County 75th Diamond Jubilee Committee.

POLK

Dunn, Hampton. *Yesterday's Lakeland*. Bay Center Corporation, 1976.

Frisbie, Louise K. *Yesterday's Polk County*. Miami: E.A. Seeman Publishing Co., 1976.

Kaucher, Dorothy. *They Built A City*. Orlando: Kristingson Publisher, 1970.

ST. JOHNS

Arana, Luis Rafael and Manucy, Albert. *The Building of Castillo De San Marcos*. Eastern National Park & Monument Association, 1983.

Historic St. Augustine Preservation Board. *Historic Properties Survey of St. Johns County Florida*. St. Augustine: 1985.

Historic St. Augustine Preservation Board. *Guidebook, Historic St. Augustine*. 1971

Turn Right at the Plaza. National Society of the Colonial Dames of America in the State of Florida, 1976.

Manucy, Albert. *The Houses of St. Augustine 1565-1821*. Jacksonville: Convention Press, 1962.

Redding, David A.. *Flagler and His Church*. Jacksonville: Paramount Press, Inc.

Graham, Thomas. *Flagler's Magnificent Ponce De Leon*. Florida Historic Quarterly, July, 1975.

SANTA ROSA

Blackwater Tour Brochures, Santa Rosa Historical Society.

SARASOTA

Matthews, Janet Snyder. *Edge of Wilderness, A Settlement History of Manatee and Sarasota Bay, 1528-1885*. Tulsa: Caprine Press, 1983. Well-written history of a unique area of Florida.

Marth, Del. *Yesterday's Sarasota*. Lindsay Curtis Publishing Co., 1984.

Venice, Yesterday, Today and Tomorrow. Lindsay Curtis Publishing Co., 1984.

Grismer, Karl H. *The Story of Sarasota*. Paschal & Paschal, Publishers, 1977.

SEMINOLE

The Tale of A Mosquito — A Story of Early Sanford. The School Baord of Seminole County, 1970.

SUMTER

Valentine, Doris. *Looking Back: Sumter County, A Photographic Essay*. Sumter County Historical Society.

Pamphlet, *Sumter County, Florida*. Sumter County Historical Society, Bushnell, Florida.

SUWANNEE

Board of County Commissioners, 1958 (Souvenir Program) Nichols, George N. *Suwannee County, Florida*.

VOLUSIA

Fitzgerald, T.E. *Volusia County, Past and Present*.

Gold, P.D. *History of Volusia County, Florida*. Centennial History of Volusia County.

WAKULLA

Green, Charles M. with Gerrell, Pete. *Wakulla County: A Glance Through the Past*. Wakulla Community Portrait Committee. 1985.